RAPIDES PARISH LIBRARY
324.9 MAG c.4                    mrla
Maginnis, John/Cross to bear

3 3331 00212 5318

W9-CCH-511

La                    c.4
324.9
Maginnis.
    Cross to bear.

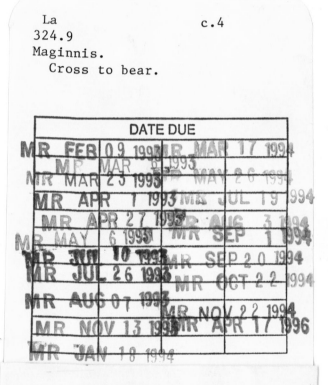

| DATE DUE | | |
|---|---|---|
| MR FEB 09 1993 | MR MAR 17 1994 | |
| MR MAR 1993 | | |
| MR MAR 23 1995 | MAY 26 1994 | |
| MR APR 7 1993 | MR JUL 19 1994 | |
| MR APR 27 1995 | MR AUG 3 1994 | |
| MR MAY 6 1995 | MR SEP 1 1994 | |
| MR JUL 10 1993 | MR SEP 20 1994 | |
| MR JUL 26 1995 | MR OCT 22 1994 | |
| MR AUG 07 1995 | MR NOV 22 1994 | |
| MR NOV 13 1995 | MR APR 17 1996 | |
| MR JAN 18 1994 | | |

WITHDRAWN FROM
RAPIDES PARISH LIBRARY

**RAPIDES PARISH LIBRARY**
ALEXANDRIA, LOUISIANA

# CROSS to BEAR

John Maginnis

**DARKHORSE PRESS**
**BATON ROUGE, LOUISIANA**

WITHDRAWN FROM
RAPIDES PARISH LIBRARY

Copyright 1992 © by **John Maginnis**
All rights reserved
including the right to reproduce this work
or parts thereof in any form.
ISBN 0-9614138-2-4

Published by Darkhorse Press
Edited by Barbara Phillips and J. F. Cado
Research assistance by Steven Watsky
Designed by Paol Bozemann
Cover Design by Stan Taylor and Jon B. Barry
Cover Photos by Tim Mueller
Layout by Louisiana Graphics
Printed by Edwards Brothers, Ann Arbor, Michigan

ACKNOWLEDGEMENT
To Jodie Cado and Paol Bozemann,
for seeing this through to the end.

Published in the United States of America

*In* memory of

*Willis Noland (1944-1990)*
*and*
*Scott Welch (1956-90)*

*Sorry you missed this one.*

# LOUISIANA

| | | |
|---|---|---|
| 1 New Orleans | 8 Clinton | 15 Lake Charles |
| 2 Metairie | 9 Denham Springs | 16 Alexandria |
| 3 Chalmette | 10 Ponchatoula | 17 Rayville |
| 4 Houma | 11 Franklinton | 18 Monroe |
| 5 Thibodaux | 12 Lafayette | 19 Jonesboro |
| 6 Morgan City | 13 Crowley | 20 Natchitoches |
| 7 Baton Rouge | 14 Jennings | 21 Shreveport |

A. Mississippi River    C. Lake Pontchartrain
B. Red River    D. Atchafalaya River

# CONTENTS

1. The Lost Hayride     1
2. Homecoming     14
3. Hamlet, Prince of Politics     30
4. The Dukewatch     54
5. Campaigns in Exile     90
6. Primary Experience     104
7. The Undead of Summer     120
8. Jesus Wept Here     134
9. Morality Power Plays     145
10. Hot as a Dog     153
11. The Insider Game     166
12. Where Voters Lie     186
13. The Thermal Index     200
14. Lower Than The People     217
15. "Skin Him Up"     232
16. Wake Up the Streets     255
17. Nebuchadnezzar at the Door     267
18. New Edwin     285
19. Matters of Faith     310
20. Victory Laps     331
21. The Way They Were     344
22. Circus Maximus     361

# 1. The Lost Hayride

It's morning in Walden, a bucolic, upper-class South Baton Rouge neighborhood with curving lanes and lakes and cul-de-sacs. It's a comfortable community where professionals and upscale retirees are insulated from crime and traffic and other ills of urban life and overdevelopment. That's reflected in the conservative voting patterns of the inhabitants, who went heavily for Ronald Reagan, George Bush, Dave Treen and Buddy Roemer throughout the '80s.

On this brilliant spring day in April 1991, at the charming little lakeside gray bungalow with the white picket fence, the back door is opened by a young woman in a white bathrobe. "Edwin will be right down," says Candy Picou. "Just make yourself comfortable." A country-western tune plays on the radio upstairs. The study overlooking the lake contains few of the artifacts of a politician's life: no photographs with presidents or foreign potentates, no oversized gavels or portraits. On the bookshelf, T. Harry Williams' *Huey Long* shares space with a handsome set of *Encyclopaedia Britannica*. On the next shelf are some carved ducks and a statue of Confucius.

The house in Walden is about a third the size of the ranch-style house Edwards built on a hill on Highland Road in 1980. He had sold the big place after his 1989 divorce from Elaine Edwards, his wife of 39 years. He was proud of that house and hated to let it go—all the more so when he discovered the buyer was a nephew of his old Republican nemesis, the late Jimmy Boyce. So he sells his old dream home to a Republican and moves into a veritable nest of them in toney Walden. A truly successful populist politician can only have so much in common with his people.

Edwards comes downstairs wearing blue jeans and a knit shirt. Candy pours him a glass of juice. In their time together, the 63-year-old politician makes no effort to hide his 26-year-old girlfriend. She accompanies him often, even to political functions—where girlfriends rarely tread. When it comes to the character issue, Edwards' greatest personal attribute always has been his open disdain for middle-class morality.

Introducing Candy to *Los Angeles Times* reporter Rick Meyer, he once explained, "At my age a man wants either a nurse or a beautiful young girlfriend." *Pause.* "I have combined the two." Edwards told friends that he did not even desire to cohabit, but gradually his resistance wore down ("She brought over a change of clothes for school the next day, and then another...") and the two settled into a quiet life in Walden. Apparently that's not been hard with Candy. "Sometimes we'll just sit on the porch at night and rock and look at the stars and talk," she says. "He can be so relaxed then."

But there's a limit. Today Edwin Edwards won't be rocking on the porch or puttering about the house. Today there is a parade.

Edwards is finishing his cup of coffee when a slender black man named Jaubert Ambeaux appears at the back door. Through 20 years of running for and being governor, Edwards has grown to take most of the perks and privileges of power for granted—except one: there is nothing like having a chauffeur. In 1990, a Baton Rouge woman, a Republican, was startled to see Edwin Edwards behind the wheel of a white land barge, unsuccessfully trying to pull out of a fast-food parking lot and merge into busy traffic on Perkins Road. He appeared tentative and frustrated after several missed chances. Just when the traffic cleared briefly, his path again was blocked by an old black man, tired and disheveled, walking very slowly across the street. The traffic light a block away turned green, sending a new wall of cars Edwards' way. The temptation for any frazzled motorist would be to give the old boy a good blast of the horn to pick up his gait. Instead, Edwards rolled down the window, motioned the fellow over and handed him some money. At least he knew how to do that.

"Man, get a driver," Edwards once chastised Baton Rouge Mayor Tom Ed McHugh. "The people don't think any more of you if you drive yourself." The difference is Tom Ed likes to drive. Edwards endures it.

No longer. Today the candidate rides shotgun as Ambeaux slows down to cross the railroad tracks and enter downtown Ponchatoula, which is crowded this one time a year for the annual Strawberry Festival and Parade. This is Edwards' fifth campaign for governor, and he will spend much of it waving to crowds and shaking hands at countless parades, fairs and festivals, just as he's done in every race before this. Except 1987, the dark year. "You know four years ago I only went to two parades." Positively unnatural.

Edwards wanders through the form-up area, looking for his contact. "One day they are going to organize a parade that starts on time." He climbs up on a few barge floats for pictures. He shakes a few hands. Maybe he's rusty at this, but he also looks lost. And the reporter is asking dumb questions.

"So what's the point of going to a parade six months before the election?"

"Two things: Radio and TV publicity. And it gives people a chance to see you. That's why I walk. Plus, it's important to your local supporters. They insist that you come. It's a symbol of their ability to reach you."

Finally, the parade is ready to roll. Edwards will ride in an antique convertible roadster, right behind the Ponchatoula High boosters and the Marine Corps band. He has loaded up with strawberry candies to throw to the crowd. It takes a certain skill, born of years of riding in small-town parades, to be both generous and nondiscriminatory in one's throws, but also not to run out before the parade ends.

And we're rolling. Edwards is just getting his throwing arm limbered up when the roadster jerks, sputters, coughs and stalls dead. Edwards looks around with helpless frustration. Now what? He shrugs. What else? He gets out and helps to push the dead antique into a parking lot.

This is pathetic, and the long campaign ahead promises only more of the same. And for what? Here's what Edwin Edwards' friends can't figure. Here is the smartest man in Louisiana politics, the best guy ever at sizing up the odds — whether in a political campaign or a crapshoot — the cool operator who never lets his emotions (what emotions?) cloud his judgment or crack his poker face; here is the champ of champs, who, for some reason, is hellbent on running a race he cannot win. Here is a man with a full life behind him, and still a good life ahead of him, with easily a couple million or more in mostly liquid assets, four grown children, ten grandchildren and one fine girlfriend, out wasting a perfectly wonderful spring morning hustling for votes he's not going to get.

That's what his friends in politics would tell him if he asked their advice; but he won't ask and they want to remain his friends, so they humor him in this sad quest. The common line is "Edwin can read polls better than anyone, and when it comes down to it, if the numbers aren't there, he'll pull out." Surely he will. And now the polls are very clear: while incumbent Buddy Roemer's approval ratings have gone down some, Edwin Edwards' have not gone up. But it's more than polls, it's a matter of timing — and time. And any fool can tell you Edwin Edwards' time is long gone.

But those were some times. . . .

At the dais, the retired business lobbyist begins his speech, while at a back table, the young business lobbyist holds his head in his hands: "No, no. He's doing it again." Yes, old Ed Steimel is at it again. He is telling the truth, damn it, and it won't look good in the papers. Since his retirement, the founder of the Louisiana Association of Business and Industry has been wading into politically unspeakable currents to answer the age-old question of what makes Louisiana politics so different from America's. His answer: too many blacks and Catholics. Oh my. Only Steimel's unassailable reputation for promoting racial tolerance prevents him from being barbecued on the spit of Political Correctness. That, and the kernel of truth in his remarks.

Multiculturalism, an emerging national trend, started in Louisiana when the American settlers showed up at the beginning of the nineteenth century. The land's culture, customs and laws already had been imprinted by the French and Spanish. While the American political experience derived from distrust of monarchs and centralized authority, Louisiana's political traditions grew out of European and Catholic attitudes of submission to authority and fealty to the king, or the pope, or both. Combined with involuntary immigration from Africa, which had its own kings, the great mass of Louisiana's population shared little experience in representative democracy from the start, which made it a pushover for strong-man rule.

The second governor of Louisiana was the first to figure that out. Appropriately enough he was an Irishman: Don Alejandro O'Reilly, in service to the Spanish king and dispatched to New Orleans to deal with the unruly French in 1768. The king's newly acquired subjects, understandably feeling betrayed by the French sell-out, ran off the first Spanish governor, an anemic and humorless astronomer named de Ulloa.

O'Reilly knew simple force of arms would only arouse and incite the surly French. And he abhorred messy landings. So he sent his respects in advance and invited the leading French citizens and gentlemen planters and their ladies to a grand banquet to mark his arrival. Finally, thought the French, someone who understands us. Only too well. It was a lavish, boozy dinner. O'Reilly was a charming host. After dinner, the men retired for cigars. That's when soldiers appeared. O'Reilly apologized for the little ruse but told them they were all under arrest. They were taken away and most were shot. That point made, "Bloody" O'Reilly had little more trouble with his subjects. He threw some very nice parties and only had to shoot a few troublemakers after that.

The state never completely outgrew the monarchic experience, which is reflected in the broad powers vested in the governors — usually skilled, manipulative Anglo politicians from New Orleans or Protestant North Louisiana. Here was a politician's dream state: a very rich land with very poor people, with big-money outside interests competing to exploit its natural resources, as the docile electorate — which worked cheap and voted cheaper — accepted, even appreciated, their rulers' corruption and colorful excess. From Huey Long to his brother Earl to Big John McKeithen, the classic formula for smart North Louisiana populists endured: oil from the ground, pork to the people, votes from the poor, power to the governor.

All Edwin Edwards changed was the geography. The first Frenchman politically astute enough to put the state's two great ethnic minorities together, Edwards took office in time for the kickoff of the party of the century, the '70s. After Edwards coaxed through the Legislature a big hike in oil and gas severance taxes, which neatly coincided with the Arab oil embargo, the money began flowing into the state treasury nearly faster than the governor could spend it. But he managed, dishing out more and more state jobs and contracts for friends and contributors, and more construction projects and social programs for his constituents. Edwards filled the power of the office with all the forcefulness and excess of his strongest predecessors.

He also refracted, Louisiana-style, society's sweeping, liberating changes. He dressed as poorly as the latest fashion, even introducing leisure suits to the Capitol. Then came the stories of the girlfriends and the blatant, public passes he would make at women. For him, womanizing was merely a numbers game. Or, as he once told a legislator, "Two out of ten women will go to bed with you, but you've got to ask the other eight." His lifestyle suited the times and entertained his populist, working-class constituency of blacks, Cajuns and rednecks.

He made it all look easy. The oilfield economy made a decent education seem irrelevant. He aroused more controversy than effective opposition, most of which came from federal grand-jury investigations that he always managed to skate through. The antics of the king and his court barely bothered the prospering middle class, who paid so little in state income and property taxes that they were embarrassed to complain. Louisiana was on a dream roll. Power, sex and money were all there for the grabbing, and Edwin Edwards set the table.

No governor since Huey Long filled and exploited the power of the office more than Edwin Edwards did in his first two terms. When the voters brought Edwards back for a third term in 1983, they seemed to be trying to bring back the magic of the '70s. He tried to accommodate them, but geology was not on his side. Oil production and prices were dropping, unemployment was rising. With a gaping hole in the state budget that Other People's Money used to fill, Edwards had to turn to his people and to ram stiff personal-tax increases through the Legislature. His popularity plummeted and everything he touched turned to garbage. His pathetic response to the weakening economy was to unveil his equivalent to Gerald Ford's WIN campaign. Edwards called his LIFT—Louisianians Involved For Tomorrow. "You can feel the energy of the word—LIFT," said the morose Edwards. Like the economy, it bombed.

Then came the indictments. Edwards and seven others, including his brother Marion and Shreveport pal Gus Mijalis, were charged by U.S. Attorney John Volz with racketeering in procuring hospital permits. Even though Edwards made his money on the deal—close to $2 million—as a private citizen, he was implicated by helping his old partners once he returned to the governor's office.

Some of the tawdry details of the case were far more damaging than the main line of the prosecution. One day during the first trial, a slender, bespectacled man took the stand, identified himself as a collector for a Las Vegas casino and recounted picking up $200,000 in cash in a suitcase from Edwards at the Mansion. Other testimony revealed that Edwards used a gambling alias of T. Wong and that he ran up debts as high as $600,000 on some trips. The sums Edwards threw around the tables were beyond the ordinary citizen's comprehension. With hard times hitting Louisiana, the image of a governor playing the games of the '70s did not sit well with the voters.

Edwards worked to maintain an air of cavalier contempt toward the proceedings, such as when he offered this toast at a defendants' party in a French Quarter bar:

*When my moods are over,*
*And my time has come to pass,*
*I hope they bury me upside down,*
*So Volz can kiss my ass.*

After an initial mistrial (one juror held out for conviction), prosecutor John Volz doggedly tried again. The second time the defendants won easy acquittal, but by now, nothing was easy for Edwin Edwards. Though he wasn't nailed, his charmed political life was forever tarnished. The federal government was not able to prove the governor of Louisiana was a crook, but it did the next best thing: it made him a defendant, a visible, indisputable subject and target of the laws of the United States. That had never quite been done before.

The rest of Edwards' third term was an exercise in futility and bitterness. Edwards' only solution to the state's economic problems was to call for casino gambling and a lottery. The wary Legislature distanced itself from the fatally wounded governor.

The stench settled in at the Mansion. One of Edwards' closest friends and aides, Wayne Ray, was found to be operating his own consulting business out of the Mansion, receiving fees from engineers and contractors hoping to land state contracts. He was sentenced to a three-year jail term for tax evasion. Edwards drove him to prison in Texas.

Edwards promised his third term would be one for history. He wasn't kidding.

Abandoning the antique heap, Edwards, determined to ride in the strawberry parade, flags down the next vehicle in line, a double-decker bus carrying the parish's Italian Society. He sits on the bus's large front bumper and waves with one hand while pumping the other hand to the *oompah-pah, oompah-pah* beat of the music blaring from the speakers. As strange a sight as this is, Edwards gets only a mild response from the parade watchers. Some aren't even sure who he is. "Oh, that's Frank Edwards," says one woman, thinking of the former Tangipahoa Parish sheriff who was run out of office four years before the ex-governor was.

Off the parade route, Edwards walks toward the fairgrounds for meeting and greeting. On a side street, Edwards stops to buy some homemade strawberry jam from a street vendor. "You remember me?" says the fellow with his pint jars. Edwards can't say he does, but keeps up a friendly banter as the fellow makes change. By the time the transaction is completed, Edwards has change, two jars of strawberry preserves *and* his original ten-spot. "Now I remember you," says Edwards as he gives the bill back.

Now the governor has two pint jars of homemade Tangipahoa Parish strawberry preserves, which presents the logistical problem of how to shake hands. With a little juggling he gets it done, because there aren't a lot of hands to shake as he works from booth to booth.

His friend Dr. Charles Gideon, the mayor and local chiropractor, hunts out friendly faces in the crafts and food booths and along the walkways. Dr. Gideon has been with Edwards since 1971, when the state's chiropractors backed the Cajun congressman. One of the first measures backed by the Edwards administration was a bill, strongly opposed by the state medical society, to make Louisiana the last state in the Union to license chiropractic. Dr. Gideon and friends have never forgotten the man who made them legal.

Shifting his jam jars, Edwards shakes one woman's hand and as he moves on, her friend says, "Now you have to wash it."

A few minutes later, Edwards shakes the hand of a paunchy, middle-aged man in a baseball cap, and keeps moving. He's brought up short, though, when the old boy throws That Question at him: "Are you going to pull out this time?" Edwards turns and faces the scowling questioner, who's waiting, hands on hips, for an answer.

"Oh no. This is a different race, my man. I guarantee I'll be in it to the end."

The old boy looks unconvinced. Who would take a politician's word? So Edwards can offer only one assurance more sacred than a promise: "You find someone who wants to bet that I will pull out the race, call me and I'll cover half of it."


The atmosphere was poisonous at the Edwards party in the Monteleone Hotel ballroom in October 1987. With the returns showing Buddy Roemer piling up a solid five-point primary lead over the incumbent, Edwards supporters flipped back and forth from shock to anger. With each new depressing vote total, the combination of hurt and alcohol led to heated words about who had screwed up in what parish.

In his suite on the 15th floor, Edwards did not trifle with fault-finding. He knew there was nobody to blame, nobody, but Bob Livingston.

Livingston was the only reason Edwards entered a race he really did not want to run. He would have just walked away from it, but that would have meant ending his career on a very sad, bitter note. Had he given up, his populist base of blacks and Cajuns likely would have passed to a younger, unscarred Democrat, and Edwards would never get it back. If there was anyone Edwards could beat in a runoff it would be Republican Congressman Livingston: a taller, stiffer, angrier version of Dave Treen. For a humanizing effect, he played the harmonica. If Edwards couldn't beat Livingston in 1987, he probably could in 1991, after the people would have had their fill of doctrinaire Livingston's failed reforms. Edwards, in turn, was the only candidate Livingston could beat. They both needed, and deserved, each other.

In the open primary that Edwin Edwards designed — his most lasting contribution to Louisiana politics — all candidates regardless of party run together, and the top two finishers meet in a runoff. Livingston began the 1987 campaign with a firm 19 percent in the polls. Too firm. He never cracked 20. Late in the campaign, when conservative Democrat Buddy Roemer started to move, Edwards grew worried and annoyed at Livingston's stalled campaign. "I'm trying to help him, but I can't do it all," the governor complained to friends. He worried that Livingston was such a dud "that not even the Republicans would vote for him."

Roemer breezed past Livingston in the polls and, by election night, he ran well ahead of Edwards. At close to midnight, the governor and entourage descended to the ballroom, where the press and cameras were surrounded and besieged by angry Edwards supporters. He began curiously, "The Chinese have a saying that if you wait on the riverbank long enough, the bodies of all your dead enemies will float by." His backers didn't know what he was talking about, but his next words hit home: "I have determined — being the politician that I am—that under the circumstances, since I did not run first it would be inappropriate for me to continue with this election." A chorus of "No, no" rose from dismayed followers. Around him, family members wiped away tears. Except one. At his side, his wife Elaine beamed. Her life in the fishbowl, along with her husband's public infidelities, had worn her spirits down. She seemed to welcome the relief of no longer being a political wife—but she did not know that her days as any kind of wife were numbered as well.

Moments later, the doors closed for what Cecil Brown would remember as the longest elevator ride he would ever take. The Opelousas businessman and Edwards friend broke the dead silence. "I can say I had a great governor for four years."

"My man," he said Edwards told him, "I'll be back."

He may have been the only one on the elevator to believe that. The consensus, even among his supporters, was that it would take more than Buddy Roemer at his worst to revive Edwards' ruined political career. *Shreveport Journal* columnist Lanny Keller put it this way: "The only way Edwards can ever be reelected is to run against Adolf Hitler."

Cruising the festival grounds, the candidate solves his surplus jam jar problem when he comes upon a young black mother sitting on a blanket with her children. He responds to her warm greeting by giving her one of the jars. This is as genuine a political gesture as Earl Long handing out hams to sharecroppers. And he still has one to take home. So he thought. Leaning against a nearby tree is a young white man in blue jeans and a white t-shirt. He looks like the type who used to vote for Edwards, but now votes for Duke. He holds out his hand. The politician has no choice.

"Too bad," says Edwards, walking back to the car. "I really wanted that jam."

Edwards spends most of the drive home from Ponchatoula dwelling on his usual subject for reporters: the lies of Buddy Roemer and how the press covers for him. "If I had done that, it would be all over the front page of the paper" is how he ends every example of Roemer's misspeaks.

But doesn't Edwin Edwards have more than Buddy Roemer to worry about? A number of moderate Democrats are getting in the race as alternatives to both Roemer and Edwards. Edwards dismisses the notion as just more wishful thinking from the press. "No, the more candidates that get in, the better it is for me. I'm going to get my vote. Roemer is the one who has to worry about a big field."

"What about David Duke?"

Duke's problem, says Edwards, is "the more he tries to broaden his appeal, the more he risks losing his base supporters. If a real Klansman got in the race it would really hurt him."

Assuming Roemer survives the primary, Edwards plans to use Roemer's own 1987 rhetoric against him. "I just have to play back those silly, stupid commercials of his and jam his own words back down his throat." The absolute firmness of his conviction is matched only by the deep, unbridled bitterness toward Buddy Roemer. It marks every statement, every retort; it finds its way into conversations on topics having nothing to do with Roemer. Apparently it guides every waking moment. Well. Almost.

Jaubert Ambeaux turns the car into the quiet cul-de-sac and stops at the little gray cottage with the white picket fence. It's a lovely spring afternoon in Walden. Candy's home.

Just one last dumb question: "Do you want to win this election to be governor or to beat Roemer?"

He pauses half a beat. "No, I want to be governor . . . after I beat Roemer." But a nerve has been hit. He considers again. Then: "The best thing that can happen to me is to win this election and to die the next day."

He walks into the garage, then turns: "I'd invite you in, but you might accept."

# 2. Homecoming

The long-haired student organizer is having trouble being heard as he tries to explain why David Duke, candidate for governor, is speaking at LSU's Free Speech Alley today. Duke, in a long-sleeved shirt and tie in the sweltering September sun, has one foot on the concrete bench while the student explains the issue: "It comes down to an issue of free speech. We worked hard to let this man speak."

"So let him speak," yells out a student in the crowd.

Duke smiles. The organizer looks a bit bewildered. The noise is not coming from the people who don't want Duke to speak, but from those who do.

"Duke, Duke, Duke" interrupts the organizer's discourse on the First Amendment. A crowd of about 500 and growing is overflowing the Alley area in front of the Student Union. Some came to cheer Duke, some came to heckle, most came for the show. So let's get on with it.

The student relents and leaves the concrete platform for the main attraction. David Duke leaps up onto the small platform to a chorus of cheers and boos.

As the cameras close in before him, students lift placards behind him that read NOSE JOB NAZI and DAVID DUKE: NAZI FOR THE '90s. In front of him, some students and some of his younger campaign volunteers feverishly wave Navy-blue-and-white Duke placards. He is silent for a moment as he sizes up the crowd. For the past three years, he has been directing his new conservative mainstream message to the frustrations of the middle class, which these kids don't know about yet. But maybe they've read George Orwell, or the Bible. "I've been accused of thought crimes before," he begins. "I've been condemned for my past. But you should look back at your own past before you throw stones at me."

This preemptive strike on his hecklers wins him just a little speaking room. A bodyguard stands in front of the candidate and watches the crowd. Duke catches his balance on the man's shoulders as he leans forward to project his voice: "I may be controversial but I'm the only candidate with no skeletons in my closet. In fact, I don't think I even have a closet anymore."

"Skeletons? Man, you got dinosaurs," yells back a black student. "You got tarpits. Man, you got museum pieces."

Just a wrinkle of a smile passes over Duke. Ah, the college crowd. It's been a while. This is not his typical campaign appearance. This is homecoming.


"You're a racist asshole!" heckled the long-haired student in the Peace Symbol t-shirt.

On the Free Speech Alley platform, the skinny 19-year-old blinks at the insult, and then he grins like *what do you expect from a Communist?* and continues reading from the tract he has written especially for today's appearance. The subject on this crisp October day in 1969 is the same as it was last week and the week before that: the urgent need to halt race-mixing with inferior Negroes, as promoted by the International Jewish Conspiracy. What's not the same is the crowd. It's been doubling each week, from the handful at his debut to hundreds a few weeks later. The strange skinny kid with the high-pitched grating voice and racist spiel is the hottest freak show on campus. Some black and liberal students come out to argue with him, others scream insults. Most just come for the show. Alone each week (if friends are there — if he has friends — they do not make their presence known) he faces increasingly personal and malicious heckling that would drive a standup comic to honest work. But here's the weird part. Even when threatened with early, involuntary plastic surgery, Duke cracks this wry smile and continues reading his harangue. He never pulls back, or caves in, or returns a personal insult — he keeps his control, and for his 15 minutes each Wednesday he controls Free Speech Alley.

For most students, Duke's appearances are a joke, while others think he defiles this one corner of free thought and open debate about the great issues of the day. Free Speech Alley was only created by the administration so students would not feel the urge to gather and raise hell on some other part of campus, as occurs with disturbing regularity on Northern campuses.

The '60s have not happened yet in Baton Rouge. They will, for about three months, in 1971. While other campuses are seeing war protests and growing drug use, the LSU student body perfects the image of a hard-drinking, hell-raising party school. Student liberation means relaxed curfews, women being allowed to wear pants to class and freshmen no longer having their heads shaved. For the most part, you cannot call students liberal. Or conservative. They are working too hard on being cool. Politics is for geeks.

And the biggest geek is David Duke. Students can at least relate to opposition to the Vietnam War, because of the issue of getting one's ass shot off. But this kid is railing on about something that's been settled — right?


More than democracy came late to Louisiana. The state also missed much of the heat and confrontation of the civil rights struggle.

Though Louisiana was no model of social justice, its Mediterranean heritage, strong-man populism and oil economy helped to lubricate some of the friction between the races during the '50s and '60s. Louisiana officials were not nearly as efficient as their counterparts elsewhere at disenfranchising black voters in the backlash of segregation that swept the South at the turn of the century. In the Catholic southern parishes and in New Orleans the number of blacks on the voting rolls was greater than the Southern average. In the '30s, '40s and '50s, Huey and Earl Long quietly used their power in local courthouses to keep and add blacks — faithful Long voters — on the rolls. The offshore oil and petrochemical booms in the '60s mostly benefited white workers, but blacks were able to fill many of the tradesmen and laborer jobs left behind. At least the two races weren't competing for the same lousy jobs.

There was no shortage of hot-headed racist politicians on the loose in Louisiana. Plaquemines Parish boss Leander Perez, who expropriated much of the parish's enormous oil wealth, fiercely pushed segregation and had little but contempt for blacks. He tried to buy into power with a succession of governors, but Huey, Earl and John McKeithen all took his money and double-crossed him. Earl even tried to reason with him: "Leander, the feds have the atom bomb now. Why don't you just give up?" It took the Catholic Church, however, to shut the old judge down. When Perez would not back off on his public and heated opposition to the integration of New Orleans public schools, Archbishop Joseph Rummel excommunicated him. It was the moral equivalent of taking Leander out and shooting him. The practicing New Orleans Catholics who were also soft racists got the point. You didn't have to like blacks, only keep your mouth shut, to avoid the eternal fires of Hell.

Strong governors, Big Oil and Holy Mother Church did not defeat racism as much as they glossed it over and deferred trouble.

On Louisiana's college campuses in the late '60s, segregation was a private issue instead of a public one. No one was going to publicly argue that blacks should not be allowed at LSU, though it sure was convenient that Southern University was across town. Without Southern, if LSU's student body was one-fourth black, the race issue would have dominated campus life. Instead, the issue was avoided and things were cool. This was the first generation of students in the South to face the race issue, and most had ducked. Young people in the state saw the same television images of club-wielding sheriff's deputies, attack dogs and angry, screaming rednecks. College kids would not identify with the hard-bitten, angry visages of George Wallace, Bull Connor and Leander Perez. Blatant, public racism did not go out of favor as much as it went out of style. Any serious discussion of racial issues — from either side — was inappropriate and uncool.

That's what made Duke such a curiosity. Were he just up there raving about niggers like the neighborhood bigot back home, it would be offensive but familiar. But David Duke couched his white supremacist and anti-Semitic rhetoric in philosophical arguments. He did not even trifle with the common segregationist rationale of states' rights. Duke had a worldview. "I am a National Socialist," he tells the student newspaper. "You can call me a Nazi if you want."

No one really wanted to call him anything, or pay him much attention after catching his act a few times. Even after he began wearing his brown khaki Nazi uniform with swastika armband around campus, most students just tried to ignore him. It would be giving him too much credit to call him a student radical. Most folks just dismissed him as a weirdo in costume, out beyond the fringe and more laughable than disturbing.

The only days Duke would never wear his Nazi uniform were Tuesdays and Thursdays, when he donned his ROTC khaki uniform for drill. "He had outstanding leadership potential," remembers a commissioned Army officer instructor. "He was very studious, very academic in class. And he worked very hard at drill." Just at the time he was debuting at Free Speech Alley, the ROTC instructors and senior cadets named him sergeant-major, the top cadet of the sophomore class. The only rule he broke was the big one: He made waves.

As his sophomore year wore on, his activities on one side of campus were noticed on the other. And beyond. "We started receiving information on him from the Department of Defense," says the Army officer. "As we were told (by the Pentagon), he was getting contributions from around the world, even then. Here was a 19-year-old kid getting money from Germany." That and the Nazi uniforms proved to be a bit much. In the spring of 1970, the Pentagon ordered the LSU ROTC program to reject Cadet Duke's application to enter the advanced-training program.

Candidate Duke has a different view of memory lane: "I've done things in my life I'd take back."

"Prove it," shouts one student. But another asks Duke's favorite question: "Why did you change your views?"

"We all grow up. When I spoke here in college, the Vietnam War was going on. It was a radical period. People were carrying Viet Cong flags on campus." (*Wrong.*) "A lot of people opposed the war in Vietnam, but our leaders did us an injustice. We should have gone in and kicked ass."

This gets a big cheer from the students, whose idea of an ass-kicking war has just been concluded in the Persian Gulf.

While he's at it, the candidate has a few more things to take back: "I'm not blaming blacks for our problems, but earlier I did. The greatest problem facing the state today is the liberal social welfare system that doesn't encourage people to work and doesn't encourage people to be responsible."

"Most people on welfare are whites," shouts another black student.

Duke was waiting for that line. He interrupts the next questioner to turn again to the black student: "If you say most people on welfare are whites, and I'm against welfare abuse, that just proves my programs aren't racist."

19

"Beautiful," says a Duke placard bearer.

"I would like to hear you renounce the Klan now," a student presses.

Easy for Duke to say: "I renounce the Klan and any racist organization. I think the old Jim Crow laws are bad."

A student turns to his friend: "Who's Jim Crow?"


It was a Klan rally with a difference. Not everyone filing into the small gym in Walker on a spring night in 1975 had learned of this event through the Klan's usually secretive word-of-mouth network. Some heard about it on television. The announcement mentioned music, cold drinks and hot dogs for the rally and, of course, the big cross burning to follow. Even an unusual celebrity speaker: Mary Bacon, America's first female professional jockey, would address the gathering.

The folks looked like the typical blue-collar workers and farmers and tradesmen and housewives of conservative Livingston Parish, a noted Klan stronghold in years past. Volunteers appeared to be doing a brisk business selling Klan t-shirts and even sheets. As the country-western band played, the mood of the crowd was relaxed, even festive. The TV cameras provided a bit of importance and glamor to the gathering. Only train wrecks attracted this kind of attention in Walker.

The Walker rally was the local debut of the new Grand Wizard and national director of the Knights of the Ku Klux Klan, David Duke, who has taken over after the unsolved murder of his friend and mentor, John Lindsay. The wealthy New Orleans real estate investor ran the White Citizens Council in New Orleans in the 1960s and introduced ninth-grader Duke, who says he was researching a school paper on integration, to white supremacist and Nazi ideology. The teenager, whose own father was working for an oil company in Southeast Asia, found a father figure in Lindsay, a known Nazi sympathizer. Through his years at John F. Kennedy

High School, his friends and teachers talked openly about Nazi philosophy.

A neighbor, Phillis Wilenzick, heard strange stories of the boy from the housekeeper she shared with the family. One day Mrs. Wilenzick saw for herself: "Sure enough there was this giant Nazi flag on the wall, helmet on the night table. He had some kinds of guns. It looked like some kind of scene from World War II." The Dukes, Mrs. Wilenzick recalls, formed "a strange household — the parents were kind of sad people" with a father who was gone most of the time and a mother who was reclusive and drank heavily. "Maxine (Mrs. Duke) was extremely afraid he (David, then an LSU student) would come home on the weekends. I know she was scared." Years later, the housekeeper would tell *Times-Picayune* reporter Tyler Bridges that young David would berate his mother for drinking and once threatened to set her on fire.

Prodigy and mentor remained close during Duke's college years, when Lindsay formed his Knights of the Ku Klux Klan, and during Duke's wanderings in the early '70s. Duke and his wife Chloe were living with his sister in Seattle in 1973 when, Duke says, "I woke up from a nap and I knew exactly what I needed to do." He returned to Louisiana to work in Lindsay's Klan, serving as state Grand Dragon and national information director. Then in 1975 Lindsay was gunned down in a motel parking lot in Kenner just after meeting with his estranged wife. A grand jury investigated, but she was never charged with the murder.

In 1975, the new wizard set out to increase and broaden his Klan base. At the Walker rally, though a few older men were wearing their white Klan sheets (with the hoods off since they were inside), most were young couples who looked like they could be attending a PTA meeting. Then there were a few younger fellows in khaki uniforms and shiny boots.

"Are you Jewish?" the young man in khaki asked the reporter.

"No. Why?"

The young man leaned to the side to get a better look at the reporter's nose. "Are you sure?"

The band wound down and people filled the folding chairs and bleacher seats. A clergyman asked God's blessing and his intervention to halt the further mixing of the white race. Next, a sheeted speaker with a bald head and bulging red neck blazed on about the rising threat of "mongrelization," which the federal government is abetting by forcing "little blond, blue-eyed girls to go to school with niggers!"

This all seemed pretty funny to two reporters leaning on the side of the stage, until the previous speaker, blood now risen to his bald head, shook his fist at them: "You laugh one more time and you'll get your ass whipped."

It was not Free Speech Alley.

With the crowd suitably warmed up and the lights dimmed, an announcer introduced the "national director of the Knights of the Ku Klux Klan, David Duke." While the band played, a spotlight followed David Duke, dressed in a business suit, up the center aisle.

His speech, which was not preserved for posterity, ignored the International Jewish Conspiracy and focused directly on the evils of forced integration with blacks. Apparently there was no point in confusing his audience with too many menaces at once. His delivery was better than in his college days. He was careful not to use the word "nigger," as opposed to the earlier speakers who tossed it about liberally.

Next up was the celebrity attraction: blond, pretty Mary Bacon. For the past few months, she had been a hot personality story for breaking the gender barrier at racetracks in Florida and New York, but this side of her had not been covered in the press. She has spent enough time around blacks in the stables, she told the crowd, to not want the races any closer. "How would you like your sister to be raped by one of them?" Strong stuff. Bacon, however, didn't realize what a good job the young wizard had done promoting her appearance in the media. As she walked off the stage, cheers and applause ringing in her ears, she had no way of knowing that she had ridden her last mount at Saratoga.

The light of the cross-burning that followed captured the intent gleam of the wizard as he saluted the flames with outstretched right arm. If, as future researchers would attest, the Klan was merely an organizing and money-making front for Duke's Nazi activities, it was working beautifully. The time was right for tapping into the simmering discontent among whites, especially in the old rural Klan strongholds. The liberating '70s and the advance of civil rights left these folks cold. They were seeing more long-haired hippies, more black men with white women, more Negroes on job sites, more black women with children in tow piling up shopping carts and paying with food stamps, more busing and integration in schools. The federal government was taking over life in the South — and the politicians like Edwin Edwards, a Catholic *and* a coonass, were selling out the white race for black votes and liberal, probably Communist, money.

Duke had hit upon a virulent and forgotten constituency of conservative whites who felt the world was tilting against them and in favor of blacks and radicals. If their jobs were not in danger, then it was only a matter of time. The world was changing fast, their South was in full retreat — and no one was standing up to fight. Except this David Duke, the smooth and articulate new voice of the Klan, a fine-looking young man who dressed well, who smiled and who could frame in complete sentences all the frustration and anger they were feeling. Under his wizardry, he said, membership would jump 500 to 10,000. And once a name was on his list, it never got off.

The candidate is fielding questions. The Arab student wants Duke's opinion of foreign aid. The familiar political response is to bemoan sending so much money overseas when there are such pressing problems at home. Not Duke: "The problem with foreign aid is the U.S. is giving billions to Israel to kill Palestinians."

The black female student wants to know more about the transformation of the young radical: "What made you change your attitude from 20 years ago?"

"My relationship with people and my relationship with Christ."

"Gimme a break," yells the young fellow in sunglasses.

"When did you accept Christ?" asks someone else.

"When I was 13 and I've been reborn every day."

"Hypocrite!"

Duke raises his hand. "There wouldn't be churches without sinners."

A black student challenges him: "Would you have a rally at Southern?"

"I'd be glad to if I could come out alive." That doesn't quite sound right. He tries again: "I would think students there would want me governor because I will work to preserve the identity of Southern."

"Louisiana doesn't want David Duke," yells a student.

"Yes, we do," a few yell back.

Duke has accomplished what he came to do. He will get singular news coverage tonight for his appearance, with the slant that he was warmly received by the student body. "He did fantastic," says the preppie-looking student in the button-down shirt and longish hair. "He's a verbal assassin. No one can touch him."

Well, almost. Duke's parting shot—"You know I represent more change than any other candidate"—comes zinging back at him from the rear of the crowd: "Yeah, all that plastic surgery."


Change was not always David Duke's friend.

At an Alexandria truckstop on this first Wednesday morning of November 1980, the old boy in the baseball cap was one happy redneck. "I know one thing Reagan's gonna do," he told his pals drinking coffee at the counter. "He's gonna get all them niggers off welfare."

Talk about cruisin' for disillusion — but at the dawn of the Reagan era, anything seemed possible in the Deep White South. The news was not good for welfare queens but it could not be much worse for David Duke. With the Great Communicator on the watch, who needed a neo-Nazi to save Western Civilization?

The success David Duke's KKK and Nazi satellites had in the 1970s, feeding on fears of godless liberalism and rising welfare hordes, stood to be victims of Reagan feel-good conservatism.

By 1979 Duke was ready to move on from the Klan. It didn't help that a rival Klansman was claiming that Duke had offered to sell him the oath-secret Klan mailing list for $35,000. Without the Klan, and with Reagan pulling the far right closer to the mainstream, Duke had to look for a niche on the fringe where people were still mad as hell and willing to send money. He formed a new group in 1980, the National Association for the Advancement of White People (NAAWP), which he described as a "civil rights organization." Basically, it was the Klan without the sheets.

Besides providing a steady income and a link to the far right, the NAAWP, through its organ the *NAAWP News*, gave Duke an outlet for his writing, which he is proud of. Though not proud enough to attach his name to two earlier books he wrote. Under the pseudonym "Mohammed X" he wrote *African Atto* in 1973, a 70-page manual which is supposed to teach blacks how to fight "Whitey" in the streets (Mohammed advises that you shout fighting words like "Hotto!" when attacking to terrorize your prey). The idea, he said, was to supply the Klan with the names and addresses of black radicals fool enough to buy the manual. In 1976 came the soft-porn self-help sex manual *Finderskeepers*, which is fairly tame stuff except for the passage on oral sex and the modern woman: "Many actually develop a taste for it. That's quite a bedtime snack. At least it's low on calories." Duke insists he only wrote the chapters on diet and fitness under the pseudonym "James Konrad," leaving the hard stuff to "Dorothy Vanderbilt."

25

The NAAWP proved to be a good money-maker, and Duke was able to siphon out thousands a year to his company, BC&E, for consulting. He ran Americana Books on the side, which offered pro-Nazi and anti-Semitic books on special order. Some quick-profit opportunities presented themselves. When he was arrested with Klansmen during anti-civil rights demonstrations in Forsyth County, Georgia, he raised $20,000 for a legal defense fund to pay a $50 fine. He did not claim enough income earned in the 1980s to file a state income tax return (the minimum was $12,000), but he did manage to play the stock market and, now divorced, enjoy the bachelor's life. A Las Vegas regular remembered being struck by a sight on the *Pride of Mississippi* gambling cruise boat. "There was David Duke. But he looked like Edwin. He had a babe on each arm and he was shooting craps and betting pretty heavy."

Yes, he did look different. In 1988, a leading New Orleans plastic surgeon performed several procedures on Duke, including a nose reduction, a chin implant and chemical peels to remove bags and wrinkles around his eyes. Duke would tell the *Times-Picayune* that the nose surgery was necessary because it had been broken. He said he did not recall the chemical peels, which are second-degree facial burns. He changed his hairstyle from the combed-down-and-parted traditional look to a fluffed-up, blow-dried cut.

Though Duke had learned how to make a steady income from his ideals, his political progress stalled out in the Reagan era. He was soundly defeated in 1975 and 1979 state Senate races against conservative incumbents. When he announced his candidacy for president in 1988 on the Populist Party ticket, he predicted he would receive more votes than Jesse Jackson did in the primaries. Not even close: Duke polled about 44,000 votes in 12 states, about .005 percent of the popular vote. As George Bush and the conservative wing of the Republican Party extended the comfortable Reagan era, David Duke appeared stranded on the eroding fringe of the forgotten far, far right. Duke so faded in the late '80s that Lance Hill, a Tulane graduate student who tracked the white supremacist movement, came to the conclusion "this guy will never go anywhere" and dumped most of his research files on Duke.

The angry Silent Majority that started the decade was sleeker, more prosperous and contented than it had been in many years. Only a few pockets of the country were suffering from a depressed economy and an unstable political climate. Lucky for Duke, the worst of those was close to home.

His big break came in the form of two magic words for any aspiring politician: *open seat*. The Republican state representative in Metairie's District 81 resigned to run for a judgeship, creating the need for a special election in January 1989. Duke's only problem was that the house he owned on Cypress Street was two blocks outside of the district. So he rented an apartment in the district, changed his registration to the Republican Party and announced for state representative.

District 81 in suburban Jefferson Parish runs the demographic gamut of upper-class country club Republicans to lower-middle-class Reagan Democrats. The voters are among the most conservative urban dwellers in the state. One of the parish's most popular politicians, Democratic Sheriff Harry Lee, secured his political career by ordering his deputies to stop and question any black youths driving through white neighborhoods and by suggesting blockades at the parish line on streets that connect New Orleans to Metairie.

Duke created a media stir by announcing his candidacy, but polls showed little support for the ex-Klansman in these quiet suburban streets. A few miles away, however, the streets of downtown New Orleans weren't nearly so quiet. During a parade in the city on Martin Luther King Jr. Day, several fights broke out and some whites were beaten up by young blacks. The incidents were played up on the local TV news, along with several other high-profile violent crimes, hitting a deep vein of the fear and hostility in the nearby white suburban enclave. Duke, running with his anti-crime, anti-tax message, reaped the benefits of the incidents without having to mention them.

On the day after Ronald Reagan left office in January 1989, David Duke ran well ahead of six candidates and landed in the runoff with quiet, staid John Treen, the brother of the former governor.

Metairie had gone and done it now. The nation's most famous Klansman was on the verge of legitimate power. There followed the descent of the national media, which had not seen much of Louisiana since the fall of Edwin Edwards. The national Republican Party's post-inaugural glow turned to deep embarrassment. The party reacted predictably and badly. Republican officials from George Bush to Ronald Reagan joined the Archbishop of New Orleans, the Jewish Anti-Defamation League of New York and the NAACP to form an indignant chorus of denunciation and to demand that voters reject the evil, racist David Duke. The outside attack only heightened Duke's maverick appeal at home. The establishment had dared the voter. Never dare the voter.

Despite denunciations, the Washington Republicans couldn't keep Duke out of their mainstream. He expropriated the slogan "Read my lips, no new taxes," bringing him loud cheers from growing campaign audiences, which were always augmented by Duke ringers.

On election day, David Duke stood on the median of Veterans Highway waving to the honking motorists. Several groups of young volunteers waving blue Duke signs in the back of pickup trucks rode the streets all day. When outnumbered Treen supporters manned a street corner on Metairie Road to wave signs for their candidate, three Duke supporters across the street shouted "Go home nigger lover" at them for more than two hours.

Driving into town, UPI reporter Steven Watsky noted that the anti-litter "Don't Mess With Jefferson" sign had been transformed with a sticker to read "Don't Mess With DUKE." Fair warning.

That night at the Duke victory party at the Metairie VFW Hall, young beer-drinking Duke supporters started unloading on reporters in the roped-off media section. Watsky watched as they called the black cameramen and reporters "niggers." When the hecklers discovered Watsky's name, they chanted, "We missed one of you in the gas chambers." A black cameraman told the reporter, "Shit, we need to get out of here before they lynch us."

With the returns flowing in and Duke clinging to a tiny lead, the candidate appeared to claim victory and, curiously, immediately shifted his target: "Mr. Buddy Roemer, read my lips, no new taxes."

Watsky had seen all he could take, but as he tried to get out of the cramped hall, one of the hecklers punched him in the chest. "I remember seeing stars and dropping to my knees in pain," said Watsky, who had suffered bruised ribs in a recent car accident. "I was pissed. I rose, cocked my fist and looked at the jerk. But then a photographer came up and grabbed my arms from behind. 'Don't do it. They'll kill you,' he said."

Onstage, David Duke announced it was "a new day for America." He won by 227 votes.

# 3. Hamlet, Prince of Politics

Good morning, Governor," says the TV reporter. Buddy Roemer smiles — now that's the first time anyone's called him that — as he opens the door of his Shreveport hotel suite just after 1 o'clock on the morning after the 1987 gubernatorial primary. It's his first press conference as Kingfish-elect.

Moments before, the candidate, his wife and his closest campaign aides were debating over whether to call it a night or to call Edwin Edwards when the governor and his entourage appeared on the TV screen. "We felt this amazing sense of drama, the thought that something was going to happen," remembers top aide Len Sanderson. The feeling had built all day, starting when the morning rain — the traditional killer of North Louisiana candidates — did not stop the heavy turnout around Shreveport. "Then we felt we had made the runoff. Then we felt we were going to lead," says Sanderson. Then when Edwards said the words, "Buddy just looked at me and clenched his right fist and he nodded. We won." It hardly seems real at first. Then the governor calls and says, according to the governor-elect, "I'll do whatever you want me to do, but I'm gone." Then the press comes beating at the door. Then the state troopers show up. Before dawn, power begins to shift. The Kingfish is dead. Long live the Kingfish.

The 44-year-old congressman's victory is singular and unprecedented in that it comes without the strings that tethered all his predecessors, except maybe Huey Long. He didn't rely on the courthouse gang and the network of sheriffs, assessors and mayors considered essential for getting out the rural vote. Nor did he buy into the major black political groups to get the votes in the cities. He isn't a Republican, so he didn't have the state's only organized party working for him. He did not start, or end, with the circle of big contributors vying to back the right horse. And he hardly projected the typical reformer image of the blandly wholesome, apolitical, All-American boy. No, overthrowing the system took someone as tough, as wily, as ambitious — damn it, as mean — as the guy who started it. Sanderson would say, "What people liked about Buddy was he was a cocky bantam rooster like Huey Long, who could look you in the eye and say, 'I can handle this. Let me at it.' "

But something is not connecting. If Edwin Edwards was the legitimate political heir to the populist power of the Longs, what has Buddy Roemer inherited? And from whom? He hit the statewide scene in 1987 as the dragonslayer, the maverick, the revolutionary at the palace gates. But he started the journey years before that, as the young political insider who grew up in the very system he now pledged to take apart. During his 1987 campaign, to shrink the state bureaucracy, the revolutionary candidate promised to "brick up the top three floors of the Education Building." No wonder. That's where his office used to be.


When Edwin Edwards was informed by phone in the spring of 1971 that the Roemer family, after a day of auditioning candidates for governor, would back the Cajun congresssman, he specifically asked if Charles Roemer's oldest son, Buddy, would get personally involved with campaigning. The young Harvard grad was eager to jump into his first statewide race. Though he got mixed reviews on taking orders and following through, he did well pinch-hitting for Edwards at some speaking engagements and seemed adept at analyzing polls.

The Bossier Parish family's role grew as the race wore on. By the time the chaotic Edwards campaign lurched into the second primary with a four-point lead over newcomer Bennett Johnston, Edwards asked Charlie Roemer to come to New Orleans to take over management of the state organization.

Charles Roemer was a complex man who embodied many of the contradictions of the Edwards campaign and, later, administration. He had taken over a cotton farming and ginning operation from his mother, who, after a divorce, had married Henry Meyer, owner of Scopena Plantation in Bossier Parish. Charles Roemer II and his wife Adeline moved into the rambling, ranch-style plantation compound with his mother, the strong family matriarch, now widowed. Charles Elson Roemer III, the first of five children, was born there in 1943. "He was the apple of his parents' eyes," recalls a family friend. "Buddy could do no wrong." Indeed, he excelled in school, both in public school and in Sunday school, where, at age 12, he was chosen to deliver a sermon to the congregation of First Methodist Church in Shreveport. He graduated valedictorian of his high school class and, at age 16, enrolled at Harvard. Back in Bossier with his MBA, Buddy got a crash post-graduate education in politics with his front-row view of the Edwards campaign.

The 1971 runoff was a watershed election that reversed the traditional dynamics of recent governor's races. This time the populist with the rural sheriffs and courthouse gang support was Edwin Edwards, a South Louisiana Catholic, while the urban reform candidate was Bennett Johnston, a Protestant from Shreveport. Johnston appeared to have the momentum rolling into the final week. The state senator was doing so well in Uptown New Orleans and Baton Rouge that he decided to concentrate in the end on the more populous southern cities instead of returning to his base in the north. Edwards stuck close to home, got his vote out and won by 4,488 votes, a margin of less than .3 percent.

Charlie Roemer ruffled his share of feathers in the runoff, but he pleased the one who counted. Edwards tapped Charlie Roemer for the No. 2 post in state government, commissioner of administration, because the executive impressed him more as a smooth administrator than a political operative. According to associates, Roemer had a larger view of his own political skills, which was fine with Edwards, who knew how to deal with people who thought they were good politicians. Roemer's ego and ambition gave him the command authority to fill the huge job of effectively running the giant engine of government without bothering Edwards with a lot of nonpolitical details.

In the *laissez-faire* ethical atmosphere of the first Edwards administration, what followed was not unexpected.

In August of 1972, Charles Roemer negotiated a $1.3 million computer services contract with Software, Inc., a Texas company owned by Dr. B. G. Schumacher. Two months after that deal was struck, Schumacher offered to pay Buddy Roemer $80,000 to provide some data processing programs for a new company that Schumacher was setting up for his teenaged daughters.

Buddy Roemer would say later he did not know that his father had negotiated a state contract with Schumacher. He said he only told Dad about the $80,000 deal ($60,000 of it was paid) after Buddy appeared before a federal grand jury in New Orleans that was investigating Software, Inc., for allegedly laundering federal welfare payments to the state-run Family Health Foundation.

When the elder Roemer did learn of the deal, he told the press he felt like he had "been hit by a ton of bricks. . . . There's no way I can come out of this without egg on my face."

The embarrassment did not stop the Roemers from getting into another excellent deal with a company supplying computers to the state. The U.S. Justice Department investigated the possible relationship between Honeywell, Inc., selling the state $16 million

33

in computer equipment and a deal whereby the Roemers' family business, Innovative Data Systems (IDS), paid Honeywell a fraction of the value of a $1 million computer system.

This time Buddy spent three hours before a Baton Rouge grand jury explaining his business dealings with Honeywell. Hours after flying home, young Roemer was spotted driving erratically on Interstate 20 near Marshall, Texas. When a state trooper tried to flag him down, Roemer rammed into the back of the Highway Patrol squad car. Roemer explained that he was suffering from insulin shock associated with his juvenile diabetes. He was treated and released.

After a lengthy investigation and an exhaustive investigative series in the *New Orleans Times-Picayune,* the grand jury took no action and the matter died.

After two grand jury visits, the younger Roemer reasoned that there had to be less stressful ways to make money in politics. A new election cycle was coming around and, this time, Buddy would not be working cheap. From 1974 to 1976, Buddy Roemer became Louisiana's most successful political consultant. His winning streak included victories over three incumbents: Kelly Nix over Superintendent of Education Louis Michot, Gil Dozier over Agriculture Commissioner Dave Peace and Jerry Huckaby over veteran Congressman Otto Passman.

"We never lost one," says Roemer, who knew to work with the best in the business: late Shreveport ad man Jim Leslie and creative director Deno Seder. "We made a lot of money, but that never turned me on," says Roemer. "I'm not a money person. For me, it was a way to get into politics."

No kidding. IDS could offer a candidate services that other firms could not match. As one former Roemer associate recalls, "His father could raise money and Buddy could read polls. It was a neat package. The old man could raise money faster than Gillis Long." (The late congressman is the acknowledged legend in political fundraising.) As commissioner of administration, Charlie Roemer was in the best position of anyone in state politics to raise $100,000 in an afternoon for a candidate he really liked. He especially liked the ones who hired his son. And if $100,000 wasn't enough, and it never was, the Roemers would encourage a candidate to borrow all he could from the bank to pay for more polling and more ads. Paying it back would be no problem, as long as you won.

Kelly Nix won the superintendent of education race in 1975, and woke up the next morning $500,000 in debt. But the Roemers hardly abandoned him. Who would want to abandon the superintendent of education, with one of the largest discretionary budgets in state government?

Buddy Roemer says he worked for Kelly Nix for one month "to help him get organized. I spent 31 days there. I got out never to return to state government."

Kelly Nix, however, recalls that Buddy Roemer worked in the department "for about six months" and was paid personally by Nix as a consultant. According to Nix, Buddy helped to set up the financial department and negotiated business contracts with suppliers while Nix worked on education programs. According to another Roemer associate at the time, "Buddy Roemer was the *de facto* deputy superintendent. Basically, he cut the deals. Buddy ran the business end. Kelly stuck to education." To help Nix retire his campaign debt, Roemer says he spoke at one fundraiser for the superintendent. According to others in the department, though, "You couldn't get to Kelly's office without going past Buddy's desk, and you couldn't get past Buddy without buying a ticket to a fundraiser or something like that."

Nix, a former college professor, was unequipped to manage the complex business and personnel affairs of the massive department. When he took office, he had over 1,200 unclassified appointments (not under Civil Service) to fill. According to a department source, AFL-CIO leader Victor Bussie was given half of the appointments to fill, those in vo-tech education, while the other 500 to 600 became Charlie Roemer's patronage. In time, the Civil Service

Commission gained control of these positions. "But (Charlie) Roemer had already hired them, so they were frozen into place as classified employees," says the former associate.

After a while Nix began to wonder who was working for *him*. When the superintendent fired one of Roemer's hirelings, the employee was back on the job within a week.

By his second term, Nix began to break with Roemer, but past ties to the commissioner helped to break Nix in the end. In 1982, Nix was named as an unindicted co-conspirator in a case in which the state's special education director, Henry L. Smith, was convicted of skimming $360,000 from a state contract and sent to federal prison for two and a half years. Though Smith was a Charlie Roemer placement, no evidence pointed to the former commissioner's involvement. That was fine, for Mr. Roemer was facing larger problems at the time.


Carlos Marcello's first notion that something was going terribly wrong came on a phone call from his friend Aubrey Young, who had just heard from Charlie Roemer, who had just spoken to Edwin Edwards, who had just been subpoenaed to testify before a federal grand jury regarding the state's insurance business.

Oh shit.

The old Mafia boss, who ran the country's most insulated, hard-to-penetrate organized crime operation, realized he had just been stung by an old friend (Joe Hauser had turned FBI informant) and two young agents posing as crooked insurance men. Marcello had taken to the two men, Hauser's "nephews," called them "his boys" and agreed to help them snare some big government insurance contracts. One day Marcello called them very excited about a strong nibble he received from the state commissioner of administration.

Charlie Roemer had dabbled with the idea of running for governor himself at the end of Edwards' second term (the governor is limited by the constitution to two successive terms), but decided instead to back state Senator Sonny Mouton in 1979. Acting as Mouton's campaign manager while still Edwards' commissioner, Roemer received $25,000 from Joe Hauser and the undercover agents. Roemer would maintain that it was only a campaign contribution with no strings attached. Hauser and the agents would testify that Roemer agreed to give state employee insurance contracts to the agents in return for a $43,000-a-month kickback.

Even when tipped off, Marcello still couldn't believe he had been taken. Dismissing the investigation, Marcello told Young on the phone he was confident that Charlie Roemer would hold to the cover story that the two only discussed oil and hazardous waste business, never insurance. "He ain't scared," growled Marcello.

Aubrey Young agreed, "He, he's got some balls."

But the feds had tapes, and at the trial, Marcello's and Roemer's defenses were shredded by them. The tapes revealed Marcello's own bragging about his friendship with Louisiana politicians, from Earl Long to Jimmie Davis to John McKeithen, and their fear of association with him. About Edwards, he said, "He's the strongest sonofabitchin' governor we ever had. He fucks with women and plays dice, but won't drink. How do you like dat?"

After a lengthy, sensational trial, Carlos Marcello was found guilty of one count of racketeering, as was Charlie Roemer. Roemer would later be sentenced to three years in prison and would serve 15 months. Charlie Roemer's family surrounded him in the courtroom, except one, Buddy, who had remained at the hotel.

Throughout his prison sentence, Roemer said he was frequently visited by FBI agents who told him he did not need to be doing this time, if he would only talk about his old boss Edwards. But Charlie Roemer did his time in silence.

In 1989, years later, after his release and his son's election, Roemer's conviction was overturned by a federal court, which found the Brilab application of the racketeering statute to be unconstitutional.

After WBRZ newsman Barry Erwin interviewed Charlie Roemer live, the two watched the station play Governor Buddy Roemer's reaction to the news. Choking back tears, Buddy said what happened to his father was unfair, "but he took it like a man."

"Gee, Buddy seemed pretty emotional," said Erwin to the elder Roemer.

"Yeah," said Charlie, "and he's the only one in the family who thought I was guilty."


Well before Brilab, Buddy Roemer was looking to establish a political career of his own and to cut his ties to his father in state politics. He almost did so in 1978, finishing third in a close three-way race to succeed retiring Joe D. Waggoner in Congress. Roemer led in the polls until the final week of the campaign, the week when campaigns are decided. Roemer was faced with the choice of putting up money to get the endorsements of some major black groups, or seeing that support and those votes go to state Representative Buddy Leach. Len Sanderson remembers that Buddy took a long walk through the cotton fields of Scopena, and came back with his decision: "We'll run third." He did. Leach won but was indicted, and later acquitted, on vote-buying charges from the election. In 1980, Leach was wounded and bitter. Buddy had been lionized in the Shreveport press for losing with principles. On his second try he won election to Congress on the same day Ronald Reagan won the presidency.

Congress allowed the 37-year-old Roemer to recast his political career. He moved out of the shadow of his father and Edwin Edwards and into that of Ronald Reagan. Roemer went to Washington determined to show his fierce independence. It didn't take long. The freshman Democrat's first vote was against Tip O'Neill for Speaker of the House. Later recognizing he had gone a bit overboard, Roemer repented his sins to veteran Congressman Gillis Long to escape exile to forgotten committees. The House

Democratic leadership, though highly annoyed with the headstrong Roemer (O'Neill called him "often wrong but never in doubt"), had to deal with the growing boll weevil movement (Democratic congressmen who vote Republican) in the South. In 1985, Roemer tied for first among Democrats on voting for Reagan administration measures. Though Roemer used the bluff that he might switch parties, he recognized, says Sanderson, that "the best thing to be in Washington was a conservative Democrat because both parties had to come to you." He parlayed that middle position into a seat on the House Banking Committee, which was always a keen interest of his. His 1980 campaign finance report included donations from owners and officers of banks and savings and loans throughout his district. A 1990 story in the *Shreveport Journal* also revealed that Roemer had major loans at seven financial institutions in his district that, according to reported ranges, fell between $200,000 and $550,000.

Though he tried to keep his fences mended on the Hill, House colleagues, rating their peers in *Congressional Quarterly*, described Roemer as an "unguided missile on the House floor." His colleagues did not fault his principles or his brains, or his adherence to the most important rule: getting reelected. After his hard-fought 1980 victory, Roemer fielded no opposition in 1982, 1984 and 1986. It was time for his next step.

When a group of Louisiana savings and loan executives trekked to Washington in 1986, they were surprised to hear Congressman Roemer depart from talking banking issues to say, "I'm not running for governor, but if I were, I would walk the state talking about our children."

Buddy Roemer was saddling up. From the beginning, he was using *that* word. He told Sanderson, "I want to run a revolutionary race, not the way things have been run in the past. That would not be fun. That would not be interesting." When Roemer was looking at running for the Senate, he considered a contribution limit of $100 to separate him from the pack. That may have separated him too much in the governor's race. "We compromised on a $5,000 limit." He also decided against accepting PAC money, though corporate checks would be okay.

In purely conventional terms, Roemer knew he had as solid a base as any other congressmen running would have in their districts. Beyond home turf, though, Roemer knew, "he could not play the retail game," says Sanderson. "He knew he was not good at that kind of campaigning and he would piss off people and the retail people (sheriffs, assessors, local politicians) would eat him alive. We thought if we kept a strong wholesale message we could win. We would do the same thing Reagan did nationally. We'd be Reagan with brains. And the side benefit was we would not have to run a campaign that his father would be involved in."

When the campaign started, Sanderson was Roemer's 35-year-old administrative aide in Washington who had been with Buddy since the first congressional campaign. Before that, as a reporter for the *Baton Rouge Morning Advocate*, Sanderson wrote investigative stories on Koreagate that once inspired Edwin Edwards to say the reporter had "a sick, deranged mind." Thereafter, Sanderson always kept in his desk a jersey with the governor's words emblazoned thereon. A few more shirts could be filled with descriptive remarks about the Alexandria native, like "sarcastic," "rude," "abrupt," as well as "absolute taskmaster" and "excellent organizer." A bad car wreck in January had cost Sanderson one lung, which made it difficult to spend much time in the Louisiana environment. By the time he came down to stay in July, though, the impact was immediate. "The only divisiveness in this campaign occurs when Len Sanderson gets up in the morning," noted consultant Raymond Strother. In many ways, the bright, acerbic Sanderson was the soulmate of the bright, acerbic Roemer. "We can call each other names," says Sanderson.

They could agree, however, along with Strother, on how to run an outsider campaign — and were very nearly wrong. The Roemer team felt that spending money early would be a waste in a race against a well-known incumbent and a crowded field. Yet the other three challengers (Congressmen Bob Livingston and Billy Tauzin and Secretary of State Jim Brown) raised their visibility by going on TV early, which bumped up their polls numbers a little, helping them raise more money.

Roemer remained mired in fifth place and single digits in the polls. "The gloom, the ongoing depression, it was terrible," remembers press secretary Mark McKinnon. "Buddy just stood in the corner and hung in." Outside the inner circle, key supporters demanded that he go on TV just to show he was still in the race. Roemer had to face down one group that wanted to raise money for third-party spots for him.

Campaign staffers had to insulate Roemer from the constant outside second-guessing, especially from Charlie Roemer, who could not get his phone calls to his son returned. "He hated us," said a staffer. "He thought we were doing it all wrong."

He wasn't alone. Not even the staff was convinced the radical campaign strategy would work. Not even the candidate. After Strother prepared a batch of radical TV commercials, with Buddy giving the camera the Hot Eyeball and claiming, "I love Louisiana, but I hate Louisiana politics," the campaign tested the spots on different focus groups composed of target voters. The results rocked him. Says Sanderson, "Generally, what we spent money on, Edwin Edwards could have told us with his eyes closed. That people want their kids educated, but they don't want to test them against kids in Texas because they're afraid ours won't be as smart; that they want good jobs, but they don't want to have to learn computers; that they want qualified politicians but not ones so smart that they can't talk to them. Besides, we've got good food and music and a $3 license plate, so don't bother us."

Roemer recalls being "shocked" that "their expectations were much lower than I envisioned." The apathetic responses were so unsettling, says Roemer, "that I was wondering if I should be in the race." What kept him in was the 1978 experience, when he finished third but impressed people that he stood for something. Even if he couldn't crack the apparent Edwards-Livingston lock on the runoff, he would run a race that folks would remember in 1991, or in a 1990 challenge to U.S. Senator Bennett Johnston. To be safe, though, the first spot he did air had him railing about potholes in highways.

The saying around headquarters was "go long." After the initial statewide advertising buy, the campaign was flat out of money. But not out of luck. On the day before his spots began in New Orleans, the *Times-Picayune* endorsed Roemer. That was a body blow to home boy Bob Livingston, as it hinted that the paper had lost faith in the Republican's ability to beat Edwards or to deal with the Democratic Legislature. Roemer hit the phones and pressed the editors of the state's other major dailies. One by one, all but the *Lafayette Advertiser* endorsed him within the next two weeks.

The combination of the endorsements followed by the commercials opened the financial floodgates. In that week, $200,000 came in; on Friday alone, $96,500.

Roemer started edging up in the polls into the Anyone But Edwards traffic jam, where both Congressman Billy Tauzin and Secretary of State Brown were starting to pull in undecided voters. Cajun Tauzin could not escape the mark of Edwards, but Brown was beginning to build on his bland reform appeal. He could have seized the advantage but for a dreadful decision to air the most remarkable and self-destructive ad of the campaign. The middle challengers had fallen into a silly argument over who could beat Edwards in a runoff and who couldn't. To settle what he should have ignored, Brown aired a spot using a clip from an old news interview of Edwards saying that of all the candidates "the one with the best chance of beating me is Jim Brown." If Brown thought Edwards' words would bolster his electability, he overlooked what the comment did to his credibility.

That stopped Brown's momentum in time for his second gaffe to begin the great slide. When reporters at a Baton Rouge Press Club forum pressed the challengers on what they would do if they were eliminated from the runoff, Brown said he would not rule out endorsing any candidate. Standard waffle, but the open-ended response drove the Anyone But Edwards sensors wild. Maybe there was a secret Edwards-Brown pact. In another gift of good timing, the last candidate to stand and answer the question was Roemer. "No," he said determinedly, "the issue in this campaign is Edwin Edwards. We've got to slay the dragon. I would endorse anyone but Edwards." Wham. The next day Brown would say he was misquoted, while Roemer would order "Slay the Dragon" buttons. The Anyone But Edwards movement had found its Anyone.

By early October, it was too late to stop Roemer, the only candidate moving in the right direction. He played to the spotlight in masterly fashion, telling audiences, "It's not my footsteps the other candidates are hearing, it's you-r-r-s," his voice trembling with preacherly humility. The press, who had always liked Roemer, could now tout him as a contender — and his press clips glowed. It was the kind of reaction Edwin Edwards had foretold months before when he said, "If everyone in the state meets Buddy Roemer just one time, he will be the next governor." It was not meant as a compliment. /

Four days after the election, the only sign at Roemer's anonymous storefront headquarters that something official has happened are the two state police troopers lounging in the reception area. Taking a break from a backroom conference, Buddy Roemer strolls through the quiet outer office and, still in pep rally mode, pumps his fist and yelps, "Can you believe it? We did it!"

Len Sanderson and Steve Cochran look up wearily from their desks, which are quickly being taken over by phone messages and job applications. "I really wish there had been a runoff," says Sanderson. "We needed to bring in more people."

It would have helped. Having laid one questionable gift on Roemer, Governor Edwards was about to drop a surprise bonus. After the two met at the Mansion, Roemer came away shaking his head. "Wow, I couldn't believe how negative he was." (Years later, Roemer would recount that conversation: "He said, 'This job can't be done.' He said, 'I have no faith in this state or its people.' He said, 'The news media will eat you alive.' He said, 'You will be the best governor of this century, but they won't see it. They will nickel and dime you to death. They have their own agenda.' He was very hateful toward the news media. He was just so turned off by the whole proposition that I was surprised he ran again.") Edwards was not even interested in finishing his term. He acceded to the governor-elect's request to appoint Roemer's future commissioner of administration, Brian Kendrick, to that position for the last three months of Edwards' term. Then the governor took a long vacation. It seemed like Edwards was doing the right thing. Right for whom? By pulling out of the runoff, Edwards prevented Roemer from finishing Edwards off and putting together a governing coalition. By turning over *de facto* control of government early, Edwards robbed Roemer of a transition and a honeymoon. Overnight, the state's crushing problems became Roemer's.

Not just dollars-and-cents problems, which consumed the transition. "The life-or-death question — I wasn't prepared," Roemer would say later. "The first night I spent in the Mansion, the outgoing governor had given me a present, an execution (scheduled for midnight). I remember people were on the lawn dancing while I was upstairs with lawyers and family members deciding. . . . It's something governors and kings are unprepared for. I didn't want to do that the first night." But he did. The execution went on.

Politicians were similarly unprepared for the Roemer Treatment, which began the day after his election. Where a sensible winning candidate starts mending fences, Roemer came out with wire cutters. President of the Senate Sammy Nunez and Speaker of the House John Alario, both Edwards' allies, were moving quickly to lock up legislators' support to hold onto their leadership positions. Roemer showed he could move fast too. "I was surprised to come to work on Monday (after the election) and find that deal was being made. Nuh-uh, I said, no way, bullshit." The governor-elect came out with his own conservative choices for the leadership posts, Senator Allen Bares of Lafayette and Representative Jimmy Dimos of Monroe. Like the military dictator who suspends free elections until the electorate can be educated, Roemer could tolerate an independent Legislature up to a point, that point being the leadership. The two old leaders were entrenched, but a new governor is a powerful earth mover and he convinced the Legislature to dislodge both. The Revolution had won its first major political victory, one that would haunt Roemer for four more years.

A little scorched earth didn't seem to bother the Roemer team. They had won a radical campaign. They would deliver a radical administration. If Louisiana politicians did not like what they saw, who cared? The whole world was watching to see if the revolutionary politician could keep the people with him to transform hidebound Louisiana. A successful two years, thought some, could set up Roemer for a race against the vulnerable Bennett Johnston. Not true, says Sanderson. "It was bigger than that. Buddy wanted to be president. We had proved that a Democrat could put together a wholesale race without catering to the special interests. If it could be done statewide, it could be done nationally. We always felt between Mabus (of Mississippi), Clinton (of Arkansas) and Roemer, one of them had a real shot."

Expectations on the homefront were enormous, especially among his political neophyte supporters in the cities, who were still aglow with revolution and ready to bask in reform. In those early days, a Hammond businessman could feel the change in the air. "I get up every morning and run out to get the paper to see what the Revolution is doing."

The Revolution was doing fine as the radical new administration entered its first legislative session. Roemer's direct-to-the-people style and the state's fiscal crisis allowed him to roll right over the Legislature and gain extraordinary new powers — unprecedented since Huey Long — to slash program budgets and raise fees. Cuts in social programs, though they alarmed black legislators, enabled him to pump new money into environmental enforcement, the universities and economic development. He passed a teacher pay raise hand-in-hand with a teacher evaluation plan that promised to yank the certification of unqualified instructors. His most radical change cut to the gut of Louisiana politics: campaign finance reform. His new law prohibited cash contributions completely and set a $5,000 limit on donations to statewide campaigns.

Every step along the way, he was careful to keep his cover, the people. In that first session, Roemer would do satellite uplinks and even some electronic town meetings to advance his reforms. Like it or not, legislators got with the program. The governor had no electoral mandate, but legislators feared he was building an electronic one. "Whether it was true or illusion," says Sanderson, "there was a fear among legislators that made them think—this guy is so good at going to the people that I have to vote with him or the voters will kill me.' "

Many trace Buddy Roemer's decline to the failure of fiscal reform in the spring of 1989, but it started months before that. At the end of his first regular session of the Legislature, the Revolution was on a roll while the traditional powers—labor, sheriffs, black leaders, polluters and the friends of Edwin Edwards—were in steep retreat. Then something happened. Or stopped happening. When the session ended, Buddy Roemer disappeared from public view. With the greatest challenge, fiscal reform, still ahead, the governor stopped sending out the revolutionary message.

"Buddy's a sprinter, not a marathoner," observes his friend Sanderson. Roemer's demanding, high-pressure work schedule, combined with his longtime bout with juvenile diabetes, sapped his strength.

Aside from that, the governor was finding that holding that revolutionary fervor is difficult once inside the castle walls. Roemer would learn that those walls aren't easy to call out from. "One of the dangers of holding high political office is you spend your time trying to make the office efficient and you divorce yourself from the people you get there with," Roemer would say years later. "You got there wearing cowboy boots and listening to people. You got there by capturing the feeling that you can do a certain thing. You are one of us. Then you go off to office. And if you're not careful, if the office is under attack, if it's on fire, you have to put the fucking fire out. You don't get down to the people."

Roemer lacked the stamina to be a revolutionary and the temperament to be a king. He avoided the high public profile expected of a governor. Even Dave Treen could throw a good party. Roemer quickly got bored with Mansion affairs and would retreat upstairs to watch ESPN and leave his wife Patti to deal with the guests. Instead of spending some time out of the office seeing the people and keeping the big revolutionary picture before them, he burrowed into the budget and lost himself, and his Revolution, in the details.

"Do I really want this job?" Buddy Roemer says it as an aside, but loud enough for reporters to hear, and to get the message. Midnight at the Revolution. Roemer's fiscal reform constitutional proposal, which he had touted as the solution to the state's budget problems, has been downed by the voters by a 55-45 percent margin. One way to read the people's message is: just because we voted for a revolution doesn't mean we want a change. Not in the one thing in this miserable economy that the people perceive is on their side: a populist tax structure that shields the broad middle class. Buddy wasn't quite sure of the message because he had stopped talking to them and selling them on the Revolution, as he had during that first session. Or maybe he just confused fiscal reform with the Revolution. The people were just informing him that they still had it straight, but maybe he had lost it.

According to Roemer the 1987 candidate, "The problem is not with our revenues. It's with our spending." What he found to be the real problem was that the deficit was bigger than he thought and that wringing waste and corruption from the system did not save as many millions as he predicted. The savings he did achieve were absorbed by new spending on teacher pay raises and the environment.

Governor Roemer fell victim to candidate Roemer's rhetoric. He had sold two revolutions to two constituencies. He had sold his good-government, educated, middle-class base on improving education and cleaning up pollution. He had sold the hardcore conservative, anti-tax, "aginner" voters on paring down government to the essentials. Still Roemer felt he could bind his coalition the way he won the election, with a strong finishing kick on TV. Problem was, he wasn't running against Edwin Edwards this time, but against the very anti-tax, anti-incumbent emotion he rode in 1987. In 1989, he spoke for the progressive, reform side of his base and left his angry voters behind, where someone was waiting for them.

It didn't take long for David Duke to get bored with the Legislature. By his affable manner he managed to achieve at least a superficial personal acceptance from colleagues, even blacks, who at least felt they knew where he was coming from. And what did it get him? His agenda on welfare reform and repeal of affirmative action would get headlines when introduced, but then would be tabled in committee without a hearing. The looming tax vote gave him someone else's target to shoot at. Opposing the governor's tax plan not only would bolster Duke's anti-tax reputation, which was preferable to his other reputation, but it would also expose him to a wider audience. He could rub shoulders with other respectable tax fighters. Appearing onstage with Jefferson Parish Assessor Lawrence Chehardy, the high priest of the homestead exemption, Duke ripped into Roemer's old campaign pledges: "Buddy Roemer promised he would scrub the budget. Instead he gave it a bubble bath."

When Roemer hit the airwaves to push his tax program, Duke hit the road, actually retracing his old Klan organizing trail through rural and small-town Louisiana — the same places where Roemer fared so well in tapping voter anger. This time the people came out to see Duke in numbers that surprised and disturbed local legislators, who were staying the hell out of the way.

Despite carping by his critics, Roemer believed he could sell anything to the people, if he just got back on TV and talked to them. But it had been a while since he had been in their living rooms, when he was an angry revolutionary, not a taxing governor. In personalizing the appeal, Roemer attracted the growing number of people who wanted a piece of him, from conservative Republicans who felt betrayed to black leaders who felt threatened.

Some would claim that the defeat of fiscal reform marked the death of the Roemer Revolution. But it didn't have to be that way. Buddy Roemer had just given the people an option: progressive, growth-oriented tax reform, or drastic cuts in government as we know it. The people chose B. That was the revolution they were looking for. Was Buddy ready to deliver it or not? B again. He patched together the next year's budget with renewed, so-called "temporary" sales taxes, moderate cuts, surplus funds and accounting maneuvers. The state would muddle along, but the governor's credibility would be muddled in the process. After his dire predictions of what would happen to the state if fiscal reform did not pass, fiscal reform did not pass . . . and nothing happened. Buddy had pushed tax reform with the slogan, "Louisiana's Worth It," but the people disagreed. Still ringing in their ears was his scrub-and-burn rhetoric of 1987. Roemer alienated his angry constituency by not following through on the deep bloody cuts they were expecting when they voted him in and then voted his fiscal reform plan down. Two chances are all you get with this crowd. Especially when there was a new agent of anger out on the stump co-opting Roemer's old seductive message. The response to that message from backwoods Louisiana even surprised Duke, and inspired him. "That campaign against the amendment showed me for the first time that I had a statewide appeal," Duke would say later. "That's what started my campaign for the Senate."

With fiscal reform dead, with Louisiana most needing its strongman ruler for hard times, the governor retreated into a deep fugue in the Mansion, all but avoiding contact with the Legislature, even his floorleaders. It was a side of his friend Len Sanderson had seen before. "I think he likes playing tragic hero. He lost his own anger. You can't play Hamlet with the situation the state was in. This state needs myths as big as we can get them. Hamlet was not who we needed." And someone who could call his bullshit was not who Buddy Roemer wanted. One of Roemer's first suggestions at a staff budget-cutting meeting was to close the state's Washington office that Sanderson headed. More old revolutionary hands began to drift away, replaced by old governmental hands like the new chief of staff, P. J. Mills, who had worked in the past with Charlie Roemer, who was coming around more himself.

With Roemer holed up at the house, more than his Revolution was crumbling around him. The move to the Mansion had not shaped up as a happy turn in the 15-year Roemer marriage. Patti Crocker was a 19-year-old divorcée working as a page at the 1973 constitutional convention when she met 30-year-old delegate Roemer, also recently divorced.

Friends think she could have handled the social demands of being the First Lady, had there been any. The Mansion went dark after the Roemers moved in. If Buddy Roemer wasn't going to return supporters' and politicians' phone calls, he certainly didn't feel like having them over for parties. Even in the staid administration of Dave Treen, he and Dodie kept up an active social schedule at the Mansion. Edwin Edwards didn't throw many parties, but if you had one, he'd more than likely show up. There was little of either in the Roemer years. The governor worked late, and to relax he would read or watch baseball on TV.

In early 1989, a woman in the administration expressed concern for Mrs. Roemer: "She's going crazy locked up in the Mansion. I've taken her to a George Michael concert and sometimes we sneak out late at night and go dancing, but she really wants to be around people." Patti once even told an acquaintance of how she used to sneak out of the Mansion at night and go to Capitol Grocery, a half mile away, for a soda. "What I remember most about that conversation is how desperate she seemed for normal company and to do normal things," said the friend, "even if she had to slip out of her own home and walk through a dangerous neighborhood just to have something to do."

The more Roemer withdrew after the spring of 1989, the greater the pressure built up on the marriage. By the fall, rumors were spreading that the marriage was in trouble. In October, Patti packed and left the Mansion with nine-year-old Dakota, the couple's only child.

The separation at last triggered a response in Buddy Roemer. Re-creating himself had worked for his politics — maybe it could help his grim personal life. In late 1989 and early 1990 the governor embarked on a crash journey of personal growth, which some saw as a desperate attempt to save his marriage and which others dismissed as an all-too-public mid-life crisis.

His guide turned out to be his boyhood friend and motivational speaker, Danny Walker, who ran some seminars called Adventures in Attitudes. Walker says he asked the governor after a depressed lunch one day: "Buddy, is what you're doing getting you the results you want? . . . I mean politically? With your family? Spiritually? Careerwise? If not, then change something."

Change something. Like your life. That appealed to Roemer, who was hardly leading a good one. But it wasn't enough for the governor to embark on an Adventure in Attitudes alone. He brought his whole staff in on it, for Walker noted they, like the boss, were spiritually closed. Soon the whole staff was packed off on retreat to communicate better, to honor more and to challenge negative thoughts. The last was achieved with the most famous prop of Roemer's personal growth phase, a rubber band on the wrist that one was to snap and mutter "cancel, cancel" whenever negative thoughts arose. The staff retreat was an adventure in transference, for the governor subjected all of his employees to his own therapy. It did not go well for the few who challenged the new orthodoxy and were told they were not with the program. As a part of the staff, Patti too attended. Two staff members said the exercise appeared to them to be Roemer's attempt to repatch his marriage as much as to reinvigorate the staff. She may have gotten the same impression, for she left early.

In a 1990 news interview in the Mansion, Roemer sat with his feet up on the desk. On it were several letters addressed to "Patti Roemer c/o Howard Johnson's Inn, Grand Junction, Colo." The only other item there was a picture of Patti.

Like many individuals following broken relationships, Roemer threw himself deeper into self-help. He took dancing lessons — one day he was seen showing off his Harlem Shuffle to a reporter in the Capitol rotunda. He put away his regular demanding nonfiction reading in favor of Robert Fulghum's tracts on love and honor, books like *It Was on Fire When I Lay Down on It* and *Everything I Need to Know I Learned in Kindergarten*. Things like the basics of respect and honor. All the things that Buddy should have learned in kindergarten.

News reports of the governor's personal growth odyssey did not bolster much confidence in him among his old voters. Appearing at a meeting in Denham Springs of angry citizens experiencing chronic flooding, Roemer took a page from Fulghum to explain his predicament. "This bed was on fire when I lay down on it."

From the back of the room came the predictable response: "And it's still on fire."

Inflicting his new awareness on his staff and even the people was one thing, but going touchy-feely on the Legislature was the last straw. Addressing a ceremonial opening of the 1990 legislative session in the Old State Capitol, the governor, after paying homage to his wife and even his mother-in-law, urged legislators, who sat slab-faced, to join hands with him and "meet me at the campfire, so that we can build a future for our children."

The legislators who understood what he was saying couldn't believe it was coming from the governor of Louisiana. So began the most infamous, out-of-control session of the Legislature since Uncle Earl lost it in the well of the House and had to be carted off to the asylum in Galveston. Within a month, Roemer's hand-picked president of the Senate was deposed in a counter-revolutionary coup. In the breakdown of leadership, one of David Duke's bills, a measure to outlaw affirmative action, actually made it to the House floor, and passed. Representative James David Cain ("I have three names and they're all in the Bible") presented—almost as a joke—a bill to set a maximum fine of $25 for anyone convicted of beating up a flag burner. The punch line was it passed. That was followed by a measure to jail record-store owners for selling albums containing nasty lyrics to minors—a bill even Tipper Gore labeled repressive. Then came the abortion armies, thousands of demonstrators on both sides, who occupied the Capitol steps and corridors for debate on the most restrictive anti-abortion law in the country. And, of course, the budget was a mess. Floorleaders received no direction from the Mansion, only homilies. Even the most hidebound legislators began feeling nostalgia for the old Revolution.

The *Atlanta Journal-Constitution*, in its self-appointed role as the conscience of the New South, flamed on its editorial page that the Louisiana Legislature was out to prove that it was "racist, sexist, backwards and oppressive." No one even noticed that it did not mention "corrupt."

# 4. The Dukewatch

It almost seems like he knew they were there.

The four people who met that evening in Beth Rickey's apartment on Coliseum Street in New Orleans all had been acting on their own to expose if not stop David Duke. Tulane history professor Larry Powell lived in Duke's legislative district and had been involved in voting rights litigation for black citizens in heavily white Jefferson Parish. Lance Hill had tracked Duke from his Klan days to the NAAWP as part of Hill's ten-year academic research at Tulane. Reverend Jim Stovall, the head of the Louisiana Interchurch Conference, felt compelled to drive down from Baton Rouge to walk the neighborhoods of Metairie asking people not to vote for David Duke in 1989. Beth Rickey, trying to alert her own Republican Party to the menace within, had exposed Duke for selling racist and anti-Semitic books from his legislative headquarters.

One thing they all had learned in the past year was that their independent efforts were not enough. They had seen Duke rise from fringe obscurity to elected office with ambitions to go higher. They had been stunned, not only by the fanaticism of his supporters, especially the young ones, but also by the casual attitude toward Duke — in fact, the flat refusal to get involved — from many people who should have known better. And they were disturbed that the harder they tried to spread the message on Duke the stronger he seemed to grow. They agreed a coordinated effort was needed to oppose him when he made his next move, whatever that would be.

The phone rang and Rickey answered.

"Beth, hi, this is David Duke." It's a joke, she thought at first, but there was no mistaking the voice. He was among them.

Perhaps state Representative Duke was following the code of another all-white secret society, the Mafia, which held: Keep your friends close and your enemies closer. If so, he had good reason to sidle up to Beth Rickey.

Having grown up in Republican politics, she was far less keen on political activism than on conventional politics. She campaigned for George Bush and, while going to graduate school at Tulane, had won election to the Republican State Central Committee. She barely knew who David Duke was when she agreed to do some opposition research for Republican legislative candidate John Treen. Rickey was in the right place. The Tulane Library houses one of the most extensive collections of Klan and neo-Nazi literature. A great body of it was written, edited or published by David Duke. Reading *The Crusader*, she confirmed her notion that Duke was a mean-spirited, racist nutcase, hardly to be taken seriously. Reading more, she was stunned, then repulsed, at Duke's early fascination with Adolf Hitler and Nazism; his continued publication of racist and anti-Semitic articles in the *NAAWP News*; the ads for his mail-order business specializing in racist and Nazi literature and tapes; and his association with the Populist Party, a haven for white supremacists, and with the Institute for Historical Review, a group devoted to disproving the Holocaust.

"I was determined to expose this man for the hate monger that he is," Rickey would later write. "I was sure that once my colleagues on the Republican State Central Committee heard that a Nazi was in their midst, they would all rise in collective indignation and denounce him."

She had so much to learn.


Following Duke's House election, Rickey, feeling a compulsion to do something about him, bought an airplane ticket to Chicago to follow Duke to a Populist Party convention. The party of Duke's presidential run was headed by Willis Carto, the leader of the rabidly anti-Semitic Liberty Lobby and the Institute for Historical Review.

Having faked her way through security, Rickey found herself sitting in the middle of a contingent of skinheads, except for the young man in the neatly pressed Nazi uniform next to her. "What am I doing here?" she asked herself.

But soon she got what she came looking for. "We did it!" shouted the newly elected state representative from Louisiana as Rickey's tape rolled. "My victory in Louisiana was a victory for the white majority movement in this country." With the crowd around her standing and chanting for the speaker, she noticed one of Duke's bodyguards staring at her. Paranoia rising, she stood and chanted along, "Duke, Duke, Duke."

His words that were most frightening to her came in closing: "Listen, the Republican Party of Louisiana is in our camp, ladies and gentlemen. I had to run within that process, because, well, that's where our people are."

As Duke basked in the cheers and salutes of skinheads, brownshirts and Klansmen, Rickey felt "like I was in on a dirty little secret."

The dirtier little secret, though, wasn't out yet. Representative Duke was forced to apologize to the House when his taped comments from the convention were reported in the press. By tradition, however, the House observes a high level of tolerance for scoundrels who have been blessed by the support of the people. Not just Duke's constituents. When Representative Don Bacque unsuccessfully challenged Duke's seating for failing to live in his own district, he received a torrent of angry mail and phone calls from his upscale Lafayette district. Then there was the story that quickly got around the Capitol of Duke strolling into Murphy's, a college bar, and being mobbed by students chanting "Duke, Duke" while some female students pressed on him pieces of paper on which they had written their phone numbers.

Rickey and her Tulane colleague Lance Hill were determined to cut Duke out of the herd. On the hunch that Duke was still in the hate-book business, the two went to Duke's house in Metairie, to the basement office of the NAAWP, asked for and purchased several anti-Semitic books. The most famous was *The Turner Diaries*, which foretells the white man's revolution and describes the scene of final victory, where lynched blacks and Jews hang from trees all over Southern California, along with the white women who dared to sleep with them. When the two sent back a researcher to buy *Hitler Was My Friend*, a young man there named Chris Winter said he was out of *Hitler Was My Friend* but explained that *Mein Kampf* was the one book about Hitler everyone should read. He charged her $7 and threw in a few for free, including *Did Six Million Really Die?* What made the discovery of Duke's sideline more interesting was that the NAAWP shared space in the basement with Duke's legislative district office, for which the state of Louisiana paid monthly rent.

Rickey and Hill felt they now possessed the missing link to connect Duke to his past. To detonate the new charge, they waited for the opening of the exhibit of Simon Wiesenthal's photographs of the Holocaust, which Buddy Roemer had invited to the State Capitol as a way to gig Duke.

As a part of the crowd that came up from New Orleans for the exhibit opening, Anne Levy sensed something more disturbing than the pictures. From the corner of her eye, she caught the image of the tall blond man, holding his hands behind his back, inspecting the photographs. "That triggered something in me, a flashback. That's the way the Nazis stood when they watched us," said Levy, who was smuggled out of the Warsaw ghetto with her family just before the war.

Anne Levy approached David Duke and tapped his shoulder. "What are you doing looking at this exhibit?" she demanded. He ignored her. She would not be ignored: "I thought you said this didn't happen."

"I didn't say it didn't happen," Duke snapped. "I said it was exaggerated."

"That's when I lost it," Levy said later. That's when the press noticed the confrontation and headed over. Duke beat a fast retreat to the House floor.

The next day at the Capitol, as Rickey and David Hagy were distributing to reporters a press release about Duke's book sales, Duke emerged from a nearby committee room. Oblivious to the bombshell being dropped on him, he stopped to sign a few autographs for tourists. Robyn Ekings of WVUE-TV approached him, cameras rolling, with a copy of *Did Six Million Really Die?*

"Who gave you that?" said the red-faced Duke. Ekings pointed to Rickey, who waved.

Duke blurted at her, "You're treating me like Salman Rushdie!" and then repeated his earlier getaway, with TV film crews in hot pursuit, to the sanctity of the House floor.

Until now for David Duke there had been no such thing as bad publicity. Press and liberal attacks, as in his House race, only gave him more exposure and maverick appeal. The Klan and Nazi stuff was part of his radical youth, his past, and no one had linked that past to his present. This Rickey woman and her friends, though, were getting close as well as on his nerves—and he was about to turn it around.

She told him she had company and would he please call back later. When he did, they talked — or mostly he did — for three hours, about: Roosevelt's "treason" at Pearl Harbor, Greek culture, blondes in India, the superior culture in Iceland, sperm banks, Duke's own love of nature, inequality of the races, and so on, while in the background he played over and over the Mike and the Mechanics song "Can You Hear Me Running?" Beth Rickey hung up the phone spent and disoriented. The object of her research, sleuthing and guerrilla operations, once as distant and impersonal as old newspaper clippings, now had come to life, and was pressing to get into hers.

An odd courtship ensued. "We established a friendship of sorts. There was an intellectual exercise going on," said Rickey, who wasn't blind to his motives. "If someone is being a friend, you don't discount the fact that he's trying to neutralize you. . . . His motive was to make himself a real person to me." To a degree it was working. "On one level I liked him and I think he liked me. It made it difficult. I knew it was getting to me. Several times I had to go to friends and get deprogrammed."

He would visit with her in the back of the House chamber. They'd do lunch. He'd call late at night and talk for hours. She would tape him. This was, after all, research, and he was, as much as ever, the enemy. "I kept the tapes in case he ever sued me for libel."

What did he want from her? When she asked him that, Rickey said Duke told her: "I want you to hold a press conference and say you were wrong about me." That, she said, was unlikely. She says his demeanor turned slightly menacing when he told her, "Well, Beth, remember, I haven't attacked you . . . yet."

The courtship continued, with surreal encounters. Once on the way to lunch, recalled Rickey, Duke said he would play her his favorite song. "He put in a cassette of *Man of La Mancha* and began singing 'To Dream the Impossible Dream' at the top of his lungs, driving a convertible on I-10."

He slipped into the seat beside her in the House chamber one afternoon and, she said, whispered in her ear, "I know you like me. You just don't want to show it."

Once he came over to her apartment with his daughters Erika and Kristin, and spent two hours flipping through the Bible to argue over passages that he interpreted to condemn race mixing. "The little girls fell asleep, they were so bored," said Rickey.

There was no small talk. "From the start with us it was always Jews. Blacks were not interesting to him. He was always upset about something, about a new conspiracy theory: World War I, World War II, the civil rights movement, bombings — he linked it all to the Jews."

During an August lunch at Ming Palace in Metairie, "he propped up *Six Million* on the table and pointed out passages from the Talmud that he claimed proved the Satanic qualities of Jewish people." This was the Rosetta Stone conversation as Duke expressed his admiration for death camp Doctor Josef Mengele and condemned the persecution of Adolf Eichmann. He drew a map of the Mauthausen "labor" camp he had visited and explained that the deadly gas Zyklon-B was only used in delousing. The bodies found were victims of starvation and typhus, he calmly explained, and most of the photographs were doctored.

Rickey would write in her memoir of that summer:

> As he got deeper and deeper into his story, his eyes lit up and he became more animated.
>
> "You see, Beth, the extermination camps were a myth concocted by Hollywood to help create the state of Israel." When I asked him why Hollywood would concoct such a story he replied, "Because they are controlled by Jews!"

Rickey was approaching overload. By summer's end, she felt both fear and sorry for David Duke, a man torn between a messianic complex and an inferiority complex. "I think he started off on a mission for white people and ended up on a mission for

David Duke. He surrounds himself with people who are beneath him. He still sees himself as a skinny kid who is not very popular. He does not operate well with people on his own level. You can see that in his table manners. He impressed me as a real loser and the classic loner in a crowd."

Yet, if Duke was trying to neutralize Rickey, part of it stuck. "No, I didn't manage to stay above it all," she says. "I got pulled into it. He invaded my space. I wonder if he did it on purpose. I'll never know how much of it was manipulation and how much I went for it. . . . I still feel residual guilt. Did I really make it clear to him, or did I trap him? How can I like someone who is so reprehensible?"

That question gets to the heart of what makes politics and politicians like David Duke work. Abstract ideas and even past actions pale next to the smiling face and the outstretched hand of friendship. It's what often makes Mafia dons heroes in their communities. Here was David Duke, a handsome young man with a nice smile, saying what other politicians wouldn't and what people wanted to hear. What they read about his past did not square with the pleasing image they saw. And seeing, not reading, is believing.

Mr. Nice Guy's full-court press affected Rickey to the point that she almost dropped her plan to ask the State Central Committee to censure Duke at the September meeting. The possibility concerned Chairman Billy Nungesser and his leadership circle, who did not want a repeat of the outburst when Republican National Committee Chairman Lee Atwater announced a censure of Duke after his Chicago adventure. Angry calls and mail poured into Louisiana party headquarters then, not just from nutcases but also from contributors. One example, a letter from Bogalusa: "Because of the despicable attack upon Mr. Duke by Lee Atwater and other national Republican leaders, I have decided to withhold my support of the Republican Party until such time as this position is reconsidered and reversed."

Nungesser had already labeled Duke a "charlatan" and "opportunist" in the press, but he feared a local censure move would backfire on the party, and direct more attention and sympathy toward Duke, whose popularity seemed to grow with every attack.

What Nungesser did not say was that he was trying to keep the divided State Central Committee from completely splitting apart, especially since Billy was straddling the middle.

Hardly the patrician model of Republican leadership, Billy Nungesser more resembled a Democratic ward boss or union leader, with his gravelly voice and Ninth Ward accent, the ever-present cigarette planted in his weathered face, and his slicked-back red hair which matched his red suits. Not a downtown lawyer or banker, he ran an offshore catering business from his office on the West Bank. He was the beating heart of the Republican Party, ever since the bleak old phone-booth days (when that was as large a place needed, the legend goes, to hold a party meeting). Because his leadership style (not to mention his clothes) rankled many party members, he was the target of numerous coups, all of which he survived. Usually when challengers found out how much money it cost to be chairman and how much more one was expected to raise, they quietly backed off.

Not that the central committee had any control over primaries, candidates or GOP state legislators. It operated more like a political action committee, overseeing the internal workings of the party, fundraising efforts and voter registration drives. But when the group did take a stand, it was duly reported, and that's what bothered Nungesser about a possible Duke censure. Another public furor over Duke could upset the delicate balance of power he had achieved with the arch-conservative evangelicals, or, worse, it could incite a new wave of Duke supporters to seek election to the central committee.

Rickey and fellow committee member Neil Curran decided more was at stake here than party contributions and insider committee politics. At the September 1989 State Central Committee held in the chamber of the state House of Representatives, the two introduced a motion to censure Duke. But Nungesser and the evangelicals outmanuevered them. Retired Navy Admiral Tag Livingston immediately moved that the censure motion be tabled and it carried on a voice vote. The leadership spin prevailed. Don't rock our little boat.

Angry committee members confronted Rickey on her way out of the chamber. "You would have thought that I had just made a motion to censure Ronald Reagan." In the past half year, Rickey had sparred with angry Duke supporters on radio talk shows, had argued with Klansmen and neo-Nazis and had received threatening phone calls. But the inaction of her Republican Party surprised and disappointed her more. "That's cowardice. If you accept the burden of public office, you've got to accept that it will be a real pain in the ass. But you just have to take a stand and stick with it."

Indeed, David Duke would get no more publicity from a censure debate. The party headquarters would receive no more angry phone calls. Fundraising for the party challenge in the 1990 U.S. Senate race would not be disrupted. The leadership was relieved that the party had just dodged a bullet—not realizing another was speeding toward its head.

His campaign against fiscal reform took Duke to the North Louisiana countryside, where he was surprised to find the reception for him and his message as strong as, or stronger than, in his suburban district. His Klan past made him a curiosity and a celebrity, his angry anti-tax, anti-government, anti-welfare stance made him a hero. When fiscal reform was smothered in April 1989, Duke, who claimed credit, knew the next step he would take.

The small band of Duke watchers also prepared their next step. Jim Stovall, Lance Hill, Beth Rickey and Larry Powell formed the Louisiana Coalition Against Racism and Nazism (LCARN), which — though it sounded like it had a broad agenda — focused on one target. Pulling together his information gathered over a decade, Hill opened a file on Duke that would be the envy of George Bush's opposition research team. Perhaps, they hoped, with a preemptive strike, people would get the full ugly picture of Duke and his influence, and that would halt him. But the flame was about to jump the fire line. In November, Duke announced he would run for the U.S. Senate.

Besides his unique maverick appeal, which complemented the restlessness and anger rolling through the countryside, Duke knew he had what it took for a creditable statewide run: a strong volunteer home base that was readily expandable, a nationwide mailing list, the cloak of elected office, and, most important, he had the perfect opponent.

Juban's Restaurant in Baton Rouge is not the place to go looking for a down-home meal. But Bennett Johnston briefly surveyed the menu of French and Creole seafood delicacies: "Yes, I'll have the red beans and rice with sausage. You know it's very good here."

Now to matters at hand. "What kind of vote can Duke get?" the senior senator asked the reporter.

"Well, Woody Jenkins got 41 against you without a very good campaign. Maybe that."

"No way," shot back Johnston. "Woody ran a very organized campaign. Duke's negatives are too high. He won't do that well."

Johnston had good reason to be confident. For years state Republican Party officials like the late John Cade labeled U.S. Senator J. Bennett Johnston "the weak sister" of the congressional delegation — a comment which only reflected the GOP's greater weakness in never mounting a serious challenge to him. Arch-conservative Democratic state Representative Woody Jenkins in 1978 was the only challenger to get within 20 points.

Since 1984, however, Johnston had lost two elections within the Beltway. He tried and failed to unseat Senate Majority Leader Robert Byrd in 1986. When the post was open in 1988, Johnston fell far short in a race against George Mitchell of Maine. Though he was the powerful chairman of the Senate Energy Committee, though he had rallied young Southern Democratic senators to vote against the Supreme Court confirmation of Robert Bork, Johnston was never fully accepted as a mainstream national Democrat. Problem is, he was accepted — and unacceptable — that way among conservative Louisiana voters.

"They laugh up here when I say I'm considered liberal at home," Johnston once explained the split view of him. But they weren't laughing back home. Johnston's problem was that he had to shift his original constituency from conservative, pro-business suburban and rural whites, who began voting Republican, to a political base of blacks, labor and courthouse officials — populist Democrats who weren't warmed by Johnston's country-club image.

Given the polarizing effects of Louisiana's open primary, the centrist incumbent, vulnerable on the left and the right, could be scrambling just to make the runoff if faced with strong Democratic and Republican challengers. Johnston's seniority in Washington, his chairmanship of the Senate Energy Committee and his No. 2 position on the Appropriations Committee made a challenge from a Democratic congressman, like Billy Tauzin, seem self-defeating. Edwin Edwards cited the same reason for his refusing to run, besides not wanting to move to Washington and have the *Post* for a hometown paper. Friends believed Edwards had a better chance of being elected senator than governor, but he told them he had no interest in being one of one hundred. Having been Number One, nothing else would do. As the Senate race developed and Johnston's appeal remained lukewarm, some urged 33-year-old State Treasurer Mary Landrieu to grab the rare opportunity. But Mary wanted to be a mother first and then governor. Johnston's graver threat would pass in late 1989 with the unexpected death of former New Orleans Mayor Dutch Morial. The first black mayor of New Orleans was seriously considering the Senate race when he died of a heart attack on Christmas Eve. Not since U.S. Senator Allen Ellender dropped dead in the middle of his 1972 reelection bid had Bennett gotten such a break. Had Morial lived and run, he would have taken away Johnston's black base and perhaps made the runoff against David Duke. A Southern runoff between a black and an ex-Klansman—it would have been Louisiana politics at its most dangerous and fantastic, but it was not to be.

Another reason Johnston had been spared serious opposition was the relatively low profile of his office. Though a titan like Russell Long commanded inherited personal appeal, the office of U.S. senator is remote from most state voters. The governor is who counts in Louisiana. Or as a seasoned Louisiana politician once told Johnston, "Bennett, if the people gave half a damn about who the U.S. senator was, you would have been gone a long time ago."

Duke's announcement made an international splash, but back home the politics of his race didn't add up. He would have to compete for the 40 percent anti-incumbent vote against a well-financed, Republican candidate with a statewide organization. Duke could only expand beyond his Metairie base with the help of his old Klan network, and that was sure to be uncovered by the pack of watchdogs on his trail. He started with the building blocks of his 1989 House race, Howie Farrell and Kenny Knight, two former New Orleans policemen who had been booted from the force for their questionable law enforcement techniques. Farrell was Duke's closest adviser and the campaign manager, as much as any Duke campaign could be managed. As in the House race, all the major decisions and most of the minor ones would be made by the candidate.

Farrell was selling medical supplies to doctors in the New Orleans area when he signed on for Duke's 1988 presidential race.

From working in many conservative political campaigns for 20 years, Farrell was the most seasoned political operative in the Duke group.

He was an Army veteran and a veteran of the New Orleans Police Department until he was kicked off the force in the early '70s. He would claim his dismissal was for union organizing, but reporter Tyler Bridges uncovered police records showing Farrell was fired for bullying and then arresting an 18-year-old man he had stopped for speeding. An internal investigation showed that Farrell had not even clocked the car's speed.

Duke's volunteer organizer, Kenny Knight, was booted from the force in 1973 for stealing lumber from a construction site, Bridges reported.

So much for the local talent. Expanding statewide, Duke recruited one of his old Klan members, Shreveport attorney David Touchstone, to run the office in northwest Louisiana.

The Baton Rouge office was opened by Babs Minhinnette Wilson, a housewife who befriended Duke in college when he was advancing the white race and she was leading a host of local right-wing causes, including: Females Opposed to Equality (to fight the equal rights amendment), the Concerned Parents Association (to fight sex education), the Taxpayers Education Association (to fight school taxes) and the Citizens for Clean Water (to fight the fluoridation of Baton Rouge drinking water). She and her husband would have the student out to her house for meals and to share their worldviews. She proved to be a loyal lieutenant throughout Duke's career, first as a Klan organizer and then as Duke's successor as head of the National Association for the Advancement of White People.

He left behind some of his more radical out-of-state friends like Ralph Forbes, his 1988 presidential campaign manager who was the Western Commander of the American Nazi Party, and Don Black, an employee in his legislative race, who had assumed leadership of the Knights of the Ku Klux Klan after Duke had left it in 1980, and who had married Duke's ex-wife. Black had also been convicted and imprisoned for plotting to lead a mercenary force to take over the Caribbean island of Dominica in 1981.

This time around, Duke was looking for more respectable associates and found one in his attorney Jim McPherson. To his friends in the legal community, it seemed the respected criminal defense lawyer had taken a short leave of his senses to be one of Duke's closest advisers. McPherson gained national recognition in 1980 for winning the release of his client, Timothy Leary, famous early proponent of psychedelic drugs, from his 12-year prison sentence for possession of a marijuana cigarette.

McPherson, on another lawyer's referral, agreed to represent Duke when a federal grand jury wanted to know more about his involvement in the Dominica plot. Though Don Black and other plotters would go to jail, the U.S. Attorney agreed there was no case against Duke.

McPherson continued as Duke's lawyer, then became his friend and racquetball partner. He helped Duke in the House race, though he didn't think he had a chance. By the Senate race, the ex-Marine and established lawyer lent credibility and gave commonsense advice to Duke's small inner circle.

Though volunteers would flock to it, Duke's campaign organization was not big, or particularly well organized. "He was a one-man show. He made all the decisions," said McPherson, "but as far as what it takes to run a one-man campaign, it was probably the best thing for him. It was simpler. And no one had a better concept of the campaign or was better tapped into what the people liked about him."

As Duke stepped up his organizing, so did the Louisiana Coalition. Researcher Hill quickly assembled a deep file on Duke. In the University of New Orleans archives, he located the map that appeared in the *NAAWP News* of the plan to divide the country into ethnic areas. (That would soon find its way into *Esquire Magazine*.) Though he had junked much of his Duke file in the '80s when it appeared Duke's career was fading, Hill had kept the best stuff, including: his full catalog of Duke's student activities and his Klan days, excerpts from his most incendiary writings, his arrest record and documentation on his involvement with racist and neo-Nazi groups well into the '80s. Hill found a lot of ammunition in a special collection of files that Duke had donated to Tulane. "Probably for tax write-off," assumes Hill, "I'm sure he regretted it."

And it kept on coming. Hill was able to suggest a list of questions to a Tulane student who was about to interview Duke. The taped interview contained such pearls as Duke's belief that the United States should not have gone into World War II, his support for a government-sponsored eugenics program to encourage whites with high I.Q.'s to have more children and his belief that blacks are genetically predisposed to crime. The student and the Coalition released the interview to the press.

Earlier in the year, Beth Rickey had stumbled upon perhaps the richest vein of anti-Duke research. In the files of the Center for Democratic Renewal in Boston, she found transcripts of interviews with Duke and other white supremacists in 1985 and 1986. In one interview, Duke discounts the Holocaust.

> Did you ever notice how many survivors they have? Did you ever notice that? Everybody — every time you turn around, 15,000 survivors meet here, 400 survivors convention there. I mean, did you ever notice? Nazis sure were inefficient, weren't they? Boy, boy boy! You almost have no survivors that ever say they saw a gas chamber or saw the workings of a gas chamber . . . they'll say these preposterous stories that anybody can check out to be a lie, an absolute lie.

Rickey thought she had both the smoking gun and the silver bullet to pierce Duke's claims of his radicalism being buried in his past. The latest of these tapes were made two years before he started his campaign for the Legislature. Yet there was a problem. The interviewer, identified only as a doctoral student, wanted to remain anonymous and would not permit the public use of the research.

Still, there was plenty of material. Finding the stuff was not the problem — deciding what to do with it created the first arguments within the growing group. "The old-liners wanted to take a stand against what he stood for and the new ones wanted to find him in bed with a dead goat," remembers Rickey.

The old-liners prevailed. "We made up our minds early to not try to defeat Duke on a fluke or a character fault, like womanizing," says Rev. Stovall. The Coalition had but did not release *Finderskeepers*, the soft-porn self-help manual Duke co-wrote. Says Rickey, "It was a silly book. Our job was not to dig up every little piece of dirt on Duke. We still have tons of it we haven't used."

The Coalition's problem was not getting material on Duke. The trouble was people's ambivalent attitude toward it. Jim Stovall was troubled because "we felt people were not taking him seriously on either count (as a candidate or an extreme racist). They did not see the moral implications of his KKK association or the greater danger of his Nazi connections. Part of it is the fact that our own convictions have been been diluted. Many of us have lost our strong commitment toward human dignity and human rights." Stovall was frustrated that many of the church and business leaders he asked for public support did not want to get involved.

The news media did not prove to be much more help when Hill readied his research file on Duke. "We passed it around to the press and generally got no response," says Hill. By early 1990, reporters regarded Duke as something more than a curiosity but less than a threat to society. He was a public official and an announced candidate — members of the press did not feel it was their role to make more of him than that.

J. Bennett Johnston's campaign was building nearly as thick a file on Duke, but, true to classic political strategy, did not intend to direct even negative attention to an opponent with so little support in the polls.

That left the Republicans, who had the most to lose by Duke emerging as the primary Republican candidate. Rickey held out little hope that the GOP would move early to neutralize Duke's candidacy. What really alarmed her, though, was the idea of some Republicans that Duke could be manipulated to help topple Johnston and to win the office for a mainstream Republican. From her research and experience, she knew Duke was the wrong guy to manipulate and the Louisiana Republican Party was the wrong crowd to try.

The rules for gaining the Republican endorsement are written by the influential Anal Retentive Wing of the party. The caucus-convention process is purposely complicated to ensure the endorsee is acceptable to the party leadership and, if possible, controlled by the same. Some trust and peer pressure are central to the process, since the party endorsement does not bar unendorsed Republicans from entering the state's open primary. In the past, these matters could all be settled in a genteel smoke-filled room and sealed by a gentlemen's agreement. Knowing they were dealing with no gentleman, the Republicans realized they needed a strong candidate not only to beat Johnston but to discourage Duke from even running.

Late in 1990, state Senator Ben Bagert of New Orleans switched to the Republican party. From an old New Orleans political family, Bagert enjoyed impressive political support across the board, from the business community to union halls to black churches. He was regarded as a gutsy, often slippery infighter in the state Senate, where his convictions usually took a back seat to opportunities. "Whenever a close vote was coming up," recalls one of Governor

Roemer's aides, "we knew we had to go find Bagert and see what he wanted."

The Republicans had more viable candidates than Bagert. Secretary of State Fox McKeithen, with his North Louisiana base and crossover appeal, or oil-man Pat Taylor, with his remarkable business and civic achievements and national stature, eclipsed Bagert's appeal. Benny's only advantages were that he had the desire and that he had read the rules.

The endorsement would be awarded at the party convention, but most voting delegates would be chosen at caucuses in each parish. Duke and Bagert were the only candidates to take the caucus system seriously. Duke's handicap was that his strength lay with conservative Democrats, not Republican party regulars. Bagert, positioning himself as the conservative, non-Duke alternative, successfully recruited the mid-level party activists and swept the caucuses.

At the convention itself, Billy Nungesser and company made one last clumsy attempt to deny Bagert the nomination, but the move was hooted down by Bagert delegates. Fox McKeithen could see the parliamentary moves and back-room plots were going nowhere. "I'm just trying to find a way out of here," he said, before disappearing down a hotel corridor.

The Coalition members hoped the streetfighter in Bagert would take on Duke, but they were dismayed to learn Bagert planned to adopt Duke's platform and to run without his baggage. Bagert introduced a set of bills almost identical to Duke's legislative package, including an anti–affirmative action bill, even though Benny had voted in favor of maintaining affirmative action the year before.

The image of the new right-wing Benny Bagert, just as hard-line as David Duke but without the past, was noted with some humor among his colleagues in the Senate, especially the Democrats.

"What are you going to do about Duke?" Leonard Chabert asked Bagert in the Senate dining room.

"Don't worry about Mr. Duke," replied Bagert breezily. "I have a plan for him."

"Oh yeah," snorted Chabert, well experienced with Benny's bullshit. "Hope it works down the bayou. He's strong as hell down there."

The organizers of the West Monroe rally were very proud of having planned the event in fine detail. First there would be the music, then the prayer and pledge. With the introduction, a spotlight would go to the back of the hall and follow David Duke up the center aisle. But the main attraction managed to blow his carefully choreographed entrance. Before any music or prayers, Duke walked down the side aisle, craning his neck at the audience. Then he went up on stage, and the audience went wild. Backstage, the organizers looked on distressed and puzzled. Standing next to Duke onstage, Billy Hankins hadn't a clue either. "David, what are we doing up here?"

"Billy, look, in the third row. The blonde. Let's meet her."

Another day's important decision made in the Duke for Senate campaign.

From the outside, the David Duke Senate campaign was an ongoing media event that sparked questions and fears about the meaning and reach of his appeal. From the inside, it was an ideological crusade pushed on by tireless true believers new to politics. On the road, though, where Duke spent most of his time, it was more like a rock 'n' roll tour, complete with screaming fans and nightly groupies.

"When we pulled into town," says Hankins, "they were ready for a show. Every night he gave the same speech over and over again. But the crowd reaction was like he was giving it the first time." Well, it was the first time for Plaucheville, Glenmora, Vivian, Holly Beach or Dubach. Legislators would be stunned to hear that 300 or more of their constituents came out to see David Duke in tiny communities that statewide candidates had not visited in years.

The David Duke Senate campaign brought back old-time stump campaigning, attracting crowds that had long since stopped coming to political rallies. Duke was far more than a politician. He was the celebrity attacked by the press for saying the things these people thought and said. His old Klan membership did not bother them — many folks in these small towns had fathers who belonged to it or knew someone who did. He was the one politician they liked, and they regarded the attacks on him by the press and the Yankees and the other politicians as attacks on them. Certainly old Bennett had not shown up in these parts in years — he knew better.

Duke usually started his speeches with as true a statement as he would make all night: "Ladies and gentlemen, isn't this a great country when someone with a controversial background like myself can run for the United States Senate?" Sometimes it wasn't easy to tell if he was running for anything. He topped the applause meter condemning affirmative action, welfare abuse, crime and irresponsible breeding among the poor, often no more than mentioning Bennett Johnston. When he would blast his opponent for voting against the confirmation of Supreme Court nominee Robert Bork, it did not elicit nearly the response of missiles aimed at Jesse Jackson and Ted Kennedy.

"Every time I went with him to a rally," says Jim McPherson, "people would come up to us before and after with their stories. These were genuine solid people of all economic strata." One woman told McPherson that her family did not have the money to send their son to college. Yet a college recruiter came to a black family to try to encourage their son, who did not want to go to college, to enroll at LSU. When the woman approached the recruiter on behalf of her son, says McPherson, "He told her, 'Look, lady, I have a quota.'" Whether the story was true or not didn't matter — it was all over Louisiana that summer.

Most who attended the rallies were not as interested in politics as they were disgusted and fed up with it. Sometimes too fed up. Hankins remembers one fellow showing up in Oakdale and bragging about having burned a cross. Duke steered clear of him. Hankins described kook control: "With an undesirable like that, David would try to have me discourage them from hanging around. If they wanted to pass out literature and hats, we would tell them we were low on supplies."

On the other hand, says Hankins, "He loved hecklers. It got the blood flowing. Who wants to have everyone for you? It gave him a chance to debate the issues with an opponent." Of course the hecklers were sport for Duke — he had the mike and the audience.

Hankins, then a 21-year-old graduate student who wanted to make a career in politics, was exactly the kind of young mainstream conservative Duke wanted to attract to his campaign. The tall, cleancut, sociable Hankins, whose grandfather had been a labor-oriented state legislator, could have been an advance man for any candidate — and Duke really valued that. Many of his more rabidly ideological supporters were best kept at headquarters licking envelopes. Duke almost seemed to want to shield his young aide from the other side of his movement. Hankins remembers that Duke got angry when he learned that Howie Farrell had given Hankins a copy of *Did Six Million Really Die?* and urged him to read it.

Once Hankins signed on, there was little time to read. The candidate and driver/advance man were constantly traveling. Forever speeding, they soon discovered that the highways belong to candidates. "The state cops would stop us two or three times a day," says Hankins. "And we never got a ticket, never, not even when a black trooper stopped us. In fact, a lot of troopers would say 'We're all supporting you' and we'd give them t-shirts."

Not everyone wanted t-shirts. Duke received death threats before he spoke at the Student Union at the University of Southwestern Louisiana, where the angry chants and yells of black students forced Duke to cut his speech short and follow a police escort out of town.

"Do you fear for your life?" Hankins asked Duke on one of their early trips. Duke's response impressed him at first: "I don't think my life is in any more danger than a policeman or a fireman." Later Hankins reconsidered. "I thought he had to be brave or stupid to parade around like that. If anyone wanted us, they could have had us. Someone could have been paid to put a bomb in the car. There were no precautions. We carried bullet-proof vests in the back all year and never once took them out. He said he wouldn't wear them 'because they make me look sloppy in the stomach area.' He was always concerned about that."

Despite the rigors of the road, Duke hit every stop tanned, rested and up for showtime. All Billy had to do was wake him. "He'd be asleep in the car as we were coming into a town. I'd wake him and he'd look like crap. But he'd fluff back his hair and put on some tan bronzer. By the time he got out of the car, he looked relaxed and full of energy."

After rallies, recalls Hankins, early to bed was out of the question. "There was so much energy after a rally," says Hankins, and too many opportunities. "Mothers would bring their daughters to meet him. That was my job. The women would go through me. . . . He went to bars because he liked to be recognized. At the end of an evening, he likes to settle down with a woman. I've heard the rumors that he's gay, but that's absolutely not true."

Rumors and stories about David Duke surpassed those about the newly monogamous Edwin Edwards that summer. The Louisiana Coalition refused to use dirt to bring down Duke, but some journalists considered the mass of stories and rumors legitimate news concerns, or at least good reading. The most playful and salacious, *Spy Magazine* in New York, called Duke "a man whose libido never left the 1970s" in its story "Conduct Unbecoming a Racist." It quoted one of Duke's Klan lieutenants, Karl Hand, from a Louisiana jail telephone: "He had no qualms about putting the make on anyone's wife or girlfriend. . . . We had to get David out. He was seducing all the wives."

The reputation followed him to the Louisiana Legislature, where Duke showed up at parties with younger and younger staffers and pages. That went on until one day an angry citizen appeared in the House chamber looking for Duke to warn him to stay away from his 17-year-old daughter. An attractive legislative aide, who had a few dates with Duke, remembers sitting with him at lunch one day "when he started explaining to me that blond, blue-eyed Scandinavian-looking people were God's chosen people, that they were made in his image. He said that God didn't want us to dilute this perfection, so we should only mate with others of our kind. He then asked me if I wanted to mate with him. It was the weirdest come-on line I've ever heard."

He did not need to be as creative on the road. "After a rally, the women would flock around him," Jim McPherson would tell an attorney friend. "He just took his pick."

Hankins said they would stay out until three in the morning and still be up at 5:30 to make a morning TV show. But not always. A Monroe organizer, Linda Melton, told *Spy* one reason she quit the campaign was Duke's missing an important fundraising meeting "because he was out till three or four in the morning in a real sleazy, sleazy, I mean we're talking redneck sleazy, after-hours club in West Monroe with some real trashy-looking girl."

"It got in the way," admits his friend McPherson. "David is like the orphan kid, always with his nose up to the glass, and then he's in the banquet hall with all the goodies laid out before him."

Duke's after-hours jaunts made the headquarters staff predictably nervous. After an incident in a Shreveport bar where Duke was cursed and shoved, campaign manager Howie Farrell chastised Hankins for encouraging Duke's behavior. Young Billy was hardly a restraining force: "I must admit I was in my glory. I was into it as much as he was."

In Shreveport, regional coordinator David Touchstone, a former Klan organizer, became alarmed that Duke's companions seemed to get younger as he went on. Hankins recalls a staff confrontation in the back room of the local headquarters: "Touchstone said he did not want Duke seeing 20-year-olds. He said 25 should be the cutoff." Duke resisted and looked to his running mate for support, but Billy had to side with the staff. "I told him, 'David, I think maybe 20 is too young.' Duke didn't want to hear that. He was sitting on the floor and he was rubbing his eyes. You could see he was tired and he was frustrated by this whole thing. He said, 'Look, isn't it enough that I'm trying to save the white race, can't I see who I want to see?' "

Finally help came from an outside source, says the aide. "We got a report that a pipefitter union would try to get an underaged girl to get to Duke and plant Ecstasy on him. That settled us down some."

Hankins' other important duty was holding the money. "At the rallies, they would pass the bucket, I would get the money and then take it to the office. David would say, 'I don't want anything to do with the money. I don't want anyone to say I pocketed anything.' I'd be driving around with five or six thousand dollars in the back of the car." Duke told his aide he was worried someone would try to pin some financial wrongdoing on him. "He told me, 'I could be sitting in the U.S. Senate or in jail when this is over.' "

Not that he was oblivious to cash flow. Duke was innovative and relentless in his mail fundraising appeals, and even in the middle of highly charged rallies, he paid close attention to passing the oyster bucket. Linda Melton said that Duke called a meeting of volunteers after a Bossier City rally: "David called us upstairs and chewed us out for not properly collecting his money. He accused us of missing some sections." She later quit the campaign and worked against Duke in the governor's race.

The Duke rallies in the Senate campaign were finely tuned money-making operations. At the Baton Rouge rally, workers did a brisk business selling t-shirts, hats, even bumperstickers, which most candidates struggle to give away. The public even had the chance to buy an official press kit, including a glossy photo and campaign fact sheet: only $7.

While most of Duke's itemized contributions came from out of state, many responding to his direct mail pieces, he collected more in cash, most of that from his Louisiana rallies and appearances.

How he spent his money was harder to track. In a *Louisiana Political Review* story, Stephanie Riegel reported substantial self-dealings between the Duke campaign, his other organizations and his companies. A Duke company, BC&E, owned the house on Cypress Street in Metairie that served as campaign headquarters, his legislative offices, NAAWP headquarters and, for a while, Duke's residence. BC&E collected $21,900 in one payment from Duke's 1988 presidential campaign. A few months later, the NAAWP paid $119,000 to BC&E. Duke's Senate campaign paid the NAAWP $4,500 for one mailing list in December 1989 and $4,000 for another in May. The campaign paid $12,000 in 1990 for computer services to a firm called Atlantic Southern Company, which was owned by Jim McPherson's law partner, Philip K. Wallace.

Hankins saw the revolving payment operation from the inside. "He paid everyone beans and worked them to death. We'd go to a campaign rally and bring back names, which the girls in the office would punch into the (Duke's mailing list company) computer and then the company would sell the names back to the campaign."

Senate campaign spokesman James McPherson, who would run for attorney general in 1991, joined the Wallace firm in 1990. Early that year, the campaign paid the Wallace law firm $52,000 in legal fees, though neither Duke nor the campaign was involved in serious litigation. Duke told reporter Riegel he paid Wallace to advise the campaign of its equal-time rights in dealing with TV stations that were reluctant to run the campaign's 30-minute commercials. Wallace's law partner McPherson contradicted that, saying Wallace did not practice communications law but that he did handle tax matters for Duke.

The campaign kept flagrantly sloppy records of expenses paid to outside companies, apparently meant to cloud the trail to Duke's campaign suppliers and contractors. One Gonzales computer company the campaign dealt with was listed at a French Quarter address that houses the No AIDS Task Force.

The money poured into the headquarters and to David Duke at the Capitol, who would unnerve his colleagues during debates by sitting at his desk and opening one envelope after another containing checks.

The campaign spent nearly $1 million on direct-mail pieces and postage, according to five Federal Elections Commission reports. The mass mailers, sent to white registered voter households, read more like sweepstakes offers than campaign ads. One envelope in August read, "I urgently need you to open the enclosed, sealed envelope marked 'Confidential' . . . Please, DO NOT LAY THESE DOCUMENTS ASIDE . . . Right now, not next week or even tomorrow."

Duke said he wrote the pieces, but McPherson said the campaign borrowed liberally from samples the printer sent them. "It could have been pantyhose advertisements, but if it had an idea we could use, we did."

One common direct-mail practice the campaign discontinued was to pay for return postage. Some pieces, obviously fallen into the wrong hands, returned with strange objects enclosed, such as, in one case, a used condom.

Mostly, though, the envelopes contained checks or cash. The sheer volume of his retail fundraising, so much of it cash, as well as the campaign's payments to companies Duke owned, convinced many that Duke was socking away a fortune while running a shoestring campaign. Yet, even Duke's hardest opponent doubts he was in it for the money. "I think that was just a perk," says Lance Hill, "I think he would have done this if it left him in poverty." Of course, it didn't. He made a living while financing a statewide organization and media campaign. The entrepreneurial candidate had learned how to use his message to raise money, which enabled him to extend his reach to millions. His message made him a movement leader. His marketing skills made him a candidate.

David Duke may have been lighting up the countryside, but the polls did not show it. The ex-Klansman's numbers did not break out of the 20s in any survey in the race. Bennett Johnston steadily hovered around 50 percent while the officially endorsed Republican candidate, Ben Bagert, never broke double digits. Twenty percent remained doggedly undecided. Though the polls did not show much voter excitement about his own campaign, Johnston was comforted that Duke's negative rating stayed well over 50 percent all year.

Classic campaign doctrine, supported by polling numbers, dictated that Johnston should run above the rabble of his noisy opposition. He ran a pork barrel media campaign, set in the venues of his largesse: Bennett in a bomber jacket inspecting B-52s at Barksdale Air Force Base, Bennett in shirtsleeves chatting with students in the LSU Quadrangle, Bennett in a jail corridor talking tough with law enforcement officers. The accomplishments message was supposed to motivate the Democratic coalition to vote for him, while it ignored the ideological issues his challengers on the right attacked on. Johnston did not feel he had much choice. To answer attacks on his voting record would be a defensive reaction. And what would he say? Though his voting record was moderate by Washington standards, trying to explain civil rights votes in an emotionally charged campaign would be a no-win proposition. The unspoken message of his pork ads was that the price of bringing all these goods home was to play ball in Washington. But what about these goods? Johnston's catalog of jobs created did not ring true in the debilitated Louisiana economy. As an energy senator, unemployed oilfield workers could as easily lay their woes at Johnston's feet. Consultant Raymond Strother was not impressed: "Bennett says we're winning the war on drugs, yet you can't go outside your house."

The summer grew long and dark for the Coalition. The Senate race was the great battleground on which Duke would have to be vanquished. By August, though, no one had laid a glove on him. "We were overwhelmed at the way David Duke could attract big crowds and receive acceptance from some significant people," says Beth Rickey. Just as the people appeared underwhelmed with Duke's opposition. "We realized that we had to build broad citizen support to defeat David Duke, but our problem was that a lot of people had become disillusioned with Bennett." Traveling the state, Rev. Jim Stovall could see the long-depressed economy was building political resentment toward Johnston and helping Duke. "So many people had seen the average family was not getting half a chance. A lot of farm people lost their farms. They saw Johnston as the problem. Duke was the escape."

With Johnston trying to ignore Duke and Bagert trying to copy him, the Coalition knew it would have to press the offensive on its own. Hill had amassed and refined the first of his many "Resource Packets" that he especially wanted to get into the hands of the news media. All they lacked was money. A speaking engagement by Rickey and Hill in Shreveport turned into the first real commitment by any group of business leaders to seriously fund the Coalition. Fletcher Thorn-Thompson, as the group's point man, brought in other donors. Businessman and World War II veteran Albert Sklar, ill with cancer, literally got out of bed and on the phone to raise money around Shreveport and around the country.

In Baton Rouge, as in other cities, businessmen had avoided getting their companies' names involved in the anti-Duke movement. Even those who loathed Duke were not about to mix their company's name with Louisiana politics. The late Josef Sternberg, who escaped Nazi Germany with his family in the 1930s, was the first to cross the line. The family partner in Louisiana's largest locally owned retail chain, Maison Blanche, told Jim Stovall: "This is different. I am ready to use my name or my business to stop this man." At a dinner at Sternberg's home, the Coalition raised $60,000, which led to fundraisers in other towns and a final total of $500,000 for the Senate campaign.

With the first money, thousands of spiral-bound resource packets were printed and distributed to all the Louisiana media and any outside journalist or group that was interested. The beauty of the packets was that they provided journalists with well-documented, instant familiarity with Duke's Klan and Nazi connections, often using Duke's own words. The packets reached Louisiana's smallest weekly newspapers, which served at least to tone down the strong coverage the candidate received from his rallies in the outback.

But there is only so much a non-candidate can do.

Near the end of the campaign, Johnston finally decided to go negative. He ran a spot with sensational video of a Klan cross-burning and a young David Duke, face lit by the fire, solemnly giving the Klan salute. The commercials provoked a lot of comment but little sense of outrage. Pollster Joe Walker thinks the spots were a mistake. "When you say that Duke is anti-black, you are not hurting him," he said. "He prospers on that, just like Hitler prospered on the Jews. . . . It's wrong to attack him on racism. You attack him on Nazism."

Duke even used the Johnston commercial footage of the burning cross crashing to the ground (suggesting Johnston was anti-Christian?) as proof of his opponent's "desperation fear tactics."

The Klan spots, however, were not aired to pull white voters from Duke, said Johnston campaign sources, but to motivate a heavy black turnout. If so, that did not work. Black turnout in the primary would be about eight percent less than white turnout, which is about par for a primary election with no black candidate. Johnston might have done better to stick with the traditional methods of paying the black organizations in New Orleans to get their vote out. His campaign figured that a hotly contested congressional race in New Orleans with a field of strong black candidates would have boosted turnout there, but it didn't. The Klan spots may have disturbed black voters, but Johnston's refusal to lay out the street money was disturbing as well. As one black politician put it, "Duke's not our problem. He's a joke to us. He embarrasses white people. He's their problem."

He was mostly the Republicans' problem, and Benny Bagert was making it worse. With their tight control over their endorsement process, the Republicans not only had kicked away their golden opportunity to capture their first Senate seat from Louisiana this century, they totally had failed to neutralize David Duke. Bagert's candidacy, polls showed, was boosting Duke's chances of making a runoff against Johnston.

The prospect of David Duke running as a Republican in the general election in November threatened Republican candidates in tight races across the country. Without understanding Louisiana's open primary with crossover voting, the average Illinois voter would just assume that the Republicans had nominated Klansman David Duke as the party candidate. Duke couldn't beat Johnston in a runoff, but he could cost the GOP dozens of tight elections in other states.

Or could Duke beat Johnston? In a runoff, warned a legislator, "the armor comes off." Invincibility turns to vulnerability. The only way to avoid that was to pull the plug on the official Republican campaign.

Yet Benny Bagert would not budge, doggedly sticking to the line that his campaign was on the upswing, that everything was falling into place. He knew things were falling apart. Republican businessmen, especially those with oil and gas interests, weren't about to open their checkbooks on anything but a solid bet to beat the chairman of the Energy Committee. Names of some Republican "Eagles," the national club of top GOP donors, had shown up on Johnston's campaign finance reports.

Bagert resisted Republican carrots of help in a 1991 race for attorney general. Finally there came the stick. Bagert denies it, but GOP insiders say some Washington party leaders told him he was a marked man if he stayed in this race and caused Duke to make the runoff: "We'll come after you' is how they put it," claims a Louisiana Republican.

A week before the election, Bagert cratered and pulled out — too late to take his name off the ballot.

The Bagert pullout hit Duke hard, and it came on the heels of a jolting financial setback. The Senate race established David Duke as Louisiana's most effective grass-roots fundraiser behind Jimmy Swaggart. The direct mail appeals, the oyster bucket collections, the paraphernalia sales were small-time techniques applied on a grand scale. His most significant fundraising innovation, though, was the 1-900 number he unveiled on his 30-minute TV commercial. Callers automatically were billed $15 per minute to listen to a recording of Duke's voice urging them to send more. Viewers responded with $90,000 worth of billable calls. Then the hammer dropped. South Central Bell refused to bill customers for the calls, citing its policy against using 1-900 numbers for political campaigns. "It was the only time I saw Duke totally devastated," says Hankins. "That was the money we were counting on for the last big media push. He figured it was the government's way of stopping him. All he said was, 'The powers that be will be.' "

On election day, a confident Bennett Johnston, eating lunch with his family at the Piccadilly in Shreveport, touted polls showing Duke's negatives were well over 60 percent. Figuring all those votes as his, he told a journalist that his vote total could go well over 60 percent, which would be good for the state.

By that night, with a strained smile, the senior senator told a subdued victory party that his 54 percent vote was a decisive victory. His 10-point margin over David Duke (with the balance going to three minor candidates), technically speaking, was a minor landslide. Neither candidate's headquarters took it that way. At the VFW Hall in Metairie, Duke's faithful held out to the end expecting a victory. Some turned angry when it was apparent their man would fall short. TV reporter Marsanne Golsby was shoved during her live report, while CNN's Charles Zewe took some verbal threats for referring to some Duke supporters as "neo-Nazi sympathizers."

Duke was upset not only that his challenge fell short, but that it cut him short. It was clear from the results that had Bagert stayed in the race, it would have put Duke in a runoff. That would have meant four weeks of international media attention and mountains of checks and cash in the mail.

Still, the media focused on his surprising 600,000 votes and 43.5 percent share as an upset of conventional political thinking. That was the night that the Duke "hidden vote" was discovered. He practically took all of the undecided and Bagert votes (those who voted) and nearly doubled his numbers from the final polls. The pollsters who focused on Duke's negatives overlooked the fact that many voters felt more negatively about Johnston. Even some people who disapproved of Duke voted for him.

One of the gloomier victory parties took place in a room the New Orleans Sheraton had donated to the Louisiana Coalition Against Racism and Nazism. Jim Stovall remembers feeling nothing to celebrate: "We got beat. Duke won. He carried a majority of the white vote. It was the third election we had lost to him." He felt worse when he got home to Baton Rouge and discovered that his own precinct in the comfortable Broadmoor neighborhood went for Duke with 55 percent of the vote.

Lance Hill reasoned that Johnston's ads were not hard-hitting enough and though LCARN's one TV commercial went for Duke's throat, "our own financial resources were not adequate to blanket the state."

Beth Rickey wasn't sure. "I felt ambivalent about what we did." She had debated the importance of exposing Duke versus the danger of giving him more publicity and martyr/maverick appeal. "I thought it was bad news to embrace or tolerate him. I don't agree with the argument that one should not speak out because it gives the subject more visibility. At times, though, we probably helped to fuel him."

Senator Johnston figured that voters were trying to "send ol' Bennett a message." Though many observers saw the results as much a Johnston weakness as a Duke strength, there was a broader message in the voting patterns. Duke had taken 55 percent of the white vote. He beat Johnston in some traditionally Democratic strongholds, including the river parishes where Johnston fared even more poorly than Michael Dukakis had in 1988.

A closer inspection revealed a larger pattern of what *Times of Acadiana* editor Richard Baudouin labeled the RAW vote: Restless, Anti-establishment, White. They are the voters who are mad as hell and ready to take it out on the established order, whoever that is. Baudouin isolated three working-class communities that exemplified the "aginner" vote. In St. Amant near Baton Rouge, in Krotz Springs in Acadiana and in Bawcomville near Monroe, Baudouin found majorities that:

— voted for Edwin Edwards over incumbent governor Dave Treen in 1983;

— voted for Buddy Roemer over incumbent Edwin Edwards in 1987;

— voted against Governor Roemer's fiscal reform package in 1989;

— voted for David Duke over incumbent Bennett Johnston in 1990.

Three towns that had voted for Edwin Edwards, Buddy Roemer and David Duke within seven years. What did that mean for 1991?

A poll and focus group by Garin-Hart Research Group, entitled "How 'It Can't Happen Here' Almost Happened in Louisiana," points out that voters' feelings of political alienation figured more strongly in Duke's vote than did economic frustration or racial prejudice. In the poll, Duke voters were evenly split on the question of whether the squeeze on the middle class comes mostly from tax breaks for the rich and unfair advantages to big business or from the cost of welfare programs and unfair advantages to minorities. According to the poll, only 31 percent of Duke voters said they supported him because he takes pro-white stands and wants to end affirmative action programs. Twenty-four percent favored Duke because he "took a strong stand on cleaning up the welfare mess" and 26 percent said they registered protest votes ("to send a message that we need to shake things up and stop politics as usual"). Though the poll analysis recognizes that some voters use welfare "as a polite code word when they really want to talk about race . . . this research suggests it would be a serious mistake for progressive candidates to ignore the substance of voters' complaints about welfare."

According to the poll, more than half of Duke's voters moved to him from the middle to the end of the campaign, with almost half saying they voted for Duke "with mixed feelings." The poll also shows that 62 percent of Duke's voters found his background unappealing, but that 76 percent of his voters in the poll believed that he no longer held his old Ku Klux Klan views.

The softness of the Duke vote and the mixed feelings that nearly half of his voters felt toward him reinforce the view of many observers that if Duke, as rumored, did run for governor, he would not fare nearly as well. For starters, Buddy Roemer is no Bennett Johnston. Buddy would not ignore Duke—he would confront him and cut him like he did Edwin. Also, in Louisiana, the governor's office conveys a deeper meaning to the people. A race for the U.S. Senate is for sending messages, while a governor's election determines the economic and educational climate, as well as who gets political jobs and contracts. The conventional wisdom holds that Duke voters, having had their kicks, will settle down to a real political decision in the fall of 1991. Very comforting. But Richard Baudouin isn't so sure. "It may be like the mark of the devil. If you've gone to Satan once, you know, it's not hard to do it again."

# 5. Campaigns in Exile

A not-very-close look at the giant blue-and-white DUKE FOR GOVERNOR sign reveals the words FOR SENATE papered over. No sense making a new sign every year.

The small attendance at the press conference at the Baton Rouge Hilton to announce his candidacy may have unnerved the candidate, who launches the new campaign with some bad monologue: "Ladies and gentlemen. You know, this is quite a governor's race. Of the three major candidates, all have had failed marriages, but only two have failed as governors." *Dah-dah-dum.*

A baby cries as David Duke stumbles through a lackluster reading of his third straight call to arms in as many years. The familiar litany of all that ails society — affirmative action, welfare fraud, illegitimacy — sounds a bit shopworn and out of step with the economic realities of post-oil Louisiana. Though he slaps on Buddy Roemer's promise to scrub the budget, he admits, "In a sense, I am a one-issue candidate. That issue is the rising welfare underclass." That's good enough for this crowd, which, though small, regularly breaks Duke's monotone with the "Duke, Duke" chorus.

Standing by the wall, a retired school principal agrees with the slam on Roemer. "If Duke wasn't running, I'd vote for Edwards because he is the first one to give retired principals adjustments in retirement benefits. Roemer and Treen, you can bury them under the Mississippi River. I could write a book about it. What Roemer is doing to the teachers is horrible. That and the homosexuals in the school system—I could write a book about it."

The man likes what Duke stands for and what Edwards did for him. The contradiction doesn't seem to matter. The retired principal belongs to a phenomenon no one can quite figure: the old Edwards populist white vote that has found Duke. If anyone has a bead on it, it's David Duke: "I am a populist like Huey Long. But we need a Huey in reverse. We need a populist for less government and more power to the people."

David Duke, neo-populist, now aims for the children and grandchildren of Huey Long's old voters. Indeed, he carried most of the same parishes in his 1990 Senate race that Huey carried in his 60 years ago. For these voters, big business is not the oppressor; big government is. The rich are not the favored class; poor people, of all people, are. The problem, as these people see it, is that nothing the government does works, especially uplifting the underclass with social programs.

The alienated vote is still out there, but where's the old Duke? The candidate limps to the end of his announcement and smiles wanly to the applause of his handful of supporters. This speech is miles from the frenzy of the Senate race, and that feeling is reflected in the Duke campaign itself. Though the core leadership of Howie Farrell, Kenny Knight, Babs Minhinnette Wilson and Jim McPherson is still on board, many committed volunteers have burned out and drifted off. There is no telling if they, or the contributors, will be back. McPherson feared back-to-back races would make him appear to be more of a professional campaigner than a movement leader. "I personally thought he shouldn't run, that he should go back in the Legislature and then run for

Congress. But David saw such a vacuum in the governor's race, between Edwards' background and Roemer's foreground."

The pollsters don't show the same vacuum Duke sees. The *Baton Rouge Morning Advocate* kicks off the campaign year with a cattle-call poll of declared, undeclared, possible and imagined candidates. The poll by Ed Renwick, dean of Louisiana pollsters, shows: Edwin Edwards, 27 percent; Buddy Roemer, 26; David Treen, 13; David Duke, 11; Louis Lambert, 10; Aaron Broussard, 4; Richard Baker, 3; Undecided, 6. The numbers are worse for Duke when the field is trimmed to a three-man race. Then the poll shows: Roemer, 45 percent; Edwards, 33; Duke, 15.

A *Shreveport Journal* poll hits the other end of the scale of voter indecision with a huge undecided vote of 44 percent and the candidates coming in at: Edwards, 20; Roemer, 14; Treen, 3; Duke, 2.

Sure, the last poll in the Senate race showed Duke in the 20s before receiving 43.5 percent of the vote. Those surveys, however, came before Bagert withdrew from the race. So, the figuring goes, maybe Duke has a 12 to 15 percent hidden factor, if that much. The governor's race won't be a three-man contest and one thing this poll clearly shows is that the more alternatives voters have, the poorer Duke fares. Even when Republicans Treen and Baker are taken out of the poll, conservatives appear to flock to the conservative Democrat Roemer. If anything, David Duke's candidacy seems to be working for Roemer by splitting the conservative protest vote without posing enough of a threat to the incumbent. Also, Duke's been campaigning for over a year, and Roemer hasn't started yet.

The other relatively good news for Roemer is that his favorite populist, Edwin Edwards, still owns the left. The governor could be vulnerable to a new face, but so far the leading poll challengers are comfortably familiar.

A middle-aged woman bristles when the reporter asks if she supports Edwin Edwards: "No, I don't support him, I just came to see him." For Edwin Edwards, just being a curiosity again is an improvement. As opposed to David Duke's fumbling, uninspired announcement, his fourth in three years, Edwin Edwards treats his fifth declaration of candidacy like it is his first. You could call his 1983 campaign a comeback, but he had never really left. Nineteen ninety-one marks more than a comeback, it is a resurrection, and he thinks enough of it this time to pack his own house. A crowd about five times the size of Duke's overflows the same ballroom of the Baton Rouge Hilton. Color posters recycled from 1983 line the walls, and a new slogan banner — THE SOLUTION TO THE REVOLUTION — serves as backdrop.

Many supporters are more supportive than optimistic. "He has to prove to people that he's not going to quit again," says a school board member from the river parishes. "But I'm gonna help him anyway. He was there for us."

Edwin Edwards has been waiting four years to give this speech, much of which will be recycled for a 30-minute telecast. One more time he lays the blame for most of his troubles on "politically motivated U.S. attorneys" while taking only a small part of the blame himself for bad appearances: "I made the mistake of being overconfident and too brash. I didn't do what I could do to disperse the clouds above me. I had confidence in my integrity and I suffered from hubris. . . . I learned from my mistakes." He has learned this much: if David Duke could get his past behind him, there's hope for Edwin Edwards.

But just in case anyone isn't satisfied, Edwards gives a final call: "If anyone has information that I have violated the public trust, now is the time to come forward or forever hold your peace." Pause for effect. Not to overdo the contrition, he adds: "I don't intend to give up my way of life, but I'll be careful not to fall into crap I fell into in the past. . . . This is a closed chapter in my life."

Now back to kicking Roemer. "He said read my lips. He meant kiss my hips. He promised us jobs and gave us jaws. . . . We lost a congressional seat and Roemer had the audacity to praise the drop in unemployment."

But one is coming to change that: "Oh yes, Louisiana, there is a Santa Claus."

Duke is not mentioned, until a reporter asks him to, and then he soft-pedals, "He is not a respectable Republican. I cannot believe that anybody who wears a Nazi uniform or wore a Klan sheet is respectable. I hope he has changed, but it is not for me to decide."

The Duke strategy. He knows he doesn't need to trash Duke to keep his loyal black support. But in a runoff with Roemer, the Duke voters will swing the election. Polls show him that many likely Duke voters used to be part of Edwards' rural populist base. When the new demagogue is through with them, the old one wants them back.

Edwards seems looser than he has been in months. By announcing, he has taken the first public step to redeem his image as a loser and a quitter. His has been a long exile as a non-candidate. You hear that in his remarkably straightforward answer to the most lied-to question in politics: "Why do you want to be governor?"

"Because it's what I want to do when I get up in the morning. It's what turns me on."

The Edwards entourage and his fans spill out into the brilliant sunlight on this clear, crisp February day. Working through the crowd, the candidate comes upon his old podnah Price LeBlanc, the Toyota dealer famous for his TV commercials, his free country sausage and his tagline *Dahlin'*.

Edwards baits him: "Who has the best selection of Toyotas?"

"Price LeBlanc, dahlin'," says Price, clenching his fist and bending his knee.

"Who has the best deals on Toyota cars and trucks?"

"Price LeBlanc, dahlin'."

"Who's gonna stop spending money on his silly TV commercials and give some to me?"

Price laughs. Everyone laughs. Edwards does not laugh. This is the part that does not turn him on. Raising money will be harder this year than ever. He almost sounds like he means it when he makes the same challenge to his opponents that he has in his last two campaigns: to join with him in forgoing *all* campaign contributions, to spend no money on advertising, and to rely strictly on personal appearances, news coverage and televised debates. He set March 1 as the deadline for all candidates to accept the challenge. "Then on March 2 we will have our first fundraiser."

Roemer shoots back a counter-challenge that afternoon: "Don't quit on me, Edwards. You did that before. You said you would run. Now let's go."


Candy looks spectacular in her tight, strapless evening gown as she stands next to Edwards, who is trying to hold court while she feeds him cake. The candidate does not look too hungry. He seems to be looking for his court. There is going to be a lot of food left over tonight after the gala kickoff fundraiser at the Monteleone. The spin is that heavy rains have kept two planeloads of Texas friends from making the flight. Fine. But what happened to the Louisiana friends?

Far fewer than 100 guests, many of them non-paying staffers, family and friends, circulate in the small hotel ballroom. This event is a fraction of the size of the behemoth blowouts he hosted early in the 1983 campaign, where well over 500 of his closest friends paid top dollar to get closer. Not only is tonight's gathering small, but Edwards is seeing the last of many of these people's checkbooks for the rest of the primary.

"You can thank Roemer that you only have to give $5,000," Edwards tells his friends. "You don't have to give any more and you can come to all the future functions." They may need to just to halfway fill the room next time. Between Roemer's rules and the rotten economy, the old Edwin Edwards buckfest is becoming an endangered political species.

Until now, Edwards' biggest obstacle has been the nagging doubts that he will stay in the race all the way. Now a bigger roadblock looms ahead, courtesy of Buddy Roemer's Revolution, and the one 1987 campaign promise that he kept with a vengeance.

As Roemer's influence with the Legislature crested in his first year, he pushed through a bill to transform Louisiana's campaign finance laws from among the loosest in the country to close to the tightest. Modeled on his own campaign's self-imposed rules, Roemer's law limits individual contributions to $5,000, lowers the reporting thresholds and outlaws cash contributions.

Louisiana campaigns without cash? Don't ask if it's advisable. Is it possible? In the old days, it was all cash. The stacks of money were piled high on the glass-top table in the Edwards campaign suite in the Monteleone in 1971. It was common for Edwards to come out of a crowd with $5 and $20 and $100 bills hanging out of all of his pockets. Cash was a big part of the thrill, and thanks to Roemer, the thrill is gone.

Reporting of contributions did not begin until 1975, and then with high thresholds and bigger loopholes. The big rollers did not seem to mind going public. Louis Roussel Jr. was very proud to be Edwards' long-running leading benefactor, pumping in at least $100,000 in 1983 on his name alone. For others, the most common form of high-rolling was the $25,000 note, which turned into loans paid back with interest if the candidate won.

The new law has sidelined Edwards' heaviest hitters while the economy has taken care of many middle-range supporters who cannot even come up with $5,000. Much of Edwards' 1983 money flowed in from friends making fortunes in the oilfield service, real estate and construction industries. Now many of them were in Chapter 11. "We went over the old contributor list from '83, and three-fourths of them were busted or Edwin was too embarrassed to ask them," says aide Bob d'Hemecourt morosely.

On the other end of the scale, the new law's cash prohibition dealt Duke's campaign just as heavy a blow. Strangely, and for the first time, Louisiana campaign finance laws were more stringent than federal rules. In the Senate race, he could pass the oyster buckets at rallies to raise trashbags full of cash. The oyster bucket was outlawed in the state race, as were cash ticket sales to the rallies that featured food and music. Since the cash paid for event expenses, Duke held fewer rallies, which had enabled him to draw big crowds in the most remote places.

While campaign finance reform outlawed Edwards' high rollers and Duke's oyster buckets, it fit neatly with Roemer's financial strategy. As the governor, he could build on the broad base of upper-middle-class contributors, political neophytes who would not give a political candidate more than $5,000 as a matter of taste. Those who really wanted to give more could funnel a few additional thousands through spouses and children.

Buddy Roemer wasn't kidding when he said he hated Louisiana politics — now he was out to starve the system.

Maybe that's why David Duke seemed offspeed in his campaign opener. Money would be harder to attract and some of his old supporters would not be back from the Senate race. Looking out over the small crowd, he can see Rev. Jim Stovall staring back at him. His old enemies, rest assured, will stick with him.

Stovall and Lance Hill of the Louisiana Coalition would concede they had lost the last round to Duke when he polled 43.5 percent of the vote in the Senate race, including over 55 percent of the white vote. LCARN was experiencing the trickiness of trying to defeat a movement in the context of a political election when the movement leader doubles as a skilled politician. Outside sniping and inside doubts force Hill to defend the group's objectives to not just beat Duke at any cost but to stick with a long-range strategy "which politically and morally isolates him." In a memo to board members early in 1991 he writes, "We are not naive idealists as some of our critics charge. The real dreamers are those who believe that the hate movement will disappear if Duke drops a few points in the polls." Duke has to be defeated because of his political beliefs, not in spite of them, argues Hill. "If Duke loses an election because he had plastic surgery, we may have struck a blow to vanity but not to racism and anti-Semitism."

Hill reasons, "To ignore Duke's bigotry . . . can lead to a failure to mobilize the anti-Duke vote as well as the undecided." That happened in the Senate race. Hill calculates that had blacks and Republicans turned out in the same percentage as the Duke vote, "Duke's vote would have been only 39 percent, rather than 44."

Hill concludes that the Coalition needs to focus on further exposing Duke's extremism as being far outside the conservative mainstream, since he assumes, "Several of the candidates in the governor's race are willing to engage Duke on both his public and symbolic racist issues." But his next sentence contains the contradiction that will undermine his own strategy: "Given Duke's slim chances of winning a runoff election, most candidates would prefer to be in a runoff with him." Indeed, all the candidates fantasize about landing in the runoff with Duke, and then attacking him mercilessly and crushing him in order to be the savior of the Free World *and* the governor of Louisiana. What a deal! But that dream only comes true by ignoring Duke's public and symbolic racist issues and hoping he knocks some other major candidate out of a runoff spot. If it looks like Duke will not make the runoff, again the best political strategy is to ignore him rather than to alienate his old voters who may be looking for a new candidate. Once again, the Coalition will be left to do the front-line dirty work alone.

If Hill's point is that David Duke must be treated as a dangerous extremist operating far outside the bounds of decency and good will, that message has not gotten through to the Baton Rouge

Downtown Kiwanis Club, which gives Duke a courteous if not big Kiwanis Club welcome. Without his cash-cow rallies, Duke is relegated to the civic club circuit. But there are advantages: every appearance before a mainstream group reaffirms his identity as a mainstream conservative and undercuts the "extremist radical" charge LCARN is still trying to lay on him.

Duke is not even being isolated and attacked by the other candidates, as LCARN hoped. Instead, he's eager to bring up the new rumor that he is in league with Edwin Edwards against Buddy Roemer.

"That happened when I went to lunch with a black reporter from the *Boston Globe* at Gino's. And who was in the foyer but Edwin Edwards. Seems he was waiting for a sweet young thing." Duke chuckles. "So Edwin says, 'Let's make it a foursome.' That's where the rumors come from. Can you see Edwin and I plotting against Roemer at the same table with a black reporter from Boston?"

The little story allows Duke to spike another charge against him, a newspaper report that he did not pay property taxes for four years in the 1980s. "I saw Roemer was late paying his property taxes too. So I asked Edwin, 'Did you ever pay your property taxes late.' He told me, 'Duke, you know I don't pay property taxes.'"

Positioning himself as just one of the boys, Duke confesses again to being a one-issue candidate: "My issue is the growing welfare underclass. I think we should require able-bodied persons to work for their welfare checks," which brings a healthy round of applause from the Kiwanians. And another with his stand for the "death penalty for drug pushers." And a few strong nods for the need "to reduce the illegitimate birth rate."

He concludes, "The only thing you can accuse me of is having wrong opinions."

Kiwanian Mike Graham, a TV weatherman, would like to test that. He has prepared a few questions:

"Do you believe blacks are genetically inferior to whites?"

"Not inferior but different. I think blacks have different talents."

"Do you believe there is a conspiracy by Jews?"

"No, I don't believe there is a conspiracy by Jews."

"Do you believe the Holocaust occurred?"

"Yes, there was a Holocaust in which Jews and Christians perished."

Well, that settles it. Who would lie to the Kiwanis Club? David Duke lunches with Edwin Edwards at Gino's, pays his property taxes when Buddy Roemer does and believes in the Holocaust. A regular guy.


Now this is what Campaign '91 is supposed to be all about. David Duke at the NAACP forum. If the Kiwanis Club is polite to Duke, if the other candidates won't take him on, the NAACP at least should provide some moral indignation for this sleepy campaign.

More wishful thinking.

*Baton Rouge Morning Advocate* reporter John LaPlante has been sitting in the front row for an hour waiting for something to happen and is about to give up: "I forgot how much I hated these things."

About 100 NAACP members in a House committee room observe the row of five candidates in dark suits. The seating at the committee desk is arranged so that four candidates sit on the side with their profiles to the audience while David Duke sits at the end, the only candidate directly facing the crowd. It could make for a decent confrontation. Instead politeness is the prime consideration, decorum is second, time restraints are a distant third and anything interesting is far back in the pack.

NAACP state president Rupert Richardson is conducting a lame, all-holds-barred interrogation of the candidates. They are allowed a criminal eternity of five minutes to respond, with no time discipline from the moderator. The candidates take the opportunity to turn all their answers into marshmallows, especially the lesser-known Louis Lambert, Aaron Broussard, Fred Dent and Sam Jones. These forums are their only chance to get any recognition, and Edwin Edwards and David Duke, who need no more ink, don't seem to mind. The focus of attack, instead of David Duke, is on incumbent Buddy Roemer. He doesn't seem to mind either. He isn't there.

"I knew I must be in the right place," says Aaron Broussard entering one forum, "because Buddy Roemer is not here."

"There have been more sightings of Elvis than of Buddy," chimes in Sam Jones.

The challengers try to make the best of having no live incumbent to kick around, but without him, they are the traveling bitch-bitch chorus. Without Roemer there to try to answer their criticism, the press after a while barely even covers the forums, making attendance at them all the more futile.

Once in a while the governor will titillate the wolves by actually accepting an invitation to a forum, but he still never shows. That gets Anna Edwards the angriest. "Daddy and I both got out of sick beds to make a forum because Roemer said he'd be there and he didn't come. The son of a bitch."

The governor is a few blocks away at the Mansion enjoying his Saturday morning while the earnest candidates slog through their positions on education, high-tech economic development and, of course, their commitment to minorities.

Louis Lambert, who last ran statewide in 1979, is making a painful readjustment to the demands and irrelevance of forum rhetoric. After showing up unprepared for several such events, he unveils his vision thing to the NAACP. Louis has an economic development plan. This will solve all our problems. You see, he will seek out the best scientists in the country for research. The lure of the big bucks will cause scientists to abandon Harvard and MIT to come to Nicholls and McNeese State and bring their grant money with them. "Then their inventions can be turned over to various businesses in the area to develop into products and this will cause a proliferation of jobs." Louis is very proud of his recitation and just a little surprised that no one has thought of it.

LaPlante softly moans.

Now comes time for all candidates to jump through the moderator's hoop to detail the racial and gender breakdown of their campaign staffs. All fumble about for politically correct ways to count every part-time secretary and runner as important players on their multicultural teams.

Duke doesn't bite: "My campaign staff is all volunteer." (Except for the eight or ten paid positions.) "If you want to volunteer, you're welcome. I'll say the same things to your face as behind closed doors." His administration will not discriminate: "When I'm elected, I'll be looking for black people."

The audience begins laughing.

Duke looks hurt that he is misunderstood. "Wait a minute," he protests. Unlike Buddy Roemer, he won't be looking all over the country for talent he can find at home. "The only person I may bring in from out of state would be James Meredith to run the welfare system." Meredith is the civil rights embarrassment, the black student who integrated Ole Miss in 1962 in the face of riots and then veered hard right. He has endorsed Duke's views and candidacy.

The only candidate who seems to know how to work a forum is Sam Jones, the mayor of Franklin, who can at least get off a laugh line. After the rest of the panel sleepwalks through another lame question, Jones tells his opposition: "Each night I go to bed and say a prayer for all of you."

Jones also is the only candidate who will go after Duke, which seems to be a sensible strategy for a bunch of Democrats at an NAACP forum. "David Duke is running a fraudulent campaign. He says he's for the working people and he's never worked a day in his life. He's as bad as the welfare cheats he talks about."

Duke gets red in the face as he details his work history, which includes a paper route as a boy and his "experience running a nonprofit organization."

Edwards finds all this very funny. He would find these forums excruciatingly boring without Sam Jones. "That's the kind of guy you will vote for," the ex-governor tells a reporter afterwards. "He's completely unrealistic. He's a nice guy and he can't win. But if he had two or three million dollars, he'd be dangerous."

Jones is an annoyance to Duke, but he's basically unknown and hardly a threat. The Coalition is troubled that early in the campaign Duke can be applauded at civic clubs, politely tolerated at an NAACP forum, joined at lunch by Edwin Edwards and ignored by nearly everyone else. If that doesn't trouble an old Nazi hunter, the worse news is that once again the Republican Party is about to get involved.

# 6. Primary Experience

In his first two terms, Edwin Edwards maintained a Jacksonian attitude toward the Governor's Mansion. He truly thought of it as the people's house, and that even went for Republicans. Well, Republican women. How else would the Republican Women's Club be holding a luncheon in the Governor's Mansion in 1978? The governor even dropped in to say hello. The topic of conversation was the beneficial effects of the state's new open primary law, which already was leading to the election of Republican candidates with more gains sure to come.

Edwards was benignly gracious, but then began to speak in riddles. "You are happy with the open primary now, but there will come a day when you will not be." And then he left the room. The women looked at each other. Then they laughed.

It would take about a dozen years for them to see what he meant.

Louisiana's open primary is unique, and like Louisiana's other unique political institutions it is openly scorned beyond the state's borders. Outside commentators ridicule Louisiana's "peculiar," "screwball," even "dangerous" election process, as though it were a French mutant perversion of the Magna Carta. Local and national party leaders loathe it. The U.S. Justice Department won't let Mississippi adopt it. And after the 1990 Senate race in Louisiana, surely no other state will even consider it. Not in this century.

Indeed, Louisiana's open primary is different. It is the future. As backward and stunted as is Louisiana's democratic experience, the state is far ahead of the Union in granting its citizens free, open, unencumbered voting rights. The open primary is so simple, so direct, so of the people, that of course party leaders view it as dangerous. The beauty and terror of it are that it gives the people exactly what they ask for, without the filtering by political parties. All candidates — Democrat, Republican and come what may — run on the same primary ballot for consideration by all voters. The top two finishers, regardless of party, meet in a runoff. Majority rules. Basically, it is a nonpartisan primary, similar to the way many local elections are held, especially in the Midwest. The difference is that the Louisiana system is statewide — from police jury elections to races for governor and the U.S. Senate.

Party leaders, even in Louisiana, especially despise it, since the law strips the political parties of any legal standing or a guaranteed slot on the general election ballot. Seen another way, the electorate is not divided by closed party primaries, which are subtle yet effective filters on the electorate's ultimate choice.

Primaries themselves, most notably the New Hampshire presidential primary established in 1952, have been the historical vehicle for the people's direct election of nominees. In three decades, that system completely took over the presidential nomination process and penetrated deep into state and local levels, though there are still holdouts where party conventions, caucuses and meetings in smoke-filled rooms choose the candidates to appear on the general election ballot.

Some states allow voters to cross party lines to choose from candidates in either primary, a basic voting right denied most

American citizens. Good, but not enough. Louisiana simply erases all the lines that divide voters and candidates in the first critical electoral step. The system grants full freedom of choice to voters and to candidates to not be shackled by a party label. For Republican candidates, that has meant the ability to compete for the votes of conservative Democrats and independents—and to get primary exposure with those groups instead of appearing as a brand-new, often unknown face in the general election. It does not penalize the candidate of broad, crossover appeal who may not make it to the general election because half of his or her base voted in the other primary.

Political parties used to intercede between the people and the government, before radio and TV gave entrepreneurial candidates direct access to the masses. Ever since, the parties have been trying to find their place in the changing political landscape. In Louisiana, it's been found for them.

It was easy for Edwin Edwards to strip the parties of their official electoral roles, since one so completely dominated the other (the Democratic Party held a 20-1 registration edge in Louisiana in 1972) and the governor always controlled the one that counted.

In state matters, Republicans did not become even faintly relevant until Eisenhower was elected and someone was needed to direct federal patronage in Louisiana. By the '60s, when Lyndon Johnson turned into a national Democrat and conservative Republicans turned into Dixiecrats, the notion of registering Republican grew. It was suppressed, just as registrars of voters had felt compelled to do for years. Peggy Kinsey remembers when the Caddo Parish registrar of voters flatly refused to let her sign up as a Republican in 1949: "She bawled me out for just suggesting such things and threatened to call my daddy."

Nothing would have changed unless the Republicans started getting pushy. Though it was no contest, the general election became an expensive formality in 1972 when the conservative Dave Treen took 43 percent of the vote after Edwards had squeaked through two grueling, expensive Democratic primaries. It really irked Edwards that as a Democrat, exhausted, scarred and broke from two hard primaries, who had to raise money and win support the hard way—promising every job three times—he would still have to face a well-funded, well-rested Republican and a final protest vote.

Edwards could tolerate the Republican Party as a good place to keep arch-conservatives away from Democratic primaries. But when they tried playing hardball with him—by directly challenging him as a party—it was time to crush them.

The idea was to eliminate the nuisance factor of the minuscule Republican Party. Edwards did not foresee how his law would instead breathe life into the GOP by allowing Republicans to vote the same ballot as normal people. By the stroke of Edwin Edwards' pen, Republicans were more than enfranchised, they were emancipated from having to be Democrats in order to be relevant. GOP registration more than doubled in four years. More important, Republican candidates, instead of being smothered in the open primary, began making runoffs in legislative districts and judgeships and winning. Edwards grossly underestimated how many Louisiana Democrats would switch parties or simply vote Republican. Or maybe he didn't.

In the 1979 governor's race, with Edwards barred by the constitution from a third consecutive term, Democrat Louis Lambert carried the black vote to edge past four moderate Democrats into a runoff with lone Republican Dave Treen. Under the old system, Lambert most likely would have been eliminated in the second Democratic primary by a moderate, such as third-place finisher Jimmie Fitzmorris, who then would have beaten the Republican in the general election. Instead, Dave Treen, running against the most liberal Democrat, eked out a 9,500-vote win to become Louisiana's first Republican governor since the end of Reconstruction—and the perfect set-up for Edwin Edwards to knock over four years later.

The open primary was good for Edwin Edwards, but it still was not bad for the Republicans, whose registration continued growing, and who won half the congressional districts, two dozen legislative seats and hundreds of local posts. They became contenders. They can hate him but they must also honor him as the father of the Louisiana Republican Party, Edwin Washington Edwards.


"Switch, switch, switch." Buddy Roemer grinned sheepishly when greeted by the chorus from the state's delegation to the 1988 Republican National Convention in New Orleans. Very flattering, but why should he switch? As a conservative Democratic congressman, he had both sides approaching him. As a conservative Democratic candidate for governor, he received half the vote of the registered Republicans and a respectable black vote at the same time. As a Democratic governor, he was gaining bipartisan legislative support for his reforms. As a darling of the Eastern press, Buddy Roemer knew where he came from and he knew where he was going. He was going to be president.

Nothing so strange about that. Every sixth-grade class president thinks he or she is going to be President of the United States one day. The defining moment in their political careers comes when they realize they won't be. Then those who stay in the game begin looking for a nice nest to feather and settle into. For Edwin Edwards, that happened in 1972 when he showed up at the National Governors Conference, wearing a white suit and shoes and making passes at female reporters. The judgment was that Edwards, like cheese, did not travel well.

The clarifying moment had yet to come for Buddy Roemer in 1988. He had survived several major political cuts, had served in and escaped Congress, became governor, and now, amid the ruins of the national Democratic Party, he saw clear running room ahead. He and about a dozen or so others, but that's okay. The Great Mentioner had mentioned him. It was in the *New York Times*.

Though not a card-carrying member, he fit the mold the new Democratic Leadership Caucus was hoping to fill in 1992: a fiscal conservative with a decent record on ethics, the environment, civil rights and with an Eastern education. He had shown he could win a state race the Reagan way: with a message that sells and a delivery that stirs. If he could win that way statewide, he told friends in 1988, he could go national.

Three years later, however, the governor's office was turning into a slippery stepping-stone. His pro-Reagan voting record in Congress went over great in his district and went unnoticed elsewhere. But as the ambitious governor of an anti-tax state going broke, his fiscal conservatism was noticed. His reform-based budget cuts and his efforts to consolidate management of the university systems had raised howls from black leaders and resonated badly, for him, among black voters. His best shot was to do the job he was elected to do, clean up corruption and stabilize finances, and move on before having to face the consequences of his reforms. He fell about 100,000 votes short, the margin of defeat of the fiscal reform constitutional amendment in 1989. With the budget still leaking and with no consensus on plugging it, Buddy Roemer found himself managing by veto and condemned to a second term. There was always 1996.

Despite growing political setbacks, the polls in early 1991 still show Roemer pulling a solid conservative vote against David Duke and even Dave Treen. Voices within the Republican Party suggest the blasphemy of rolling over. "This is not our year," says George Despot, a former party chairman who would die in 1991. He reasons that with Roemer and David Duke cornering the Republican base, there is no room for an endorsed Republican candidate to be any more than a spoiler, if that. The Republicans either can embarrass themselves, as they did last year with Ben Bagert, or they can, at best, split Roemer's base, put Duke in the runoff, and enable Edwin Edwards to be reelected. But that logic was drowned out by the party line, expressed by chairman Billy Nungesser: "We are in the business of electing Republicans."

It would be swell if Buddy were to switch, but so far his quoted response on that has been, "There is only one thing that kept me from being a Republican — the Republicans" and "I love the Democratic Party as much as I love my country."

So state party leaders are shocked in early 1991 to learn that Governor Roemer has been talking party affiliation with the White House. Two things seem to be moving Roemer: his ambition and his survival.

Roemer is not one to underestimate the GOP's ability to pursue boneheaded strategy, even two years in a row. "I felt the Republicans almost had to put up somebody and that somebody gets 15 percent of the vote. My 15 percent." A chorus of footsteps is heard shuffling on the right, including those of: Lieutenant Governor Paul Hardy, a recent party switcher and former gubernatorial candidate; Congressman Clyde Holloway, who had strong fundamentalist support; Secretary of State Fox McKeithen, who had switched the year before but who could still draw Democratic, even black, votes with his father's name; Congressman Richard Baker, a rising party star in favor with the White House; former Governor Dave Treen, who badly wanted a rematch with Edwin Edwards after a humiliating defeat in 1983; and former congressman and current Deputy Secretary of Energy Henson Moore, who lost a close U.S. Senate race in 1986. Any of the last three could seriously undercut both Roemer's and Duke's bases. With Duke and a respectable Republican on the right and Edwards and Aaron Broussard on the left, the open primary would act like a vise on Roemer in the middle. As a Republican convert, though, he could clear out some room on the right.

Then there is Buddy's revised timetable beyond 1991. Taking his present conservative pro-business course into a second term would push him too far to the right to even be near the national

Democratic Party's new moderate center. There is a platoon of other Southern Democrats, from Al Gore to Bill Clinton to Ann Richards, hewing closer to that center line.

Not only are his policies alienating him from the Democratic Party, his politics already have won him powerful new enemies. A big Democratic sore spot is how he spoiled the party's hopes to get behind a moderate Democrat to fill Roemer's vacant seat in the Fourth Congressional District in 1988. Party leaders were ready to close ranks behind Allen Bradley of DeRidder when Roemer asked them to delay a week until he could better assess the race. Sure. It was, after all, his old seat. The next thing the Democrats heard was Adeline Roemer's announcing she would run for Congress.

Bradley pulled out. The Democrats fumed. Mrs. Roemer's campaign went nowhere. Buddy didn't mind. He had another seat-warmer in the race. His former administrative aide Jim McCrery was pulling Buddy's old conservative backers. Soon Roemer seemed to lose interest in raising money for Mom, reinforcing his reputation in the Capitol for broken promises. The headline on Lanny Keller's column in the *Shreveport Journal* said it: THROW MAMA FROM THE TRAIN.

In 1991, his Democratic bridges turned to cinders, Roemer begins to reconsider his long-term possibilities in the GOP. As the Democrats try to tighten up, the Republicans under closet moderate Bush seem to be following America to the center. After George Bush finishes up in 1996, there is — who? Quayle? Kemp, maybe? Pete Wilson, as short as Roemer and not as eloquent? As the pendulum swings back to the center, the prospective candidates dwindle. Not that the party chiefs would come looking for Roemer, but assuming a wide-open race in 1996, a well-positioned darkhorse and dynamic campaigner could just catch on in the Southern primaries, and from there . . .

Well, it is not the kind of vision one confides to cigar-chomping state party boss Billy Nungesser or his crowd. News that Roemer is negotiating with White House Chief of Staff John Sununu does not sit well at home. Party Chairman Nungesser doesn't appreciate being frozen out of discussions or having his cooperation taken for granted. Sununu does not speak for the state party, which has its own unique process for endorsing a candidate. Maybe Roemer is toying with the White House with no real intention of switching. He sure seems to be taking his time, as time for Republicans' options is running out. As rumors of a party switch turn to drawn-out speculation, so does the talk that at least one prominent Republican will go for the party endorsement whether Roemer switches or not.

A Louisiana voter survey by White House pollster Robert Teeter shows Roemer's party switch would have a slightly negative effect on his approval ratings. Yet the poll does not measure how much of the vote a name Republican like Henson Moore would slice away from Buddy Roemer in a crowded field including Edwin Edwards and David Duke. Roemer's parents and some leftover aides from 1987 argue strongly against the switch, sensing, perhaps, that Buddy will not get along with the Republicans any better than he has with Democrats. But in a state where party lines are blurred, the question comes down to defensive positioning, to keeping his right-center flank clear, and to opening up political opportunities beyond the next election.

As it becomes clearer that Roemer is leaning to switching, so too is it that the other GOP contenders are not going to roll over for him. On the night before he publicly announces his switch, Roemer meets at the Mansion with Nungesser, Holloway, Hardy and Baker to break the news. Though they resent the governor's silent treatment of the state party, within days all the Republican hopefuls declare themselves noncandidates, except for Holloway, who does not attend the ceremony the next day. Still hanging in the air at the outdoor press conference at the Mansion is resentment over how Roemer brushed off and bruised Republican egos. Roemer, shrewd poker player, has called the local bluff. Hard feelings, however, count for more in politics than they do in poker.

Buddy Roemer hits the road after announcing his switch on March 11: "I want to get around this state so the people can touch and feel." For two weeks he does just that, traveling the state, meeting with local Republican leaders, asking for their help. A young Republican, Michelle Shauer, is pumped. "He got people excited. He was up on tables. He was saying, 'I need everyone.' He was very strong." The drawn-out decision over the switch and the ruffled local egos appear to be behind him. But there is one little problem.

The party may now have a Republican governor again, but it also has its rules. After the debacle of the Senate race, instead of throwing away its futile endorsement process, the Anal Retentive Wing resolves to tighten it further. Not only will the party endorse a candidate at its statewide convention, but candidates must now sign a written affidavit to not run if not endorsed, and they must sign before they can participate in the caucuses to select delegates. Duke says he has no intention of signing. Buddy Roemer says nothing.

In the afterglow of his switch, the governor would be the heavy favorite to sweep the caucuses and the convention and keep all other Republicans from the ballot, except for the maverick Duke. But there's the hitch with the affidavit. Caucuses are highly unpredictable, in that a small but well-organized special interest group, such as the evangelicals, could pull off an upset with Clyde Holloway, whom they love. George Bush still remembers the nearly fatal thumping he took from Pat Robertson in the 1988 Iowa caucuses.

The governor's supporters make the valid point that, as governor, his first responsibility is to the state and not to a handful of party activists. The governor, still saying nothing publicly, undertakes a quiet campaign to torpedo the convention.

First he tries to be nice. He invites the entire State Central Committee to the Mansion for a friendly luncheon reception. Clyde Holloway counters by inviting them all over to the Hilton afterwards for a spirited little keeping-options-open rally. The conservative State Central Committee members, many of them fundamentalist Christians, relish the attention from Roemer and his possible rival. "I've never had a dream to be governor," Holloway tells the Republican leaders, who are still wearing their name tags from the Mansion fete. "I will not be divisive," though a little divisiveness is just what a lot of this crowd has in mind. Holloway basks in their enthusiasm for him but doesn't know quite what to do with it. "This is the toughest decision I've ever made," he says. Lucky for him, Buddy Roemer was about to make it for him.

There are four Democrats trying to take away Edwin Edwards' base and he doesn't seem a bit concerned. "Louis Lambert can spend all the money he wants," he says after Lambert releases a flight of commercials to reintroduce himself to the Louisiana people. Apparently the reintroduction conjures up enough bad memories that Lambert remains mired in single-digit land and soon drops out of the race. Edwards predicts the same for Aaron Broussard, who is buying early airtime and going nowhere in the polls.

The pretenders' machinations bore him. Confident that he will rule the left, Edwards turns his attention to stirring up and cluttering up the right.

"Did you know Buddy Roemer voted for Michael Dukakis?" asks Edwards on the way to another parade.

"Did he say that?"

"It was in the *Advocate* three years ago." Buddy Roemer, who can't resist an impromptu question, told a reporter in fall 1988 that he would reluctantly vote for Dukakis. "Dan Quayle helped me make up my mind," he added.

Choice research, too good to be used by a Democrat, so Edwards passes it along to Clyde Holloway. Maybe it will encourage him. Any news about the Alexandria congressman is of prime interest to Edwards. Hearing that a reporter will attend Holloway's reception, Edwards jots on a pad. "Here, this is my home number. Call me if he says he's running."

"Would it matter? He'll just hurt Duke, if that."

"No, no. If Clyde runs, Roemer won't make the runoff. Clyde's a real Republican."


At first Charlie Roemer wasn't going to go to the party for the legislators at the Mansion on the evening after the opening of the session. "Then he said maybe we'd come by for just a few minutes," says Adeline Roemer. "Now look at him. He's loving this." Under the party tents on the Mansion side lawn the legislators and the lobbyists feast on the shrimp and crawfish. "And try that crabmeat," advises the elder Roemer, clearly in his element as he jokes with older legislators and younger staffers. This is one of the governor's father's first appearances at an official governor's function.

With the departure of the bulk of the old revolutionary guard and the influx of the political pros on the governor's staff, Charlie Roemer draws closer to his son's circle. The former commissioner likes the reorganization: "Yeah, he's gotten rid of about 18 of the 20 who ought to go."

The old man's back, runs the Capitol gossip while the true cynics add: When did he leave?

The veterans from 1987 attest that the son listened to but rarely heeded his father's political advice. Charlie argued hotly against the party switch, to no avail. But on the caucus question in 1991, the two seem of like mind.

A guest suggests, "It might be a good idea for Buddy to put together an organization for the Republican caucuses that he can use in the campaign."

Roemer stops mid-shrimp. The guest has turned into a bug. "Oh, you think so? He should just stand out there naked and let anyone shoot at him? What a great idea!" Anyway, he's right about the crabmeat.

The younger Roemer is more circumspect but just as reluctant to succumb to the GOP caucus experience. But neither he nor his campaign staff will make a public statement on why he, as governor, should not lay his office on the line for internal party politics.

Billy Nungesser has lobbied hard for Roemer to go along with the caucus process, sure that he would get the party endorsement if he would just work for it a little. In one Mansion meeting, though, according to Billy Nungesser, a shouting match ensued over the convention. "He's beating on his desk and telling me, 'Goddammit, sonofabitch, I don't need you or Dave Treen or the Republicans or the Democrats. I won without any of you last time.' " Another lasting Roemer impression.

The governor's operatives and his supporters in the practical, moderate wing of the party go to work to get the State Central Committee to call off the caucuses and the convention. The battle lines are drawn for a State Central Committee meeting in May.

David Duke, not a committee member, is on the sidelines working spin control on the press. "Holloway will hurt Roemer much more than he will me," he says. "If Holloway stays in, it's the end for Roemer." Duke grins and glides to the next reporter.

"He's blowing smoke," observes a committee member. "If Holloway gets the endorsement, that's a problem for Duke. People like Clyde. If he starts moving, Duke may have to get out."

The fight over calling off the convention barely lasts past Nungesser's opening gavel. John Treen has prefiled a motion to cancel the state party caucuses, a motion his brother Dave, the former governor and a lion of the party, will present. John Treen has covered every angle but one. The deliberate Treen (it's a family trait) studied and refined and reworked the motion before he filed it—one day after the deadline for accepting items for new business. Rules are rules, clucks Billy Nungesser. Old pals Dave Treen and Nungesser get in a shouting match behind the podium. Treen stalks off. His motion to suspend the rules is rejected. The caucuses are on.

Afterwards, the drinking conservatives convene to celebrate in the back room of T. J. Ribs. Clyde Holloway gets a rousing toast as he drops by to convey his thanks. These guys should thank him for the chance to kick Roemer for the slights they perceive and keep a close running count of. "He blew it when it took him six weeks to make up his mind," says one member. Others say he slighted the local party by dealing with the White House. Others say he did not state his position against the caucuses. After a few more objections, it is clear that nothing was going to stop this payback. What if the Treens had got their motion in on time? State Representative Art Sour of Shreveport considers that briefly. *Naa-a-a-h-hh.* "We'd have found something else."

The black gentleman wearing the Roemer sticker quietly confers on common strategy with the guy in the red-white-and-blue-striped vest and David Duke straw boater. The Lafayette Cajundome is the site of the Convention of the Weird.

Though Holloway has won most of the caucus delegates to the state convention, many Duke and Roemer supporters were elected as uncommitted delegates. The governor also has a lot of support among party officials who are automatic delegates. There is only one official candidate, Clyde Holloway, seeking the party endorsement, but he faces the No Endorsement challenge of the Duke and Roemer supporters, locked in their alliance from Hell.

The endorsement vote itself is preceded, of course, by an internal squabble over who gets to address the convention. Only the Republicans would consider allowing a nominating speech for No Endorsement, and David Duke wants to give it. Billy Nungesser, resplendent in his white suit and pink shirt and tie, at first acquiesces but then rules against Duke. The final ruling: one Duke supporter and one Roemer supporter will be allowed to give seconding speeches for No Endorsement. But not the candidates themselves, who, of course, are not official Republican candidates according to official Republican rules.

117

Most in the crowd are not as enamored of the stultifying convention process. They have come psyched up for Holloway or for Duke, who has filled the bleachers with non-delegate volunteers to make noise for their man. Holloway delegates are the most vocal on the floor, regularly breaking into frenzied outbursts to be countered by the ominous "Duke, Duke, Duke" chant from the rear gallery. The Roemer supporters suffer silently — they could be playing tennis.

Bryan Wagner urges delegates to vote for Clyde Holloway, a man who is what he is: "Clyde Holloway walks like a duck, he talks like a duck. . . ."

"Clyde Holloway is a duck!" screams a Dukester, setting off another round of dueling chants.

State Senator John Hainkel speaks for the governor. At the first mention of Roemer's name, the boos roll through the Lafayette Cajundome.

Now it's the Duke camp's turn. Duke whispers in Howie Farrell's ear as he accompanies his campaign manager to the side of the stage. Nungesser, suspecting that something is up, positions himself near the side steps to make sure only Farrell comes on-stage. Farrell is introduced. The Dukesters break out in cheers. Duke puts a move on Nungesser. He darts to the back center of the stage, takes the steps in one leap and charges for the mike as Farrell pivots aside. Nungesser, caught off guard, races to intercept him. He, Duke and convention sergeant-at-arms Tommy Gaudet collide at the mike at the same time. Duke gets out a "Ladies and gentlemen" before Nungesser seizes the microphone and shoulders Duke aside.

The convention floor erupts, and Duke supporters rush the stage. Nungesser pounds the gavel for order. "This is out of order and we're going on. That's the way it's gonna be, it ain't gonna be no other way." But Nungesser is drowned out by boos and chants as he vainly gavels for order. Duke remains at the side of the dais, regally waving to the Cajundome as disciples beneath him chant his name and shake fists at Nungesser.

The convention will not come to order. Party official Rod Miller yells at the Dukesters: "Is this the bunch that's going to bring law and order? If y'all don't knock it off, we'll be here forever." Not Fox McKeithen, who, for the second year in a row, makes a beeline for an early exit: "I'm like the tomcat dating the female skunk. I've had all I can stand." And he's gone.

Someone on the dais is thinking on his feet. College professor David Thibodeaux is produced to begin singing "God Bless the U.S.A." The song soothes the savage crowd. Holloway and Duke delegates, screaming at each other the moment before, now sway in unison and hold up lit cigarette lighters. It works well enough that Thibodeaux is urged to continue the musicale through the endorsement balloting. Next we hear "The Battle Hymn of the Republic" and "Dixie" (many Rebel yells here).

State Representative Charlie Lancaster is spinning on a TV reporter: "This is a very positive development. This proves that no one controls this party." Who would try?

"I must be at the wrong convention," says a departing female delegate from New Orleans. "I thought I'd never see the day."

By the time Thibodeaux launches into "Wind Beneath My Wings," former party treasurer Matt Isch approaches the press table holding his hands over his ears. "Any sharpened pencils?" he asks, pained.

It could be worse, says Richard Baudouin. "They could be singing 'Tomorrow Belongs to Us.' "

The vote totaling starts off close between Holloway and No Endorsement, but then swings narrowly to the congressman. The party's official endorsee, who looks like he's had all he can take too, maintains a brave face as he tells reporters, "This is a great day for the Louisiana Republican Party."

And for its father.

# 7. The Undead of Summer

With Patti Roemer gone and not coming back, with most of Roemer's old revolutionary guard departed, with the governor coming down from his Adventures in Attitudes and other outward signs of his mid-life crisis, life at the Mansion begins to settle into a more familiar atmosphere for Buddy Roemer. It begins to resemble Scopena.

At the small desk just outside the governor's Mansion office door, Adeline Roemer is on the phone planning an upcoming Mansion event. Her role? "Oh, this is like a big fraternity house and I'm the housemother. Buddy likes to have the nieces and nephews around but there has to be protocol. That's what grandmothers are for."

Did someone say protocol? The *New Orleans Times-Picayune* has been panting about the subject all week. The city, which considers itself a cosmopolitan island in the cultural swamp of Louisiana, is aghast at Governor Buddy Roemer's treatment of the new Japanese consul, Yasuhiro Hamada. The same governor who campaigned on and briefly fulfilled a promise to open a trade office in Japan showed little interest in receiving the foreign dignitary upon his arrival at his New Orleans station. The governor's office put off requests for a courtesy call for several months. On the day of the visit, Roemer kept the consul waiting an undiplomatic 20 minutes and then received him wearing blue jeans and cowboy boots, which were propped up on the desk.

The consul contained his ire until he returned to New Orleans, where he promptly unloaded on Roemer to the *Times-Picayune*. According to Hamada, the substance of the visit was no better than the governor's attire: "He said, 'I am very frustrated that Japanese companies are not coming here.' I thought, no wonder! If you receive the Japanese businessmen in such manner, it creates incredibility. They think, this man cannot be trusted."

Class-conscious New Orleans is mortified that the governor of Louisiana would comport himself like the rednecks who voted for him. The incident underscores the alienation of the upper middle class from the governor who seems insensitive to the needs and values of the state's largest city. Roemer held his own in Uptown New Orleans against Bob Livingston in 1987, but some speculate had he started his commercials there earlier — *with that voice* — he would have driven voters away. Exactly what he appears to be doing four years later.

Of course, many working-class New Orleanians don't mind that Buddy snubbed some Japanese high hat. But Roemer has a way of alienating them too. The *Picayune* reports in a breathless front-page exposé that Buddy Roemer went to the Saints' thrilling final game of 1990, sat in the governor's skybox . . . and read a book. The common touch.

His challengers are out beating the roads every day, and beating up on him. Buddy Roemer is barely concerned enough to make his scheduled fundraisers, several of which he postpones on short notice. His campaign staff is starting to get concerned, but the calm, resolute governor is not going to be rushed into something uncomfortable . . . like a reelection campaign.

Before the first polls measure the effect of Roemer's party switch, the bookies adjust their odds. Based on about 200 bets placed with bookmakers in three states, Edwin Edwards is installed as a 7-2 favorite, followed by Roemer at 4-1, Duke at 8-1 and Aaron Broussard at 40-1.

"The race is going to make history," the Associated Press quotes Kenneth Johnston, a North Louisiana handicapper. "People in Chicago may not know who the pope is, but they know Edwin Edwards and David Duke."

A running joke among campaign veterans who have managed races around the country is the sage advice of locals: "You know, politics are a little different here." Politics, of course, differ as much from place to place as does human nature, which is not a lot. What keeps the myth alive is the incompetent performance of outside political operatives who would make just as bad mistakes in their own backyards, which they probably were run out of.

In Louisiana, the worst reputation for outside incompetence belongs to the Republican National Committee for its performance in Henson Moore's 1986 Senate race. Moore was criticized not for using RNC campaign professionals but for practically turning campaign strategy over to them. Their clumsy, blistering attack against John Breaux in the crowded open primary field helped to elevate the Cajun congressman to a strong second-place primary finish. Then the Republicans' attempt to purge the voter rolls backfired into a civil rights crusade and the huge black turnout that smothered Moore in the runoff.

The antithesis of the outsider campaign was Buddy Roemer's in 1987, which was directed by Roemer himself, an experienced political consultant and pollster, and was managed by his homegrown cadre.

In 1991, with his old campaign staff chased off and with some other key supporters barely speaking to him, Governor Roemer, not

122

to be bothered with political details, turns to Washington. Sam Dawson from South Carolina, a disciple of Lee Atwater's, is brought in as campaign manager. Gordon Hensley comes in from Washington to be communications director.

"I am not RNC," says Hensley, with a drag on his cigarette. "I wish I was. They have a good health plan." Roemer's campaign communications director lives in Washington and hires out to Republican political campaigns around the country. He is part of a network of Republican political operatives who have become friends on the endless campaign trail. As Hensley describes it, "It's a bonding thing. We've been through so many losing campaigns together."

Hensley's last defeat was the Clayton Williams debacle in Texas, the conservative millionaire who blew a big lead and made Ann Richards the governor. Before that, he worked for Pete Dupont's nonstarting race in the 1988 Republican presidential primaries. There, at least, he got to know Dupont's New Jersey and saw firsthand what Louisiana-born consultant James Carville did to Republican favorite Pete Dawkins in the New Jersey Senate race. Carville at the time is the hottest consultant in the country, a slash-and-burner who can use a stiletto but prefers the meataxe. That was Hensley's only qualm about accepting the Roemer job: "I called down here to be sure Carville was not working here."

Even Republican field workers have tasted defeat in foreign lands. The manager of Roemer's New Orleans headquarters, Michelle Shauer, last worked in the disastrous Republican campaign for governor of Minnesota. A few weeks before the general election, the GOP nominee was accused of skinny-dipping with some teenage girls four years before. Shauer was surprised that the headquarters staff was freaking so. "Here I was from Louisiana saying, 'What's the big deal? He didn't even have sex with her. This will blow over.'" But instead it blew the Republicans out of the race.

Outsiders though the staff may be, a home boy is calling the shots. "Roemer is the strategist," says Hensley. "We're just technicians." They may not know the players in Louisiana politics, or even where all the cities are, but they know the basics of media management, about which the opposition seems not to have a clue. Hensley is amazed that Roemer's challengers, for all the bashing of him at poorly covered forums, make no consistent effort to get their share of "earned media," a professional euphemism for news coverage. Hensley sees his job as having his candidate "making news in the morning and having your opponent responding in the afternoon." That's the way to control the agenda of a campaign without being ambushed at forums or spending early money on TV.

Hensley has that much right. Louisiana politicians got lazy over the years by having so much money to spend on TV commercials. With the money well dried up this year, other candidates appear to be at a loss on how to get their messages out. When they do, Hensley and Dawson are on it right away, to see if a response or a counterattack is called for. Sometimes it's as easy as counting. When Edwards issued his 10-point education plan, Hensley counted only 9 points. "This is great," crows Hensley. "He puts out an education plan and he can't count." He is proud that the *Washington Post* picks up his tidbit but is mystified why the state newspapers ignore it. They don't know good spin when they see it.

No matter. The Roemer campaign is not out to attack Edwards. They don't need to, says Hensley. "His negatives are so high he has little credibility. He'll try to cobble together the old-style Democratic coalition—African-American voters and yellow-dog Democrats—but things have changed. The Democrats he needs are up for grabs, between Roemer and Duke."

Sure, he acknowledges, "Roemer is getting bad press, but it's cyclical. When the voters focus on who are their choices . . ."

The governor may get his lumps over the Japanese consul and another round of sparring with the Legislature, but he chooses not to take any body blows by subjecting himself to the bloodlust of forums. For the record, Roemer says he will not begin campaigning until after the Legislature adjourns in July, and if there is a special session, he'll wait longer still. Polls show Roemer and Edwards within two points of each other, but more important, they are both strong with their respective bases. Clyde Holloway, who promised once not to be divisive, finds he is not even when he tries to be. Following his hard-fought convention endorsement, a new poll gives him 5 percent of the vote, barely denting either Roemer or David Duke.

The news is also good for Roemer on his left flank, where the governor's worst nightmare would be for a moderate Democrat to overtake Edwards and give voters a reasonable alternative to Roemer. It's not happening. Louis Lambert drops out. Aaron Broussard, having spent a wad and seen nothing for it, is about to follow. Fred Dent and Sam Jones continue to register trace elements of support.

Kathleen Blanco enters the race with plenty of fanfare and about $150,000. She is the first viable female candidate for governor in a year when women stand for competence and reform. But Kathleen, the Catholic mother of six, refuses to soften her anti-abortion views, and that undermines her natural base. Blanco's TV commercials state the obvious — "I'm not one of the good ol' boys" — but who she is never quite comes into focus. Amid the pumped-up excitement of an early fundraiser in Lafayette, a local attorney observes, "I think we are witnessing a stillbirth."

Anyone who saw what happened to Billy Tauzin in 1987 should not be surprised at what is happening to the new-face Democrats. As Edwards' aide Bob d'Hemecourt explains, "When the king is dead, they can pick a new king. Until then, long live the king and don't forget it."

That's fine for the governor for the old dragon to have just enough fire in him so Buddy can slay him one more time. By early summer, the polls are static. Money is harder than ever to raise.

Edwards is a broken record. Duke is on good behavior. The press is taking a nap. The campaign billed as the Race from Hell, the most colorful ever, is a dud. And Buddy Roemer would just as soon keep it that way.

While the other candidates are out schlepping around where there are more trees than people, Buddy Roemer is indulging in the pre-election ritual of handing out money to local governments. The press office has set up an assembly line of block-grant check presentations with dozens of local officials, all duly photographed to be sent to the hometown newspapers. Next to signing pardons, this is the closest any governor gets to God. Roemer flashes a smile for the camera as he hands over another check: "Is this a great job or what?"


"Don't go. Don't go. Don't go."

A band of about two dozen protestors shout to cars pulling into the Fourth of July celebration in New Orleans City Park. For a mere $15, fun-seekers can enjoy all the food they can eat, all the beer they can drink, all the music they can dance to, and all of David Duke they want to hear.

For weeks, the posters had been papering telephone poles in the white neighborhoods of the New Orleans area: DUKEFEST. CALL TICKETMASTER.

It worked very well the year before, when over 4,000 paid $15 each for the combination rock festival-county fair-political rally. It's another innovation Duke has introduced to Louisiana politics, along with the 1-900 number, paraphernalia merchandising and aggressive direct-mail appeals. Duke's use of Ticketmaster, the premier ticket service for rock concerts and sporting events, is another clever, ironic touch. Ticketmaster outlets were all over the city, including the Maison Blanche stores, owned by outspoken Duke opponents, the Sternberg family.

The event was a successful money raiser and showpiece political rally for Duke in 1990. It could be even more important in this unprecedented money drought of the governor's race. One small problem: the law. This is strange getting used to—a Louisiana campaign finance law more restrictive than the federal government's. But this is what Buddy Roemer has wrought. Ticketmaster stops selling Dukefest tickets when it discovers it is illegal to accept cash on behalf of a political campaign, specifically including ticket sales for political events.

Duke again bemoans the repressive Roemer campaign finance law that is crippling small grass-roots campaigns the most. Even cash ticket sales at the gate are illegal. Duke conceives a clever bypass. Staffers and volunteers manning the gate are giving each entering Dukefester a couple of Duke stickers as a $15 "purchase of paraphernalia."

That gets the gates open and the money flowing. But not like last year. Threatening thunderclouds during a week of showers may be one reason that less than 1,000 show up, far off the 1990 attendance. But the show must go on. Small groups of mostly young people in tanktops and muscle shirts and shorts dot the huge expanse between the food and beer booths and the music stage. The beer booth is doing brisk business as volunteers keep the draught taps pouring. One confused festgoer offers money for brew, but the sixtyish volunteer waves it off. "It's on the Fuehrer," he laughs—his little joke.

Onstage, the band knocks off for short remarks by the candidate. David Duke masks any disappointment over the small crowd as he rips into his standard litany of the woes facing Louisiana: "The greatest problem facing this state is the rising welfare underclass . . ."

"The niggers," yells the bare-chested young man in sunglasses.

If Duke hears that, he pretends not to. "People say I'm anti-black. I'm not. They're suffering too with the drugs and crime and the poor education. They want to be proud of their heritage and to preserve their heritage like we're proud of ours."

127

Duke has some special guests to introduce. On stage come two young girls. "Ladies and gentlemen, I want you to meet my daughters. This is Kristin and this is Erika. You think I have it bad, think what they've got to put up with." The girls live in Lakeland, Florida, with Duke's ex-wife Chloe and her second husband, white supremacist Don Black, whom Duke considers a friend.

Daddy's notoriety has not stopped young Erika from taking her first step in politics, as Duke proudly announces, "She is an elected representative on her student council."

But we're here to have fun, since apparently no one is making money. Duke leaves the stage to mingle through the crowd, those who can get past the cordon of bodyguards and New Orleans policemen.

The band's vocalist is warming up the crowd before the next set. "How many people here paid your property taxes late?" he yells. Between the homestead exemption and the looks of this crowd, it's doubtful few have even seen a tax bill, much less paid one. But that's okay, says the rocker, "When David Duke gets elected governor, like Ray Charles says, 'You got the right one, baby.'"

As the Duke wedge moves out, a young woman in a tanktop and a Harley cap penetrates the security lines to get the candidate's autograph and returns all excited to her blanket by the bandstand. Her name is Shortstuff. She and her pal Oona have their own reasons for digging David Duke. "David Duke is so fine they should put him in *Playgirl* for us ladies," says Oona, barely contained within her tanktop. "On St. Patrick's Day I kissed him and my old man left me. I mean I really kissed him." Oona leans forward and extends her arm, curved so to demonstrate how she hooked the back of the candidate's neck and laid a wet one on him.

You can see how it would have disturbed the old man. "His name is Clarence — with a name like that and he's white."

Any other real men in this campaign? Roemer?

Oona shows contempt. "He's an asshole and a jerkoff. His old lady left him because he ain't worth a shit."

Edwards?

"I liked him all right, but he's old."

Shortstuff howls, "Old? Look at your old man." As for a real man, says Shortstuff, "I love David Duke. He's so cool." And as if her endorsement is not enough, she adds, "The bike groups love him. I'm 30 years old and I've never been into politics. I never could back anybody till David Duke. He'll straighten things out. He'll get the blacks off of welfare. Fucking blacks live on my street. I got a gun and I'm waitin' for 'em."

A tall bearded young man with a Harley cap and an NAAWP t-shirt comes up with three cups of beer. Oona introduces her prodigal beau: "This is Clarence."

Clarence shares his own history with David Duke: "David signed me up in the Junior Klan when I was 16 years old. Out on Metairie Road. Me and David go back 15 years. Back when I joined the Klan I lived in a neighborhood that was half black and half white. I was in a bind. I couldn't walk into a place and not get jumped. That's what gave me prejudice."

Clarence, who works in an auto trim shop, chooses his words carefully on the race question. Not Shortstuff: "I hate niggers."

"Duke is no b.s.," continues Clarence. "A lot of people hide behind a political shield and only think 'fight.' David is out there fighting for himself but for everyone else too. He worries about the little people. He believes in equal rights for all. Too much privilege goes to blacks."

"Damn niggers," interjects Shortstuff.

"My grandfather is good friends with Edwin Edwards," says Clarence. "I can't say nothing bad about him. He's had a little corruption, but that's history."

The Duke wedge continues an erratic odyssey near the food booths. The cops keep a nervous lookout. One almost draws his weapon when an incoming frisbee knocks his hat off. In addition to the policemen, four bodyguards in dark suits and dark glasses vigilantly check out the Duke fans. A woman holds up her baby, decked in American flag pants, for a kiss from the candidate.

Another young woman, who says she's from Philadelphia and works at a local hospital (she doesn't want to divulge any more information than that), gets her boyfriend to take her photo with Duke. Now she wants a souvenir shot with the security detail.

"Are you a bodyguard?" she asks the guy wearing sunglasses and a black suit and sweating profusely.

"No, no, I'm just out here," says the suit, who gets a bit rattled and has to walk away for a moment to regain his anonymity.

The music has ended. The small crowd is getting smaller. Duke and security entourage load up in two cars and depart in a cloud of dust.

Duke would call it a successful event, only a bit dampened by the threat of rain. "There were about 3,000 there," he would wildly exaggerate later. Press secretary Glenn Montecino is more realistic. "We lost a lot of money on it. It was a big bust. That was the real low point of the campaign. Afterwards we went back to headquarters and just cried."

In not many states would you find the association of chiefs of police running the hospitality bar at a convention for local officials. At the Louisiana Municipal Association gathering in Lake Charles, two chiefs are working the bar while another is cooking some boudin in the back. The South Louisiana sausage delicacy draws a crowd of mayors and police jurors. Alexandria Mayor Ned Randolph and his neighbor across the Red River, Mayor Frank Baden of Pineville, are enjoying their Cajun hors d'oeuvres. "Man, man, I could eat this all day," grunts the earthy Baden. "Meat in a condom I call it." Ned Randolph, his mouth full, gets this queasy look on his face. Nearby, a couple of women are dipping their hot boudin into Steen's cane syrup. "Oh, it's the only way to eat it," one observes, though she admits the cane syrup issue divides the boudin universe.

The chiefs at least provide some diversion for this convention of very unhappy campers. Budgets are tight and options are few to meet the fiscal crisis in local government. The state seems to pile on more mandated expenses while continuing to tie municipal officials' hands on raising revenues. Certainly they will get some answers today, for there will be a forum of gubernatorial candidates.

Even Buddy Roemer has accepted the invitation, but you know how that goes. His office calls to slightly amend his schedule. The governor would like to address the convention in the morning, alone, so he can take the afternoon off to go fishing with his sons Chas and Dakota.

This one starts on as flat a note as the other dreary sessions. The new addition to the race, Kathleen Blanco, can still work up some indignation: "I'm running for governor because I can't stand the corruption and the lies anymore." The police jurors look bored as she bemoans Louisiana's poor image. "I'm tired of the looks of pity," she continues. A mayor stifles a yawn.

A murmur runs through the crowd as David Duke joins the panel late, shaking Edwin Edwards' and Sam Jones' hands before sitting down. When his turn comes, he returns to the question of image. "I've heard it said that David Duke will be bad for the image of Louisiana." He looks incredulous. "Bad for the image of Louisiana? Ladies and gentlemen, Louisiana's biggest problem is not its image, it's its reality. That's what I'm here to change. At least my image is not Buddy Roemer's blue jeans or popping rubber bands or Edwin Edwards' taste in women, though I happen to like his taste in women."

This rates a nod from Edwards, who keeps the playful tone alive: "My friend David Duke keeps trying to make me a wizard under the sheets. But at 64, I just don't qualify for that anymore. But I'm a pretty good governor. . . ."

Sam Jones' turn: "I know I must be doing good. Duke told me, 'Go get Edwin.' Edwin told me, 'Go get Duke.'" Sam settles on

Duke. "I've seen Edwin's girlfriends and I've seen David's — and it's true, Edwin's taste is better. That is, if all yours are girls, David."

Duke blushes and with an expression of hurt and pain looks for sympathy in the audience, which at least is getting a bit of entertainment from this road show that is growing punch drunk.

After the forum, Jones is more serious. "Forget the polls, man. Duke has a place in the runoff. It's all I hear people talk about. Duke is the present. Edwards is the past. Roemer is old news. People out there are talking about Duke. There needs to be someone who can stop him."

Jones sort of has himself in mind, since he is certain Buddy and Edwin are history. And speaking of history, "Doesn't this phenomenon with Duke, the way people react to him, doesn't this remind you of something in the past?"

"Well, Hitler had a few more guns."

"I'm not talking about Hitler. I'm talking about Huey Long. Once he got in there, he had the power and he got what he wanted. Don't think Duke can't too."

Jones sounds like a man trying to set off an alarm. "I've got a poll going out in the field that will be very interesting. It will be very different. It will tell how people really feel. The people are hiding their feelings."

Jones is not the only one trying to resurrect Huey Long. In a slow summer's weird side drama, Dr. James Staars of George Washington University, a forensic scientist specializing in historical murders, wants to exhume Huey Long's body to try to determine who really killed him. Russell Long's response, basically, is forget it. The Long family dismisses and resents speculation that Huey was not killed by Dr. Carl Weiss but by a ricocheting bullet from a trigger-happy bodyguard. Or, according to another barroom theory, Weiss was a dupe in a broader conspiracy to stop Huey. The Weiss family has approved the exhumation of Weiss' body, so that Staars can look for evidence of drugs in his system or a nervous disorder that could have explained his action. Staars knows he is digging up the wrong body, but hopes he can find something to further his investigation and to pressure the Long family to permit Huey's exhumation.

The idea has some public appeal. "If they dig up Huey before October 19," says state trooper Marshall Lyles in Jonesboro, "we're gonna put him on the ballot and vote for him."

Another far-fetched conspiracy theory prompts the exhumation of the body of President Zachary Taylor. Though a Kentuckian, General Taylor was residing in Baton Rouge at the time of his 1848 election, and hence is claimed as Louisiana's only president. The scientists seek to confirm a theory that Taylor, who supposedly died of indigestion, actually was poisoned.

The exhumations turn up nothing, but for a couple of weeks the dead politicians make more news than the live ones. A member of the bored Legislature rises in mock alarm. "They're digging up our politicians," cries Ralph Miller on the floor of the House. "They're trying to dig up Buddy Roemer, but they can't find where he's buried."

# 8. Morality Power Plays

For day after steaming day, under the broiling sun and driving rains, for two summer-long seasons, the competing troupes transformed the Capitol steps into a stage for the morality power play on God and women in Louisiana. Anti-abortion protestors outnumbered abortion rights protestors, but they all got their stage time at the Theater of the Unborn.

For days three charismatic Christians shouted biblical verses *at* the State Capitol: "The Legislature's judgment is not God's judgment. It is God who is the Supreme Court! Abortion is murder! Repent!" Telling the State Capitol to repent—talk about a lost cause. The cries of the demonstrators were heard all the way up on the 24th floor, driving Capitol workers to distraction and to revenge fantasies, some involving boiling oil. Other performances ranged from Bible readings and Rosary recitations to speaking in tongues. Several women laid hands on the building and prayed and bobbed their heads. More pro-lifers linked hands and surrounded the Capitol and sang. A Christian radio station reporter interpreted the piece for his secular colleagues: "The walls of Jericho thing, you know."

Abortion rights activists demonstrated too, but they were outnumbered and outshouted by the pro-lifers. A woman holding a sign, "Support vasectomies," was told by pro-lifers, "Your father should have had one." Not to be outdone, a group of players from California appeared on the steps to stage a botched abortion. A woman wore a white gown with blood smeared over its midsection. Pro-choice leaders were horrified, but the Theater of the Unborn trifles not with matters of taste or even politics.

The abortion politics of 1990 and 1991 posed problems and opportunities for the candidates for governor, especially the incumbent. During the reign of *Roe v. Wade*, Congressman Roemer found it easy to side with the mobilized pro-life forces opposing abortion. When the Supreme Court in its 1989 Webster decision reopened the question of how much states could regulate abortion, anti-abortion activists nationwide identified Louisiana as the one state most likely to impose the most complete ban on abortions. The same factors that made Louisiana more liberal than other Southern states in civil rights made it most conservative on the abortion question. The large rural Catholic population and their priests, a font of tolerance on the race question, cut no slack on the mortal sin of abortion. Even Catholic politicians with liberal and black constituencies, like New Orleans District Attorney Harry Connick Sr., pressed for the strongest anti-abortion law.

In 1990, anti-abortion activists forged an unprecedented, ecumenical coalition of Louisiana bishops, evangelical Christians and the national Eagle Forum to mount a grass-roots offensive on the Legislature. Conservative Representative Woody Jenkins led the charge with a bill to make abortion a crime of second-degree murder punishable with ten years at hard labor, with only one exception for danger to the life of the mother.

Jenkins and company equated a so-called moderate position, allowing for exceptions of rape and incest, as tantamount to abortion on demand. While public opinion polls showed that less than 20 percent of the people favored "abortion on demand," over

60 percent favored the three main exceptions. But the legislators weren't reading public opinion polls as much as they were their own mail and phone messages, or as much as they could hear the cries to repent coming from the Capitol steps. Intensity counts. Politicians know a hard-core minority can hurt you much more in an election than can the disengaged majority.

Disengaged and silent. While the pro-choice movement was waking up in other states, it was very slow overcoming social pressures in Louisiana to oppose the church-based pro-life forces. Many people confused their personal opposition to abortion with the issue of the government deciding who can have one. Many others felt strongly that abortion was an intensely private matter and did not wish to parade their views before hordes of pro-life demonstrators and state politicians.

The Legislature was not much help. Of its 144 members, 141 were men in 1990. Many of those could vote to ban abortions for the population but would make sure their wives or daughters could have one to end an unwanted pregnancy. That's the fourth great exception: life of the mother, rape, incest and me.

So the pro-life forces seized an early advantage and did not let go. Reasonable objections were cast aside. A conservative lawmaker pointed out that the bill's 10-year prison sentence for doctors for the separate crime of second-degree murder could result in court tests for other second-degree murder statutes that carry life sentences. "I've got some guys up at Angola who are clapping and cheering about the bill," said Representative Robert Garrity. "They want to see it passed because the first thing they're going to do is come in and file a writ saying, 'If he (the doctor) gets 10 years, then I want 10 years.' "

The objection was ignored, as was concern that the broad language, "Whoever commits the crime of abortion," could make a woman who induces her own abortion liable for 10 years at hard labor.

Some legislators confused the demonstrators on the steps with the electorate and lost their grip. Most notably, Carl Gunter of Pineville, rising to oppose the incest amendment, began with the five most dangerous words in the Legislature. "When I got to thinking," he said, "the way we get thoroughbred horses and thoroughbred dogs is through inbreeding. Maybe we could get a super-sharp kid." Some representatives were seen burying their heads in their hands. Even Gunter quickly realized he had gone beyond the threshold of the Merely Stupid, but it was too late.

Representative Jenkins, holding up plastic models of fetuses, his "little people," fended off all efforts to weaken or to even clarify his bill. It passed the House 74-27, sailed through the Senate and went to the governor's desk. He vetoed it. "Women cannot and should not be forced to bear the consequences of these traumatic, illegal acts," Roemer restated his earlier stand. "These exceptions are very important to me and, I believe, important to the women of Louisiana whose rights and lives must also be protected."

The governor's word should have been the last. It had been on every other bill vetoed by every other governor in this century. The historical, preeminent power and authority of the Louisiana governor, especially his control over which roads are built and which relatives are hired, had prevented the Legislature from overriding any gubernatorial veto. But Buddy was not your normal governor, nor were these normal times. After the defeat of fiscal reform and the failure of his marriage, Roemer was still listing through a personal and political mid-life crisis. He had started the session with a New Age call to legislators to join him to "build a campfire," and they had promptly pissed on it. With the governor appearing weak when not absent, the Senate hatched a countercoup that deposed Roemer's hand-picked president of the Senate. The session was in full drift, with a $500 million hole in the budget and no consensus for filling it. With leadership divided or nonexistent, freelance demagoguery ran amok. David Duke had whites and blacks in the House squaring off over his anti-affirmative action bill, which passed the lower chamber. So did the ban on trash lyrics and the beat-the-flag-burner bills. Fear and frustration stalked the halls. Legislators heard ominous reports of the crowds David Duke was drawing in their districts and of the fiery anti-abortion sermons in Baptist and Catholic churches. The center was not holding. The vaunted power of the governor was unraveling. And Woody Jenkins, once again, was mobilizing.

"Welcome to the land of the barbarians," muttered a suburban legislator when the House voted to override the governor's veto. The battle turned to the Senate. By now, though, the anti-abortion juggernaut was slowing down. Senators began hearing from constituents, especially in the cities and in less-Catholic North Louisiana, who demanded the rape and incest exceptions, or who wanted the government to stay out of the abortion question altogether. When it came to a vote in the 39-member Senate, 8 of 11 North Louisiana members stuck with the governor and voted to sustain his veto — the full Senate fell two votes short of the override.

Jenkins regrouped for one last push, at any cost. Already the Senate had received a telegram purportedly from Mother Teresa, offering to take any unwanted children. The telegram was discovered to have come from a priest in Lafayette. Then Senate President Nunez received a call purportedly from the Vatican. When Nunez asked for a number to call back and verify, he was given a 504-area-code number. Woody Jenkins' aides placed photographs of aborted fetuses on the desks of some swing-vote senators. Someone spray-painted the Capitol's front wall: "Stop Killing the Innocent."

Finally the override effort collapsed. Then reality sank in and a new sense of panic seized the Legislature. Jenkins and allies have prevented the slightly milder rape-and-incest-exceptions bill from moving. Now, with it too late in the session to get it passed, legislators realized they are on record for a draconian bill that would force 15-year-old rape victims to continue pregnancies to term, and still there is no law on the books to curb abortion on demand.

Most legislators had no one but themselves to blame for being stampeded to vote for the no-exceptions bill. But you can never tell a politician there is no one else to blame. In a fitting end to an insane session, the Senate seized the only available bill languishing on the calendar, James David Cain's beat-the-flag-burner bill, and created the crime of "battery by abortion" with exceptions for rape and incest. The bastardized bill rolled through the Senate and, over Jenkins' stern objections, the House too.

Now the governor was back in a box. He had said he would sign a bill with the exceptions. But this bill? His aides predicted he would take the easy way out, let the bill become law without his signature and then let state and federal courts figure it out.

As the 1990 session adjourned at midnight, an old friend of Roemer's stood at the bottom of the Capitol steps, now empty save for reporters ritualistically quaffing cheap champagne. Buddy not sign the bill? "Forget it," said the friend. "Buddy Roemer won't take the quiet way out. He judges every controversial decision by its size relative to the size of his balls."

"This bill does not honor women," Roemer would tell a packed press conference two weeks later as he red-lined his second anti-abortion bill. In the preceding weeks, he had immersed himself in conversations with women, his ex-wife among them, who had urged him to veto the bill. He said his consciousness had been raised further by other possible exceptions, including fetal deformity, the mental health of the mother and other situations that would appeal to "common sense and common decency."

Conservatives predicted Roemer would pay for having flip-flopped on his earlier position. Yet the major state newspapers backed him up for putting down the mutant bill. And women around the state poured in their thanks for standing up for them before the stampeding herd of yahoos. Something else was at work here. The veto message marked Roemer's strongest public stand since his political and personal life began falling apart a year ago. By saying no (also on the Trash Lyrics Bill and some excessive

139

spending items), Roemer seemed to sedate a Legislature gone wild and to anchor his own drifting governorship. After Louisiana's rollercoaster ride into madness, the driver was awake and in control again. His welcomed message was: almost anything goes in Louisiana, but not this.

But it wasn't an election year.


"Watch out, Clinton, it's coming."

"What's that, Buddy?"

"Abortion. It's coming."

Fresh from his abortion vetoes, Roemer arrived as the newsmaker of the National Governors Conference in Mobile. Peter Jennings featured Roemer in a segment of an ABC special on America's abortion debate. Roemer was lionized by the national press, even national abortion rights groups, for turning back the most direct threat yet to *Roe v. Wade*. Which is strange, considering the bill that Roemer had vetoed was so defective it would not have survived a *state* court challenge and that Roemer's very public stand was more conservative than that of every other governor who had vetoed or even signed anti-abortion legislation that year. Outside Louisiana, you could only call him moderate in comparison to the Republican Party's 1988 platform. Contrary to Roemer's prediction, pro-life's post-Webster tide was receding fast around the country. The Florida Legislature's rejection of its Republican governor's anti-abortion bill showed how quickly the pro-choice movement had rebounded.

If the abortion storm was headed anywhere, it was on its way back to Louisiana just in time for the election.


In 1991, the Catholic bishops, frustrated and embarrassed by Jenkins' and the fundamentalists' strategy and tactics, decouple their pro-life alliance and back an anti-abortion bill with exceptions for the life of the mother, rape and incest. In vetoing last year's bills, Roemer had vowed to get with pro-life legislators to work out a bill he could back and sign. By the time Allen Bares introduces the Catholic-favored bill in 1991, he still has not heard from the governor. The majority of the Legislature, already well on record on the issue, quickly fall into line. So do the candidates for governor, supporting the new anti-abortion bill to a man, and woman. Only Sam Jones, last seen at 2 percent in the polls, opposes government restrictions.

Outnumbered and isolated by legislators and candidates, Roemer finds his views are growing more in line with only one group, the voters. Though a majority favor some restrictions, polls show more and more people unsure about how much the state should get involved in private family decisions — especially theirs. That old fourth exception. Roemer is making the same political odyssey as other formerly pro-life male politicians facing for the first time the crosscurrents of how people feel about abortion and how they feel about government regulation of abortion. He also feels that on a personal level, now that he is back into pleasing women, whether his ex-wife, whom he misses, or the young women he is dating, most of whom are under 30.

Politically, he can still say he's pro-life while being the only candidate to have done something for pro-choice voters. There's no point in his veering back to the right. By now, he couldn't sway hard-core pro-lifers even if he gave birth himself.

Fortunately for him, his opponents, bunched up on the right, are giving him plenty of room to float toward the center. Even the lone major female candidate, Kathleen Blanco, has refused to budge from her support of the restrictive bill. "I talked till I was blue in the face," admits her husband and adviser, Ray "Coach" Blanco. He admires his wife's principles, he wouldn't have "Mom" any other way, but he knows she needs a little more wiggle room to build her base with women.

The pro-choice option was the last hope for Aaron Broussard's dying campaign, but not only is the Kenner mayor a devout Catholic, he's a frequent flyer to Medjugorje.

Given his fears of the rising underclass, it would seem David Duke would find abortion useful. Instead he hews to the conservative line, "I am firmly pro-life," with his own twist "and firmly pro-contraception." He has proposed a bill to pay women on welfare to have the Norplant contraceptive device implanted in their arms. It does not pass.


Woody Jenkins returns with his plastic fetuses and busloads of Christians to occupy the Capitol steps. Their no-politics, no-compromise stand barely gets past the front doors this year, for legislators are determined to get this issue behind them quickly and neatly. The bishops' bill passes both houses easily. Issues of fetal deformity and the mental health of the mother are briefly raised before they are shot down. The so-called moderate bill gives victims of rape and incest seven days to report their situation and get an abortion. Publicly, Roemer holds his stance of struggling to protect the unborn while honoring women. He doesn't offer any suggestions — after all, they might be accepted and he would then be attached to the bill. Instead, he waits until it reaches his desk, seizes on the seven-day period as too short and vetoes his third abortion bill. When reporters try to pin him down by asking what exceptions he would include were it his bill to write, he wiggles loose: "I just can't say. I could come up with a list of exceptions, but then there could be a dozen more."

The Legislature, though, has had enough. This time, both houses override his veto, the first time that has happened to any Louisiana governor in this century. Despite the historic rebuke, the other candidates do not jump Roemer for being out of step with the Legislature. They too are hearing the moral tap-dancing of the people as the new law, immediately challenged and blocked in federal court, is packed off for eventual hearing by the U.S. Supreme Court.

Even Edwin Edwards, who once endorsed wiping the old anti-abortion law from the books in the wake of *Roe v. Wade* (the initiative stalled in the Legislature in the '70s), says he too would sign the current bill. But he doesn't see any gain in pushing his pro-life position. "Actually, Roemer's stand would benefit me more because I don't have an anti-abortion record like he does," says Edwards in the front seat. With d'Hemecourt at the wheel, we speed past canefields eerily lit by an ammonia plant on the way to the Sunshine Bridge. "I'm not saying it's a bad issue," analyzes Edwards. "We're just talking politics here. Forget morality."

Forgotten.

"Roemer might as well say he's pro-choice. He's boxed himself in on the issue." Besides that, says Edwards, Roemer already angered the conservatives by backing riverboat gambling. "Once Roemer crossed the Rubicon on gambling, he might as well as have vetoed the abortion bill, because he already lost the religious people."


Another charter bus pulls up in front of the Mansion, and a couple of dozen more women, from 20s to 70s in age, disembark and join the long receiving line to shake the governor's hand and stay for lunch.

The override of Roemer's veto was taken as further proof that the governor was losing his grip on the power of his office. Seen another way, though, abortion was a moral issue that rose above traditional political concerns. About half of the people in the Capitol took it very personally. The day the override passed, Dee Dee Fulmer, a senior research analyst in the Senate, felt the anger and frustration of women from the Treasurer's Office to the proofing room. "Every woman in the Capitol felt devalued," said Fulmer, who picked up the phone and was able to get through to the governor: "All right, Roemer, I'm with you." Governor Roemer's loss was candidate Roemer's gain. For the first time since taking office, Roemer had a large group of angry people on his side.

The Mansion luncheon is one of the first events planned by Women for Roemer, which would be a committed force for him, though it did not always mesh with his Republican campaign organization.

You can see that on Gordon Hensley's face. He's growing impatient at the inordinate time Roemer is taking for one-on-one conversations instead of getting in today's sound bites for the media.

"Lighten up, Gordon," says Marianne Freeman. "You've had your panties in a wad all day." Daughter Caroline brings Dad a Diet Coke. She's been riding and walking in most of the parades Roemer has missed this summer, so she's glad he's paying this attention to the Women for Roemer movement, which she and her campaign pals call "Babes for Buddy."

When it does come time to speak, Roemer preaches the politics of inclusion, as he seems to borrow his old party's vision of the state as a big tent, which holds, he says, "Men and women, black and white, all treated with respect and honor, and all with a place at the table."

Some women are ready to sign on while others are candidate shopping. A spunky, elderly woman wearing the button "Elect More Uppity Women" observes Roemer close up but is not ready to buy. "They're all politicians. They're all alike." Somewhat less uppity, Virginia Molaisson of Terrebonne Parish thinks Roemer is different: "I didn't agree with him on abortion, but he was strong to do that. He knew he would lose votes for that, but he was man enough to stand up for it."

# 9. Jesus Wept Here

Jimmy Swaggart is so full of grace that when he encounters a reporter in the courthouse bathroom he smiles broadly and asks, "How's life treating you, podnah?"

"Well, Reverend Swaggart, this trial is taking a toll on my personal life," the reporter responds.

"How's that?"

"Well, my fiancée told me that if she catches me fooling around, I don't get a trial."

Swaggart, who is washing his hands, throws back his head and laughs. Then, pulling down the paper towels, he offers advice not found in the Bible: "You know what they say. When you say, 'I do,' make sure you do." He laughs again and heads back to court.

So what's Jimmy Swaggart have to laugh about? He is being sued for $90 million by a minister who already has cost Swaggart's ministry more than that by exposing Jimmy's tryst with a hooker at an Airline Highway motel. Once the most viewed televangelist in the world, Jimmy Swaggart has had to sob his confession on TV and struggle to pick up the pieces of his shattered empire. The man whose support presidential candidates once sought now finds himself the butt of crude jokes from — *aaauugh* — Louisiana politicians. That's a fall.

Now, in the dull heat of a slow-starting governor's race, Swaggart on trial is considered a hotter ticket than what was supposed to be this great governor's race.

"So how is our friend the ex-governor doing," chirps Swaggart during a court recess. Frances Swaggart steps in front of her husband and says in a low voice, "That's a reporter."

"I don't care," booms the smiling Swaggart. "Everything we're saying is the truth."

Maybe this time the truth will set him free. For three years Jimmy Swaggart has talked of wrestling with giant serpents and holding extended conversations with God. He has short-circuited the prescribed counseling period to return to the pulpit and prop up the ministry's sagging TV ratings and its cash flow. Now comes a turning point, finally, the legal confrontation with his exposer. Jimmy Swaggart is the defendant in this defamation suit, but the defendant is very much on the attack. The defense is confident that when this trial is over, the plaintiff Marvin Gorman will be proven the more miserable sinner, the ministry-defiling philanderer Swaggart accused him of being six years ago, back when both preachers were riding high, before they slimed each other. Swaggart may have fallen farther but Gorman fell lower — driven from his pulpit and into bankruptcy. Jimmy Swaggart Ministries lost nothing but ratings and love offerings, and both are trending back upwards. Surely His justice was served. Jimmy, though challenged, was saved: he knows not for what purpose but only that the Lord is not through with him yet.


While Jim Bakker of PTL was being dragged through the muck of his sex scandal with church secretary Jessica Hahn, Jimmy Swaggart's star was rising higher. Having described himself as "just an old-fashioned sweatin', shoutin', weepin', soul-winnin', Holy

Ghost-filled, Gospel-preachin' preacher," he ran a ministry that grossed $142 million in 1985, with profits of $38 million and assets of $150 million. His telecasts, seen in 2.1 million American households and in 70 countries worldwide, were produced in his Baton Rouge world ministry complex that seemed to sprout new white buildings like mushrooms. His appeal was that he never seemed to have drifted too far from his rough-cut beginnings in Ferriday, Louisiana, where he chose a different path from the one taken by his cousin and childhood piano-lesson partner Jerry Lee Lewis. From the back of his beat-up jalopy to his first television broadcast of his worldwide electronic ministry, he never lost that redneck gut rage that condemned sin where he saw it and took on the appeasers in the war against Satan, whether they be Catholics or secular humanists or freethinkers or liberated women or, the worst, psychologists.

By the mid-1980s Swaggart began to assert himself in Louisiana politics before moving on to the national stage. In the 1986 Senate race, the *Baton Rouge Morning Advocate* reported that he sent out a "report card" letter to the faithful, rating the candidates on the vital issues. While making no endorsement, the report card pointed out that Republican Henson Moore opposed "homosexual rights" while Democrat John Breaux did not, and that Moore opposed the "Library of Congress printing *Playboy* in Braille" and that Breaux did not. Enough said.

Early in the 1988 presidential primaries, he dismissed religious broadcaster Pat Robertson and then embraced him before finally promoting Vice President George Bush. In an hour-long meeting with Bush, he said he told him televangelists would strongly influence the election contest. "We go into their homes every week. . . . They won't all vote the way I like them to vote, but most of them will."

There was press sniping about the size of his house, the relatives on his payroll (14 family members making a total of $344,000 in 1985) and Frances' $11,000 desk. He returned fire, calling the local reporters "snakes" and "reprobates." He said that people he knew with contacts in the Mafia had told him that the Gucciones of *Penthouse Magazine* were out to get him "any way they could" because Swaggart had led the crusade to remove their pornographic magazines from local 7-Eleven stores.

Sin was sin wherever he found it, and God told him to root it out. Especially in the Assemblies of God. Swaggart had learned that a family friend, a minister's wife, had had an affair with Marvin Gorman, a popular Assemblies of God minister with a fast-growing televangelism ministry in suburban New Orleans.

It could not be tolerated. Swaggart collected information on Gorman and, with other ministers, confronted him. His choice was to turn himself in to the national Assemblies of God, or his wife would get a phone call that night. Gorman was defrocked and his mini-empire crumbled around him. "We lost everything, except our clothes and our bed," related Gorman after bankruptcy. Gorman retaliated with a $90 million defamation suit against Swaggart that one judge threw out of court. The suit was reinstated but it went nowhere, and Swaggart pressed on with God's work and the love offerings of hundreds of thousands. But Jimmy didn't fathom the depth of Marvin Gorman's desire to crawl up from the muck and to drag Swaggart back into it.

In the wake of the Pearly Gate scandals, Jimmy Swaggart held out little hope that Jim Bakker could ever do the Lord's work effectively again. In a 1987 newspaper interview Swaggart said: "We've got a lot of scoundrels in the ministry. A person can return, but what they can do for God is negligible."

At about that time, Swaggart was making regular visits to the seamy strip of Airline Highway in Jefferson Parish dotted with no-tell motels that rent rooms for $10 an hour. In a story she later told *Penthouse*, prostitute Debra Murphree talked about a man who looked like Jimmy Swaggart but insisted on calling himself "Billy." From early encounters in his Lincoln Town Car to room 7 in the Travel Inn Motel, she said they met 20 to 25 times. She would pull down her pants and masturbate as he did the same and sometimes she performed oral sex on Swaggart. She confided her adventures to a sheriff's deputy she dated, a preacher's boy, name of Randy Gorman.

On October 17, 1987, in the closing days of the Louisiana governor's race, Marvin Gorman was alerted by phone that Swaggart and Murphree were in a motel room together. At the Travel Inn, Swaggart and Murphree had not got into their usual activity when Swaggart sensed something suspicious was going on outside. As they walked out of the motel room a private detective took the couple's photograph. At his car, Swaggart found a flat tire . . . and Marvin Gorman. The men talked. Swaggart admitted to affairs with prostitutes. The next day, he repeated his admissions in a meeting with Gorman and his lawyer and Swaggart's wife Frances and son Donnie.

Then nothing happened. Except that Swaggart signed contracts for $12.9 million in construction on the Jimmy Swaggart Bible College campus. Four months went by with no word from Swaggart to church officials. Then Gorman mailed the photographs to the Assemblies of God headquarters in Springfield, Missouri.

The shocking revelations led to Swaggart's famous, tearful confession — "I have sinned" — on his most-watched broadcast. Jimmy submitted to stepping down from the pulpit and to seeking counseling. He abandoned the construction projects and started cutting back ministry operations.

But Jimmy just could not shut up. The *Morning Advocate* made a regular beat assignment of all Family Worship Center services. Weeks later, Jimmy Swaggart, worshipper, rose to share a few thoughts. Having spent the day struggling with "the darkest, most debilitating powers of Hell," he related another encounter with the Holy Spirit: "Then, instantly, without any explanation or warning, just like that, it was like every demon of Hell left." Friends who saw him that day, he said, were stunned: "I was supposed to be dying. I was supposed to be out of my mind. Instead I'm shouting, 'Let me tell you something. I pray God you never find out, but when your back's against the wall and your knees are buckling, this Gospel works. It works.' "


Something works. Jimmy Swaggart may be the butt of jokes of even politicians (at a political roast, Jefferson Parish Sheriff Harry Lee talks about the new brand of Jimmy Swaggart golf balls: "They go to the hole but they don't go in"), but he is coming back. By July 1991, the Arbitron ratings show he is reaching 403,000 households, less than 20 percent of what he had before the fall, but enough to place him ahead of James Robison and Pat Robertson as one of America's most watched preachers. The enrollment decline has leveled off at the Bible college and Christian academy. A vacant building is leased to the state to house the Department of Environmental Quality. He erects a large digital sign on the Interstate that gives biblical quotations night and day. He won't give up. Marvin Gorman won't either. Their summer trial matches two men who have nearly destroyed each other. Now they contest who gets the final bitter laugh.

The trial begins badly for Gorman when the judge rules against his efforts to introduce evidence about Jimmy Swaggart's extramarital sexual affairs. So Gorman's photographic exposé of Swaggart will have no legal bearing on this case, though it already has cost Jimmy more than he can lose in this trial.

Gorman can only focus on Swaggart's spreading rumors about Gorman having flings with as many as 100 women. Defense strategy is to show that Marvin Gorman did engage in multiple affairs. Swaggart's lead counsel, Phil Wittman, says Gorman had at least five affairs and three of the women will testify. The fourth, he says, is in hiding. "She's trying to avoid being served with a subpoena. She's embarrassed. So am I."

Crowds line up each day to hear what they expect to be lurid, sexually charged testimony. They will seize on anything. A titter runs through the court when the bailiff orders, "All rise."

During early testimony on an exorcism, the lights in the courtroom flicker.

A courtroom drama, however, this is not. Much of the trial is a bean-counting exercise to determine how much money Marvin Gorman Ministries would have made had not Swaggart defamed him. Testimony that gets the least bit juicy is bound to be interrupted by frequent bench conferences. The judge grows impatient by the hour, and usually by mid-afternoon one or two jurors begin to nod off.

The star witness, Lynda Savage, testifies that she had sex with Gorman eight or nine times between 1978 and 1981. Lynette Goux did not testify, but Gorman admits to petting her breast (he said he only petted one). A Shreveport woman says on the stand that she had sex with Gorman several times on the floor of Gorman's office in 1973. Two other women say they hugged and French-kissed Gorman in counseling sessions.

The testimony, however, especially Gorman's, makes one thing clear: televangelists do not do it better. Gorman's sexual encounters are belabored and dissected in court to the point where one wonders who, if anyone, had any fun. And nothing is less appealing than a man swearing it was all the woman's fault. Under cross-examination, Gorman describes opening a motel door during a crusade and finding Lynette Goux, who, he says, "fell into my arms and started kissing me." Gorman denies he could have encouraged her in previous counseling sessions: "If I held her, it would have been in prayer, I may have caught her hand."

But now he has a handful of Goux. "Did you stop kissing before you went to bed?" asks defense counsel Wayne Lee.

"I don't imagine we went to bed kissing," Gorman struggles to recall. "She said, 'I'm gonna take off my blouse and slip off my skirt.' She lay down. I sat beside her. We started kissing again."

"Who started it?"

"I don't remember."

"Do you recall fondling her breast?"

"No. I may have touched the naked skin of her breast. I don't recall."

Marvin apparently does not know the power he has over women, as he relates how another woman in counseling made a pass: "She grabbed me and started kissing me. She grabbed my crotch."

"How many other women have grabbed your crotch?"

"Only my wife."

More hairs are split. Gorman admits on the stand that what he did was a sin but refuses to say it was immoral, which opens vast new theological ground for preachers and politicians alike to explore.

Testimony continues in this deadening vein for weeks. It's hard to find anyone who cares how this trial ends, only that it does.

Finally even that happens. The prosecution has established that Swaggart and company bullied Gorman into confessing his affairs. The defense has fairly well established that Marvin, whether he enjoyed them or not, was not good at avoiding the near occasion of sin. Often trials like these are decided on whom the jury likes more. Another tough one.

The jury deliberates 26 hours and comes back with a shocker. It decides that Swaggart and his ministry did conspire to defame Gorman and awards $9 million to bankrupt Marvin Gorman Ministries and $1 million to Gorman himself. (The judge later reduces the award to $6.64 million.)

Marvin Gorman's retribution is complete and very satisfying.

Swaggart tells reporters he was afraid it was going to be a bad day when on the way to court a state trooper pulled him over for speeding. The verdict is a public relations blow to Swaggart, but, he claims, no more than that: "It didn't cost us anything. We have insurance. I'm sure they will appeal it."

As far as he is concerned, this case is behind him. Jimmy Swaggart can get on with rebuilding his ministry and spreading God's word. Until the next highway patrolman stops him.

Charles Roemer II, state commissioner of administration in 1978.

DENNIS HARKCOM

Buddy Roemer and his mother Adeline.

Patti Roemer.

Raymond Strother.

JAMES TERRY III

What's wrong with this picture? Len Sanderson (left), Roemer's top aide from the Revolution, confers with state Senator B. B. "Sixty" Rayburn, the Dean of the Senate.

JAMES TERRY III

Buddy Roemer as governor in 1988.

State Republican Party Chairman Billy Nungesser.

Ben Bagert.

David Treen, governor of Louisiana, 1980–84.

Kathleen Blanco.

Before the Fall: Edwin Edwards in Paris, 1983.

With Candy Picou.

Those were the days: Marion Edwards (left), with Gus Mijalis, at defense party during 1985 federal hospital trial.

Edwards with son David.

Edwards at his 1985 arraignment.

Not Guilty: Edwards after his acquittal in the hospital trial.

PLATER ROBINSON

Edwards received over 90 percent of the black vote in the 12-candidate primary field.

JAMES TERRY III

Edwards having fun with the missing incumbent.

DAMON NASH

Andrew Martin.

J. F. CADO

Billy Broadhurst.

J. F. CADO

Sherman Copelin.

JAMES TERRY III

The late state Senator Leonard Chabert.

B. ROBINSON

Bob d'Hemecourt.

Over 500 LSU students turn out for David Duke campus rally in 1991.

Duke, with bodyguard in front, answers questions and hecklers at LSU rally.

Duke conferring with State Rep. Willie Singleton of Shreveport.

David Duke lobbies for one of his bills in the Louisiana House of Representatives.

With campaign manager Howie Farrell.

David Duke greets Buddy Roemer at Capitol.

Longtime Duke supporter Babs Minhinnette Wilson.

ALL PHOTOS BY JAMES TERRY III

ALEXANDRIA DAILY TOWN TALK

Edwards' stigmata tableau at 1984 Alexandria Gridiron show.

Jack Kent's anti–Roemer commercial in the primary.

The Coalition's anti–Duke commercial in the runoff.

A. J. SISCO

Duke prepares for New Orleans television appearance.

# 10. Hot as a Dog

Can there be a happier day for Buddy Roemer? Today the Legislature goes home for the last time. After four bruising regular sessions and seven endless special sessions, Buddy Roemer won't have the Legislature to kick him around anymore. For months he has been promising staff and supporters that when the Legislature leaves town, at last the great race will begin and watch those poll numbers turn.

The legislators are burned out on the Buddy Roemer experience and would prefer to spend time with their opponents, who are waiting in the newly reconfigured districts. Some lawmakers who sleep over at the Pentagon Barracks have their cars packed and ready for the final Saturday morning vote.

A mere formality remains. The governor only has to sign the reapportionment deal that he and top dogs shook hands on last night. It's been a very, very tough deal to cut. At the beginning of the session, the Legislature thought it had acted nobly in drawing about half of the new minority districts that the pushy Sherman Copelin of the Legislative Black Caucus had demanded. Then the U.S. Justice Department, which still has the Bomb, sent back the plan, torn in little pieces, with the suggestion that they work out something along the lines that Mr. Copelin likes.

Welcome to the New Reconstruction, a reconspiracy of Washington Republicans and black Democrats to realign Southern politics. The Party of Lincoln gave up a long time ago at seriously trying to attract African-American votes, which is especially difficult in the absence of a black middle class. So they did the next best thing. The Republican U.S. Justice Department, through its enforcement of the Voting Rights Act in Southern states, forced on legislatures the maximum possible number of predominantly black districts. Besides giving blacks political representation equal to their numbers — something they never thought they would get — that strategy makes the predominantly white districts superwhite and far more winnable for Republicans.

The traditional community-based legislative districts — the ones that made some sense geographically — resulted in fewer minority seats but spread the influence of black voters through many majority-white districts. That, of course, favored the white moderate Democrats, who could count on getting almost all of the black votes — 20 to 30 percent — against a Republican or a conservative Democrat. The moderating influence of black voters on white Democrats was the cornerstone of Louisiana populist politics, from Huey Long to Edwin Edwards.

The unspoken Republican strategy used Lyndon Johnson's landmark 1965 Voting Rights Act to isolate the white moderate Democrats by offering blacks their own political homelands. Legislative reapportionment in Louisiana and Mississippi would serve as a dress rehearsal for congressional reapportionment for the 1992 elections, where the national GOP would get its reward.

Black politicians are ready for their reward too, with many new predominantly black congressional districts sure to follow legislative reapportionment. White moderates preach the evils of polarization and how blacks are being used. But few black voices join the chorus. Whatever the ulterior political motives, an important political milestone is being reached in the South. For the first time since the first Reconstruction, African-Americans will achieve proportionate representation. Not just in the Legislature, but in Congress and on school boards and city councils and county commissions across the South. As a result of a federal judge's ruling in Louisiana, even judgeships will be placed under the representative principle of one man, one vote. It took an alliance from Hell with the Republicans and some weirdly gerrymandered districts to achieve; and it likely will result in more polarized politics. But it's what blacks, through their representatives, wanted and it's what they got. Equality in commerce and society may lag behind, but the minorities at last have received their proper piece of the political pie in the South in 1991.

The populist Democrats who run the Louisiana Legislature can understand and appreciate artful alliances backed by naked force. Along with the requirement to draw more black districts, there are the internal mandates that the state Senate especially is determined to satisfy: 1) to protect the leadership's majority and 2) to destroy its opponents. The Senate leadership has plotted all summer to twist the GOP grand strategy in order to create more black seats but also to protect its own populist majority (that is, the guys who voted to throw out Roemer's president and to reinstate Sammy Nunez). The Senate president explains how the deal is done: "All you've got to do is massage it and massage it until everyone realizes that two or three guys have to get screwed — and you go ahead and do it." Once marked, there is little a screwee can do to save himself. Take the troublesome loose cannon Benny Bagert, whom even the Republicans have little use for. His New Orleans district will be reconstituted as majority black. Nunez is sympathetic, to a point: "Poor Benny, even if he was a personal friend I couldn't help him." That strategy is employed wherever possible, drawing the new black districts where uncooperative senators (read: Buddy Roemer supporters) used to be.

The governor, of course, has a say in this, called veto power. It's all he has left to rein in the runaway Legislature. Reapportionment, however, is more politics than policy. The last thing Roemer wants to do is to get into the map room and fight over precincts to favor one politician, even a friend, over another. Not when his campaign kickoff is past due and when legislators are as anxious to leave Baton Rouge as he is to see them go. Though he may lose a few allies in reapportionment, he'll need them less when he is reelected.

Finally the new map is drawn, which creates enough new minority districts and preserves the Senate's populist majority. Even Roemer's conservative Senate friends, the ones who have been spared, prevail upon him to go along. Finally, in a Friday night meeting in the governor's bedroom, Roemer relents. The deal is struck. He will sign the redrafted bill the following morning in time for most guys to get home to ride in afternoon parades.


Sammy Nunez's face is turning from red to purple. "He won't sign." Donnie Kelly wants to spit. The senators can't believe it, but they can believe it. Four years of head-butting and impasse come down to this. Buddy Roemer has lied again.

"That's not true," explains Roemer, emerging from the Speaker's office. "I said it looked good and we would all sleep on it."

Not even his long-suffering ally Allen Bares can swallow that one. "We were all up in his bedroom. He was at his desk. I can tell you where everyone was. He said, 'If y'all can pass it, I will sign it.' "

Apparently, though, Buddy did not sleep well.

"Captain Chaos," says Mike Foster, "is at it again." Foster says he tried to be a political friend of the governor until "I found out that no one gets anywhere with Buddy Roemer by going along with him."

One who's still trying to be a friend, Randy Ewing, shakes his head: "Whenever he is the focal point of anything, he will take it to the brink."

We are beyond the brink. Some legislators hope to turn into grand marshals by the afternoon. Their opponents are out working against them. The campaign season is hard upon them and Buddy Roemer is really getting on their nerves.

"He's perched up there in his blue jeans playing God, deciding who lives and dies," fumes Jimmy Cox, who is not happy with the games either Roemer or Nunez is playing. "Buddy's in there playing poker and Sammy's playing 52 Pickup."

Hardly a time for games. Certainly no one needs to be out working the trail more than Buddy Roemer does. It's as though the governor doesn't want his own reelection campaign to begin.

The governor has made sure it won't begin on a positive note for himself. With even his friends claiming he has broken his word, the story line for the Sunday papers will be: Buddy Lied. The usually friendly *Baton Rouge Sunday Advocate* and *Shreveport Times* will unload on him the next day for visibly backing down on a deal. This is not a good time for the press to validate the worst of what his challengers have been bashing him with for months. Edwin Edwards has been showing off a poll of legislators conducted by the *South Baton Rouge Journal* that shows 78 percent of them trust Edwards more than Roemer while only 17 percent trust Roemer more. Five percent said they trusted neither. "I hope those are our guys," say two lobbyists, comparing notes on the poll.

Besides lack of credibility, Roemer's problems with the Legislature now include the reapportionment standoff. He may have lost his Revolution, he may have lost the gut anger, but he never lost that iron-willed stubborn resistance to compromise. This is the man who said, "I will break but I will not bend," in one of the several legislative showdowns he lost in 1990. "With Buddy, you could agree with him on ten of eleven items, but if you couldn't go along with Point Eleven, then you were just another whore politician," says an exasperated legislator who tried to help, but eventually just gave up. That type of attitude barely works even when backed by a solid mandate of the people and a working majority of the Legislature, neither of which Roemer ever enjoyed. His last defiant stand was especially laughable, since the other side has more than a mandate — it has the federal government.

As legislators stew and converge in little pockets around the Capitol, phone calls shoot back and forth from the Senate to the Justice Department in Washington. The Senate majority is slim but it is hard, and Buddy Roemer is not going to break it. By the afternoon he relents. The plan will fly. Still the day drags on while the final document is being prepared.

"What's the holdup?" complains a senator, checking his watch.

"We're running a lab test on the ink in the governor's pen," says Mike Cross with a straight face, "to make sure we can still read it tomorrow."

Something's up. Buddy is being nice to his friends. His friends are the press. Reporters like Roemer because he's confrontational and quotable, and while he might not return contributors' and mayors' phone calls, he usually has time for the press. Often he will spend more time talking to reporters than he will speaking to real people at some function he breezes in and out of. So he gets along with the press. But today he's going overboard. Trays of blueberry muffins and coffee are laid out for reporters during this chat in his rarely used Fourth Floor office. The governor's Capitol office is in the old Supreme Court chambers, with its 20-foot ceilings and carved wood paneling. Now, though, some of the paneling is covered by a banner that reads: "Honor."

In cities and towns around Louisiana today, Buddy Roemer's challengers are shaking hands and making speeches and hoping for any favorable mention in even the smallest country gazette. Buddy, meanwhile, has 20 reporters in his office eating muffins. The governor peels a banana and invites any wrapup questions on the session past and the campaign ahead.

Credibility is the lead question. What about the charge that he doesn't keep promises?

"There is some truth to that. Sometimes I get new facts or my feelings change. . . . Not kept my word? That's not true. Sometimes I don't listen and I wish others would admit that. There are moments when people don't hear the subtleties."

He doesn't apologize for his battles with the Legislature, but will he do it over again if he's reelected?

"It depends on what it takes to move our program farther. If it takes shaking up, I'm a shaker. If it means building up, I'm a builder."

"Governor," Ed Anderson of the *Picayune* raises his hand.

"What are you, Ed, are you a shaker or a builder?"

"I'm a runner, Governor," says Anderson wearily.

"Ed's a runner," chortles Roemer, breaking off another piece of banana. Buddy is buoyant. It shows what getting the Legislature out of town can do for one's attitude. Not even an abortion question fazes him, as Marsanne Golsby asks, "People have the impression you are pro-choice . . ."

"I'm not saying that."

"You haven't said that . . ."

"Do you want me to say that now? You're as goofy as I am, Marsanne. You ought to come work with us."

But seriously, folks. "The window must be tightened, but it must be done in a way that honors women. I wish I knew of a law written to protect the rights of women and the unborn. I've not seen it. Is it worth working on? You betcha."

Hamlet of the Unborn is about six weeks late, as the toughest abortion law in the country already is in federal court.

What about appearing at some forums?

"I have a minimal interest in it, quite frankly. . . . At this stage in my career, I have some power to make some choices about what is most illuminating and what is most heat producing."

In the corner, Gordon Hensley nods approvingly. The campaign press secretary finally has a nearly full-time candidate. The polls are bearing more good news. Robert Teeter, Bush's pollster, has just delivered his latest survey results showing Roemer widening his lead over Edwards to 33-27, with Duke at 12 and Holloway lost in the pack. The reapportionment flap did not hurt the governor at all. In fact, his strategy of doing his job instead of jumping into campaigning has paid off. And Roemer hasn't even turned on his campaign juice yet. Hensley, for once, is starting to feel like a winner.

"Ladies and gentlemen, the man who gave us our pride back, the honorable governor of the great state of Louisiana. . . ." Congressman Richard Baker, Republican golden boy and heir apparent, gives the mike to candidate Buddy Roemer at the last stop of his announcement tour, which has gone very well.

The Baton Rouge event is attended by a flock of Roemeristas, mostly young professionals and business people who endured the long march of 1987 to its storybook conclusion. Nancy Roberts, now a member of the Board of Trustees of Colleges and Universities, remembers carefully peeling off the "Roemer" stickers each night to be reused the next day. There is no shortage of campaign resources now. Paid staff have replaced the inexperienced 1987 volunteers, who have been called upon primarily for fundraising this time around.

The message, too, has changed, from anger to progress, from how-far-behind-we-are to how-far-we've-come.

New theme lines roll off the candidate's tongue:

"It's not happening quickly but it's happening.

"We cannot turn back the clock. Our children cannot endure it. Our consciences cannot accept it.

"Those were the dark days, the days of politics for sale, suitcases full of cash, contributors hiding in the shadows. We will not go back to the time when our major exports were our jobs and our children."

And, finally, a big hit with the urban crowd: "I'm a farmer. You plant and you harvest. Before we harvest we must make another commitment to campaign. . . . Remember the lesson. You taught it to me. Anything is possible if we do it together."

It's a grand little speech and the old fieldhands respond heartily. So far, however, Buddy has only called them together to raise money. But that's the nature of the new campaign. The more committed reform activists don't mind if they personally have not heard much from Buddy since 1987. They did not work so unselfishly for a governor who would return political favors, though a returned phone call or two would have been nice. But he's barely even had time to get into his own campaign. The main thing keeping the reform vote and middle-class money solidly with Roemer is the nature of his opposition. After Edwards and Duke announced, Roemer joked, "A really good candidate could get in the race and beat the hell out of all of us." Yet the so-called new faces have all been non-starters. Kathleen Blanco's pro-life stand is keeping her from breaking into the women's vote. Aaron Broussard can tout his experience, but the voters seem as leery as ever about experienced politicians. Clyde Holloway is said to grow on people, but it's very slow growth.

According to the polls, Holloway has not even dented Duke, much less Roemer. So Buddy can infuriate the Legislature, neglect his own politics, ignore his old supporters, kick off his campaign two months before balloting and still be headed straight for a runoff with the same discredited politician he booted last time.

The governor takes stock of his political fortunes: "Am I the luckiest guy in America or what?"


The Pickin' and Ginnin' Festival in Rayville celebrates King Cotton, White Gold, the source of generations of wealth, employment and misery for the Louisiana Delta. The streets are jammed with folks from Monroe and the little Delta towns up and down the river. There is some reason to celebrate. The organizers have gone all out to make this first-ever celebration a major attraction with promises of food, music, agricultural exhibits and old-time political speeches, precisely in that order of interest. Huge, gleaming, green John Deere combines command the intersections along Louisa Street, and booths displaying carved wood and cotton handicrafts line the main drag.

The festival officially will begin when a locomotive rolls into town to deposit the governor and various dignitaries including area legislators, mayors and Miss Louisiana.

Buddy Roemer, in blue jeans and cowboy boots, disembarks and shakes a few hands, then turns to an oddly familiar voice.

"Welcome to Duke Country, Governor."

The governor shakes his opponent's hand. "Well, thanks, Dave, I thought this was Louisiana."

"Louisiana is Duke Country, Governor."

A photographer asks for a photograph and captures the frozen smiles. Looking over the photographer's shoulder, the governor can see what his opponent is talking about. In the crowd jamming downtown Rayville, nearly one in three festival-goers is wearing blue and white Duke stickers. Duke's well-trained volunteers have been working the crowd all morning, affixing the Duke squares often without even asking. At least two or three blacks walk the streets with the stickers, apparently unaware of their newest accessory.

Duke, in his long-sleeved white shirt and botanical tie, has been attracting big crowds at his booth like the celebrity he is here. "I just want you to know I was with you last time and I'll be with you again," says the young mother with Duke-stickered children in tow. Several folks present their children to shake Duke's hand. "We're all for you down at the gin," says the elderly, sun-burned farmer. Another shares the obvious joke of the day: "How many votes do you think Roemer's been getting sitting in that air-conditioned train?"

The governor has other ideas about how to get votes in Rayville. With the town mayor and half the police jury behind him on the music tent stage, the governor proudly announces a $750,000 water system grant to Richland Parish, which the crowd, seated in folding chairs and waiting patiently for more country music, applauds politely. Roemer practically apologizes for appearing before them as a mere candidate. "I'm not much of a politician," which is sort of true. "I'm a farm boy. A cotton farm is where my heart is, it's where my roots are."

This is not the same Buddy who swept through town four years ago, promising to scrub clean the waste and corruption in Baton Rouge. He's here today to show, with his check, that the state's resources are working their way back to Rayville.

The three black police jurors onstage are the most blacks in one place at this festival of mostly white faces. Black folks apparently do not share as endearing a bond to King Cotton. But courtesy of the Justice Department, they do have a voice in the local government and how the state's $750,000 will be spent. The governor sees a lot of progress here: "If we can live together, black and white, north and south, this will be the greatest state."

But enough of speeches. The governor wants a big hand to welcome Miss Louisiana, who hails from Marshall, Texas, to resume the musical entertainment. Roemer looks on slightly amazed as Miss Christi Page, who started out as Miss Caney Lake not far away, belts out a knockdown version of "Great Balls of Fire" with her crown bobbing to her ferocious piano riff.

Offstage, the governor tells KNOE's Jeanne Burns, "Did you hear him say, 'Welcome to Duke Country'? I cut his ass with a smile." Sure you did. Other reporters edge in with questions. As Miss Louisiana wails out "I Fall to Pieces" the governor describes his late-starting campaign as "very aggressive, encompassing and positive."

"So when do you start?" inquires radio reporter Mitch Goldman.

"Why, I think I have," the governor answers testily. "I mean I'm out here on a Saturday, it's hot as a dog and it's going well." What's a fella have to do? Well, there's a street full of votes out there — a good place to start. It's even convenient, since he has a meeting at the bank. State Representative Francis Thompson leads the way down the sidewalk of Louisa Street, stopping to introduce the governor to storeowners and people standing in the shade of shop awnings. The woman at the Duke booth breaks from her brisk t-shirt sales to give the governor a wide, knowing smile. Buddy smiles and waves. "Am I being overly friendly? Do I have no principles left?" Roemer is not exactly going out of his way to meet and greet, but he does shake hands if people present themselves to him. The governor consents to pose with a woman for a photograph when he realizes what is going to be wrong with this picture. "What've you got on your chest?" He points to her Duke sticker. He doesn't even bother to mention the same thing to another woman, who shakes his hand and asks for his help with her Social Security problem. Finally, he runs into a vote he can count on, a state Department of Health case worker who voted for him in 1987. She wants to tell the governor about the front lines: "Can I tell you about the child abuse problems we have here?" He would rather she write him a letter. But she presses on about caseload and scant resources. Roemer honors her as best he can. "Linda, I know you can talk. Now let's see if you can write." She agrees but turns away looking disappointed. We'll call her a maybe.

Finally he makes it to the air-conditioned safety of the Richland State Bank lobby, which has been converted into the VIP center. Ferriday newspaper publisher Sam Hanna waits there for a meeting the governor has requested. If the governor hasn't figured it out yet, the polls that show him with a narrow lead in this area might be overly optimistic. "It's all Edwards and Duke up here," says Hanna. "He needs to wake up."

Out in the heat of the street, David Duke autographs t-shirts under a shade tree. Yes, it's been a good day, but, he says, "It's not just here. It's been like this all over the state: Thibodaux, Bunkie, Bossier." He agrees that it's still a quiet governor's campaign for this stage: "My theory is that it's quiet because a lot of people are for me." For all that satisfied support, however, contributions are still far off from last year at this point. But of course there is a reason for that too. "They're not ready to give me money and to put their names out there."

His teenage daughters Erika and Kristin are in from Florida for an extended stay during summer vacation. Kristin is with the volunteers up the street, but 15-year-old Erika is close by Daddy's side as usual. He strokes her long blond hair as he speaks to the ever-widening circle around him.

Come October, says Duke, "I'm going to run first, well over 30 percent."

And who will he face in the runoff?

"It doesn't matter. I'll beat Edwards. He's too identified with the blacks. And labor is not with him because he signed Right to Work. Roemer is not seen as a conservative. Edwards belongs to the NAACP, they both do. He and Edwards are the same side of the coin."

As he speaks, a little girl of about 10 appears at Erika's side and smiles up at Duke. He goes on talking, but now he is stroking and twisting the younger girl's hair as Erika watches.

"The teachers are all angry with Roemer over evaluation — it was a terrible idea. . . ." He looks down in surprise. "Oh!" he says, letting go of the little girl's hair. "I thought you were Erika."

The crowds have been enthusiastic for Duke all day and he is reciprocating as he heads back up the street again to the thick of the festival. The barber in his shop waves, so Duke drops in to shake hands. "Let me have some of those stickers," says the proprietor. "I'll give some away." The air conditioning feels great. Indeed, it is hot as a dog out there. But that's where the people are. So off Duke goes looking for more hands to shake and to check that the volunteers are still getting those stickers out. Buddy Roemer, meanwhile, having spent all of about 20 minutes outside of air conditioning, departs the VIP center and Rayville to return to the Mansion. His heart and his roots may be in cotton country, but he'll have to find his votes somewhere else.

# 11. The Insider Game

Summer in the South is not so bad, says the writer from *Vogue*, "because the air conditioning is very good." It would be better today had the staff at the Sheraton turned on the blowers in the meeting rooms before 750 Edwin Edwards supporters jammed in for an afternoon organizational meeting. And who says campaign novelty items are useless? The yellow "Swat the Revolution" flyswatters turn into pretty good fans in a pinch.

Now if heat were the only problem in the Edwards campaign. Not even in the very old days has Edwards run a campaign without early money—and the change is not becoming. In 1983 Edwards spent $1 million just on billboards. By late July 1991 he hasn't raised that much overall. Instead of ordering yardsigns, campaign workers are attempting to make them on their own in the Baton Rouge headquarters. In his $13 million 1983 budget, Edwards sprang for $80 satin baby-blue jumpsuits for the campaign softball team. This year the paid staff can barely field a team, even if they were in a playful mood, which this bunch is not. There have been no TV or radio ads, which has not helped silence the doubters who think the candidate will not go the distance. Unlike Duke, Edwards never went in for grass-roots fundraising, so he has discouraged supporters from asking him to appear at dozens of local rallies. The money drought also means there will be no early money to lock up the black organizations. This is causing some rumblings in New Orleans.

Hundreds responded to Edwards' fifth call to arms in February, ready for a new beginning or even just more of the same, only to be sitting on their hands five months later. All they hear from the candidate is his nonstop bitter diatribe against Buddy Roemer, but where's the campaign?

That's the point of today's little gathering of workers from around the state. It is billed as an organizational and strategy meeting, but the ulterior motive is to pump up the supporters' flat morale by showing them, yes, there is an Edwards campaign.

This is probably not Edwin Edwards' idea. Motivational management is too close to rubber band-popping for him to take too seriously. No matter. He approaches the makeshift dais with all the life of El Cid on the final charge, but the mere sight of him in the saddle stirs the troops. They cheer his opener: "Ninety days from now you will put me in a second primary with a fella that's in a lot of trouble."

Now for the point of this meeting: "We want you to get to know each other, because you will be running the state. If you look around, you will see mostly new faces here." Looking around, one sees Louis Roussel Jr., Harry Lee, Bobby d'Hemecourt, Andrew Martin, Roland Manuel and dozens more of the usual accomplices.

But he's also right, a lot of old faces aren't here this time: there is no Billy Broadhurst or George Fischer or Gus Mijalis or Wayne Ray.

Wayne Ray, Edwards' constant sidekick from 1983, recently has been released from federal prison in Texas after doing time for income tax evasion. Like an old friend, Ray for the most part has stayed away since.

George Fischer appreciates the value of keeping a little distance. He was quietly setting up Edwards' 1983 campaign while he was Dave Treen's secretary of the Department of Health and Hospitals.

Some don't grasp the concept of distance as well. Billy Broadhurst, who made such a splash in Gary Hart's presidential campaign as first mate on the good ship *Monkey Business*, doesn't understand why the press makes such a big deal whenever he's spotted near Edwards. "Maybe I made some mistakes," he admits, "but I did nothing illegal and that's all in the past." That's where other Edwards' staffers would like to keep Billy B. Several know the drill to nudge Broadhurst out of the way when cameras are around.

Edwards hates to even mention the subject to these friends. Pals like Gus Mijalis aren't as shy. The codefendant with Edwards in the 1985-86 federal racketeering trials was heard to complain to staffers: "I was indicted and acquitted. Why should I be treated like I'm guilty." Mijalis, a seafood importer, rolled big dice in real estate and banking in Shreveport and went bankrupt. The bad association cuts both ways up in Northwest Louisiana: "He hasn't been so easy to carry for the past five years either," said Mijalis in a huff.

Family has not been as hard for the candidate to deal with. The ex-governor and his younger brother agreed that Marion would not play the role of his brother's keeper that he did so loyally and strongly in campaigns past. Marion will not jeopardize his governmental affairs position with Jim Bob Moffett's Freeport McMoRan, which has afforded Marion first-rate health care in his successful bout with cancer.

In Marion's place, the candidate has pulled his immediate family closer. His daughter Anna, he tells the meeting of supporters, "will be manning the headquarters 24 hours a day." *I'll be doing what?* is the look on her face. Daddy shrugs: "Well, Anna, you haven't worked in 40 years. . . ."

The oldest daughter always took a far back seat in previous campaigns. In 1983, No. 2 daughter Victoria handled the TV advertising and even stumped alongside her father while Anna was out of sight. Now Vicki is in New York, still pursuing parts in commercials and soap operas, and Anna is running the statewide headquarters. J. C. Wyllie, a Republican and a former state trooper, is the official campaign manager. But everyone gives Anna wide berth around the office. Anna can curse like a sailor, or, worse, like her father. "Oh God, what do you want?" is one of her warmer greetings for reporters she likes. Beneath the tough exterior is a tougher core. She is loyal and protective of her staff. Working for Anna, one often feels the need for protection.

Now the candidate gets down to business with his campaign rules to win by. "You have 60 days to get people registered. If you don't think they will vote right, don't encourage them.

"Organize locally and decide for yourselves," instructs Edwards. "You know what is best to do. We don't have the time or the inclination to tell you what to do." This is a nice way of telling volunteers that nothing they do as an organization in the next two months really matters.

"We are only planning eight big rallies around the state. It's hard to tell people in Mamou and Ville Platte and in Tallulah and Bastrop that there will only be one rally in that area. But I don't have the time or the energy to have more than one rally in one district."

As for television exposure, Edwards is about to start airing his 30-minute commercial on different channels and time slots around the state. In order to get people to tune in, he says, "We're asking people to go to your local papers and get an ad published." And notice he didn't say to send the bill to Anna.

As for the enemy: "Everyone will run into friends who are voting for someone else. You say to them, 'That's fine, they're nice. If your candidate doesn't make it, we want to talk to you.' Remember, the more you antagonize them about how dumb and stupid they are, the harder it is to win them over."

He touches on other nagging details, like the law: "The rules are complex. But we can win following the rules. We don't have to break them. I'm running to win for the state, but I also want to do something for myself. I don't want to have something look bad when I win."

So much for directions, on to politics. The candidate's assessment: "It seems the campaign is in two tiers. Edwards, Duke and Roemer are in first phalanx. In this short a time and with the media not getting behind anyone else, no lesser candidate will break through. Unless there is a dramatic change, I will be in a runoff with Roemer. Roemer would have to erode tremendously for Duke to make the runoff. Now I've been lucky in politics, but I don't think I can be that lucky."

In 1983, Marion would have done this work. Not that Edwin's bad at it. He can even get his audience — for that's still what this is — involved when he says, "Now I'd like to hear your views."

The flyswatters stir as folks wait for someone to go first. Someone from Central Louisiana says Holloway and Duke are about even there. Farther north, Duke looks strong in Franklin and LaSalle parishes, says another. Edwards nods with no surprise. Local reports put Duke first in Livingston and Bossier and West Monroe.

A former state trooper says Duke may be losing important core support: "According to my sources, the Klan is not unified behind Duke. One of my best informants says the Klansmen think he is out for himself." Edwards doesn't press him on whom the disillusioned Klansmen *are* out for — but, as with Pentecostals, the ex-governor likely will land an improbable share.

A young man from Lafayette says he thinks Blanco is strong there. That gets a rise out of the portly older Cajun gentleman holding his cane. "No!" he turns around. "Who said that?"

When a fellow from Jefferson Parish says Duke is running first there, Edwards asks Sheriff Lee behind him: "Harry?" Not according to the Renwick poll Lee just paid for: it's Edwards, Roemer, Duke, with home boy Broussard in fourth.

The consensus is that Duke is running well in the white areas of the small towns and the country parishes. Duke's strength doesn't bother Edwards, since he knows it comes at the expense of Roemer's impressive rural showing in 1987.

Edwards feels the need to point out that the base is secure: "The black vote is coming together. Roemer lost whatever chance he had for black support—and my opponent had the second highest percentage of black votes last time."

A supporter is concerned that Edwards is going overboard ragging Roemer. He comes as close as anyone to actually criticizing Edwards today: "Let's not be negative. You're No. 1."

Edwards acknowledges that: "I will run first. Every poll shows Roemer gets weaker and I get stronger." He says nothing about easing up on attacking the incumbent.

"You're putting too much emphasis on Roemer," says a South Louisiana supporter. "He won't make the runoff."

"I'm trying to help him all I can," jokes Edwards.

But friend Perry Segura, another former codefendant from the hospital trials, isn't kidding: "Roemer is not going to make the second. That scares me, because someone else unknown may sneak in."

Now wait a minute, says the candidate: "You don't seriously think Roemer will not make the runoff?" When he asks for a show of hands on the question, half the people there raise theirs, along with a few yellow flyswatters.

For the first time today Edwards looks genuinely surprised or rather amazed. He puts his hands behind his head as if to say: *I can't believe this.*

The voter surveys do not bear out what his own people are saying, and Edwards respects the numbers too much to ignore them. Yet, as a seasoned politician, he also won't ignore the pulse on the streets—and never has he seen the two wider apart.

He's heard enough and he's told his people what he needed to say. One more sop to the announced purpose of this meeting. "Now I want you to join hands and meet with other people here from your areas and decide how you are going to plan your fundraisers."

He walks out of the room. His headquarters entourage follows. The local soldiers mill about for a couple of minutes, and then they leave too. It wasn't much of a planning session. People gathered from around the state, heard a pep talk from Edwards, threw in their own observations and a little advice, and everyone went home. That's probably all Edwards intended to do. They will go home and tell their friends they met with Edwin in Baton Rouge and told him how things were going here. Edwin Edwards has never heard of Robert Fulghum, much less read that crap, but he has effectively recharged and motivated a very loose-knit organization: he has told them what he expects of them, he has shared information on reaching the common goal, and — though he would be embarrassed to use the word — he has honored them by seeking their opinions and advice — most of which he has dismissed and forgotten by the time his car pulls away.

You wouldn't expect a Louisiana sheriff to admire a floral centerpiece, but the ones at the Sheriffs' Convention are truly festive: miniature cowboy hats set in yellow daisies, attached to cards bearing the lyrics of "You Are My Sunshine."

The special luncheon is a high point of the convention, a tribute to former Governor Jimmie Davis. Jimmie was first elected governor of Louisiana in 1944, the year after Buddy Roemer was born. He finished his second term in 1964 before any sheriff in the room was first elected. Frail at age 91 ("When I bend over to tie my shoelaces, I look around to see if there is something else I can do while I'm down there"), he still carries a tune clearly, as when he leads the sheriffs in his Louisiana classic. On the last note, a tingle runs through the room — the shared experience of how grand it is to be a Louisiana politician, especially a sheriff.

A special bond exists between Louisiana governors and sheriffs — for years those were the only political offices worth holding in this state, since everyone else, in one way or another, worked for one of them. As the tax collector and the only law enforcement officer, sheriffs *are* the government in rural Louisiana.

For years they were the feudal lords of politics to the king, the governor. When a sheriff dies, the governor names his successor, which can be a delicate decision. Governor Earl Long's aide once worried how the governor would replace a deceased sheriff in North Louisiana. "You have so many good friends in that parish," said the aide. "Who will you pick?"

Earl growled: "The first one of my good friends to get here with $10,000."

The sacred link between governor and sheriff is reforged with every four-year election cycle, when both offices are on the ballot together. The gubernatorial candidate with the sheriffs on his side traditionally carried a big advantage. Especially in rural parishes, the smart sheriff looked to his deputies and clerks, who serve at his pleasure, as his private political force for spreading the word for the sheriff's candidate. The sheriff also traditionally enjoys the best contacts with the black community. If he was getting the black vote out for himself, his candidate for governor could get on for the ride. The alliance worked to maintain control in the Legislature. Back when legislative districts were contained within parish lines, legislators often owed their elections to sheriffs; so when a governor started looking for tough votes in the Legislature, he would call on the local sheriffs to help in the roundup.

That was the old days, before the growth of the cities and the dominance of television advertising undercut the sheriffs' influence with voters. Voters these days also are looking for professional law enforcement experience, which has led to the elections of ex-state troopers over old-time sheriffs. Some sheriffs, once the lords of their parishes, are being threatened with federal, state or local investigations. In Jefferson Davis Parish, Sheriff Dallas Cormier is running under 36 indictments on various malfeasance charges. His colleagues, though, still admire Cormier's political grit. "He still leads every funeral procession," notes an admirer.

The bond between Edwards and the sheriffs is strong, and his personal attention and loyalty to these men have reinforced it.

Edwards knows what these politicians go through. Like Sheriff Huey Bourgeois of St. Mary Parish. He's with Edwards all the way. Why?

"Well, when the FBI had me indicted, Edwin called me and said he was behind me. That meant a lot."

Edwards also knows the sheriffs, though politically in decline in years past, could be more important in the coming election. The sheriff can still turn out a strong country vote, especially among blacks. With far less money being raised this year, there will be less for TV commercials and for paying drivers in rural areas. This will make the sheriff's coattails longer and stronger than ever in 1991.

Edwin Edwards understands that. He doesn't waste his time or theirs discussing issues in his brief appearance at the convention. "You can say anything you want as long as you're with me the Friday night before the election," says the former governor to a room full of knowing smiles. "That's when you fellas go to work."

That sentiment is echoed during the hospitality hour before the evening banquet. Next to the bar a few last sheriffs beat the deadline to register for the door prize, a Spectra Shield Sternum Plate, the real no-nonsense underwear marketed by Pro-Vest, an Ollie North company.

"With Edwin, we knew where we stood," says Bucky Rives, the director of the sheriffs' association. "You'd go into a meeting and he'd say, 'I understand what you need. This is what I need. You do this. I'll do that.' I worked hard for Roemer last time. This time . . ." his voice trails off diplomatically. Roemer might not be the sheriffs' man, but he is still their governor.

Sheriff Ed Layrisson also was with Roemer in 1987 and Dave Treen in 1983, but he told Edwards at the Strawberry Festival, "We'll finally be together on this one." Roemer, he said, totally backed down on a commitment for funding local jails. "We had a deal and he lied to my face. Once is enough."

Most of the sheriffs at this convention are pro-Edwards and will be with him the Friday before the election. To bolt from the incumbent could be tricky business with a governor who knows what is going on in the courthouses. Since Buddy Roemer doesn't, the sheriffs can applaud him warmly and regard him lightly. They are trying to be nice. So is Roemer, who gives a nod to the sheriffs' organization's director and its lobbyist. "I want to thank Bucky (Rives) and Reggie (Coco), whom I work with on a daily basis."

"Another lie," grins Tony Falterman, the former sheriff and now the district attorney in Assumption Parish.

So what does Buddy Roemer talk about with a room full of sheriffs. Why education and children, of course. Either Buddy Roemer really doesn't have a clue or really doesn't give a damn about the power of sheriffs. He blasts Edwin Edwards for letting public education slide while he was governor and he promises to redouble his efforts in his second term "for the children."

The lead balloon has landed. Falterman's assessment: the old thumbs down. The governor receives even less polite applause leaving than when he was introduced. No time for small talk. Roemer speaks before dinner and is gone before salad is served.

The sheriffs feel somewhat insulted, but what's new? The real message from Roemer is you can kibbitz with Edwin all you want, but elections are won on TV—and I can do that without you.


"I'm goin' fishin'," says the governor, stepping back from the dais after announcing his list of 71 vetoes. "I'm a tired matador."

You should see the bulls, or the gored oxen, or the hogs slaughtered at the trough. The 71 line-item vetoes following the 1991 legislative session leave bloody pork strewn throughout the budget. Even after his anti-abortion bill veto of 1991 was overridden, the gubernatorial *nyet* remains Roemer's most effective means of balancing the budget and dealing with an unruly Legislature. All of these vetoes will stand, since they gore separate budget items precious to separate legislators. Senate President Sammy Nunez alone lost about $10 million in district projects he had slipped into the capital outlay bill.

The vetoes underscore Roemer's public image as the tough administrator but also reinforce his reputation for being unable to work with the Legislature. They also give Edwin Edwards, touching down at the Destin, Florida, airport, the opportunity to get close to some very unhappy bulls at the beach.

Louisiana's district attorneys have amassed some of the political power that Louisiana sheriffs have lost in the past couple of decades. The sheriff can haul you in, but the district attorney has the power to prosecute you or let you go. The DA forms the center of the local criminal justice system. He (they are all he's) decides how good a case the police or the sheriff has, and can drop or add charges accordingly. Through guiding secret grand jury investigations, they can make their own cases or steer clear of making them. Even judges, once the preeminent local powers, usually defer to district attorneys, who alone have the standing to criticize a judge's sentencing practices. At a lower level, from fixing tickets to overlooking juvenile delinquency, the district attorney gets hundreds, thousands of opportunities to quietly build his influence. Come election time, the district attorney's backing counts for as much as the sheriff's — if not more.

So it only makes sense that Buddy Roemer would alienate the DAs as badly as he did the sheriffs. Worse. The theme of the DAs' convention in Destin goes beyond *Buddy Lied* to the red-line zone of *Buddy Lied and Screwed Us.* Individually and as a group. Among the governor's 71 line-item cuts were vetoes of pay raise bills for district attorneys and assistant district attorneys. This did not come out of the blue. The DAs clearly remember the governor addressing their spring dinner at the Country Club of Louisiana, where he said he could support but not guarantee pay hikes for district attorneys but that absolutely "you have my word" on the salary increase bill for assistant DAs.

Then came the legislative session. Taking nothing for granted, the DAs lobbied hard to push both bills through both houses. Yet, at every step of the way, their executive director Pete Adams encountered some subtle and not-so-subtle roadblocks of unspoken administration opposition. Knowing where that would lead, he began early trying to get his audience with the governor. He had his top officers call. No word came back from the governor, just his veto messages.

That's why, in early August, Edwin Edwards is campaigning in Florida. He asks for an informal session with the DAs, off the agenda and away from the convention site. When they meet, it's Old Home Week, as Edwards swaps stories and insults with these powerful politicians, many of whom, as conservative law-and-order types, have not backed him in the past. With the newly elected ones, Edwards compares notes on their mutual political friends back home. The cocktail hour alone is a performance in relationship building and rebuilding. Then to business. This is one group on whom he does not have to press his *Buddy Lied* chorus, since the governor has done that so effectively. He can only state what he would do: "I cannot tell you that when I am governor I will get your pay raise for you, but I can absolutely promise you I will never veto any raise that you get the Legislature to pass." Some of the convention speakers, including distinguished law professors and officials from the East and the Midwest, sneak into the back of the room to catch the real show. "I've never seen anything like that," a professor says later. The DAs had not seen anything like it in a while either. Louisiana's most famous criminal defendant and most frequent grand jury target flies home with The Law on his side.


Bob d'Hemecourt is on the portable phone with Anna Edwards, checking scores on his and Edwin's college football bets. The governor has never displayed much interest in organized team sports and he only bets, he tells audiences, at the craps tables in Nevada. But since the campaign trail has kept him out of Caesar's Palace, a fella's got to have some action. D'Hemecourt fills in Edwards on bets in progress when the two connect in the Ramada Inn parking lot in Baton Rouge before the Young Democrats forum.

No score in on Michigan yet, so Edwards kills time with Democratic rivals, so to speak, Sam Jones and Fred Dent. Dent asks the usual question posed when the three of them are together: "Have you found anyone out there who's working for Roemer?" The operative words here are "out there" meaning outside of campaign headquarters and "working for" meaning actively, publicly promoting the governor's candidacy. Edwards and Jones report none while Fred Dent has found a couple in Abbeville.

Knowledge of the governor's grass-roots organizational weakness only adds to the frustration of Dent, Jones, Kathleen Blanco and Clyde Holloway, the so-called new faces, who have been predicting that people, disillusioned with the major candidates, will turn to Somebody Else, that is, one of them. They tout Buddy Roemer's rise from nowhere to take advantage of the Anyone But Edwin movement in 1987.

Their problem is that the voters this time have too many Anyone But choices—Roemer, Edwards and Duke. People fear that if they go looking for Somebody Else, two of the Anyone Buts will make it into the runoff, resulting in Nobody Left they could vote for. Unhappy as they are about it, the swing voters in this election must pick the Lesser of Three Evils so that they aren't left with the two worst.

The strongest Somebody Else is Kathleen Blanco, but after some initial excitement, her rise in the polls has stalled. She can't make it, observes Edwards: "She thinks if she hangs in long enough, people will come to her like they did to Roemer. But she lacks three things: one, the conspiracy of the press; two, she's not as smart, articulate or conniving as Roemer; and three, she's truthful."

Sounds terminal. Compounding Blanco's problems is the persistent rumor that she is going to drop out. Tonight's no-show further fuels that speculation. Too bad for her, because the Young Democrats are serving up softballs.

To the question, what will hurt Roemer the most?, Jones almost sounds respectful: "I really hate talking about the dead."

Fred Dent: "I don't know what lie will be his downfall." Fred has compiled a list of 23 groups Roemer has lied to.

Edwards: "His downfall was his inability to deliver on his Big Lie of four years ago."

Word is just out that President Bush will attend a fundraiser for Buddy Roemer in New Orleans. This enhances Edwin's party-switch routine. "Bush is coming in to help Buddy Roemer. They are going to charge $5,000 to take a picture with Bush. While he's here, I hope Roemer takes Bush up to England Air Force Base and tells him about the 12,000 jobs we'll lose when the government closes it." The fundraiser, says Edwards, was part of the deal Roemer cut with Bush's top aide "when Sununu wasn't flying around somewhere."

Though Louisiana got nothing, says Edwards, the White House got what it needs: a Southern governor. "Bush campaigned in Texas for a Republican who was 19 points ahead. The Democrats won. Then he went to Florida. After two trips there, the Republican governor was defeated. If he comes here, it's over. After the Texas and Florida debacles, George Bush is desperately looking for a Southern governor and he's found one fool . . . ours."

Without Roemer, the candidates would have to start feeding on each other. Or start addressing real issues. When pressed, Edwards can even do that, giving an informed, detailed answer to a question about insurance reform.

Sam Jones is impressed with the erudition: "Is that Insurance 101?" But then the knife: "Didn't Champion Insurance give you a contribution in 1987?" (The owners of the defunct automotive insurer are in federal prison along with the former insurance commissioner they bought in 1987.)

"Yes," says Edwards.

"But you gave it back?"

"No," says Edwards. "That's Economics 101."

Back in the car, d'Hemecourt at the wheel, making up time on the way to the next meeting, Edwards checks a few bets by car phone — then relates some Politics 101.

Clyde Holloway, he notes, has gotten a lot of mileage from the clipping Edwards sent to him about Roemer voting for Dukakis: "I wanted to get that out, because people who voted for Dukakis won't vote for Roemer. And the people who didn't vote for Dukakis will say, 'What?' " And since no one who would consider voting for Clyde Holloway would vote for Edwin Edwards, Edwards wants to encourage him all he can in splitting Duke's and Roemer's base.

Paul Keller, president of St. James Parish, waits at the entrance to Tony's Restaurant near Donaldsonville. Inside, police jurors from up and down the river parishes are finishing their stuffed shrimp and are ready for the ex-governor's address. One rung down the ladder from sheriffs, the police jurors are the ward heelers of rural Louisiana politics. With districts as small as 2,000-3,000 residents, they are closest to the voters—and they get closer at election time. With police jury races also up this fall, these incumbents will be vital to the turnout. But some will be sitting on the sidelines. The U.S. Justice Department has not cleared dozens of local reapportionment plans in time for qualifying. That means the current officeholders will remain in place until new lines are approved and new elections are held. Some suspect a Roemer-Republican conspiracy to hold up many local elections and thus retard the country turnout that would benefit Edwards and Duke.

You'd be hard-pressed to find a Duke or Roemer voter in this room, for these folks believe in government and they remember governors who returned their phone calls. Edwards doesn't have to tell them about his commitment to funneling state money to local projects, but he does anyway. And in case they get confused by labels, he reminds, "I built the bridge at Luling and Dave Treen dedicated it. I started the bridge at Gramercy and I will dedicate it."

Bragging over public works is how politicians argue the age-old male question of whose is bigger. "Do you know how to tell the difference between a man and a boy?" Edwards asks. "It took a man to build the Interstate system while that boy can't even keep the grass cut." The jurors whoop it up over that one. When grass along local roads gets too high, they are the first to hear about it.

As for that boy, "I tell you, the fella does not like us. Anytime he has a good job to fill, he brings in someone from out of state. He went up to Chicago to hire a young lady—a very nice-looking young lady—to run our Department of Economic Development. And he paid her $90,000 a year."

The room gasps. "Paul Keller said he'd take it for eighty-nine five." It's an interchangeable punch line that he's used dozens of times around the state, always getting a laugh and making a point.

Finally a serious note among old friends. "I don't really need this job. I can live a long happy life without it. But something is burning in my gut from the election four years ago when I faced no other choice but to let him have it." Win or lose, he stresses, *that* won't happen again. "I don't want the last chapter of my life to end on that page. Others running may have another opportunity. I don't. This is my last shot."

The candidate does not leave until he shakes every hand in the room. Politics done, though, it's back to football, or gambling. "Do you have that score?" he asks d'Hemecourt at the door. Back in the car and on the phone to Anna: "How much did they win by?" He listens to the rundown of the day's bets. "So what's our net net?"

This football betting is not bad. He can campaign while he's doing it. He has picked up enough principles of the game to even comment on LSU's opening defeat. "You know you can't win with four turnovers." Not that the game matters—he didn't have any money on it.

The streets of Morgan City are roasting hot, but that's not stopping the people from lining the route long before the parade begins. This used to be called the Shrimp Festival, until the oil business began booming and the shrimp catch starting shrinking (you wonder why), and the city fathers found it right and proper to rename the celebration the Shrimp and Petroleum Festival. Yum.

The food and crafts booths are doing a brisk business in the shade under the long downtown bridge. A contingent of Duke volunteers sell raffle tickets for a giant barbecue pit on wheels, until festival organizers shut them down for not having a booth permit. They roll the giant cooker a few blocks up the parade route and resume surreptitious sales.

Excitement is in the steaming air. The big parade is rolling with festival queens on floats, marching high school bands, and local politicians on the backs of convertibles. A candidate for sheriff has built his own float. He waves from his throne position as a courtier with a megaphone urges the crowd to greet "Chester Baudoin, ladies and gentlemen, the once and future sheriff of St. Mary Parish, Chester Baudoin."

David Duke is riding on the back of a vintage convertible. He has brought along some shock troops from Metairie to show the local volunteers the fine art of crowd cultivation. They are out along the parade route, pushing the blue and white Duke stickers on the willing as well as the unsuspecting.

A few positions up the route, Edwin Edwards and company are riding on the back of a flatbed truck. In the cab, Andrew Martin drives while Bob d'Hemecourt checks pro football scores and relays them back to Edwards. Julia Reed of *Vogue* is along for the ride in the back of the truck as the candidate waves to his people and monitors his bets. Edwards points out the black woman in the crowd jumping up and waving — "We love you, Edwin" — she's wearing a Duke sticker.

Down most of the residential street, the crowds are very restrained, responding more favorably to teenage festival queens than to politicians. A group of local young Dukesters boo at a black Shriner on a motorcycle bearing a "No Dukes" sign. But their leader is not far away. The 20 young people break into "Duke, Duke, Duke" as their candidate, now standing on the back seat of the convertible, rides by and waves.

The biggest part of the crowd waits by the bridge. When he nears, the crowd goes into a Duke frenzy, people whooping it up and saluting him with raised beer cans. A dozen rush the convertible to shake his hand. Now this is what Duke had in mind.

But he's not counting on what's ahead. Near the end of the route, the parade passes through the black neighborhood. Duke's security closes in on the convertible. The ending parade ahead progresses to a crawl. Duke stops waving. The crowd starts booing. Someone throws a bottle that misses Duke. Reed of *Vogue* finds herself in the thick of an ugly incident that is about to turn violent. Then a woman comes out of the crowd and holds up her hands: "Please don't stoop to this man's level. He doesn't need any more ammunition." The shouting stops. The crowd retreats and silently watches Duke's car roll slowly by. Duke is not waving now. He is blushing, nervously eyeing the sullen crowd and looking, says Reed, "like one scared rabbit."

Edwin Edwards is heading home after a satisfying political and wagering weekend. Betting is as close as Edwards cares to get to contact athletics. In the back seat, aide Al Donovan describes the knee brace he is getting for his torn ligament so that he can continue playing basketball.

Edwards asks, "You wouldn't consider anything reasonable, like not playing basketball?"

"No, that's for wimps. That's what the brace is for."

"For fools."

As for real action, says Edwards, "I heard Raymond Strother wanted to bet $25,000 on Roemer to win. I called him and left a message to call me back and say when and where he wanted to meet. He never called me back."

"That's partially true," Strother later confirms. "It was a tactical thing. It looked like Edwards was coming on. So I leaked to two bookies I know that I was willing to bet $25,000 on Roemer. I was not going to bet on Roemer, but there were certain people that I wanted to hear that. I could tell people that Roemer's doing great, but if they heard about the bet secondhand, they would take it more seriously."

Edwards took it seriously. The message Edwards left at Strother's office was: "I want all he can get."

As Edwards' car closes in on Walden he finds the bet offer very curious. "You know I met with Strother a year ago. He said everything bad he could about Roemer. He called him a no-good liar and an s.o.b. and things worse than that." Edwards turns in his seat. He's enjoying this. "Then he says he wants to drop Roemer and work with me. I told him I'm satisfied with my arrangements and that was that. Then, that very day, he went to a 3 p.m. meeting with Roemer and he signed the agreement to do his campaign."

"Not even faintly true," says a surprised Strother. "I can't believe him lying like that." This, he says, is what happened. "I saw Edwards before I signed with Roemer. I had got a call from Edwards in my office. He said if you're ever in Baton Rouge to drop in and see him. So I did. He was sitting behind his desk, and he was talking on the phone about taking a gambling cruise from Galveston. He wanted to know about my Montana ranch and we talked about that for an hour. 'Do you have elk hunting,' he asked. 'Can I use it?' I said sure. I left and I went and had lunch with Roemer at the Mansion. I told him I had just come from seeing Edwin Edwards. And that was the last time I talked to Edwards. I can't imagine he had that kind of animosity. He doesn't do that. He's a pro's pro."

But Edwin holds to his story: "I would love to tell him I have a tape."

It is a strange story. It is a strange time. Edwards is all over the state, swinging from the heels at his invisible enemy. With other Democrats dropping around him, he has a better-than-even shot at making the runoff with Roemer, but his prospects slide after that. His own credibility stained, Edwards keeps trying to soil Roemer's. But whatever inroads he makes with the politicians, polls show he is gaining no ground with the voters. His disapproval rating continues to range between 40 and 50 percent. Roemer's "rope-a-dope" strategy continues to frustrate his challengers, especially Edwards. The constant attacks sound more hollow and bitter the longer he rags on and the longer Roemer does not acknowledge him. As much as does the rest of the state, Edwin Edwards needs a governor.

# 12. Where Voters Lie

**R**aymond Strother could feel the mugging coming. "It was quite amazing," the advertising consultant describes the campaign's handling of his 30-minute commercial for Roemer. "It was the first signal of the problem of a lack of decision-making authority in the campaign." His first sign.

Staff problems seem to bother Roemer as little as they do Edwards at this point in the campaign. That's because Edwards doesn't need a staff in order to campaign. And Roemer doesn't need to campaign. "At first we were going to start July 6," says Charlie Roemer. "Then we pushed back to August 6. We were thinking of waiting until September 6, but we didn't think we could do that." The numbers support delaying. The press only covers the campaign perfunctorily and the public ignores it. Despite heavy shelling on Roemer by challengers in the forums, his numbers do not go down. Theirs do not go up. His challengers cannot afford to go on TV early; he does not need to. His war chest is filling up steadily, now that he's making it to fundraisers, while raising money is harder than ever for his rivals.

Roemer has another good reason not to campaign early. He hates it. Always did. The vaunted grass-roots effort of 1987 was the work of committed volunteers and a small loyal staff. On many days, the candidate spent his mornings raising money and his afternoons reading novels in the back room of headquarters. His feelings didn't change by 1991. And he could read more comfortably at the Mansion. He could work there. Being the governor, on the job, above the unseemly campaign fray, was how Buddy Roemer chose to sell his candidacy through most of the summer. Then would come the TV campaign, where his commercials would dominate and dazzle. The candidate and the consultant had mapped out the advertising strategy in broad strokes the year before, using a 30-minute documentary as the foundation.

Shooting film for a year, Strother loaded his 30 minutes with friendly images: Buddy reading to children, Buddy seeing off the National Guard on their way to Desert Storm, Buddy chatting with ordinary people, and even listening. Strother believed Roemer needed the length to reestablish his battered credibility, something 30-second spots alone could not do. He felt the piece would put Roemer and his Revolution back in perspective for the voters.

But the commercial also gives the idling campaign staff something to really fight about. With Roemer in the rose garden, competing forces clashed behind him. Sam Dawson, as the professional Republican, shows little patience for the old grass-roots supporters, who in turn feel neglected. Charlie Roemer, held off by Buddy's young dogs four years before, asserts himself and tangles with Dawson over a black-vote strategy. Chief of Staff P. J. Mills wants his piece of turf. The Republican women volunteers do not get along with the pro-choice Women for Roemer. The center cannot be found, much less held.

All of the above and more are on hand when Strother airs the · rough cut of the 30-minute commercial. After a long critique, Strother can draw this conclusion from his copious notes: "A lot of people didn't like different parts of it." He recuts the whole spot and returns to show it to Roemer, who, says Strother, "never said if he liked it or not." So there.

Strother puts $100,000 into the piece, but Roemer and Dawson decide not to spend the last $20,000 on completing it. Dawson tells Strother to cut the long commercial into shorter spots. Those spots are shelved also. Then Strother and Reynaud Rochon, whom Charlie Roemer has brought in for the black strategy, recut a 10-minute version aimed at minorities. It too is scuttled when Roemer and Dawson decide against pursuing a black media strategy.

Once Roemer focuses on *how* he will open his electronic campaign, he and Strother are able to get something done. This time Roemer seems satisfied. "They are understated and that is deliberate," Roemer describes his 30-second commercials reservedly. "We wanted to calmly show what we've done." The commercials are total departures from the hot, rough-edged "Revolution" spots of 1987, but the biggest change is in the cast itself. The 1987 spots, as well as the 1989 commercials for fiscal reform, put Buddy front and center. Strother cut a dozen spots of Roemer delivering his own message. The governor believed his persuasive oratory was his greatest political asset, but, as the old political consultant, he also believed in research. Extensive focus-group testing of the spots turned up a jarring revelation: even people who might vote for Roemer did not believe him.

"People knew he was glib and intelligent and he could overwhelm them," says Strother of undecided or "weak Roemer" voters. "They considered him manipulative and they did not want to be smooth-talked." Which left Strother with a slight problem. "It's hard to have that good a spokesman and to not be able to use him. It's the first time I've seen anything like that."

The Roemer commercials also have to abandon their most effective emotion of 1987. Anger is fine for challengers but dangerous for incumbents. Buddy could not afford to make people angry again, but he did not want them to forget why they were so mad in the first place. "Remember four years ago" opens each of the set of four spots, and each revisits the sorry state of ethics, the economy, education or the environment during the prior regime. "Then came Buddy Roemer," chirps each of the commercials, as Roemer appears on-screen. "He said he would make people mad, and he did, but he didn't make deals," states one. "The Legislature became a political lynch mob, but Buddy fought and lost, and fought again. His victories grew, and slowly hope is taking root in Louisiana. . . . It's painful, but Buddy Roemer is doing what we elected him to do." Each one ends, "We can't turn the clock back now."

They are well-crafted spots, not dynamic, but with a hopeful tone and a stay-the-course message. So they aren't perfect, or even provocative, but there are a lot of them. Strother is not happy to have his 30-minute show shelved or to lose his candidate as a spokesman. The Roemer campaign's consolation is that Edwin Edwards did not get the same message.


David Duke started something when he aired a 30-minute television commercial in the 1990 Senate race. Now Edwards is ready to air his own 30-minute spot and the Roemer team can't wait. Crows Gordon Hensley: "Edwards is wasting his money. With his negatives, Edwards as a messenger is a flawed advertising concept."

But Edwards does not intend to be the only flawed messenger. Since he began talking about this campaign, he has promised "to play back Buddy Roemer's silly promises and jam them down his throat." Also, Edwards understands that his greatest challenge still is to convince his friends that he is in this race to stay. If it takes 30 minutes to do all that, so be it. At least Edwards recognizes the downside of trying to be convincing *and* interesting for 30 straight minutes. The upcoming 30-minute show, he tells supporters at the Sheraton meeting, "is not something to set the world on fire. . . . It's something I want to get off my chest and from my heart. If you don't want to listen, just turn your sets off and watch."

Bad idea. The weakest, most dangerous element of the 30-minute spot is the candidate's appearance. TV makes the face look fatter, and Edwards doesn't need to add any electronic bloating to what nature has wrought. He is sitting back in his chair, with his head tilted back to present an unattractive angle, especially with his heavy-lidded eyes. Occasionally, when he leans forward, he looks thinner and more vital, but just as quickly he leans back and resembles the last days of Elvis.

The Edwards show is not long on production values, as the client requested. The hook is the remote control device to flip on a TV monitor to rerun Buddy Roemer's 1987 commercials. It's remarkable for a man recognized as the dominant figure of a generation in Louisiana politics to spend about half his show playing the commercials of someone else. "Let's see what Buddy Roemer said last time about taxes." Edwards zaps the TV monitor on the set and up comes the fuzzy young face of Buddy Roemer in an open-neck shirt, exhorting the citizens around him. "Our problem is not money. Our problem is the way we spend our money. As governor, we will have a budget where I can look you in the eye and say, 'Money's tough and it's tight. But we've spent our money on our children. We've cleaned up our politics. We're gonna build roads in this state. And we don't need new taxes.'"

The Buddy face freezes on-screen as Edwards reminds viewers: "Need I ask you if he kept his promise not to raise taxes? Need I ask you if he kept his promise to scrub the budget?" He rolls through the Roemer list of sales taxes, gasoline taxes, telecommunications taxes, cigarette taxes. Scrub the budget? The number of state workers has just hit a record high under Roemer of 85,000 employees, clucks Edwards, who, by the way, promises for the first time in his political life "to not support any tax increases." This anti-incumbent stuff can be fun.

We go through more clips, such as Buddy on corruption. The fuzzy Buddy face is back: "I call it corruption when you run for governor and sell the influence of the office. I call it corruption when you have to make promises you can't deliver on." Well, says Edwards, what about the 1989 bill Roemer vetoed that would prohibit contributors of $500 or more from holding a position in the cabinet or on a board or commission? It's a weak slap at Roemer. Edwards, of course, would never have signed such a self-emasculating bill, but neither would he have preached about honesty. Now Edwards blatantly over-reaches: "If Buddy Roemer was willing to deceive you about his promises, if he was willing to deceive you about raising taxes, is it possible that maybe he deceived you about me too?"

Not possible. Not according to the People Meter.

The Roemer campaign tested Edwards' commercial just as it did its own, with the Audience Perception Analyzer, or People Meter. It's merely a hand-held dial viewers are given and told to turn up or down depending on "how favorable" they feel about the commercial second by second. It enables a campaign to evaluate the overall response to an ad as well as to note sharp positive or negative reactions to particular phrases or even words. The campaign tested the spots in three cities on a total of 80 voters, whose responses were tracked according to their candidate preference. Once an ad is tested, the campaign can review the commercial with the People Meter graph superimposed over the screen. It's less than science but it is highly revealing, especially in terms of intensity.

Roemer's first set of commercials tested very well, in the 80s among his voters and in the 30s and 40s among Edwards' and "all others" voters. Edwards' supporters rated their man's spots in the 80s too, but he barely got out of the teens among Roemer's and "all others" voters.

Even Edwards' "firm, unequivocal position that I will not support tax increases" and his conditional act of contrition — "Even good leaders make mistakes and I freely acknowledge I have made my share" — barely move the non-Edwards groups off the floor.

The People Meter confirms that Roemer is heading in the right direction with his media strategy and that Edwards has nowhere to go with his. Edwards has a rock-solid base among blacks, but little else. Strother describes the race as "a referendum on Roemer and Duke. It has so little to do with Edwards I can't tell you."

The opening flourish of classical music says this is no ordinary paid political broadcast. David Duke thanks you for inviting him into your living room, from what looks like his homey living room, and wants to introduce you to his daughters: Kristin, the Air Force ROTC student at her high school, and Erika, who sings in the church choir and recently has been reelected to her school council. "My sister and I are really glad you're watching," says Erika, "and we're sure you'll like what my dad has to say."

Dad has plenty to say, starting with his own conditional contrition for his radical youth: "Over the years I have grown as all of us do. My Christian faith has deepened and Christ has led me to see that working to preserve my heritage doesn't mean that I have to disparage others. . . . Sometimes I wonder about the self-righteous people who speak about loving everyone and hate me."

But enough about him. Seated in a wingback chair, Duke rips into Buddy Roemer for promising a revolution and then increasing taxes and spending. He blasts both Roemer and Edwards for their expensive fundraisers as a segue into his own pitch. "Call the toll-free number on your screen to pledge what you can to help pay for the cost of this commercial." Minutes after the 1-800 number fades from the screen, a 1-900 number appears. For $15, the caller hears a Duke message and an address to write to for a free subscription to the *David Duke Report*, "a hard-hitting newsletter" devoted to the major issues of the day: affirmative action, welfare reform, busing...

But didn't South Central Bell refuse to bill for his Senate campaign's 1-900 calls? True, but this year, the $15 does not go to the David Duke campaign, but to David Duke. Himself. It's all in the marketing.

Duke builds up to his major sight gag. Duke has boasted before about the support he's received from James Meredith, the black man whose 1962 admission to Ole Miss caused violent campus riots in which two died. Well, here he is. The wiry, graying gentleman with intense eyes asserts, "Unlike those who are paid street money for their endorsement, I came at my own expense." An appalling enigma to his old civil rights cohorts, Meredith now believes that universal suffrage was a mistake, that only property owners should vote. According to newspaper interviews, this sharecropper's son now believes he is descended from African and European royalty. In 1983, Duke published an interview with Meredith in the *NAAWP News* and praised him for advocating the resettlement of blacks in Africa. Recently, Meredith worked for a foundation supported by conservative U.S. Senator Jesse Helms until he was fired for endorsing Duke for the Senate in 1990.

"Affirmative action insults the principle of civil rights," states Meredith, who reassures his black friends: "You can trust David Duke because he always said what he believes. What he said he didn't say behind our backs. . . . I believe he is a good Christian who will stand up courageously for our family values. . . . The nation needs Clarence Thomas on the Supreme Court and David Duke as governor of Louisiana."

"Thank you, Mr. Meredith."

"Thank you, Representative Duke."

After that, what's left to add? Only the 1-800 and 1-900 numbers and "God bless you."


With Raymond Strother watching from behind a one-way mirror, a focus group of ordinary citizens talk about the candidates for governor. The group members, all residents of the New Orleans West Bank, represent targeted swing voters, blue-collar Democrats not attached to any candidate. There are few surprises from the group's first impressions: Edwards is a crook but he made the trains run on time; Roemer has good ideas but can't get others to go along; Duke says a lot of things they agreed with, but his past bothers them.

Then the group leader goes deeper and asks their reactions to facts about Duke.

Fact: He evaded the draft.

General group response: So did a lot of people, it was a lousy war.

Fact: He had cosmetic surgery.

Response: So what? Politics is a lot of show biz.

Fact: He never had a job.

Response: Well, he's a politician.

"Then when we described a hypothetical candidate in the same way, the people hated him. But when you told them that person was Duke, they made the same excuses. Basically, we found that the guy was bulletproof."

Except on one point. When members of the group are told that if Duke is elected, many major conventions would cancel their dates in New Orleans, that seems to register. "We learned from that that the only issue that really worked against Duke was the economic argument, and that took some talking," says Strother.

Roemer's respect for research reveals an important lesson for beating Duke, but his lack of respect for Duke stops him from using it.

How to head off Duke is the next battle for Strother to lose. He presses to make some anti-Duke commercials. He is not alone. "Daddy Roemer was screaming about Duke," says Strother later. "And P. J. Mills wanted us to take him on." Even Roemer's 24-year-old daughter Caroline, who's been campaigning all over the state for her father, complains the campaign is underestimating Duke's support. Not everyone agrees. Billy Rimes, the former Farm Bureau and administration lobbyist who is supposed to be lining up rural support, dismisses the Duke phenomenon as a mirage: "Duke is using out-of-state people," he scoffs. "A hundred people are following Duke, and none are from Louisiana," says Rimes.

For whatever reason, Roemer, too, doesn't buy the Duke threat. Roemer, the old consultant, believes in polls and Duke has been mired at 12 percent all summer. "He never took Duke seriously," says Strother. "He did not want to alienate conservative voters in North Louisiana — Roemer called them 'lost conservatives' — for the runoff. He would not allow any attack on Duke, ever."

Part of Roemer's reluctance is that he has not seen anyone directly attack Duke without giving him more attention and making him stronger. Strother estimates that with the millions of dollars' worth of free exposure Duke already was receiving, a Roemer attack would have composed only 10 percent of the volume of his coverage.

Roemer opts for the safe strategy, like Bennett Johnston did: an incumbent ahead in the polls should best ignore noisy challengers.


Out-of-town reporters who come to David Duke rallies expecting to see folks bouncing off the walls tend to come away disappointed. "I was surprised they looked so . . . normal," says *Los Angeles Times* writer Ron Brownstein after a visit to Duke's Baton Rouge headquarters.

Lance Hill is not surprised. In the early '80s he wrote an article on Huey Long as representative of an "incipient fascist movement." Hill sees the same thing at work today. "People say Duke's followers are normal and that they don't believe his wild ideas. Yet that's based on the assumption that in a dangerous movement the followers have the same ideas as the leaders."

You won't find many members of the NAAWP at Mudbugs today. David Duke always has been well received at this mecca for country-western music on the New Orleans West Bank. In 1990, Edwin Edwards came by to judge a dance contest and was barely acknowledged. The same day Duke was introduced there and the walls shook.

A year later Duke holds a small noontime rally in the cavernous club. As a black teenager stacks boxes behind the bar, about 200 people sit on barstools around high-top tables in front of the bandstand. These are suburban cowboys. They are well dressed, middle class, mostly in their 30s. Buddy Roemer could learn a lot, talking to this crowd, for many of them used to be his.

Meet Paul and Theresa Boyce. He's an electronics technician who moved here from Arizona. She's a sales clerk who grew up in Ohio. "I'm tired of financing other people who won't work," says Paul. "I'm not a racist. It's that way with other people, but not with me. I know white people in on two or three scams, like food stamps and AFDC." Paul likes the governor, to a point. "Roemer's like a preacher to me. He's looking out for my morals. He wasn't half bad but he needed to be stronger."

John Schillo, originally from rural Pennsylvania, "used to be a libertarian." The data-processing manager admits, "I do drive a pickup, but I'm not your typical redneck. Duke does have an educated following." He and his wife Darice like Duke's hard line on crime. "We've been robbed three times. I never had anything stolen in my life until I moved to Louisiana."

Norris Livette, a pipefitter, says he did not register to vote until he was 42, to vote for Duke. "I like the idea of welfare drug testing. The illegitimate birth rate is too high. There are too many people getting money from me." Edwin Edwards, he says, is "a liar and a crook. He's got all the ignorant people who don't know better." As for Roemer, "He's not too bad a guy, but he has too many personal problems."

Voting for Duke is one thing, saying it is another. Paul Boyce is still thinking about putting up a yardsign. "I know someone on the East Bank who put up a sign on their property and the tenants tore it down. They find it offensive, I guess." The bumpersticker on his truck draws reaction: "A lady drove by in traffic and held up this sign: RACIST PIG."

After John Schillo put on his bumpersticker, "people have shot me the finger and left me notes calling me racist. So I put on two stickers, bigger ones. You don't scare a Pennsylvania Dutchman. We're as pigheaded as they come." Other friends, he says, don't want to be noticed: "I know five people who will say they are voting for Roemer, but I know for a fact they are voting for Duke."

Numbers don't lie, but people do. In a campaign in which the lies of politicians are such an issue, who would figure that the voters might be lying too? There has always been a "won't say" response in polls. By the end of the 1991 primary, the pollsters could add a large new category: Probably Lying.

The polls remain stagnant through the summer. Even Roemer's long-awaited commercials barely cause a ripple. A Verne Kennedy poll taken between July 30 and August 2 shows: Edwards, 27.4 percent; Roemer, 25.3; Duke, 11.8; undecided, 19.3. Five weeks later, Ed Renwick's poll shows: Roemer, 26; Edwards, 25; Duke, 10; undecided, 24.

Pollsters find it odd that the undecided group would be so high in a race with three major candidates who have universal name recognition. It's also strange that Duke, who polled 43.5 percent against Bennett Johnston, remains in the subteens in governor's race polls. Consultants attribute his fall-off to Roemer's and Holloway's conservative support and to the more serious attitude Louisiana voters have toward the governor's office. Others speculate that if the folksy, hard-campaigning Clyde Holloway can get on TV and start to move in the polls, Duke will pull out. Though Duke attracts intense support, pollsters by summer's end focus on a two-way race. With nothing new to report in the primary, Verne Kennedy starts polling the runoff. He finds Edwards beating Roemer 51.7-48.3 in early August, but Roemer ahead 46-42.7 a month later.

The static polls, the lack of TV ads, the invisible incumbent, the predictable challengers, the damned heat, all shape a consensus among political observers: this is the most boring, overrated governor's race of all time.

Then one poll in August departs from the norm and rattles the prevailing wisdom for about a week until the source is considered. Sam Jones has been saying all summer that Duke is the real frontrunner. Now he has a poll that says it, though in a different way. When Jones' Chicago-based pollster Michael McKeon asks the same old question in his survey ("If the election were held today, who of the following would you vote for?"), he gets the same old answer. Then he asks a different question: "Who would you like to see elected governor of Louisiana?" Survey says: Duke, 32.3; Edwards, 23.7; Roemer, 22.8.

The polling question is criticized as unscientific, as if what's been seen this summer passes for science. Yet McKeon's question gets to what Louisiana politics, in the absence of a checkbook issue, is really about: feelings. The "who would you vote for?" question elicits a response from the head; the "who do you like?" response comes from the heart, or the gut, or whatever moves one when the curtain closes.

The poll is still just a bit too weird. Sure, McKeon has found a way to uncover the closet Duke vote, but to triple Duke's numbers, to declare him a lock for the runoff and to suggest the dynamics are right for Sam Jones "to come out of the blue" strain credulity. The Jones poll stirs dormant campaign paranoia. Clyde Holloway, dismissed in the poll, bristles: "I used to wonder about a connection between Edwards and Duke, now I wonder about Duke and Jones."

Though hardly accepted as accurate, the McKeon poll does cause other pollsters to go beyond their conventional methods to measure the "hidden vote." Verne Kennedy's September poll counts Duke at 15.5 percent but projects he "could go as high as 20." Ed Renwick, polling Duke at 10 percent, measures Duke's "maximum possible vote" at 25 percent. Roemer, says Renwick, also is moving and could surge into the mid-30s when his "leaners" break for him.

At least the McKeon poll, though hardly considered reliable, demonstrates that the campaign is far more fluid than the old static poll numbers indicated. Duke may not be in control of this race now, but the next best thing for him is that no one else is.

# 13. The Thermal Index

It is mid-September, six weeks before the election, six months since the heavy campaigning began, and Buddy Roemer is ready to appear at a forum. The candidates will appear at the LSU Student Union with a statewide telecast on Louisiana Public Broadcasting. The challengers are looking forward to this opportunity the way Roemer did in 1987. Having just been endorsed by the *Times-Picayune*, he was the emerging candidate who showcased very smartly on the televised LSU debate. Then it was at Edwin Edwards' expense. When a student asked what the governor would say to LSU graduates planning to leave Louisiana, a testy Edwards snapped, "I would say they are free to go."

Lest he be reminded of his infamous quip, Edwards uses his opening statement to apologize for the old remark that was made in frustration. As usual, Edwards practices even contrition in moderation. He can't resist the turnabout: "Now I would say go ahead and leave the state and let Buddy Roemer send for you, because he is hiring everyone else from out of state."

The first question is traditional for this forum. The candidates were asked in advance to tell what living person they most admired.

Roemer has his personal heroes, like state Senator Leonard Chabert, who died of cancer the day before, and Mother Teresa, but he settles on Boris Yeltsin, who, notes the governor, "also switched parties."

Sam Jones: "Working people."

Fred Dent: Ernest Johnson, a black lawyer in Baton Rouge who has started a savings and loan.

David Duke picks James Meredith.

Edwin Edwards stays safe: Billy Graham.

Clyde Holloway stays safer: Ronald Reagan.

The governor starts and stays on the defensive. Yes, he did scrub the budget, he insists, citing the sale of airplanes and limousines. Edwards retorts that he sold more planes than Roemer did and, anyway, it costs more for this administration to lease planes than to operate a King Air.

In a pattern all candidates will follow, Edwards disputes the facts in Roemer's TV commercial on education. He cites press critiques of Roemer's ad showing the claimed 20-1 student-teacher ratio has been reached in only a third of the classrooms. The claimed 30 percent teacher pay raise only comes out to 19.9 percent without existing longevity increases.

Roemer tries to stress the positive strides in education, even citing Superintendent Wilmer Cody's trip to the Soviet Union to study advances there.

Sam Jones turns to Roemer: "I don't know what this fixation with Russia is. I just hope he doesn't send the Department of Economic Development there."

On the environment, Duke charges that "all the polluters are contributing to Roemer while DEQ is harassing small business." Edwards adds, "The Roemer administration is spending millions to do the same things we did with no staff or money." That's a highly specious statement, but with all panelists teeing off on Roemer, he can barely keep up.

Buddy talks tough on crime, all but boasting, as his commercials do, of the five executions during his term. Even that opens an attack line for Duke. "Roemer's TV commercials say he's executed five people. The trouble is, we've had 2,000 murders in that time. Until we execute more than five, we won't solve the problem."

Roemer has taken head shots from every direction tonight. This forum is a graphic example of why Roemer has skipped them all so far. But had he gone through this drill in some smaller forums, he would be better prepared for the televised event.

The attacks on Roemer are all that gets hot in this forum. No one touches Duke, except the usual Jones cracks about Duke never holding a job. Clyde Holloway, in his first real shot on television, is singularly inarticulate and unimpressive. If he has any hope of busting into double digits and challenging Duke, he loses it tonight. This campaign forever marks the end of the Nonverbal Candidate.

Backstage, Edwards men Bob d'Hemecourt and Bill Broadhurst are watching one TV monitor while, a few feet away, Roemer's handlers Sam Dawson and Gordon Hensley watch another. As Edwards hurls another accusation at Roemer, Hensley complains to Dawson, "This is weak pussy shit."

D'Hemecourt hears that: "Yeah, well there's more to come, pal."

Hensley takes one step toward d'Hemecourt and says low and darkly, "We're gonna slit your throat."

What! D'Hemecourt has hung out with some tough characters in New Orleans street politics, but he's never heard a line like that. "Who is that guy?" he starts asking backstage.

But the action onstage is approaching its thrilling conclusion. Edwards uses his entire closing statement to reveal that Roemer personally helped negotiate a $500,000 state legal contract for Dave Treen just three days before the former governor asked the Republican State Central Committee to call off the state convention. "I am asking the press and the attorney general to look into it, because you would with me."

Now Roemer has to spend part of his closing statement to refute the charges. His staff had heard of a bombshell coming from Edwards. This was more of a hand grenade, but it could be dangerous. Roemer answers that the legal contract was necessary "to defend the state's liability for loans you approved."

The other candidates' statements are the usual mind jelly. Holloway reminds viewers that he is still married to his first wife, which in this race is more of a distinction than a qualification.

Then it's over. Reporters and handlers crowd onto the stage. Edwards is pressing the Treen legal fee charge but adds, "There is more to come. I'm going to stop being a politician and be a reporter and do your job for you." Behind him, Billy Broadhurst is passing out further documentation on the Roemer-Treen deal.

Hensley is working reverse spin. Pointing to Broadhurst, he is shouting to reporters, "This is shameless hypocrisy. This guy lined his pockets in the First Use tax case."

Edwin Edwards is ready to leave, but d'Hemecourt wants another shot at Hensley: "That jerk gets near me I'll whip his ass." When the entourage pushes its way through the stage door, Hensley follows. D'Hemecourt and Hensley are about to get into it again, but Broadhurst, the cooler head, quickly shepherds the group down the loading dock ramp toward the car.

D'Hemecourt, over his shoulder: "Our paths will cross again."

Hensley: "Yeah, pal, more to come."

The candidate is amused by all the partisanship. Standing on the curb, peeling the wrapper from a mint, he coolly observes the smoldering Hensley up on the loading dock.

"So you're one of Roemer's boys from out of state."

"That's right."

"Well, it's too bad you can't find a job anywhere else."

"I'm sure glad you found something for Broadhurst to do."

Edwards smiles: "Well, while you're here, there is a very good AIDS clinic at Charity Hospital in New Orleans."

D'Hemecourt, still highly pumped, points at a reporter: "You make sure he can spell my name right. I want to make sure he can find me."

The Edwards cars roll off, as Hensley glares into the darkness. As childish as the interplay was, it did mark a rare sign of life in the staid Roemer organization. But Roemer, now on his way to the George Strait concert, would later chide Hensley, whom he calls "The Assassin," for the confrontation. Not because it could reflect badly on the campaign, or that someone could get hurt. No, Roemer tells Hensley, "Get a life."

The morning after the LSU forum finds Buddy Roemer and Edwin Edwards sharing a pew in Sacred Heart Catholic Church in Cutoff for Leonard Chabert's funeral service. Chabert inspired the Senate with his stubborn fight against cancer. Weakening steadily, he held on to broker Senate reapportionment, including a district he could win in, and then declared he was not coming back. The Lord works in mysterious ways . . . and so does Leonard. It takes one of the state Senate's most ferocious knife-fighters to bring about a cease fire in the governor's race, which is just starting to get nasty.

Chabert and Edwards went way back, from floor fights in the Senate, to close political races in bayou country, to orgies in Las Vegas. When Chabert was in trouble in his 1983 election (Leonard was always in trouble in his Houma-based district), Edwards made two trips in the final week to campaign alongside Chabert. With mock seriousness, he explained to audiences that "the state can save $40 million a year if Leonard Chabert isn't reelected. The capital outlay budget isn't big enough for all he wants." Chabert reveled in his reputation for hardball politics. When he was described in The Last Hayride as the "Luca Brasi of the bayou," Leonard loved it. When he found out who Luca Brasi was, he really loved it.

Though Leonard led the coup to depose Roemer's Senate president in 1990, Chabert was often a rock of support for Roemer's reform bills. In eulogy, the governor says, "I believe that Leonard is in Heaven. And he is going to people and saying, 'I know this is Heaven, but can I help anybody?' "

From Heaven, the person Chabert may be helping most is his son Marty, who is running for his father's Senate seat. Marty lost when he tried to fill his father's House seat in 1983. Again, the residual negatives from his father's heavy-handed local political style are hurting Marty, and he is running third in the polls. The father's death could change that. In this land where Catholicism meets the sea, the Lord and Leonard may be at it again. "I just think," says a bayou resident mystically, "that Leonard felt the only way Marty could win was for him to die before the election. So he did."

Using their experience in 1987, the organizers of the business-sponsored 1991 gubernatorial forum have set up 400 chairs in the Stonebridge Country Club on the West Bank. With less than 25 of them filled, a deflated club organizer worries, "I wonder what this means for our attorney general forum." Not only has the public stayed away, but just one candidate has arrived on time. Edwin Edwards uses the waiting time well by cataloging Buddy's lies and the media conspiracy to a CNN producer.

Finally Holloway and Duke show up to make at least a forum quorum. Having been worked over pretty well in the LSU forum, Roemer is back to no-show status. With one annoying exception. Roemer attended an environmental forum, his strong suit, while Holloway and Edwards skipped — their absence was noted in the *Times-Picayune*. Further proof of the ongoing conspiracy, asserts Edwards: "Roemer misses 35 debates and you do not hear a word about it in the *Picayune*. Look," points Edwards, "their reporter is right here and you won't hear a word about it." He is correct.

In the back of the room, Bob d'Hemecourt, who has logged 2,280 minutes on his car phone in the past month, is concerned his phone batteries are running low. This could cut his constant link to the outside world and leave him nothing to do but listen to another silly forum.

As for politics, he says, it's been a good week. Kathleen Blanco's exit from the race "releases the elected officials in Acadiana to get behind us." Roemer likely will attract much of Blanco's vote in Lafayette and among women. The more immediate result, predicts d'Hemecourt, is: "Now that Kathleen's out of the race, it's going to get dirtier." Anything would help this race.

Anything would help this forum, now slogging through the Education Question. "Look at him," says d'Hemecourt of the boss. "He's bored stiff. He'd much rather be back here shooting the shit with us."

More good news: the New Orleans Alliance for Good Government, a reform crowd that shunned Edwards in the past, endorsed him this week. Edwards had filled out their questionnaire carefully and pushed all the right New Orleans buttons in his appearance before the membership, and then dutifully worked the room. "He stayed until the last one was gone," beams d'Hemecourt. Roemer's basic record of benign neglect toward the city did not help him going in. Then he didn't go.

So Edwards gets the good-government crowd. Now, what of the talk that the major New Orleans black group, SOUL, may go to Roemer? The story is causing big ripples on the street, for SOUL has been with Edwards since the 1971 runoff, which it may have won for him. Having backed third-place finisher Gillis Long in the 1971 first primary, SOUL was available, but not free, for the second. The Edwards and Johnston camps entered a blatant bidding war. Johnston blinked at $35,000. Edwards delivered cash. SOUL delivered about 10,000 votes. Edwards won by 4,488. In 1983, sources piecing together all payments to the group, and to companies that Sherman Copelin and Don Hubbard owned, estimated that the Edwards campaign spent $750,000 for SOUL support.

This time around, it was reported that a fight broke out among SOUL leaders when Edwards came looking for their endorsement. Copelin, for Edwards, and Hubbard, for Roemer, got into a shouting match behind a closed door. "That's fine, you don't have to endorse me," Edwards said he told the two before he left. Edwards knows there could be less than meets the eye here. Copelin and Hubbard, once called the Gold Dust Twins, have been known to work the good cop-bad cop act to pump more money out of prospective endorsees who are reluctant to meet the SOUL budget. This time, however, it may be Edwards who blinks at the price. With barely $1 million raised and most of it spent, Edwards' spending plan cuts out all early money for black groups and projects a spartan budget to get out the vote on election day. Word is that Charlie Roemer, who is close to Hubbard, is working on getting SOUL's nod.

His son, however, chooses to remain vague on the subject of paying the election expenses of black organizations. "Election expenses? I don't know. I've never done that. What do you mean, election expenses?"

If Buddy doesn't know, his daddy does. Charlie Roemer is said to be determined not to cede the entire black vote to Edwards.

Could SOUL go to Roemer?

"I hope so," says d'Hemecourt a little too breezily. "Listen, we'll tie Don Hubbard and Charlie Roemer so tight and then we'll paper over SOUL with so many other groups you won't find their ballot." It takes money to get out the black vote, but it also takes a reason. SOUL or no SOUL, says d'Hemecourt, "You'll not get a black to vote for Roemer."

But the nagging question is pressed: *Where is the street money coming from?*

D'Hemecourt waves it off. "Look, my job is New Orleans. I ain't Bennett Johnston. I'll do what I'll have to do."

A nervously pacing Andrew Martin stalks the conversation.

"Andrew thinks I talk too much," laughs d'Hemecourt.

"I know you talk too much," says Martin.

Back at the forum, the Tax Question is moving slowly from candidate to candidate. D'Hemecourt lights another cigarette. "You can't give Edwin five minutes to think about an answer. He'll slam dunk you."

Bryan Wagner, Holloway's New Orleans sponsor, materializes. D'Hemecourt compliments him for the excellent job he did standing in for Clyde at a recent forum. Then the two disappear into an adjacent meeting room to listen to a tape of a Holloway radio commercial. Why? "There's no reason not to exchange a little humor in a campaign," Wagner would say later. Was that all that was exchanged? D'Hemecourt would say later that the Edwards campaign helped raise some money for Holloway to air the spots. Wagner said that never happened, though "there were conversations with Edwards people in New Orleans as well as Roemer people and others." Wagner said Baton Rouge contractor Bert Turner helped Holloway raise most of his money. Turner also co-hosted a fundraiser for Edwards in the primary and sent out a letter supporting him.

Rumors about Edwards' collusion with Holloway were eclipsed by the stories of Edwards and Duke plotting against Roemer in frequent meetings. Whether or not the stories are true, Edwards has managed to clear out every major Democrat from the primary and so can afford to stir things up among the three Republicans.

Onstage, Edwards is trying out his response to Duke's attack on affirmative action. "I'm the beneficiary of an affirmative action program. When I got out of the Navy, I had help from the G.I. Bill to get my education and the taxpayers have been repaid many times over for that."

But Duke won't let that pass. "But you did something for your country. Affirmative action today doesn't reward anyone for service . . ." and off he goes on his favorite issue.

The two do find some common ground on the Casino Question, though Duke doubts New Orleans fits the European example of casino towns. Referring to his last trip to Austria, "There's a nice casino in Salzburg. But it's a clean city, there is no Mafia there." Even so, "I could support a single casino in New Orleans if the people wanted it."

Now it's Holloway's turn. Reminding Edwards that he quit the race when he ran second to Roemer in the primary, Clyde goes for the kill: "Will you drop out of the race if you run second to me?"

Edwards is almost contemptuous: "If I run second to you, I *will* drop out."

Now it's Duke's turn. Curiously, he asks Edwards, "Is Roemer guilty of what he accuses you of ?"

Edwards laughs. He starts to answer, then stops. "You just hit a nerve. Yes, there will be some interesting revelations about Buddy Roemer. I will not make them here, but in a debate with Roemer. It will set the state on its ear. I'll not reveal it here, but you watch his face."

"You may be surprised who you're in a runoff with," adds Duke.


Having taken blood from Buddy Roemer, with more to come, Edwin Edwards can relax a bit and insult someone else. He's the master of ceremonies for the roast of Harry Lee, the colorful, rotund, Chinese-American sheriff of Jefferson Parish, whose family runs the famous House of Lee restaurant. Edwards asks the guests to take their places. "Harry, you take these two seats here."

He's on a Don Rickles roll. "You know, folks, Harry rode with his posse in a parade last week. When Harry came by, you should have heard the crowd cheer . . . for the horse.

"And Harry's concerned about the racial tensions in Jefferson, so he's opened a new restaurant. It's called the House of Leroy."

Protocol demands that he demean the New Orleans sheriff too: "Charlie Foti is very generous. Last week he was asked to send something to the Old Folks Home. So he sent his mother." *Dah dah dum.*

David Duke meets and greets supporters and reporters on the oak-shaded lawn of the antebellum courthouse in Clinton, which, incidentally, was a shooting location in the 1961 film *Long Hot Summer*.

Before the last push of big campaign rallies, he is touring the small towns and parish seats of the Florida parishes north and east of Baton Rouge. The small group of citizens awaiting him appear to be the conservative, small-town, working-class folks who show up at his rallies. Well, almost. There's the long-haired, full-bearded, gap-toothed biker in the World of Wheels Tour t-shirt, who says the state cannot stand another four years of the incumbent: "Roemer's gonna sink this state if he gets in again." Next to him is an intense, thin-mustached man with an American flag sewn on his shirt sleeve. He is very pleased with the handmade Duke sign he has placed at the edge of courthouse lawn. As David Duke appears and begins shaking hands, a woman in a chartreuse dress whispers, "He certainly is the most handsome candidate."

Reporters from Dallas and Atlanta show up to catch Duke on the road. He alternately answers questions from supporters and reporters. What about the president's trip here to help Roemer. "Roemer's vote is soft. I think Bush will help him with money, but not with votes."

The biker concurs, "People like Bush, but not when he tells Louisiana how to vote."

"Especially since Roemer voted for Dukakis," Duke adds, in case they've not heard that up here in Clinton.

A prediction? "A runoff between Edwards and myself. And that will be one of the cleanest elections ever. It will be all issues, no mudslinging."

"Why's that?" asks the reporter.

"Because Edwards knows the things I can use and vice versa."

The lady in chartreuse observes to no one in particular, "He's gonna bring back the idea of the good politician. I don't know if that's an oxymoron." Other locals eye her warily. *Who's she calling a moron?*

Duke parries the question on His Past. "I've become more moderate over the years. It all has to do with growing up."

The thin mustache jumps in: "They holler 'Racist' and all the politicians scatter like roaches."

"But I am not a racist," Duke reminds, in case they haven't heard that either.

Duke has miles to go and hands to shake. As he turns to enter the courthouse, the lady in chartreuse makes her move, extends her hand and drawls, "Why, yes, Captain Butler, I remember you." Then she takes a ring from her finger and presses it into his. "I want to make a contribution to your campaign. This is worth about $100."

Maybe it's the heat. Or the old movie location. Or a day pass from the nearby mental hospital. She turns and sashays off. Duke, staring dumbfounded at the ring for a moment, rushes after her. "Ma'am, ma'am, I don't think the campaign finance law will allow me to accept this. Now if you'd like to write a check to the campaign. . . .  "

No wonder the campaign is becoming a little strange. The voters are starting to get interested. And Edwin Edwards is starting to serve food at his rallies. That will bring out a crowd in Houma, the coastal oil town struggling back from the bust. "There were people coming out an hour early, pressing their noses up to the glass," says one volunteer. By the time the candidate arrives, the sandwiches are disappearing, the beer line is lengthening and the dancing is starting. This is a well-integrated crowd, and requests to the band alternate between Elvis Presley and James Brown.

Edwards pauses at the door. Not wanting to shut down rock 'n' roll just yet, he swings by the neighboring bingo hall just to remind the players "who passed the law to make bingo legal."

Back at the rally, Edwards catalogs the roads, levees and hospitals he built in Terrebonne Parish and the projects that Buddy Roemer vetoed. The headquarters manager, T. Bagin, brings up the leading volunteer, 86-year-old Narcisse LaFont, who has been putting out Edwards signs all day. His reward: "I'll have you come sleep in the Mansion," says Edwards, holding the old man's shoulder. "You can have any bedroom you want. Edwin keeps his promises and Roemer doesn't."

He has whooped this crowd up good, and they want to shake his hand. Maybe an accident taught something about shaking hands from a stage. Andrew Martin has a firm grip on Edwards' belt and the back of his pants as he leans out into the crowd and pumps hands.

Overall, a good appearance before about 600 people. T. Bagin figures that Edwards is doing well around here with the old people, but he doesn't know about the young ones. And this Duke is coming on strong.

So is Marty Chabert. Two weeks after his father Leonard's death, the momentum has shifted to his son. Leonard's ultimate strategy seems to be working. As one local supporter figures it, "Of ten people who hated Leonard, two will vote for Marty."


Edwin Edwards on the vice president's visit: "Dan Quayle will not come here to join the National Guard, because ours fights."

How about Buddy Roemer on Dan Quayle? "Still have a 'problem' with him?" the governor is asked at a Women for Roemer rally in New Orleans City Park.

Roemer laughs a bit nervously. "I can't retract what I said. I thought the No. 2 man should be ready and I didn't think he was. Since then I've come to know him and George Bush has faith in him and that's good. But that's a decision I made and I can't retract it." Nor will Clyde Holloway let him forget it.

But will the voters remember Clyde Holloway? Even with Kathleen Blanco and Aaron Broussard out of the race, the officially endorsed Republican candidate can't crack ten percent in any poll anyone believes. Between the heavy-hitter money on Roemer, quiet money on Duke and some bet-hedging on Edwards, only a trickle of GOP contributions is going to Holloway. In one day in September, the Roemer campaign deposited more money than Holloway's total to date of $189,000.

A survey by University of New Orleans pollster Susan Howell shows Roemer beginning to widen his lead with 35 percent to Edwards' 30 and Duke's 12. But when Howell employs her own "thermal index" to track undecideds who respond favorably to statements about Duke, the adjusted results are: Roemer, 30; Edwards, 28; Duke, 24. Roemer and Duke appear to be the only candidates moving. Concludes Howell, "If Edwards doesn't get out blacks, Duke can slip by."

The loop around Roemer is tightening. Chief of Staff P. J. Mills has been shut out of it. And Roemer is starting to avoid Raymond Strother at the Mansion, because the ad man is pressing him to do something about Duke. Charlie Roemer's efforts to put together something, anything, in the black community are brushed off by Sam Dawson. "I've tried to get a few black groups together. That guy Dawson says we don't want those endorsements," complains the elder Roemer, angry at being shut out of a second consecutive Roemer campaign. "The Republicans have no acumen. They're the worst."

"Worse than Len Sanderson?"

"Sanderson?" sniffs Roemer. "They make him look good."

Dad may complain but his son's campaign looks on course. His rivals can keep their rallies and retail politics. On the eve of the presidential visit, Roemer is ahead in the polls, strong on TV, and about to turn up the volume.

The biggest Republican fundraising party since Bob Hope did one-liners for Dave Treen in 1983 is but an hour away. So what is Fox McKeithen doing lugging golf clubs down a corridor of the New Orleans Sheraton?

"It's for the President," beams the Republican secretary of state, proudly showing off the white golf bag and white golf-club covers with red crawfish stitched thereon. "Now I think the President's really gonna like these," says Fox.

Downstairs, Gordon Hensley is trying to run a scam on the Secret Service. The White House has agreed to have the President pose for pictures with 100 different couples, who have paid $5,000 each. But the campaign has overbooked an extra 40 couples for the picture session. That's another $200,000. If Hensley can just get them through. On top of that, 750 people have paid $1,000 each to attend the presidential banquet. Subtract costs and it's an easy $1 million without extra photos.

The problem with Republicans is that they can get excited about the wrong numbers. As Republicans queue up for their photo session, reporters in the hotel bar are buzzing about the new poll coming over the wire. A Mason-Dixon survey, the first national poll to use a thermal index on Duke, reports a virtual dead heat: Roemer, 30; Edwards, 29; Duke, 28. Some national reporters are wary that the pollsters are overcooking this thermal index thing. Duke's straight numbers in the poll are only 14 percent.

The big show is about to begin. Despite Hensley's protests, the photo line has been shut down just past the 100th couple. The ballroom of the Sheraton is studded with the prime givers, movers and shakers from Jim Bob Moffett of Freeport-McMoRan to shipbuilder and Republican national committeeman Donald "Boysie" Bollinger, as well as the financial heavyweights in the Republican Party and in the financial and social establishment of Uptown New Orleans and around the state. Hensley, surveying the crowd through the bottom of his first martini, has good reason to feel pleased. But he's also troubled. So much financial artillery in one room reminds him of the high-flying days of Clayton Williams in Texas, before the slide began. From the new poll numbers, he smells another close vote coming, which bothers him. "The problem with a close vote is that when it comes down to the end and the Democratic nutcutters come out of the woods, the Republicans head for the country club," says Hensley. "Here come the nutcutters and you look behind you and no one is there." This guy needs another drink before showtime.

The St. Augustine High School Band plays "Hail to the Chief" for the big historic moment, the first time a sitting President of the United States has campaigned on behalf of a Louisiana governor. It's a first for Buddy Roemer, too: "I'm 47 and this is the first time in my life that I feel we have a president who puts children first."

Bush in turn praises Buddy as "a man who values conviction above conscience."

"He does what?" double-takes Tom Baxter of the *Atlanta Journal-Constitution.* That's how the printed version of the speech reads too. *Conviction before conscience.* That's been said of Buddy, but you wouldn't expect the President to agree in public.

Hensley is delighted some Roemer rhetoric has found its way into the President's remarks. "I sent the White House a copy of the announcement speech," he says, lighting a cigar.

It is, of course, a very nice speech. The audience stands and applauds as Bush makes for the exit, wriggling free of Fox McKeithen at the end of the table. A relaxed mood settles over the Roemer organizers. Hensley has found two old friends from the Claytie campaign, Mona and Lisa, now on the RNC traveling staff—all three are ready for Bourbon Street.

Roemer is rolling through his patented speech about the importance of a governor who is a member of the PTA and the day when we won't have to "spend too much money on long-distance calls to our children."

"That's a Ray Mabus line," notes reporter Baxter.

Finally Buddy Roemer focuses on exactly why we're here tonight. "The next three weeks will be tough, full of bigotry, hate, distortions and mudslinging. The next three weeks may be the toughest job in my life." And what can they do about it?

"If you don't have a bumpersticker on your car, you're not committed," says the candidate. "If you don't have a sign in your yard, you're not committed." As Roemer gets into his planting and harvesting imagery, something this crowd can really relate to, more and more couples slip through the exits, on their way to expensive cars that have no Roemer bumperstickers to go home to their Uptown mansions that have no Roemer signs in the yard. Until tonight, he hasn't asked for more than their money, and that's all he's getting.

# 14. Lower Than The People

**B**uddy Roemer needs the statewide TV forum in early October, with the largest viewing audience of the campaign, to bounce back from the beating he took at the LSU forum the month before. This is an event to psych up for. But the time on the schedule brings a pained look to his face. 7:30 p.m., Saturday. Kickoff time. The sacrifices of political life. "I'll be there at halftime," says Roemer determinedly. "I will not miss an LSU game."

Carried by four major stations, the campaign forum with the live audience combines the worst features of candidate debates: attack rhetoric and a peanut gallery with an attitude. As he does with most campaign events, Duke has brought a full cheering section of young vocal supporters.

Again, the line of attack of Edwards and Holloway is straight to Roemer, and Duke tries to turn every question toward busing, affirmative action and welfare reform.

Roemer gamely tries to defend his administration and his record, but he has not developed the counter-maneuvers to overcome the in-your-face attacks. Even the old solid ground of fiscal responsibility is moving underneath him. When Roemer claims he

217

balanced the budget for four years, Edwards silently holds up to the camera a Public Affairs Research Council report that he has been quoting from lately. It shows the Roemer administration ate into cash reserves to cause deficits in the last two years. People in the audience laugh and Roemer snaps, "This is not a joke." But it is a joke. The fiscally promiscuous Edwin Edwards is using the good-government mouthpiece to attack budget scrubber Buddy Roemer. Holloway piles on by pointing out that Roemer's administrative budget increased from $13.6 million to $22.6 million in four years. "That's like adding three floors," says Clyde, referring to Buddy's old brick-up-the-top-three-floors slogan of 1987.

Roemer can't even get off admitting imperfection when he says: "I'm not an expert politician." More laughter.

Buddy Roemer is yearning for Tiger Stadium and the seclusion of the governor's box. Sam Jones, who didn't make the ratings cut to be a member of this forum, can see by watching at home that Roemer should have gone to more earlier forums or to none at all: "He made the mistake of coming out first in front of mass media and he got pounded. We'd been in 35 forums. We had our attack lines ready. He was like a pitcher who had not been to spring training and tries to come on in the seventh game of the World Series. He got mangled."

It seems Roemer, who appreciates the power of TV, would have developed at least one sound bite that would put his record in perspective and his critics in their places. As Jones later says, "If he had had one zinger, people would have said, 'There is life there.'"

Instead he takes each sting as it comes, like a man swatting hornets.

David Duke is having his own problems. The panel is insisting he stick to the questions instead of letting him launch into his own rhetoric. Late in the forum, Duke fields a lottery question and comes up throwing welfare. Shreveport TV reporter Rich Masters interrupts, "You're not answering the question."

Duke steams up, "You have not had one question on welfare or affirmative action. These are important issues. I have my time and I'm going to use it."

"No, you aren't," says moderator Ed Buggs, cutting off Duke's mike. Dukesters boo. In the front row, station manager John Spain points at the Dukester and threatens in an angry stage whisper: "I'll throw you out of here." She sneers back. There are more angry voices in the studio audience. "This is liberal press censorship," snarls the young man in the Duke cap. "Let him speak," yells another.

The forum lurches on. Holloway gets off his first interesting statement of the campaign: "The three leading candidates could be on Jimmy Swaggart's show tomorrow." Not sure what it means but it's interesting.

Duke finally gets a crime question he can work with: "Some people will be afraid to leave this hall tonight in downtown Baton Rouge. . . ." From the menacing muttering of the Duke cadre, the threat of danger does not appear to be *outside* the hall.

The show finally over, Buddy Roemer wants out of here, the press wants to get at the candidates, and the Dukesters want to get at the panelists. Rich Masters has been given an earful: "Well, so far, I've been called a faggot and Jewboy." A bookish young man in glasses growls at the reporters, "Well, it looks like Duke is a real problem for the socialist press."

Duke with entourage presses out the door, where a group of black students from Southern University want to ask him about an earlier statement that blacks are genetically different.

"Yes, I said you were better athletes," says Duke cautiously, as Howie Farrell tugs at his sleeve to keep moving.

"And I think you said we were more musical?" sneers a female student.

Duke, about ten feet away, turns to answer. He sees reporters coming out of the building. He thinks better of it, and turns to head off into the safety of the downtown Baton Rouge night.

For two years David Duke has crisscrossed North Louisiana, talking to the same voters who put in Buddy Roemer four years ago, the same children and grandchildren of Huey Long's constituency. Over one weekend, Duke held rallies, barbecues or handshaking visits in Goldanna, Fisher, Marthaville, Mer Rouge, Vivian and Oak Grove. Julia Reed of *Vogue* drove four and a half hours to tiny Chatham for David Duke Night at the stock car races, but it was rained out.

Duke's headquarters operation in Metairie gets more overwhelmed as the campaign goes on, but his volunteers around the state form the best-organized field operation in the race. The deeper one gets into the country, the more active and committed are the volunteers. Some go way back with him, like former Klansman David Touchstone in Shreveport and right-wing extremist Babs Wilson in Baton Rouge. Some of Duke's newer supporters distrusted Wilson as a dark influence from Duke's past. In the Senate race, Billy Hankins thought she distracted Duke with her own agenda. "She would tape any talk show with a black activist or liberal and would replay them for Duke. We were running for the Senate and she was talking about Communist plots." Jim McPherson, however, can see her importance to Duke. "Babs Wilson was a worker, night and day, and she didn't view any job as menial. That lady got from concept to action real quick. She was a good manager. Baton Rouge was the best-run office."

Volunteers in the rural parishes keep the grass roots growing. Jim Johnson in Farmerville, Glen Dunlap in Pineville and Donal Milton in Jena distribute steady streams of bumperstickers and road signs and get the word out for Duke's barnstorming stops.

You know when you are entering Duke Country. On North Louisiana country roads where once Buddy Roemer signs were common fixtures, David Duke signs now ride high in the pines. A state trooper notes the higher altitude of Duke signs, placed there by "country boys used to climbing these trees to shake out coons."

Thanks to Buddy Roemer's executive order, there are no billboards along new Interstate 49, but there are plenty of 4-by-8-foot Duke signs where his campaign has secured permission from property owners.

Roemer volunteers in North Louisiana can't even get yardsigns from headquarters. No problem. Buddy Roemer will bring some up himself when he makes a long-overdue campaign swing to Jonesboro.

It hasn't been a great day as Roemer heads for his plane. Lunch was spoiled by another forum, this one at the New Orleans Press Club, where Edwards finally pinned down the governor on the uncut grass along the Interstate. "You've taken credit for the interstates and bridges I built. Will you at least own up that the current crop of grass is yours." Roemer had no choice but to laugh, since the rest of the room was.

Duke shows more testiness with the press. Warren Bell, a black anchorman, asks him a relatively harmless question that Duke takes as another attack on his past. "Why don't you talk about your past, about your cocaine conviction?" snaps Duke. It is a cheap shot, considering Bell's very public ordeal of years past, his treatment and his reinstatement at the news desk.

The mood is getting ugly at these affairs. Roemer is glad he's not made a habit of them: "I can only campaign if I'm in good shape. I looked around the table today and I thought I'm in better shape physically than any of them."

He's keeping his mind agile too. Reading material for the flight to Jonesboro will include no campaign research, polls or speech drafts. The governor instead is relaxing with Nicholas Lemann's *The Promised Land*, about the formation of the underclass, and *Beyond Numeracy* by John Allen Paulos. The latter allows Roemer to have some fun with fractals and with the premise that numbers depend on circumstances. Here's an example, as he turns to the page with a map of the East Coast of the United States. "Is the distance from Maine to Florida 2,500 miles or 8,000 miles?" The answer, of course, depends on circumstances: it's only 2,500 miles to roughly follow the shoreline, but it's 8,000 miles to cover every foot of every bay, cove and inlet. After a few more brainteasing examples, Roemer closes the book. "Numbers depend on circumstances. The budget is balanced now, but after July 1 you add $300 million for inflation. Is it balanced then? Fractals. Circumstances. That's why I read numeracy."

Laurence Guidry is relaxing too. He's alternately reading the sports page and watching the Red River twist into the sunset. The governor's aide theorizes on the state of Louisiana high school football. Fewer schools are developing top athletes, he says, because there are fewer resources for athletics statewide with cutbacks in education. This pulls Roemer out of his fractals. "So you're blaming the decline of Louisiana high school football on me, you bald-headed son of a bitch."

Guidry's laughing, "I'm telling you like it is, Buddy."

"I love you, Guidry, but you're not helping me."

Roemer is silent for a while as he looks down at the fields of soybeans and cotton, then he comes up talking politics, from a governor's vantage point. "All the time I've been in office, Edwards has not talked to me. Other governors do—Dave Treen, John McKeithen. They call with ideas or to ask me about something. Edwin, I don't think he likes me."

The governor is clearly ambivalent about this job he's supposed to be working so hard to keep. "The job has its pluses and its minuses, but it has its pluses . . . and its minuses. I'm not married to this job."

That triggers a connection. It's been nearly two years since he and Patti separated, he notes. Things work out, he says. "Dakota spends most of his time at the Mansion. He has a bird and his dog there. I'm glad Caroline lives there now. I tell you, if the kids were not there, I'd be gone."

Speed Bradford, a black police juror, and Harold Thomas, a white businessman, wait as the governor's plane taxis to the end of the lonely airfield at Jonesboro. The two have been trying to get the candidate up here for weeks. Not just the candidate.

"We need materials," says Speed.

"I know," answers Roemer quickly. "We're going to have a sign blitz in 2,500 locations. Have you been called?"

Speed's been calling. The Duke signs have the two concerned about Jackson Parish, which Roemer carried handily in 1987. The first stop on the evening itinerary is a school. Roemer has consented to campaign, but has insisted that at least one stop a day be at a school. "I don't want to talk about politics," he tells a room of almost evenly mixed white and black parents at Southside School. "Let's talk about our kids." He does.

The first question he takes, however, is on welfare. Obviously, another candidate has been through who has not been talking only about the kids.

Roemer has numbers at his fingertips. In Louisiana, about 170,000 children and 70,000 adults get assistance through Aid to Families with Dependent Children (AFDC), a program run by the feds. It takes up about 2 percent of the state budget. Besides, Louisiana is a national leader in welfare reform. "If you are on AFDC, you must get trained. If a job comes up, you have to take it. When David Duke talks welfare reform, we're doing it, thank you very much." Roemer is right. The state's new workfare system achieves many of the reforms David Duke is calling for, but, outside of this classroom, Roemer has not been calling him on it.

By the time Roemer and company make the next stop, a meeting of the area woodmen, only about half of the chippers and loggers and buyers are still around having a few drinks. State Senator Randy Ewing wishes his candidate had made it here sooner: "These are Duke people, but if he shakes their hand and talks to them, he can turn them."

Roemer is probably right about the sheer enormity and impossibility of effective retail politics on a statewide basis. He could spend the next three days in this parish and still barely make an impact come election day. Maybe that's why Edwards and Duke go at personal campaigning almost nonstop. You have to if you're going to make it work. Roemer does do a TV interview. The governor's visit to this part of the state is bigger news than it should be. Buddy should be a regular electronic visitor in North Louisiana living rooms, pumping out his message. Not just for the last three months, but for the last three years. Since Buddy has last seen Jackson Parish, David Duke has been through a half dozen times.

Blue lights flashing on the police chief's cruiser, the three-car caravan glides through the empty streets of Jonesboro to the next stop, a sad little fundraiser in the junior high gym. Through adroit scheduling, the governor's $25-a-ticket hot dog fundraiser coincides with the state fair two blocks away. About 100 souls respond blankly to his challenge: "If you don't have a bumpersticker, you're not with me." He tactfully avoids mention of yardsigns.

Meanwhile, political light-years away in Lafayette, Edwin Edwards is about to go onstage in the Cajundome at the largest campaign rally for any candidate this season. Atlanta newspaperman Tom Baxter calls the crowd of 8,000 "the most integrated crowd I've ever seen at a political rally." This is where personal campaigning and organized support pay off. Edwin Edwards has not seen this many friendly faces since he ended his 1983 campaign with a monster rally in Lafayette. Having worked many limp, sparse crowds all summer, from fairs to bingo halls, Edwards is pumped at the sound of 8,000 partisans rocking the house as he bounds onstage. "Welcome to the Cajundome," roars Edwards, "which . . . I . . . built."

Last stop in Jonesboro is the state fair, where Bradford and Thomas have arranged for Roemer to speak to an audience before Percy Sledge appears onstage. If it meant more to him, Roemer would be miffed: "Fellas, you know what happens when a politician gets up onstage at a concert or at an athletic event?" Roemer moans in the front seat. "He gets screwed. But because you're my friends, I'm going to go get screwed."

Happily for Roemer, Percy has been delayed. Roemer serves as a diversion to the crowd of waiting fans.

In a brief hand-shaking lap around the fairgrounds, Roemer waves to a group of young men in their 20s, and one barks back, "Duke, Duke." A young woman reaches out from the circle to shake Roemer's hand. "Don't worry about those guys," she says. Roemer's not worried. If he's lucky, they won't vote.

The police blue lights pulsate faster as the caravan speeds back through empty streets. "The chief sure likes his lights," observes Roemer. He would object, but tomorrow is the chief's birthday and the governor doesn't come to town often.

A politician is usually either relieved or pumped after blitzing a town this way. Roemer is quiet and subdued, meditating on the pine-lined road. "Here I am," he says, "riding around Jonesboro with a black man and a white man. Roemer, you don't have a clue, you don't have a hope. And I wouldn't have it any . . . other . . . way."

Back at the plane, Bradford picks up the yardsigns the governor brought along. This trip accomplished that much.

It's such a different race than last time, he notes on the way home. And 1987 was a different race itself. "It was the only campaign where I never deviated from the game plan." He's keeping to this year's plan, but, "It's tougher. The last time I had the anger. Since then, I've been through eleven sessions of the Legislature. No one should have to go through what I've gone through. It changes you."

He says he's changed his view of leadership and quotes the *Tao Te Ching*. "The philosopher asked the farmers, 'What's the greatest body of water?' The farmers say, 'The sea.' The philosopher says, 'This is correct. Why?' The farmers say, 'Because all rivers run to the sea.' The philosopher says, 'This is correct. Why?' The farmers say, 'Because the sea is lower than the rivers.' The philosopher says, 'This is the answer to leadership. The leader must be lower than the people. And the people will come to you.' "

If this feeble campaign swing through Jonesboro shows anything, it's that the sea is not as low as it used to be.

Yet is anyone lower? He has seen some of the Duke phenomenon on this trip, but he's not seen it in the numbers, "My polls show he's at 12. So double it. (Sam) Dawson says his absolute ceiling is 25." Outside of spending a lot of money on television ads, Roemer is barely engaged in this primary. Yet his numbers are holding steady for the runoff. After he finishes off Edwards, things will get more interesting.

"If I win here," Roemer clenches his fist, "I could go all the way to California. Ninety-six is wide open."

Buddy Roemer is locked in a tightening three-way governor's race, his polls are not moving, he has no yardsigns in Jonesboro, but he's looking ahead to running for president in 1996. Roemer considers and dismisses other Republican governors and senators in the South as presidential contenders. Outside of the South, there's Pete Wilson in California.

"No," Roemer shakes his head. "Not very dynamic."


All year, the Louisiana Coalition Against Racism and Nazism has been updating, printing and mailing out thick new media resource packets on David Duke. Though its aim has been to isolate Duke as a dangerous radical, Lance Hill is frustrated by the voter mindset that accepts Duke's current blow-dried conservative image over the documented proof of Duke's recent radical writings and associations. For all its research, the Coalition has failed to uncover the "smoking gun" proof that would blow Duke's mainstream conservative cover.

The closest Hill had come were the transcripts of interviews that Beth Rickey had uncovered in Boston in 1990, but the Coalition had been unable to clear for republication. Since then, doctoral student Evelyn Rich has turned over to the Coalition her tapes of interviews with white supremacists that included one 1985 conversation with Duke, which was mildly damning but still no smoking gun. Going through Rich's material, Hill paid little attention to one tape that was labeled as an interview with avowed Nazi Ed Fields at a convention in California of the Institute for Historical Review. But when he finally plays the tape, he gets a pleasant surprise. On tape, Rich and Fields are talking about Nazis and Jews when into the room walks David Duke, who, in all the convention excitement, has locked himself out of his own hotel room. "We don't want to talk to you," Rich chides Duke playfully. "We've had enough of you for one year." She is more interested in Fields, a real Nazi, who was bold enough to wear his swastika for drinks in the hotel bar after the prior evening's banquet. His Klan outfit is all right, Fields tells Rich, but "there's something about the swastika and the brown shirt I like better."

Duke, who doesn't take rejection easily, hangs around the edges of the conversation, until it turns to Hitler's plan for the Jews.

> FIELDS: Yeah. Of course, they actually do deserve . . . (Duke laughs)
> . . . No seriously, they actually do deserve everything they get.
> And if it was extermination, they would have deserved it.
> RICH: Well, David, what do you think?
> DUKE: I think, ummmm . . .
> FIELDS: They're a pest. You know, when your house is rotting, you
> have termites, you get rid of the pests.
> DUKE: Well, as I say, people generally deserve what they push on
> other people. I think they're trying to exterminate our race. I
> think probably in a moral sense, the Jewish people have been a
> blight. I mean as a whole, not every Jew. And they probably
> deserve to go into the ashbin of history. But, saying that and
> actually shooting or killing people in masses are two different
> things. I'm not advocating some sort of extermination. I think the
> best thing is to resettle them some place where they can't exploit
> others. And I don't think they can live among themselves. I really
> don't. I think their numbers will dwindle rapidly and they'll have
> a great deal of problems.

Later, Fields stresses the need for a new National Socialist government "where the threat of the Jew wheedling his way in again would be taken care of." Duke cautions him about calling himself a National Socialist: "You need to leave your options open."

> FIELDS: They call ev–everyone's a Nazi who doesn't go along with the Jewish line.
> DUKE: But there's a difference.
> FIELDS: So why not say, "All right, I am. What are you going to do about it, Jew?"
> DUKE: Well, there really is a difference. Of course, I'm on a different tactic. I'm trying to bring new people in, like a drummer. The difference is, if they can call you a Nazi and make it stick–tough, really hard–it's going to hurt. It's going to hurt the ability of people to open their minds to what you're saying. It's going to hurt your ability to communicate with them. It's unfortunate it's like that.

Fields doubts people will begin to "come over" until a bad depression hits.

"I think that's a very defeatist philosophy," says Duke, the entrepreneur at heart.

"No, I look forward to it happening," says the committed Nazi. He continues:

> FIELDS: It doesn't take that many people though to start something rolling. Hitler started with seven men.
> DUKE: Right, that's what I'm trying to say to you.
> FIELDS: And most people didn't want to have anything to do with him.
> DUKE: Right! And don't you think it can happen right now, if we put the right package together? Don't you think that there are millions of Americans that are alienated and are looking for something, and the truth is the truth, and give 'em something to believe in?
> RICH: And guru Duke will come along!
> DUKE: Not necessarily me–somebody–my God! I might have to do it because nobody else might come along to do it.
> FIELDS: Well, maybe I wouldn't go out and say I'm a Nazi, you know, Hitler, National Socialism–but I'd never deny it. I'd never deny it.

It's like a Christian—you know. When Christianity first started
they were feeding them to the lions. They still wore their crosses.
They went to their deaths, but they never gave up. It's like a faith.
It's not just politics. It's a religion.
DUKE: Well, I try to avoid it . . .
FIELDS: You have to feel it in your soul.
DUKE: I wheedle out of it because I'm a pragmatist.

By now, Lance Hill has become one too. If the media and the
fencesitters wanted a smoking gun, this comes close. But he's been
wrong before on what works against David Duke. "A lot of people
thought we had exhausted the stuff on Nazism. We weren't sure
the Rich tape would have an impact." By now, the heightened
media coverage and the candidates' commercials were drowning
out LCARN's lonely message of Duke's moral extremism. Maybe
Duke's voice itself could cut through the din.


Edwin Edwards has always enjoyed a special relationship with the
Pentecostal church. It goes back to his own youth in Avoyelles
Parish. His mother was a Catholic and his father was devoutly anti-
Catholic. Though baptized in the One True Church, Edwin and his
brother Marion were attracted to Nazarene tent revivals that
would set up near their home on the Red River. There Edwin
learned his Scripture and a certain cadence of speech that served
him well in his career.

Later, as a candidate addressing tent revivals, Edwards would
evoke knowing smiles from the elders with his remembrances of the
brush arbor. The test of faith, he recalled, was how well people
would concentrate despite the swarms of mosquitoes in those little
outdoor meetings: "We'd watch the folks out of the corner of our
eye. If we saw them slapping, we'd know they weren't right." The
weeklong, statewide Pentecostal tent meeting in Tioga was a
required stop for politicians at election time. If you could remember
a scrap of Scripture, this was where to pull it out. Things got a bit
out of hand in 1986, though, when J. E. Jumonville Jr. got excited
and started speaking in tongues.

229

Despite the stories about women and gambling, Edwards could always count on solid Pentecostal support. After all, explained one minister in 1983, "He doesn't drink or smoke." Following his trials and his all-out promotion of legalized gambling, Edwards lost some favor with the rank-and-file faithful. But not with the pastors of the largest Pentecostal church in Louisiana, G. A. Mangun, his wife Vesta and their son Anthony. The bond has a little bit to do with politics.

At the opening of the Sunday evening service at the beautiful new church in Alexandria, Anthony Mangun asks the children who had the Holy Spirit to come up onstage. From the two dozen kids gathered there, Mangun singles out a tow-headed lad. "How do you know you have the Holy Spirit, little Jimmy?"

"I talk in tongues."

It's going around, professes Brother Mangun. "The Catholic bishop of Alexandria, he's a tongue talker. Who would think it?"

After a song by his mother, Anthony introduces the man who is no stranger to the Pentecostals. "The governor has always been kind to the Pentecostals," says Mangun, who then relates the story of how the church didn't have the $30,000-$40,000 to install sprinklers on the outside of the new church when it was built. Their only hope was to call the governor. "We called him and said not to do anything illegal. He said he would see what he could do. In 15 minutes, we got a call from the fire marshal, who said we didn't have to put in the sprinkling system. Let us stand and give thanks."

And he gives the mike to Edwards, who continues the story: "Brother Mangun, what I didn't tell you is that the fire marshal said, 'But, Governor, what you don't know is it gets hot in those meetings.' "

He thanks Sister Mangun for her beautiful music. "A fellow asked if he could sing at the inauguration. I told him I've been inaugurated three times and Sister Mangun has been there three times. I'm not taking any chances."

He points out Clyde Holloway's wife Kathy in the congregation: "I don't know a kinder, gentler, more Christian man than Clyde Holloway. Getting to know him has been one of the pluses of this campaign." That's an understatement, considering the number Holloway has been doing on Roemer and the split within the GOP.

He's laying it on thick now. So important has the word of God been in his life that he chose his children's names from the Bible: "Anna, for the sister of Mary. Victoria, for victory. Stephen, for the first Christian martyr. And David, for King David. Though I should have called him Jonathan, for I've not had a more faithful friend." His youngest son blushes.

"I'm 64. I've made my mistakes but I've tried to be available. Anytime I can be of service, let me know. I'm not a perfect human being. But when I'm ready to go from this earth to my reward, I know I will be judged by that infallible judge. A judge who knows in my heart I'll never be as great as He . . . but when the time came I stood and fought the good fight. . . ."

Edwards has perfected the art of talking in church, and the congregation responds more warmly than when he was introduced. He may not have the old Pentecostal support, but he figures enough of them will be there when he needs them. Just as surely he will be there for them. For Brother Mangun is not waiting until the election. "Governor, we need you one more time. We're busing in 600 to 700 kids a week. They've passed a law for busdrivers where you practically have to have an advanced degree to drive. We need some relief on this so our busdrivers can drive these kids. We know you will help us with that."

Edwards nods. With the prayers — and votes — of the Pentecostals, it's as good as done.

# 15. "Skin Him Up"

**B**uddy Roemer is greeting the lunchtime crowd at the Boudin King, one of Jennings' most popular eateries. He's not happy about it. He can tolerate meeting people. But does he really have to watch the sausage-making? "You know how you've seen politicians wearing Indian bonnets. I said I'd never do that. And here I am." The governor grows a bit pale as the kitchen worker mixes the rice, beef, liver, pork and seasoning in a huge vat. Then with a turn of the hand crank the sausage is shoved into the casing, which, of course, is the lining of a pig's intestines. Now to eat.

Roemer is resigned to his fate. "Call Caroline. Tell her I love her. Tell her I died with a whimper."

He responds, at least, to the economic data on boudin. "You know this place makes 6,000 pounds of this a week, and it's all eaten in Jennings."

The parish seat of Jefferson Davis Parish is believed to be a good area for Roemer to recapture his rural conservative base from 1987. This is rice country settled largely by Midwesterners—they named one town Iowa—who didn't cotton to the Legislature's renaming the parish for the president of the Confederacy.

Roemer may benefit from the reform backlash in the parish over the sheriff's race. Three-term Sheriff Dallas Cormier is facing a tough reelection challenge, especially since he has just been indicted on 36 counts of malfeasance. This is not a federal investigation. The Jennings Police Department began its probe when three state prisoners in the parish jail took off for the evening in a parish truck, got drunk and wrecked it. That led to other revelations of lax jail administration and a flock of election challengers. In a fight for his own political life, Cormier won't be of much help to Edwin Edwards.

In this kind of atmosphere, there are votes here for Buddy Roemer to get. There's also a huge Duke sign in the middle of town with no Roemer support visible. Sure, he saw it, says Roemer, as he sits down to a table full of boudin. "Duke is getting support because he's new, he's a novelty."

And what's the incumbent doing about it, especially in his own base of North Louisiana?

"I've been taking votes off of him. That's why I've been up there the past three weekends. I'm seeing it happen. People are starting to think twice."

The governor is thinking twice about this boudin, having nibbled on one end. His attitude toward the lump of sausage on his plate seems to sum up his whole distaste for retail politics. Sure, he could be a better candidate, but: "What's that Lyle Lovett song? 'If I were the man you wanted me to be, I wouldn't be the man I am.' That's about how I feel."

In this final week of the campaign, with his poll numbers not having budged in six weeks, the governor is chatting about the unmentionable. "If I don't win, my job will be to be on the phone the next day, telling these guys, 'We need you more than ever.' Let me tell you, if Duke wins, there will be a real problem in this little burg, meaning Louisiana. Can you see him and the Legislature? I may even run for that. You guys would see another side of my ass. I'd want a part of that."

Getting out on the campaign trail at least is giving Roemer a feel for Duke's growing strength. It doesn't feel good. The media and poll consensus still favors Roemer and Edwards, but it's clear none of the three has a lock on the runoff.

If a campaign has life, it will begin to show two weeks before an election when the grass roots sprout and begin covering neighborhoods and communities. Grass-roots organization may have a minimal effect in a statewide race dominated by TV advertising. But in a close race, especially a primary, turnout becomes the major factor—and that's when an organized, motivated volunteer army can push thousands more to the polls. Roemer received a groundswell of volunteers toward the end of the 1987 race, after he was on a roll and really no longer needed them. In 1991, he decided early on that the electronic media would carry his message. Despite the campaign rhetoric about planting and harvesting, staffers say the governor knew he would not put in the time cultivating the workers in the field.

Some volunteers are springing up anyway, though few individuals who offer to help are put to any good use. Little direction and assistance are coming from Baton Rouge. At the New Orleans headquarters, local manager Michelle Shauer says she was told by Sam Dawson that "yardsigns were not his concern." And apparently no one else's. In Shreveport, leading Republican organizer Harriet Belchic offered early to begin putting together a phone bank, but hears nothing more from the campaign until the final weeks. In Baton Rouge, the friction between Republican women and the pro-choice Women for Roemer limits the already limited GOP presence at headquarters. In other areas, the most active Republican volunteers either are helping Holloway or are waiting on the sidelines for the runoff. The week before the primary election, many of them leave the state for a National Republican Women's Club convention.

Roemer has no business being in this close a race, but it's been a pattern in his politics to spot his opponents an advantage and then to pull it out in the stretch. Several factors still favor the incumbent. Though he's still being pounded on the road by all of the candidates, only Edwards can afford to attack Roemer with TV commercials. And that can be a mixed threat. Edwards' ads mock Roemer's with a clock turning backwards and the announcer saying, "There's a reason Buddy Roemer doesn't want to turn back the clock. He wants you to forget the four years of higher taxes and the jobs he has given to out-of-state people. . . ." They are hard-hitting spots, but the viewer is left to consider the source. Edwards' own credibility is lower than Roemer's and his attacks on the incumbent are nothing new.

Coming into the final ten days, Roemer still controls his own message, which remains more credible than he is. If he can keep hammering away at the need to stay the course, he feels he can hold onto conservative Reagan voters and open a small lead on Edwards and Duke. Now's the time when voters are tuned into the campaign, and nothing is standing in the way of Roemer's message.

Eight days before the election, a man with a briefcase and a checkbook walks into all three major New Orleans television stations to buy every available 30-second spot left on the schedules. Jack Kent, the excitable and unpredictable owner of a hazardous waste recycling company called Marine Shale, plops down more than $500,000 for a last-minute, third-party offensive on Buddy Roemer.

The spots were brutal but not crass. Slickly produced, they carried a message wrapped in political kryptonite: humor. There's Buddy Roemer's face with a halo over his head and a message slamming the governor for being a hypocrite. There's another with Roemer beneath gathering storm clouds, representing the worsening condition of the state during his term. The spots advocate no other candidate while urging viewers to vote for anyone but Roemer.

Months before, Kent hired Washington-based consultant Deno Seder to cut the ads. He picked the right guy. Seder got his start in Louisiana politics, airing the first commercials to attack with humor. One of the first political consultants to spot and use his talent was Buddy Roemer in Kelly Nix's 1975 race for superintendent of education. Having done other work for Roemer over the years, Seder conveniently had a variety of Roemer images on file. Kent liked what he saw when he reviewed Seder's commercials. "Let's skin him up," he said.

Kent would say that Roemer is only getting his due: "He's tried to put me out of business. I can do the same to him." Kent's Marine Shale plant near Morgan City has been fined $4 million by Roemer's Department of Environmental Quality and is under investigation by the federal Environmental Protection Agency for illegal disposal of hazardous waste.

In the mid-'80s, Jack Kent claimed to have invented a kiln process that changes the molecular structure of hazardous waste to make a benign chunk of gravel, suitable for use on roadbeds, driveways and playgrounds. Alternately, it's been hailed as an environmental breakthrough and an ecological timebomb. His process is far cheaper than standard hazardous waste disposal incineration. But does it work? The state and the feds never have come up with a satisfactory answer to that after years of inspections and regulation.

Kent is an old friend of Edwards. With Edwards' allies working as his lobbyists, Kent received a permit from the state DEQ to operate a recycling plant. Former DEQ Secretary Pat Norton remembers being ushered into a Mansion meeting with Edwards, Kent and Marine Shale attorney George Eldredge in 1985. Norton said in a newspaper interview that Edwards flatly told her to grant the company the hazardous waste recycling permit. "If it hadn't been for all the pressure he (Edwards) put on me, I never would have granted the permit." When nearby residents charged that the plant was responsible for outbreaks of a rare form of cancer in children and when the feds began asking questions, Edwards authorized a state investigation. From then on, says Edwards, "Kent has hated me."

Roemer's DEQ stepped up monitoring of Marine Shale and slapped it with fines. The EPA barred federal agencies from doing business with the recycler. Though under federal criminal investigation, Marine Shale remains in business with its old state permit, and Jack Kent hopes to retire Buddy Roemer.

As soon as the spots hit the air, "paid for by John Kent," press and politicos assume there is an Edwards-Kent conspiracy. "I knew nothing about it," says Edwards. "Jack Kent can't stand the sight of me ever since I authorized DEQ to investigate him." Kent says basically the same thing, but that "anyone is better than Roemer." The attack ads saturate the New Orleans TV market, which reaches one third of the state's population. Gross rating points there top 1,000, which means that every TV viewer sees them at least ten times, twice the amount needed to make an impression on the most doltish voter. This has all the look and smell of major-league dirty tricks. But with so much going on in the final week of the campaign, there is nothing solid to refute Kent and Edwards. All the public will remember seeing is Buddy Roemer under the halo and the storm clouds, over and over again.

Finally, something has Buddy Roemer angry again. "This is disgraceful," he snarls on New Orleans TV. Privately, however, he thought the commercials were a ray of hope. As he dished out jambalaya to LSU fans before the Arkansas State game, the governor describes his real initial reaction. Bending his knee and clenching his fist, he says, "When I saw that ad I said, 'Victory!' These guys have just given me something I've needed — an enemy."

Roemer expects Kent's entry into the race will boomerang on Edwards if Roemer can tie the two together as partners in politics and pollution.

So how will he do that? Is a commercial in the works?

Roemer is signing a fan's visor. "We're talking about it. But we find that the media is a more effective way to answer that. I've found that people are skeptical of my spots. And that increases with each election I've run. So I try not to react." The daily reporters are onto the Edwards-Kent story. "I think the *Picayune* has something coming out."

He reassures some business supporters from Baton Rouge: "The numbers we have coming in show we're holding and Edwards is dropping like a rock."

Roemer appears oddly relaxed for a man fighting for his political life. When another supporter presses him on when and how the campaign would respond to Kent, Roemer cools him. "Hey, man. It's the weekend." Not only that, but it's almost game time. And Buddy's date has arrived. The tall, blond, big-haired young woman is wearing cowboy boots and a blue-jean jacket studded with rhinestones.

"Why, Sherry," says Roemer. "You look like a rock star." They cross the street and disappear into the crowd at the gate.

Across town, Edwin Edwards works a roomful of chiropractors.

The polls open in six and a half days.

In the final week of the primary campaign, the David Duke Show is rolling south from Bossier City to Alexandria to Lake Charles to Lafayette and then Baton Rouge. Over 600 supporters overflow the Baton Rouge Hilton ballroom. They are primarily working class, most either under 30 or over 50, as Duke has yet to attract yuppie voters — at least to his rallies.

The steady media barrage on Duke, like the recent CNN report heavy with Nazi imagery, seems to stiffen these folks' resolve to back Duke. "The press is out to get him because they can't control him," says a retiree. To them, the past is just that. Robert Cook is an LSU student with longish hair who says he can relate to what Duke is going through. "A year ago I was on Chimes Street, drinking and smoking and partying. I was saved. I'm a Christian. I wouldn't want someone to come back at me about my past and say I haven't changed."

The rally follows a tight format. After ample time for merchandise and t-shirt sales, the national anthem is sung by former runner-up Miss Louisiana, Julie Jones. Attorney general candidate Jim McPherson is like a lot of people here: "Four years ago I voted for Buddy Roemer. I wanted a revolution, and now I'm going to get it if we put David Duke in office." Then former congressman John Rarick introduces the candidate as "the only man who tells you what you want to hear and what the country needs."

Duke hits the stage with arms over his head, receiving the cheers and egging on more. "Are you ready for a new governor?"

"Yes!" scream back 500 people.

"The pollsters say my voters fly beneath radar. Well, we're up on the radar screens tonight." The crowd cheers for itself.

"The pundits and pollsters say the people may have voted for me for Senate but they won't for governor since that office is about getting things done. Well, they are not saying that now."

"They're scared," yells the young man in the work shirt.

Duke wastes no time getting down to all that ails society: a government out of control, the welfare state, the rising underclass. He even brings up a few issues the governor has some control over. "We have new licenses, fees and taxes coming out of the wazoo. You can't even take a cane pole down to the pond and fish without a license. A lady came up to me in church the other day. A feisty lady. She told me the next thing they're going to license is having sex and if Roemer is governor they'll raise the fee every year."

The Democrat in this race is no alternative, he assures them: "Going back to Edwards is like moving from New Orleans to Detroit to escape crime."

He hits Roemer for holding a fundraiser in New York City. "Why should someone in New York give $5,000 to the governor of Louisiana?"

"They're scared," repeats the work shirt.

"I don't have $5,000 fundraisers. I have $10 red beans and rice dinners, though it could be dangerous in a packed house." Duke laughs at his wicked little joke, then regains his indignation to remind the crowd which two candidates belong to the NAACP, a group that supports gun control.

"Shame, shame," says one woman amid the cascade of boos.

"The NAACP believes in reverse discrimination. I believe in equal rights for all." In fact, he says, "I think Clarence Thomas will make a great Supreme Court justice."

A more subdued cheer.

"I really felt badly for him. The forces that are attacking me are the same ones that are attacking Clarence Thomas because he is conservative."

Since the state lottery has been up and running for a month, Duke adds to his repertoire of welfare abuse. "It should be illegal for welfare recipients to buy lottery tickets." No one here seems to have heard about Roemer's workfare reforms, since Duke still gets good mileage out of his call to make "able-bodied welfare recipients" work for their welfare checks. "If we don't change the system, there is no future, for there will be fewer people pulling and more riding."

On to crime. Not only has Buddy Roemer executed a mere five convicted murderers, he also furloughed a convict working at the Mansion who promptly went out and murdered his ex-wife. "When I work at the Mansion," pledges Duke, "there will be no violent criminals around my kids."

His favorite crime story is about a Metairie shopowner who was accosted by two thugs in her store. By the time the police answered her 911 call, says Duke, the intruders were beating her with the telephone receiver. "The officers grabbed them and threw them against the wall and said, 'Are you guys crazy? Don't you know this is David Duke's district?' Ladies and gentlemen, won't it be great when every law enforcement officer in Louisiana can say the same thing?"

"Duke, Duke, Duke." That line is always a showstopper.

From there he rolls through busing and birth control and cutting taxes and the state's image. "They say David Duke's election will hurt the tourist industry. Ladies and gentlemen, when I make the runoff, every hotel room will be filled with reporters. Every restaurant will be hiring new cooks."

All those jobs, jobs, jobs have people on their feet. Duke has this room revved. Time has come to tell them what they can do for him.

"Roemer and Edwards are putting out a hatchet job on me. Here's what I need from you. First thing to do is go home and call somebody. Call everybody. Even make long-distance calls."

One of his opponents, he adds darkly, has "gone to the jails and signed up the prisoners to vote. The jails have voted absentee already. I need the silent majority to be less silent. Take a bumpersticker. You might get a flat tire, but that's what this country is all about. Do not be intimidated. Stand up. . . . Don't forget. I'll be checking your bumpers."

Now for the real help. "I've got to raise money to make our checks good and get these commercials on." Volunteers and staffers with oyster buckets take their positions at the head of the aisles. People are reaching for their wallets.

"Now wait a minute, this is the way it works. If you give cash, you have to get a doubloon for it. That's Buddy Roemer's law. You got that. Can you help me? If you want to give more than $25, you can write a check at the back of the room. If you can offer major help, we need it."

Minutes later, Duke, like a preacher, is standing at the door shaking hands with everyone leaving. This is an added treat for the faithful. "We've got it this time," an older man says. "Hammond's gone wild for you," says the woman behind him.

A writer asks about the commercials Dave Treen cut attacking Duke's claims of military service. "I think it backfired on him," says Duke. "Vets are calling me every day with their support."

Roemer, he says, is finished. "The turning point was his bringing Bush in. He got a lot of money but he lost a lot of votes. It hurt his rural votes terribly. . . . Roemer realized too late I would win. He made the classic mistake of preparing for the old foe instead of the young foe."

Signing a fan's shirt, Duke predicts, "I'll get 45-50 percent of the white vote, Roemer will get 35, Edwards about 10. I'll come in at about 33 to 35 percent, Edwards at 28 to 31 and Roemer at 26 to 28."

The New Orleans weekly *Gambit* has just run a long excerpt of Duke's and Nazi Ed Fields' 1986 interview with doctoral student Evelyn Rich, and WWL-TV is playing the tape itself. So what about it, a reporter asks Duke.

"That was out of context. It's a rehash of years ago. I don't hold those positions. When you have a conversation, you don't use words the way it really reflects your feelings." He continues, "I had just met the guy (Fields). When you are trying to bring people around in late-night conversations, you try to soften up someone very radical, you try to have empathy and see their point of view."

Jim McPherson confirms that: "I've seen priests talk to possible suicides and say they don't believe in God either. Sometimes you give verbal agreement to move them off of their position."

A CNN crew wants an interview. Art Harris' piece about Duke's Nazi ties has just aired and the candidate is still outraged. "Is this about the election? You're not going to show the old stuff, the swastikas, are you?"

No swastikas, he's assured.

"Where do you want me to stand?"


Getting out of his car, Edwin Edwards takes one look at the well-dressed crowd of about 1,100 people, mostly black, entering and overflowing the Shreveport Holidome. He smiles. And he dances a little jig.

The well-planned rally (the steering committee has been meeting weekly for two months in Gus Mijalis' office) has exceeded expectations. More than 500 are turned away. This is the moment Edwin Edwards has been waiting for. After a full year of nonstop campaigning on the rubber-chicken circuit, after sniping comments about how old and dispirited he looked, after speculation that he was bankrupt of money and ideas and would not finish the race and might even miss the runoff, finally the eternal candidate is seeing his campaign come together when it counts. He could still finish out of the money Saturday, but at this point his prospects are every bit as good as, maybe better than, Duke's or Roemer's.

"I've seen him when he was not as high as he is now," says Mijalis. "Back when things were not too strong. Still, he made all the functions. We'd drive sometimes till 1 a.m. and he'd be ready to go in the morning."

Now Edwards' fate comes down to turnout among black voters. He is counting on black turnout being no more than ten points below white, the normal spread in a primary. But he has to get that without the street money he normally would spread over all black communities. Gus Mijalis remembers the 1983 campaign's $500,000 budget for election week expenses in ten northwestern parishes. "This year we'll spend less than $60,000 for election week. That's ballots and transportation. And a lot of volunteers."

Many of the middle-class blacks here tonight were Roemer supporters in 1987. In four years Roemer neglected his political ties in the black community as badly as he did among white businessmen. He was in Shreveport the week before to attend a well-publicized rally on his birthday at a black-owned restaurant. Sixty attended. The governor's key black supporter in Shreveport, state Representative Alphonse Jackson, is under a cloud for accepting money to help a Democratic congressional candidate and then working for the Republican incumbent. The state Democratic Party has filed suit in the middle of Jackson's hard-fought reelection campaign. The *Shreveport Times* ran a front-page picture of Roemer and Jackson embracing at the birthday party. "It's a death grip for both," says a local pundit.

Polls show Roemer leading in Caddo Parish, but there's a difference. "Last time the streets were on fire," says a consultant. It's cold out there now.

The Sunday before the election finds Edwards mounting up a caravan of recreational vehicles for a series of rallies down Bayou Lafourche. It will be Edwards' last scheduled public appearance of the primary, as he has set aside the final week to personally make his election-day arrangements with black political organizations.

Edwards rides in the posh Picou family RV, with Candy's brother Richard at the wheel and assorted other relatives of his girlfriend along for the ride. At every stop, from Napoleonville to Galliano, he works over the incumbent: "I am tired of Buddy Roemer using our children as pawns," he responds to the governor's education spots. "You ask him what time it is. He says, 'Children first.' Listen, I was for children first when Buddy Roemer was a children." In Thibodaux, he takes a rare shot at Duke: "He calls James Meredith a hero when six years ago he was burning crosses on his yard."

At every stop, David Edwards is at his father's side. He never leaves. Even at a cookout at Irving and Elizabeth Blatt's secluded home in Thibodaux, David stands directly in front of Edwin, who stands on a half barrel and holds David's shoulders while he speaks.

Over 1,500 people meet Edwards at the final stop, at the Galliano Centroplex, for sausage and white beans and beer. The Saints won today—Edwards won his bet—and he wants to remind the folks that quarterback Bobby Hebert only wears a Saints uniform because Edwin Edwards intervened in the salary negotiations with owner Tom Benson. And of course the Saints would have packed up and left long before that had Edwards not talked Tom Benson into buying the team.

Bob d'Hemecourt, who has driven in from New Orleans, is trying to keep up with two beepers. He is pumped. "Election night, we're asking Roemer for state police security. But I want to pick them.

Look at these guys," he refers to Edwards' private security detail. "Half of them are looking at Edwin. I want them looking at the crowd." D'Hemecourt is fantasizing Edwards' victory speech. "If we get in with Duke, on election night, he's gonna say this is our race and he'll tell all the out-of-staters, including out-of-state-owned newspapers (the *Picayune,* that is), to stay out of it. This is our fight."

Onstage, Edwin Edwards is wrapping up his last campaign speech. And just in case he doesn't have Buddy Roemer to kick around anymore, he swings his last low blow. "He says he puts Children First. Go look at his ex-wife's divorce petition," Edwards refers to Roemer's 1971 divorce. "She charged him with abandonment. How is he going to put your children first if he doesn't his own?"

The crowd gasps. D'Hemecourt shakes his head: "He doesn't need to do that." But no one had ever beaten Edwards before Roemer did. Who knows what he needs to close that old wound?

As Edwards climbs in and out of RV's in little bayou communities, Buddy Roemer is enjoying the balance of his weekend. Raymond Strother has camped out at the Mansion for the final few weeks. Having cut his last spots, he has done all he feels is worth doing. Roemer's own poll shows he is leading but not moving, and Duke is coming on. Strother thinks his candidate is finished, and the candidate apparently agrees. "I'm doomed, there is no hope," Roemer told Strother more than once in the closing week. "I couldn't tell if he believed that or not," says Strother. They both agreed, however, that all that could be done had been done with the final TV commercials and that frenetic personal campaigning would change nothing.

So why blow a weekend? Sunday morning finds Strother in front of the TV in the second-floor family room watching the Saints game. Roemer wanders in wearing gym shorts. They watch the game together. Buddy gets a beer. Three hours later, the second game begins. Roemer doesn't move.

As it starts getting dark outside, Strother says, "Buddy, if we had a split screen on the TV right now and Edwin was on one side and we were on the other, what would we see?"

Roemer grunts.

"We'd be on one side watching the game," continues Strother. "On the other side, I see Edwin on the phone, saying, 'What's going on in Grant?' or 'How's the Tenth Ward of Lafourche?' or 'Get that $10,000 in here tonight.'"

Roemer feels only slightly guilty. "Well, I'm going to New Orleans tomorrow. Have to give a speech."

Strother sees Roemer the next day as he's getting back from New Orleans at around six o'clock, about time for the poker game to start upstairs.


One of the drawbacks of having regular conversations with God is that from time to time the devil will want equal time. Poor Jimmy Swaggart. After losing the $10 million jury verdict to Marvin Gorman, he's been out of the news. Ten days before the election, in fact, he is out of state and saving souls in Southern California. The morning after celebrating his and Frances' 39th wedding anniversary, he would tell his congregation later, he sat in a friend's Jaguar under a grove of palm trees praying and studying. Then "it was like two hands took me and squeezed me. I turned right, toward Indio, about three miles away. I don't think the Lord would be pleased for me to say anything else, but one thing, I thank God there was a traffic policeman there." Unfortunately, 31-year-old Rosemary Garcia, a prostitute, was there too, when the policeman pulled Swaggart over for swerving. According to Garcia, Swaggart became nervous when he saw the cop, tried to shove some adult magazines under the seat and caused the car to swerve.

Back in Louisiana, the news of Jimmy's latest fall breaks just as the campaign enters its final week, and just as Anita Hill begins her sensational testimony against Clarence Thomas' confirmation. Over the weekend, the viewing audience is hijacked and interest in the governor's race plunges. With Jack Kent's anti-Roemer spots dominating the commercial breaks, it's a bad time to depend on the media to get a message out.

The *Picayune* and the *Morning Advocate* do small stories on the Edwards-Kent-Marine Shale connection that get no farther than Edwards' version of events. "He hates me," says Edwards of his indirect benefactor. He's also able to return fire. "Marine Shale has been operating for four years while Buddy Roemer was governor. Why hasn't he done anything about it?" Roemer's DEQ has fined Marine Shale, but has taken a back seat to the federal investigation, which is moving toward a 1992 trial date. That the recycler is still operating, hauling in gunk and turning out little gray pebbles, tends to undermine Roemer's role as the victim of politics and pollution.

At Roemer headquarters, Gordon Hensley is previewing a commercial Strother cut to hammer home the connection. "This is the symbol we've been waiting for," says Hensley, lighting another cigarette. "This is going to move some numbers." There is another complication, though. Roemer will have to pull some of his other commercials to make room for the new spot. By now, the full scope of the Kent buy is hitting home at Roemer headquarters. There is hardly a vacant 30 seconds of airtime left on any major station's schedule. Kent has made sure that if Roemer wants to respond, he will have to use some slots he already has booked for his "Don't Turn Back the Clock" message. Without that positive reinforcement, Roemer's anti-Edwards commercials, trailing Kent's anti-Roemer spots, could push more conservatives to Duke.

In most campaign headquarters in the final week, the fast pace intensifies when the candidate is there. When Buddy Roemer appears next to Hensley's cubicle, the room seems to relax. He looks over the new commercial. He approves.

"What's the head count on the Thomas confirmation," he asks the room.

"Fifty-two," answers a male voice.

"Forty-eight," responds a female's.

"That's Caroline," chuckles Dad. "She wants Thomas to get maybe two votes. She's got a poll. Thomas is dropping like a rock."

Chas Roemer, who is taking 10 days off from Harvard to campaign with his father, is angry about the Edwards quote in the *Times-Picayune*.

"Edwards has no idea of our relationship with our father or his relationship with our mother. He'd just better not meet my sister anytime soon. I'm pretty laid back, but she's not."

On Wednesday, the last night of tracking, Roemer's poll shows him leading Edwards 34-32, with Duke at 24 and rising.


A couple of black workers at the Pontchartrain Center in Kenner are opening the room partition to accommodate the overflow crowd of 1,000 at David Duke's campaign-closing rally. He is joined onstage by some Jefferson Parish candidates who have received his endorsement. Waving to the crowd is Republican state Senate candidate George Ackal Jr., the son of the late public service commissioner and a prominent Democrat. Earlier in the campaign, Ackal helped silk-screen signs at Edwards' headquarters.

This crowd on Duke's home turf includes a good number of well-dressed, middle-aged voters. He's given this rambling speech dozens of times, but he hits every applause line with full gusto. And his audience responds in kind, clapping, yelling, whistling, stomping. An anti-Duke Republican has come to view the Duke phenomenon, and she's alarmed: "What you see in this room is what Buddy Roemer didn't fix four years ago."

Onstage, Duke is touching on that very subject: "Roemer and Edwards are the same side of the pancake. One side is burnt, the other is light and fluffy. It's time to throw out the pancake and get some real meat and potatoes!"

He challenges the new press stories that Duke's election will chase out businesses: "We will have so many businesspeople come to the state because business wants a policy to hire the best-qualified person and not by race."

The mention of the press brings angry boos. Duke quiets them, "We owe a debt to the media. They pointed out who we should vote for."

That, of course, is not all the press did: "They have dragged my character through the mud in a way that makes the Clarence Thomas case look mild. It takes strength, but it's not my strength. I have strength because my faith is in Jesus Christ."

Mention of his new soulmate Clarence Thomas triggers a snipe at their common oppressor: "Wasn't it ironic to see Teddy Kennedy sitting on the committee?"

Boos and hisses roll through the crowd.

"You know, Kennedy doesn't harass women. He kills them. Ted has even attacked me a few times. They have a sign at the entrance to the Palm Beach estate that says: 'Trespassers will be violated.' "

The crowd is loving Duke's standup comedy routine. Duke has the perfect target, because with Kennedy and this audience, you can never swing too low.

"You know what William Smith told that woman? He said, 'Submit to me or I'll let Uncle Ted drive you home.' "

Andrew Martin and Bob d'Hemecourt tried to get Edwin Edwards to set up shop in another hotel rather than the Monteleone in the French Quarter. Maybe a bigger, more modern hotel with a larger ballroom and more elevators that work all the time. Not to mention the bad memories of 1987. But no dice. Edwards was thinking not of 1987 but of 1971, when he was unknown in New Orleans and the Monteleone provided him free rooms to base his operations in the city. He did not forget and he will not switch, even if the place is that much older, the elevators even slower and the rooms no longer free. There is a certain charm to the old hotel at Royal and Iberville. Presidents and heads of state have visited the grand new hotels across Canal Street, but at the Monteleone, Edwin Edwards will always be the king.

His room is 1545, the corner suite just below the penthouse. Edwards moved in in August and spent more and more time there as the weeks went on. Until now, Edwards has been making nearly every civic club meeting and coffee klatch he's invited to. For the last week, the schedule is wiped clean. "If something comes up anywhere in the state that we have to take care of, the plane is waiting at Lakefront," says d'Hemecourt. Other than that, Edwards will concentrate on his base in the black community.

Nothing is on today's schedule, but Edwards is dressed and ready for politics. His hands are shoved in his suit pockets as he leans back in a small chair pulled up to the glass-top table in the corner of the suite. Four phones are on the table, with three of them in use as d'Hemecourt, Martin and Cecil Brown make and receive calls from around the state. Drivers and security men lounge about the suite. Soap operas are on all three television screens mounted in the far corner of the room.

Black turnout remains a huge question mark. If fewer than 60 percent of blacks vote and white turnout is over 70, Edwards could run third behind two Republicans. The prize is New Orleans, where over half of the state's black population resides. The key there is money for the black political organizations to pay drivers, poll watchers and phone bankers to get voters to the polls. Some may think that David Duke's presence on the ballot would be enough to motivate a strong black turnout. That's what Bennett Johnston thought, that blacks would have nowhere else to go on election day, a Saturday. He was wrong. Blacks went fishing, to the mall, to Grandma's — or they just sat on the stoop.

Some blacks consider Duke less of a threat to them, and white moderates view him as an embarrassment. David Duke, the white man's new burden. Had Ben Bagert not pulled out and polled enough votes to force a runoff between Duke and Johnston, the threat might have become more real and blacks more motivated. But a primary election with only white candidates often does not motivate black voters to go to the polls. That's where the black political organizations come in. Their networks of drivers and canvassers can get voters to the polls, with sample ballots marked.

The system works pretty well. Almost too well, says one black New Orleanian. "I think we've created a monster with this money. You can't get a good turnout in New Orleans without that money."

And Edwin Edwards has no money, if you believe his latest campaign finance report showing a total of $1 million raised and spent in this campaign. Buddy Roemer's rules have put a big dent in the way Democrats traditionally raise and spend campaign money. But Edwards already has figured his way out of that box. Months ago, he began raising money the way Republicans do. The Republican National Committee has spent $108,000 in "soft money" on behalf of Buddy Roemer. Soft money is funds raised and spent by third parties, especially political parties, on a candidate's behalf. Theoretically, the candidate does not control where the money comes from or goes, and so it is not subject to the $5,000 cap on individual contributions.

By early October, Edwards is firming up his own soft money. He has put together a condominium arrangement with the other statewide Democratic candidates to raise and spend $940,000 through the Louisiana Democratic Party: Edwards' old angels who have maxed out in contributions to him can give unlimited funds to the Democratic Party to directly help Edwards. Nearly all of the soft money will go for election day expenses, mostly in the New Orleans area. It's a brilliant scheme to raise money like Republicans and spend it like Democrats.

The soft money approach has helped Edwards hold down costs. In past elections, with Edwards' building war chest, he was expected to spend money early with the black organizations — long before it really mattered in election week. "Four weeks ago I saw no evidence of money in the black community," says local operative Bill Schultz. "There was so much money four years ago that you were giving guys $5 to put signs on telephone poles." Now when it counts, in the final week, Edwards is seeing that the Democratic money is spent when and where it helps him most.

The most boring election three months ago has turned into Louisiana's strangest, maybe its closest. The final Mason-Dixon poll, taken in the last week of the primary, shows: Roemer, 31 percent; Edwards, 30; Duke, 22; others and undecided, 17. When the undecided who do not respond negatively to David Duke are added to his total, the "thermalized" results show a dead heat: Roemer, 31; Edwards, 30; Duke 29; others and undecided, 10.

Still, organized punditry cannot fathom an incumbent governor not making the runoff. Two days before the election, the *Times-Picayune* prints the forecasts of five pollsters and consultants. All predict Roemer to lead, except for Ed Renwick, who places him behind Edwards. All show Duke running third, except for Susan Howell, who has him tied for second with Edwards.

Friday morning, election eve. All the street money that will do him any good has been dispatched. Andrew Martin is trying hard to discourage any more requests from preachers or freelancers seeking "budgets." He knows what a soft touch the boss is for someone who offers to help him. Martin takes an "emergency call" transferred up from the front desk. He grimaces and cups the receiver, "Some woman wants $200 for three drivers." Edwards laughs at the inflation rate. As Martin tries to brush her off, Edwards predictably relents: "Oh, you just as soon . . ."

Martin is agitated. "I'm gonna put him on a boat somewhere," says Martin later. "I had it all balanced this morning."

Edwards reviews the cluster of printed ballots from the organizations who are getting them out on the streets tonight. Most have Edwards' picture and ballot number on top, followed by the names and numbers of other contributing Democrats, from Melinda Schwegmann for lieutenant governor to Richard Ieyoub for attorney general, on down to Jerry Fowler for elections commissioner.

A few renegade ballots are in the pack. Edwards admires a ballot for Republican attorney general candidate Ben Bagert. The headline reads, "Vote the entire Democratic ticket," and includes Bagert's name below Edwards' and Schwegmann's. This is an old trick, like putting a white candidate's ballot number next to a black candidate's picture to fool illiterate voters. "Very slick," says Edwards. "The son of a bitch."

Not all ballots feature Edwards' name. BOLD is the only major black organization to endorse Buddy Roemer. This makes BOLD a special project for the Edwards team. A number of splinter groups have been formed and financed to outdo BOLD in the group's own neighborhoods. "Rumor is there's a bounty out on BOLD ballots," says d'Hemecourt. "I don't know anything about it." There are even reports that some BOLD ballots — well, they look like BOLD's — have number 5 (Edwards' number) next to Roemer's name. "Must be a printer's error," concludes Edwards as he inspects samples.

Candy Picou comes in from shopping and wants to show her new things to Reed of *Vogue*, who's trying to follow the politics. Candy and friends are going to a concert at the Superdome. Edwards is concerned about her getting over there. "We'll have a driver," says d'Hemecourt. "I've got everyone on tonight."

At this point for Edwards, everything is reduced to numbers. Not poll numbers, just numbers. He memorizes and views each set as some augury of Saturday's results: "The Roemer campaign says they had 300 at their Bossier rally. Our people counted 126. He had 2,500 in '87." Lake Charles, he notes, was a bigger disaster. "They expected 1,000 people and they had 92, including the 3 people I sent to count."

Now if he could only get down a bet. "I just missed one," says Edwards. "Some idiot in Lake Charles wanted to bet $25,000 Duke would come in first. I told the fella who called me, 'Cover it immediately.' Then he called back and said they were taking it themselves, the son of a bitch."

Finally, it's time for predictions. D'Hemecourt scribbles his out on a scrap of yellow paper: "EWE, 500,000; Duke, 410,000; Buddy, 365,000; Clyde, 45,000; Others, 35,000." Edwards bases his on a 67 percent turnout, 70 percent among whites and 60 among blacks. He calls it: Edwards, 34.7 percent; Duke, 30; Roemer, 26.9; others, 8.4.

JOHN MAGINNIS

Duke on primary night with his daughters Kristin (left) and Erika.

JAMES TERRY III

Mob scene: In the runoff, Duke received state police protection from troopers Brad Stewart (left) and Beauregard Torres.

Duke supporters defiant to the end.

Young supporter in Crowley.

Duke addresses Franklinton rodeo rally from mule–drawn wagon.

The old master in the runoff.

Duke and the crowds at Crowley Rice Festival parade.

JAMES TERRY III

Dukewatchers: (at left) Beth Rickey; (below, from left) Larry Powell, Lance Hill and Rev. Jim Stovall.

A. J. SISCO

JAMES TERRY III

Anti–abortion protestors demonstrate on the Capitol steps for the override of governor's veto.

Anti-abortion leader state Rep. Woody Jenkins.

After and Before Falls: Frances and Jimmy Swaggart.

# SOME CHANGE IS ONLY SKIN DEEP

## BEFORE                    AFTER

He changed his face. He changed his political image. But he can't change the truth.

David Duke is skillfully exploiting our racial resentments and fears. He's using race to elevate himself to power.

Duke has forewarned us of his secret agenda. In 1986 Duke chillingly discussed his ominous plans in a taped interview with Evelyn Rich. Duke was a mature 35 years old. He had long since left the klan and declared himself a born-again Christian.

Duke told the interviewer that he thought that "the Jewish people have been a blight . . . And they probably deserve to go into the ashbin of history . . . " Reminiscent of Hitler's anti-Semitic plans, Duke calmly suggested that Jews should be removed from America. "I think the best thing is to resettle them some place where they can't exploit others."

There's more. The topic of Hitler arose in the interview. Joe Fields, an avowed Nazi, reminded Duke that "Hitler started with seven men." Duke promptly responded:

"Right! And don't you think it can happen here, right now, if we put the right package together? . . . I might have to do it because nobody else might come along to do it."

This was David Duke's dream only five years ago.

Your vote on November 16th will decide something far greater than the governorship. It will signal to the world not only our choice of candidates, but also our choice of values. It will determine in coming years how Americans will confront the problems of poverty, crime, drugs, and unemployment.

Will we turn to one another, or against one another? Will we extend a hand of friendship, or point the finger of hate?

Many argue that we are confronted with two bad choices. But there is considerable difference between good-ole-boy politics and genocide.

Someday we will all have to account for how we chose between the two.

Imagine the future. Imagine explaining to your grandchildren the actions you took when the merchant of hate begged your support. Rogues come and go. But a Duke victory threatens more than our state treasury or environment. A Duke victory threatens to irreparably injure our state's reputation, our human dignity, and our nation's principles.

Some argue that Duke would be ineffective as Governor — thus harmless. Perhaps he would be. But think for a moment about the meaning of a Duke victory. What moral lesson would our children learn? That hatred toward minorities is acceptable — a mere blot on an otherwise fine resume.

The Governorship is not the only office at stake. The Governor's mansion will provide Duke with a springboard to develop a national movement. He is an ambitious man with no commitment to Louisiana. He has been frank about his designs on the White House. Imagine the daunting power. The Armed Forces. The Nuclear arsenal. This in the hands of a man who only five years ago embraced Hitler. Will history record that David Duke was Louisiana's contribution to humanity? A sad legacy for future generations.

The events of the past weeks have turned friend against friend, neighbor against neighbor. We have been pilloried by the world press. We are portrayed as a state of mean-spirited, half-witted bigots.

We know another Louisiana. We know the kindness of the Bayou fisherman. The hospitality of the upcountry farmer. The generous spirit of the urban dweller.

We've seen hard times in Louisiana. And we are angry. But we are not blind. We will not allow our passions and fears to deliver our State to the demagogues.

The Louisiana Coalition Against Racism and Nazism.
The Louisiana Coalition Against Racism and Nazism is a statewide organization committed to racial and religious understanding.

Yes, I want to help build a better future for Louisiana. Enclosed is my contribution for:

$100     $50     $25     $10
☐          ☐        ☐         ☐

Mail To:

Louisiana Coalition Against Racism and Nazism,
234 Loyola Suite 915, New Orleans, LA 70112

## IT IS NOT HIS PAST THAT WE FEAR. IT IS HIS FUTURE.

Sources: Evelyn Rich Interview with Joe Fields and David Duke, 1986, Culver City, California. A copy of this audio-taped interview is held in the Evelyn Rich Collection, Rare Books and Manuscripts, Howard-Tilton Memorial Library, Tulane University, New Orleans. The complete transcript is available through the Coalition.

Paid for by the Louisiana Coalition Against Racism and Nazism, a political action committee, James I. Stovall, Chairman. Not authorized by any candidate or candidate's committee. Contributions for this state campaign are not deductible for federal income tax purposes.

Coalition ad showing Duke before and after plastic surgery.

Around the glass–top table in Monteleone suite 1545: (from left) Bob d'Hemecourt, Cecil Brown and Edwards.

Edwards and Candy at 1992 Capitol Correspondents Gridiron Show. Daughter Vicki is looking over Edwards' shoulder.

Edwards campaigning in Raceland (son David in foreground).

JAMES TERRY III

Sammy Nunez.

John Alario.

Jack Kent.

Sheriff Harry Lee.

JOHN MAGINNIS

Ben Jefers.

HAROLD BACQUET

# 16. Wake Up the Streets

Three things are eating at Bill Schultz as he drives through the quiet streets of Treme, a low-income neighborhood near the French Quarter. First there are the numbers. It's 10 a.m. and the voters have not shown up yet. His check of three target precincts in poor neighborhoods shows turnouts between 14 and 20 percent. Second, it's just too quiet. "There's not the excitement on the streets. That worries me." Third, the batteries in his car phone are out, which means, for now, he can't do anything about one and two.

Schultz is a deputy civil sheriff working for Civil Sheriff Paul Valteau. He's also one of the top political operatives in New Orleans, a veteran street campaigner who understands the dynamics of getting out the vote. Today his primary mission is electing Marc Morial to the state Senate while also boosting the turnout for Edwin Edwards in the district's black neighborhoods.

Finally he commandeers a phone in a nearby law office and reaches Ben Jeffers, who is coordinating Edwards' street operation. "Look, we need to get some soldiers out in 5-5 (that's Fifth Ward, Precinct 5). It's only 20 percent. Geez, 7-27 is only 14. What's going on?" He listens to Jeffers. "Right. Let's target 5-5, 6-7 and 17-12. We gotta get the low incomes out. Okay, and I'm on my way over."

Scores of young people in Edwin Edwards t-shirts are moving in and out of the temporary headquarters on South Galvez. They arrive as dayworkers and are dispatched as soldiers, under a squad leader, to knock on doors and get voters into vans and to the precinct.

In a small paneled office behind the lobby, Jeffers and field coordinator Chuck Brown go over a wall map of the city divided into precincts. "We've put 91 people in the Lafitte Project," says Brown, as they pinpoint the other precincts to be targeted between 10 a.m. and noon. "We're making the best use of our manpower and we're concentrating on the areas where we're strong."

Brown belongs to SOUL, which, having come to terms with Edwards, has grafted its operation into Edwards' get-out-the-vote effort in New Orleans. Edwards knows the only way to afford working with the several major black political groups is to control the overall umbrella organization. That's the job of Ben Jeffers, a former Edwards' cabinet officer, who, when he ran unsuccessfully for secretary of state in 1979, received the most votes of any black candidate to run for statewide office. His low-key command skills help Edwards get the most from SOUL and its rival groups at a fraction of his 1983 investment.

Jeffers returns to his office, where he's joined by SOUL co-leader Don Hubbard, "The General," and with City Councilwoman-at-Large Dorothy Mae Taylor, one of Edwards' earliest champions. Her name is not on the ballot today, but her job is. New Orleans voters are deciding a referendum to limit City Council members to just two terms. If it passes, six of the seven council members will be out of office in 1994. The poll numbers and the talk on the street say limited terms is the one sure bet on the ballot today. Dorothy Mae has put it out of her head. "I just want one winner. We've *got* to get Edwin back. I don't care about limited terms. There are so many things I can do."

By noon, Chuck Brown's squad leaders are pumped up after blitzing the Lafitte Project. For many younger workers, this is the first election on the streets. For some with a little experience, it's the first time they've been entrusted with a leadership role. The young squad leader describes his team's deployment. "We had ten in my team. I put one in the back and one up ahead." Brown nods approvingly. Security first. "Then we said, 'Hey man, it's like football. We're gonna blitz this place!'"

Fresh numbers in by phone confirm the mission accomplished. Between 10 and noon, turnout jumped from 19 to 29 percent in 5-5. Now this is more like it. The poorer the neighborhood, the lower the turnout. The 29 percent turnout by noon in the Lafitte Project puts that precinct halfway to the 60 percent black that Edwards is counting on. And the day is young. The other axiom in street politics is that whites vote heaviest in the morning, blacks in the afternoon.

Today's spartan budget is one reason why Schultz is seeing less street activity. Yet the trimmed-down operation is still getting voters to the polls. Over at the St. Augustine gym, staging area for Morial's street troops, Sheriff Paul Valteau foresees a possible watershed election: "This election will prove that we can win without money." Well, without a lot of money.

The pace is much less frenetic in Suite 1545 at the Monteleone.

Edwin Edwards is reviewing a map with overlays. "Here, even you can understand this," he tells a reporter. The Governmental Studies Institute has prepared a map showing who carried which parishes in the 1987 election, with an overlay of the results of the 1990 Senate race. Essentially, it shows that Buddy Roemer and David Duke carried the same parishes: all of North Louisiana, the Florida parishes in the southeast and most of the southwest. (You could put a second overlay on this map showing that Huey Long carried the same places in 1928.) With Duke and Roemer sharing the same base, the map shows clearly that only one of them will survive the primary. Roemer will need to do very well in Shreveport and the South Louisiana cities (including Uptown New Orleans) to overcome Duke in the country. The morning news says it's not happening. According to the few white precincts checked earlier, the turnout in the upscale Uptown areas is not much higher than in the black community.

The greater concern for d'Hemecourt and Martin is the turnout in Suite 1545. The campaign has taken all the rooms on that part of the floor. As the last few Canadian tourists straggle down to check out, d'Hemecourt is dispensing keys to family and friends.

Marion Edwards, who was the majordomo of past campaigns but has sat this one out completely, arrives with his daughter Wanda and takes a seat across the glass-top table from his older brother. The candidate already is considering his appearance before the cameras tonight.

"Marion, tonight I only want the immediate family up on the podium."

Marion nods, "I think that is only right." The corporate vice president has his own appearances to consider.

"Anyway," says Edwin. "Your daughter has done much better than you."

Wanda is surprised at the odd and avuncular compliment. Uncle Edwin continues, "She's better and a whole lot cheaper. She did for $1 million what you did for $16 million."

Marion knows he's helping keep Edwin off the hook. If his brother is not on the stage, other close friends can hardly complain to Edwin at not being by his side.

"What's Candy doing at MB (Maison Blanche)?" asks d'Hemecourt, trying to keep track of the drivers.

Edwards: "I don't want to know."

"Is David here?" someone asks.

"No," says d'Hemecourt. "If David were here, he'd be sewn to Edwin's back." D'Hemecourt admires the youngest son's loyalty, but it worries him too. "I'm just glad he doesn't have a gun. If he wants to punch someone out, that's okay, we can take care of that. We can write checks. But let the pros take care of the real business."

Assorted numbers trickle in by phone. The absentee vote is 53,000. The turnout in Jeff Davis Parish at 2 p.m. is 49 percent. When Gervais LaFleur, one of Edwards' top black supporters in Acadiana, calls in from Ville Platte, the candidate needles him: "I don't think your man Duke is going to make it. You'll have to be with me in the runoff."

The tide of old friends washes in. Billy Broadhurst, who has kept his distance the past few months, settles into a wingback chair. Tom Nolan wonders how Raymond Strother is feeling right now: "I bet he won't handle another Republican."

"Or a Democrat," beams Broadhurst.


Buoyed by optimistic polls that showed their candidate narrowly leading, the ardent Roemer supporters are the last to feel the ground sinking below them. Roemer could sense it in his final dispirited campaign appearances. So did Strother and the top aides who read Duke's movement in the polls and Roemer's lack thereof, despite a lead, as deadly.

The Roemer campaign believes in lucky hotel rooms, too, booking the same suite for the candidate in the Shreveport Sheraton. Most of the crew from the Baton Rouge headquarters make the long trek north. The sense is the race is too close for comfort, too close to call.

By 2 p.m. in New Orleans, Michelle Shauer knows it is all over. She and volunteers are calling back wavering voters. "We kept getting, 'No comment,' 'No comment,' 'Edwards,' 'Duke.' People who a week ago were undecided or leaning to Roemer now were saying Duke."

As the polls were set to close at 8 p.m., Buddy Roemer tunes in the National League playoffs.

The Duke victory party, like his rallies, attracts all types. About 1,000, from true believers to mere partygoers, mill about the cavernous main hall of the Pontchartrain Center in Kenner. With some Dukesters, it's hard to tell if they are wearing everyday clothes or costumes. Michelle Mayeaux comes dressed as the Fairy Princess, just stopping by on her way to a Halloween party. Karl Habighorst, a 22-year-old unemployed security guard, sports a tattoo of a Confederate flag on one arm and a swastika on the other. "It don't mean nothing, my family's German." Oh.

David Duke, he says, "is good for Louisiana. He's trying to get the parasites off welfare."

"We want to get everyone off welfare," says a Baton Rouge woman, sipping a drink. She and her friend, former hairdressers now retired — "We're moms" — came dressed to party in miniskirts and sequined blouses. When David Duke appears on the TV monitor, both squeal. No, they have no qualms about Duke's background. "His past is all out of his closet. You can't get any more out than he is. And look, you'd find some stuff if you dug into Roemer's closet, and, of course, Edwards'." A middle-aged woman nearby joins in, "I voted for Edwards last time, but Duke says what I really feel."

Behind the TV camera platform, Babs Wilson and volunteers are doing a fairly brisk business in Duke t-shirts, hats and bumperstickers. Far above the party, on the top row of the pushed-back bleachers, research director Marc Ellis takes photographs of the crowd.

The group erupts into loud cheering and the "Duke, Duke, Duke" chant as the candidate, surrounded by his security cordon, enters behind the stage and slowly makes his way to the TV cameras.

Minutes later, the crowd goes wild again as Duke bounds onstage with his daughters and Jim McPherson and a few staffers. Julie Jones sings "Dixie" and "The Battle Hymn of the Republic" to the sea of blue Duke placards. Duke has not much to say to his fans, except "I love y'all." The hairdresser moms swoon. Duke retreats to a back room to view returns.

Todd Gillman of the *Dallas Morning News* is interviewing celebrants when an intense young man, holding a child, interrupts, "You know what's wrong with Buddy Roemer?" He hands his daughter off to his wife so he can poke Gillman in the chest. "He borrowed a billion dollars to balance the budget—from the Jew banks. Those New York Jews!" Gillman keeps a straight face as he takes notes: "Jew banks, uh-huh." The man adds that if Duke wins, "All them niggers on the west side of Louisiana are gonna go to Texas." The man refuses to give his name, saying the last time he "told it like it was" to a reporter, he almost lost his job teaching in Tangipahoa Parish. He concludes, "This is the beginning of the end. White Protestant Anglo-Saxons are gonna rule, because we're God's people."

Gillman turns away a bit shaken. "This guy doesn't know his code."

Security in Suite 1545 is in shambles. Throughout the campaign Edwards has been inviting his innumerable friends and allies to drop by and see him at the victory party. They take him literally. By 8 p.m., there are as many good friends jamming into the small hotel suite as there are in the ballroom downstairs. Edwards has retreated to the bedroom, where he's directing d'Hemecourt's and Martin's calls to precincts around the state, especially in Acadiana.

The first returns to flash on the TV screens don't look good. Roemer leads with 3 percent of the returns in. Edwards is last. The outer room is deadly silent. D'Hemecourt shrugs it off. New Orleans is not in yet.

The suburban vote, however, is piling in.

At Duke headquarters, only a fraction of the crowd can get near either of the two small TV monitors flanking the stage. With 10 percent of the vote in, Roemer still leads with Duke and Edwards swapping second and third.

At about 15 percent, new numbers flash up. Duke leads. The Pontchartrain Center explodes. "We're gonna win!" shrieks the hairdresser. Bedlam ensues for 20 minutes more. Duke is about to return to the stage, when the numbers go through a new upheaval. New Orleans comes rolling in. At 25 percent of precincts reporting, Edwin Edwards takes a narrow lead over Duke with Roemer slipping to a permanent third. The 15th floor of the Monteleone rocks. Edwin Edwards stares impassively at the TV screens. Bobby d'Hemecourt's shoulders sag in relief.

Three hundred miles away, Buddy Roemer switches back to baseball.

The Dukesters are chanting for their man again. He bounds back onstage and walks from one side to the other, arms over his head, pushing the crowd a few decibels higher. He hugs his daughters close as he stands at the edge of the stage and lets the cheers wash over him.

By 35 percent, the order of finish begins to solidify. Edwards holds a two-point lead over Duke, as Roemer fades to three, four, then five points out of the running.

Clyde Holloway, who was banking on pushing for a respectable finish in the low teens, is stuck at 5 percent.

For the second time in three elections, a Republican reform governor has been sent packing. Not by Edwin Edwards, though, but at the hands of renegade Republican David Duke. The Democratic crowd at John Breaux's satellite feed party in Washington find all this oddly amusing. No one more so than the senior senator from Louisiana, whose smile broadens as the returns pile in. Not only has the race eliminated Roemer as a potential future threat to Johnston, it relieves him of the embarrassment of the 1990 election. They won't be chuckling behind ol' Bennett's back anymore. *Morning Advocate* correspondent Joan McKinney describes Johnston reveling in the political incorrectness of it all, cheering on last year's nemesis: "Here he comes, our guy Duke."

The 1987 numbers are reversed as Edwards pushes over 33 percent and Roemer fades below 27. When he pulled out of the race four years ago, Edwards said, "The Chinese have a saying that if you wait on the riverbank long enough, the bodies of your dead enemies will float by." With his immediate family gathered onstage behind him, with the TV lights and faithful friends before him, perhaps Edwin Edwards in his mind's eye sees the lifeless lump of Buddy Roemer floating past. He'll miss him.

For four years, rarely has he passed up the opportunity to attack or ridicule the only man who's ever beat him. Even when the team around him saw Duke surging months ago, Edwards maintained his denial. "It would be easier to beat Duke, but I would rather beat Roemer." The returns say he did that, but he knows it's Duke who beat Roemer while Edwards simply maintained his base.

It is not easy for him to let Buddy Roemer go. So he doesn't. From listening to him, you'd think Roemer is his runoff opponent. He compliments worthy opponents "I have come to know during the long, tough candidate forums. Clyde Holloway, Fred Dent, Sam Jones and, yes, David Duke. . . . Hopefully now we can work together to take the best of what they had to offer with the best I have to offer."

As he speaks, and his people cheer, Edwards notices that Roemer is being interviewed on one of the TV monitors. He quiets the crowd as the volume is turned up. The governor interprets the returns, "The voters said, 'Buddy, thanks, but you didn't do enough.' That's fair." He thanks state employees for the job they did for Louisiana: "We'll give it in better shape than the way we got it."

That sets Edwards off again. "I don't accept that he left it better." He challenges Roemer's taking credit for the state's lowered bond rating. Edwards' aides look wearily at each other. Maybe after a good night's sleep he'll remember who his runoff opponent is. Edwards, however, won't be denied his psychic payoff. After tonight, he won't have Buddy Roemer to kick around anymore, so a few last boots can't hurt.

If Edwards is not focusing on Duke yet, plenty of others in the Monteleone ballroom tonight are. The Jewish community will waste no time in mobilizing. Hippo Katz, a premier fundraiser and political player, can already see the TV spots homing in on the economic angle. "We need to do a commercial with taxi drivers and working people. The message is economics. You may like him but can you afford him?" And the money will be there. "I'll get out my temple list tomorrow and we'll raise money from people who have never thought of contributing in politics." Hippo tips the bartender. "David Duke thinks he hates Jews now. Wait till we're through with him."

The final returns:
  Edwin Edwards–523,195; 33.77 percent
  David Duke–491,342; 31.71 percent
  Buddy Roemer–410,690; 26.51 percent
  Clyde Holloway–82,683; 5.34 percent
  Sam Jones–11,847; .76 percent
  Ed Karst–9,663; .62 percent
  Fred Dent–7,385; .48 percent
  Anne Thompson–4,118; .27 percent
  Jim Crowley–4,000; .26 percent
  Albert Powell–2,053; .13 percent
  Ronnie Johnson–1,372; .09 percent
  "Cousin" Ken Lewis–1,006; .06 percent

The open primary has worked its classic dark magic. The electorate has been polarized to the extremes. The weak incumbent, trying to work both ends, was squeezed out in the middle. Over 63 percent voted Republican, a historic first. Yet the incumbent Republican and the endorsed Republican finished out of the money.

Sixty-three percent of the electorate were not voting specifically Republican, or even completely conservative. Many voters gravitated to that end because Edwards was the only choice on the other. Much of Duke's vote, though hardly liberal, could be described as rural populist, folks who could easily vote for the right Democrat. Duke carried parishes that Democrats Edwin Edwards and Buddy Roemer had carried before, and populist Huey Long before them. Much of Roemer's vote was reform moderate, mainly city dwellers who believe in balanced budgets and, to a degree, civil liberties.

Just as last year, David Duke would not have done so well in a closed party primary. Dividing the voters would have split his wide base of alienated voters. He came close to getting more Republican votes than Roemer and smothered Edwards among white Democrats.

Edwards alone understood the true dynamics of this election system he invented. You would have thought he planned it all this way. He didn't. It's just the way he played it.

Edwards carried 26 parishes–3 with outright majorities, including 54 percent in New Orleans. His 64,000-vote lead over Duke in New Orleans accounted for double his statewide margin. His prediction beat all pollsters' forecasts: he was two points high on his and Roemer's vote and two points low on Duke. But it's a troubling two percent spread.

Duke carried 31 parishes, 4 with majorities. He swept rural white North Louisiana, taking nearly every rural parish there that Roemer carried in 1987. Roemer carried pluralities in only seven urban parishes and actually ran four behind Holloway in three parishes. The incumbent governor received only 8 percent of the vote in the parish of Evangeline.

Republicans at Roemer headquarters have few kind words for Clyde. The numbers alone don't support their anger. Were Roemer to have received every one of Holloway's votes, Roemer barely would have nipped Duke. Were Holloway not in the race, however, the vast majority of his pro-life, fundamentalist support would not have gone to the governor who vetoed three anti-abortion bills. Holloway did rob Roemer of a unified Republican effort, which could have given the governor more momentum. However, Roemer's attitude toward the party from the time he switched indicates that he would have done little to motivate GOP activists, with or without the Holloway challenge.

Others attribute Roemer's defeat to the party switch itself. Surely that would have hurt him in a runoff against Edwards, but he might not have fared much better as a Democrat. Had he not switched parties, an even stronger Republican, such as Dave Treen or Henson Moore, might have split Roemer's conservative vote even more.

The view of Raymond Strother and others is that nothing could have saved Roemer once David Duke got in the race. Unless, of course, Buddy Roemer tried to do more to save himself. The shock and tears at the Roemer parties in Shreveport, Baton Rouge and New Orleans turn to anger by morning light. "He just didn't try" and "He didn't want to win" are consensus views of Roemer supporters. Even his most forgiving champion knows where the campaign failed. When Strother comes downstairs at the Mansion Sunday morning, Adeline Roemer hugs him and says, "We had everything going for us but a candidate."

# 17. Nebuchadnezzar
# at the Door

Louisiana wakes up stunned. The Roemer voters were the last to know their man was going down.

Tears flow at the final campaign staff meeting from the hurt, the shock, the anger and the choice left to them. They feel that more than a campaign has been lost—gone is the opportunity for real reform, for a normal government like other states have. It is a bad scene. The only person there who seems to be taking things very well was the ex-candidate.

"I never saw Buddy so relieved and happy as when I saw him after the election," says Michelle Shauer, the New Orleans headquarters manager. "It was as though a great weight had been lifted from him." Lifted from him and placed squarely back on the people who had battled for him. They are burdened with the awful decision about what to do next.

Most are flat burned out on politics and say they might not even vote in the November runoff. Those who can just go home are the lucky ones. Others still have some politics to get out of their system, or want to remain in a campaign. Some will quietly support Edwin Edwards. Others, like assistant press secretary Peyton Smith, will join the Edwards campaign.

"At first I was going to leave the state," says Michelle Shauer. Montana, where her parents live, looked good to her. But she can't quite get this campaign behind her. As a young Republican who grew up outside Louisiana, she could not consider working for Edwin Edwards, the antithesis of GOP values. She decides to at least talk to Howie Farrell at Duke's campaign.

Shauer knows her personal defenses were down after her conflicts with campaign manager Sam Dawson and the lack of response from candidate Roemer. "Howie is not Sam Dawson," she says later. "He's a nice guy. He's straightforward. He told me, 'I spent 14 years in the Republican Party. I know what you're going through.' He told me, 'The time has come for us' to broaden the campaign. He said, 'We need people from the establishment who know how to do things like run phone banks.' "

Apparently Farrell knew just what nerves to hit. "He told me, 'Michelle, y'all could have beaten us.' " A few days later she joins the Duke campaign.


The campaign fundraiser's dream has come true. "We've heard from friends we didn't know we had," says Bob d'Hemecourt in the candidate's suite. "People were calling at 3:30 a.m. and started again at 6. That's politics in Louisiana. One guy loses, you pick another horse."

Early Sunday morning, the Edwards campaign team assembles. Time and money dominate the discussion. So much for lean and mean. Edwards wants $2 million for the runoff and has only 26 days to get it. That means he can't get around the state to dozens of small fundraisers. He will concentrate on where the money is: Baton Rouge, New Orleans and New York.

Some returns are highly puzzling, and troubling. How in the world did David Duke finish first in French-speaking Terrebonne and Lafourche? Andrew Martin recognizes that the campaign made a mistake in relying on the local organization of two-term Sheriff Duffy Breaux, who was believed to be an easy winner despite some ongoing nettlesome federal investigations. Breaux was shocked by ex-state trooper Craig Webre, who lands in a runoff in a virtual tie with Breaux. Though Webre was no supporter of Duke, their anti-incumbent appeals dovetailed. "We're gonna straighten that out this time," says Martin — meaning, Old Duffy is a goner and Edwards will cut free of him.

No specific strategy for dealing with Duke is discussed. Edwards is more concerned with his allies. Two decisions come out early: 1) to keep the Jewish groups under control, and 2) for Edwards to avoid being seen with large black audiences. There is no need to reinforce the images Duke already has planted.

Toward the end of the primary, as Duke came on stronger, Edwards fantasized briefly about telling the hated *Times-Picayune*, as an out-of-state-owned interest, to butt out of this campaign. And the same for Buddy Roemer. With the runoff before him, however, and with his own negative ratings only slightly lower than Duke's, Edwards' political instincts quiet his heart. That morning he calls *Picayune* editor Jim Amoss to lobby for the paper's endorsement. Then he dials the Governor's Mansion.

Sunday afternoon, divisive politics are put aside for the celebration of the state religion: football. The Saints even are obliging this year with an unprecedented division-leading season. Everyone comes together at the temple of the Superdome. Indeed, isn't that Edwin Edwards chatting with David Duke? Their two entourages, armed street gangs, come upon each other outside of Edwards' skybox. Maintaining their cordial primary relationship, the two congratulate each other. "I was surprised you did as well," says Edwards. "That's right," says Duke, "we're neck and neck." While they chat, bantamweight Cecil Brown sizes up stocky Duke bodyguard Errol Simmons and audibly growls.

Buddy Roemer, last seen in the Superdome reading a book, is not at the game today. His consultant, Ray Strother, joins his old friend Billy Broadhurst and Edwards' advertising consultant Bill Morgan in the Edwards skybox. After the game, Strother catches a ride back to Baton Rouge with Morgan. "How do we beat him?" asks Morgan. "The economic issue is the only thing that works on him," says Strother, glad to share the advice that Roemer ignored. Yet, Edwin Edwards, who keeps his own counsel, seems to have other ideas.

On primary election day, there are over 800,000 Louisiana adults who are not in jail and who are not registered to vote. Come Monday morning, the first of 67,000 start to change that. Lines snake outside of registrars' offices all over the state. In Baton Rouge, Southern University calls off classes as hundreds of students head downtown to queue up for hours, while being serenaded by the Jaguar band. In the three days that the rolls are open, over 35,000 whites and over 32,000 blacks register to vote. What many whites saw was TV video of lines of mostly black registrants in New Orleans and Baton Rouge. Letters to the editor question the authority of officials at Southern to dismiss classes. School board members call for an investigation of the principal of predominantly black Capitol High School using the schoolbus to take students to register to vote. Until the numbers are released — and even then — conservative whites see the specter of the old bloc vote rising.

"Get down, Channel 9." The elderly gentleman tries to get the attention of the news crew blocking his view of the speakers' platform at the Baton Rouge Hilton. It's futile. Two months ago, TV reporters were complaining that the campaign was dead asleep. Now nearly a dozen film crews, from in state and out, stake out this confrontation at the state convention of the American Association of Retired People.

Older citizens have long been a prime constituency of Edwin Edwards, who prides himself on not turning his back on their needs. In his opening statement, he reminds the crowd that there are 69,000 older citizens on welfare in Louisiana and promises to "never get so big, so mighty that I won't take time to help the unfortunate."

Edwin Edwards is having trouble getting his message across. For one thing, his microphone is not working. His first statements are interrupted with calls to "Speak up!" His other problem is that few if any of those 69,000 elderly welfare cases or otherwise "unfortunates" are here today. This is a conservative crowd, and David Duke seems to have their number, and Edwards'.

Duke will have no trouble being seen or heard. He stands, looking every inch the fine young man, and launches an assault on the corruption and waste of Edwards-style government. He compares his own demand for tougher sentencing of those convicted of violent crimes against the elderly to Edwards' own history of numerous pardons and paroles. He conjures up his favorite image of the retired schoolteacher surviving on a $378-a-month state pension who can't afford to turn on her air conditioner while "convicted criminals have central a/c and color TV."

The retired crowd warms quickly to Duke. Of course, it doesn't hurt that some of his own older supporters pepper the audience and are leading the cheering.

Edwards tries to stick to the specifics of his promises, ticking off five categories of Medicaid services that he will expand with the use of federal matching funds.

Duke is not going to bite and try to out-promise Edwards. The real problems, he claims, are the welfare system, the rising welfare underclass and the growing illegitimate birth rate. Loud applause.

Edwards makes a stab at reason: "It's not the child's fault it is born illegitimate."

Duke counters, "True, illegitimacy is not the fault of the child, but neither is it the fault of those who must pay for it." Louder applause.

Edwards looks clearly ill at ease. He has given up on his microphone by now and must awkwardly share the moderator's. What really must be disconcerting is to find himself trying to use fact and reason while his challenger is running wild and free over the audience's fears and resentments. He had looked forward to basing his runoff campaign on Roemer's record, but now he's having a hard time defending his own.

After Edwards stresses his commitment to consumer rights and ethics, Duke returns the serve: "That's the best speech against white-collar crime since Doug Green said he would clean up the insurance industry." The insurance commissioner, the most recently imprisoned state official, won his 1987 election with $2 million in contributions funneled to him by Champion Insurance, also a major Edwards campaign contributor.

Deftly hitting applause lines, Duke is on a roll. This is easier than attacking Buddy Roemer: "Government is out of control in Louisiana. We need protection from government. Consumer protection, yes. Taxpayer protection, yes."

This gets the first chuckle out of Edwards: "I don't know why you complain about taxes so much. Until they caught you, you didn't pay yours." Duke gets his only boos as he tries to explain that his income was below the state tax threshold for reporting.

Edwards, though, is getting the worst of it, especially with Duke's jeering section razzing him. At least Edwards will have the last word in his closing statement. He stands: "Let me tell you a couple of things about this fella." Duke throws up his arms in here-we-go-again disgust as the crowd—not just Duke's crowd—hits Edwards with boos. "Don't get personal," yells out one woman.

Edwards marshals his facts. Duke voted against funds for the disabled with his vote against the state budget. "You think he likes elderly people? He was one of nine legislators who voted against letting people 60 years or older not have to buy duck stamps." Duck stamps? Duke rolls his eyes.

Welfare fraud? Did you know, asks Edwards, "that a welfare mother only receives an extra $11 a week with each extra child she bears. Can you see a woman sitting around the kitchen table scheming to get pregnant to get another $11 a week?"

"Yes!" shout a few people. Edwards blinks. This is a tough crowd.

He tries reason again, saying "only three percent of the state budget goes to all forms of public assistance."

"That's three percent too much," comes back the response.

The debate over, Edwards quickly leaves by the back door as Duke wades into the crowd for handshakes and autographs and to beam at the TV cameras.

Edwin Edwards debated David Duke on Duke's issues and Duke smoked him. The facts were on Edwards' side. The crowd wasn't.

Edwards' performance doesn't improve much for the first statewide televised debate between the candidates that weekend. Duke again confronts Edwards with wasting taxpayers' dollars and being "the biggest enemy to the environment." He brushes off a question about how his election would affect tourism and business. "They said the same things about George Wallace and Lester Maddox," he answers, without much damage to Alabama and Georgia.

An odd question surfaces when both are asked to name the church they attend and its pastor.

For Edwards it's St. Jude Catholic Church in Baton Rouge and Father Collins, though he ecumenically hedges his bet in saying he sometimes goes to a Pentecostal church. Duke says he attends the "Evangelical Bible Church." As much as he promotes his Christian faith, this is the first time he mentions a specific church, which, it turns out, doesn't exist.

Duke goes back on the attack, charging that Edwards is selling every board and commission, "some three and four times." That gets at least one game response from the ex-governor: "Boy, you're gonna lose your newfound religion if you don't stop lying."

In his closing statement, Edwards appeals to the voters' better nature, which can be risky business in Louisiana. "We need a governor who is as good as the people of this state."

This leads perfectly into Duke's slamming close. He pulls out a sheaf of papers: "This is a small portion of pardons and paroles he signed while governor," and spends his entire three minutes pounding Edwards' vulnerable record for releasing prisoners.

It's a strong finish for Duke and another disorienting performance for Edwards, who has been worked over while barely laying a glove on Duke in two debates.

This time, the pollsters will not be burned again. They are ferreting out David Duke's hidden vote by assigning every poll respondent to his column who registers any warmth to him or bare acceptance or even lack of contempt. The Mason-Dixon poll after the primary, once thermalized, shows Edwards barely ahead, 46-42, with 12 percent undecided. Of that 12 percent, 10 percent are white and 2 percent are black. Duke is taking 58 percent of the white vote to Edwards' 28 percent. Of the undecided vote, 58 percent say they think Duke is more honest, while only 5 percent say that of Edwards.

The Roemer vote is breaking evenly, which means Duke is cracking the middle-aged, middle-class group that has eluded him. One Baton Rouge homemaker and Roemer voter is more concerned about Edwards' competence than Duke's reputation. "As I see it, if Duke wins he'll only be in four years and won't get anything done. If Edwards gets in, he's in for eight and it will take years after that to get out of the hole he put us in."

Most voters are still in shock at their predicament. "After the last time, I said I'd cut off my right arm before I vote for him again," says a Baton Rouge dentist of Edwards. Now the dentist has a problem.

*USA Today* is researching a story on what Governor Duke would be like. "Wouldn't he control the state police?" queries reporter Matt Cooper. Now there's a thought, but the Dukesters have far more guns than do the state police. Despite the governor's appointment power, what can Duke really do that would threaten those who fear him? Those who know the snakepit of the Legislature recognize Governor Duke would not get far advancing an ultra-conservative agenda, especially the hidden white supremacist agenda that the Louisiana Coalition is convinced he is still committed to.

In Pineville, though, just across the Red River from Alexandria, an overflow crowd cheers what Duke promises to not do. "People say, 'Well, what can he get done?' One thing he can get done is to make sure the Legislature doesn't put any more taxes on the people because I'll veto them." And not just taxes. "The governor has the line-item veto in Louisiana — thank God for that. I can go through and cut waste and fat line by line. And there has not been one budget veto overridden in the history of this state." Huge applause. "If President Bush can veto the liberal policies in Congress, I can do the same thing in Louisiana."

These small-town and rural voters are the children and grandchildren of Huey Long's poor lower-class constituency that looked to government to improve their lot. Having inched up the ladder into the squeezed middle class, many feel government has forsaken them for a new and less deserving lower class. Meanwhile, the public institutions the middle class relies on — schools, law enforcement and roads — deteriorate. They bought into the Roemer Revolution, but dumped him when he did not deliver on his rabid slash-and-burn rhetoric. Duke still sounds like the Huey-in-reverse he promises to be.

The momentum is all Duke's. He is boxing Edwin Edwards' ears every day, and the old boy doesn't seem to have a clue about dealing with Duke's accelerating campaign. Trying to engage Duke on the issues isn't working because Duke's issues are also Reagan's.

Attacking Duke's character and past would sound fairly ridiculous coming from Edwin Edwards.

It can too happen here.


David Duke is the hottest talk-show ticket going. Conversation on him dominates drive time from Long Island to Los Angeles. WJR-AM in Detroit does a call-in poll, with 60 percent of respondents saying they would vote for Duke. Before he was a media novelty. Now his huge new celebrity status vaults him to the top rung of infotainment, where the real voters and money are. In quick succession, Duke appears on *Crossfire*, *Larry King Live* and *Donahue*.

Edwards gives him a free ride — "I'm running for governor of Louisiana, not President, as he is" — and declines invitations to appear with Duke. That suits most producers. Including Edwards could turn an appearance into — *aauugh* — a political debate.

Senator John Breaux is recruited as Duke's counterpoint on *Crossfire*, but shrewdly allows Michael Kinsley to tackle the important cosmetic surgery issue. That sets up Duke's most memorable national sound bite: "That's the kind of cheap shot I would expect from a little worm like you." Now that's infotainment.

Duke is hot enough that he can dictate terms. Larry King, who rarely prepares for his shows, usually invites other guests to challenge controversial subjects. He tries for *Times-Picayune* reporter Tyler Bridges, but Duke nixes that. Then King wants to bring on a Holocaust survivor, but Duke won't bite. King relents and allows Duke on alone.

An interviewer not prepared for Duke ends up pitching batting practice, and King is throwing softballs. Duke crushes the affirmative action question — "I favor giving help to people on basis of need, not on basis of race" — and bunts safely on his past — "I was too intolerant. I thought that the problem was with blacks instead of with the welfare system." King could have pulled up any one of Duke's anti-Semitic quotes from the 1980s, which are legion.

Instead, King idles while Duke twice gives his address and asks people to send money.

Phil Donahue has Duke's past on tape, and begins the show with the younger, slack-jawed Duke grinning as he gives his correct title as Grand Wizard of the Ku Klux Klan. Donahue presses on the past, which Duke is waiting for: "Phil, I'm sure you would change a few things if you could. I once saw you wearing a skirt." Donahue, Duke and the audience laugh together, the infotainment family.

The audience's questions are tougher: "How can you say you want government out of our lives when you want to put Norplant in women?" The woman doesn't wait for an answer: "The only thing that has changed is your plastic surgery and it's terrible."

Instead of sitting still, Duke is walking around the stage and into the audience a little, making eye contact with his questioners, working for the soft spot.

Another woman asks, "Would you want your child to marry a black or a Jew?"

David is the concerned dad. "Most Jewish people want to marry within their faith. I would want my child to marry within her faith and heritage. It would bother me. I'm proud of my daughters. I want to see them continue their heritage."

A telephone caller pitches in: "Anyone who doesn't believe David Duke has changed does not believe in Jesus Christ." Duke smiles and blushes — infotainment works.


While David Duke does *Donahue*, Edwin Edwards is also in New York — not for TV but to raise money from investment bankers and bond underwriters.

In Metairie, Duke funds are pouring in at a rate of $10 to $50 with each envelope opened. At the Monteleone, the Edwards camp is working in bigger lots. Instead of coming by mail, his money is walking in the door. "Wednesday this place looked like a synagogue," says Andrew Martin of the campaign's strongest new constituency. "They came with money in hand."

Edwards has returned from a press conference downstairs and the suite is filling up. With the candidate retired to the back room, Bob d'Hemecourt is trying to direct traffic. "An hour ago, there were five people in here, now there are over 40." Groups of two and four people are moving in and out of the bedroom for audiences with Edwards. Labor leader Pete Babin and labor lawyer Louis Robein leave as New Orleans politico Sal Anzelmo ushers in a judge.

"How do you feel about forced heirship?" asks a young lawyer, a Roemer supporter.

Edwards answers diplomatically. "If I had a rich father I'd like it."

The lawyer makes his point. "Well, I have and I do."

Sheriff Harry Lee relaxes on the couch. He was so confident of reelection that he spent $100,000 on one commercial that he allowed Edwin Edwards to star in. Here's Edwin, standing in front of the Superdome, claiming credit with Harry for finding Texan Tom Benson and encouraging him to buy the NFL Saints and keep them in New Orleans. "With Edwin Edwards as quarterback and Harry Lee as the front four, we scored a touchdown for New Orleans." Edwards then walks off camera and Lee walks on for his one line: "Who dat?" It was one of the most brilliant uses of soft money and cleverest perversions of the campaign finance law.

Lee's love for Edwin paled next to Jack Kent's hatred for Buddy Roemer — the difference came to about $400,000. The big joke in the suite is that Kent continued running the commercials of Buddy with the halo for days after the election. "He wanted him to know who beat him," laughs George Fischer. The whole room laughs. If there was ever a link or even a wink between Edwin Edwards and Jack Kent over the $500,000 character assassination of Buddy Roemer, the press never smoked it out. Maybe that's what makes it so funny.

D'Hemecourt emerges from the bedroom and hushes the room. The candidate is taking a nap. Edwards has renewed energy since making the runoff. Still he works in rest stops throughout the day. "He'll lie down for 30 minutes, then he remembers someone he needs to call and he's up again," says d'Hemecourt.

"Old Lawrence Chehardy is the most energetic campaigner I ever saw," recalls George Fischer. "He could sleep in a car." The nice thing about Edwards' campaigns is there are always a few veterans around to supply lore. Fischer is one of the old faces Edwards says you won't see around this new campaign. The ex-governor's former Health and Hospitals secretary and campaign manager stays out of the public eye and on the phone. Today he is working the engineer list. "Roemer got money from nearly every engineer I know. I've got some friends on the list. Some say they will vote with us, some will give a buck or two, some say go to hell. You can't get too personal with all this stuff."

Talk about old faces. Wayne Ray makes a brief appearance in the suite. Edwards' old sidekick from 1983 has stayed far away from any campaign function since his release from federal prison on tax evasion charges. Eight years ago he was at the middle of the action in this suite. Today he's not sure he should be here. "It was a humbling experience," he says at about one third his old decibel level. "I've been on a weight loss plan I wouldn't recommend to anybody."

Cars are crowding the parking lot at Duke's Baton Rouge headquarters. A couple of teenagers in football jerseys sit waiting for Duke yardsigns that will find a suburban home. The sign for the state's hottest new bumpersticker reads, "Tired of the 'No Dukes' signs, get 'More Dukes.' $2." Also on sale for $6 are tapes of Duke speeches, along with the familiar line of Duke t-shirts, caps and visors.

The Baton Rouge office is located near one of the city's busiest business intersections, with a large Duke sign rising high to greet traffic. Down in Metairie, though, Michelle Shauer is shocked at her first look at campaign central. "This is the headquarters!" is her reaction to the warren on the bottom floor of Duke's old residence.

Howie Farrell has cautioned her on what to expect: "He told me, 'This is an ideological campaign, not an establishment campaign.' "

Shauer soon learns that the new Republican recruits weren't brought in to reorganize the campaign. "Howie didn't let the Republican people organize. He has his own way of doing things. And when you get within striking distance like we were, people start protecting their turf. But they had the spirit and that's the kind of thing you hope for in a campaign. They were so committed and they worked hard every day for nothing. Duke was written on their eyeballs," says Shauer. "People would just quote the Bible and Christ and link that to Duke. One lady told me that white supremacists and the KKK are really good people — 'just wait till you meet them,' she told me." Sometimes when Duke entered the headquarters, says Shauer, people would stand up and applaud.

David Duke paces a storefront parking lot as the big Crowley Rice Festival parade organizes. He pauses to watch the Edwin Edwards van, flanked by supporters, pass by toward its parade route position.

"Look at the difference between Edwin's people and mine," he sniffs.

"What do you mean?"

"Well, just look at the element. Look how they're dressed. And look how little enthusiasm there is."

On the street, the Edwards "element" looks much the same as Duke's, except that the former includes blacks as well as whites. It is too hot and humid on this last weekend in October to dress any way but barely on Crowley's steaming streets.

Crowley, in Acadia Parish, is Edwards' second hometown, after his birthplace of Marksville and before his current residence in Baton Rouge and the hotel suite in New Orleans. Crowley is where he got his start as a lawyer and a politician. In 1959, he walked these streets with Senator John Kennedy. This is where he started his law practice and won election to the City Council, then the State Senate, then Congress. It's where his children were born and, at the height of the 1983 campaign, it's where his brother Nolan was murdered. Gunned down in his office by a client who then turned his gun on himself. The man was a former drug offender Nolan had represented and Edwin had pardoned.

That loss of his youngest brother started the long dark period for Edwards, broken only briefly by his 1983 landslide. Personally and politically, things were never the same for Edwin Edwards again, even at home. In 1987, Buddy Roemer shocked him by very nearly beating him in Acadia Parish. Many of those voters switched to David Duke in 1991, who trailed Edwards 42-32 percent locally and carried the white vote.

"I knew him when he first moved here," says the woman in her 50s, sitting in a folding chair near the courthouse. "I voted for him last time, but he couldn't do anything. Edwards is burned out."

The man next to her pipes up, "We had Edwards for 12 years for better or worse, and it can't get much worse."

Several sheriff's and state police sharpshooters look down from second- and third-story rooftops on Parkerson Avenue, the main drag and parade route off the courthouse square. The country-western band on the stage near the courthouse finishes its set, and the food booths do brisk business in boudin balls and shrimp on a stick. A giant Duke sign commands the top of a storefront where another group of folks have set up their folding chairs.

One of them is a man in his 60s, a retired farmer and World War II veteran visiting his family from North Louisiana. Like a lot of rural voters, he has voted the straight "aginner" ticket of Edwards in 1983, Roemer in 1987 and Duke in 1991. He doesn't care what he's heard about his candidate. "You can't pin nothing on him. Years ago my father and my grandfather belonged to secret organizations, and they were no different from the Klan."

But how about Nazis?

He brushes the air with his hand, like swatting a mosquito: "There are too many people looking at him. If they could prove he was a Nazi, which I doubt, they would have proved it by now." The man's daughter, a woman in her 30s, agrees: "I've never heard the man say anything against blacks. He's a gentleman, not a sneak. If he wasn't, he wouldn't have gone as far as he has today."

The "they ain't caught him" defense served Edwards pretty well too, until he was indicted.

A pipeline engineer from Opelousas recognizes Duke can't achieve his whole platform, but, "If he could just do a small part of what he's saying, we need it."

Up Parkerson Avenue, the parade is about ready to roll. Duke has been working the bands and floats formed up behind him. Among the Crowley High cheerleaders, the black girls sport their Edwards fans. Duke jokes with the white cheerleaders: "Can we balance this float? Will you wear my sticker?"

Crossing the street, he passes through the ranks of a drill team of black teenaged girls. The team leader bellows, "I said stand at attention," which startles Duke as the marchers snap to around him.

Edwin Edwards will ride in the front seat of a van with a walking security cordon to keep anyone from getting within six feet. David Duke will ride standing up in the back seat of a 1956 red Thunderbird. He explains to his assigned trooper, Beau Torres, "I want the people to have access to me." Torres agrees that it is okay for people to shake his hand as long as he does not get out of the car. Over a dozen reporters and photographers, from Sweden to North Carolina, are taking pictures and asking questions as he paces back and forth between the Thunderbird and the truck float that will carry his local supporters. From the float a speaker blares out the new campaign theme song:

*When David Duke*
*Comes marching in*
*He's the work-ing man's best friend.*

Duke is not through with the details. In this jumpy environment, the police have warned his sticker people against their usual method of slapping a Duke sticker on anyone without asking. "They can't tell you not to give out stickers," Duke tells the sticker squad. He peels off a sticker on his finger and extends it. "Here's what you do. See?" He instructs the squad leader. "You don't worry about giving out stickers. You just see that they are well up ahead of me. And get that literature out." He is the most famous statewide candidate in the world, a man with hundreds of volunteers and thousands of contributors, and here he is supervising the distribution of stickers in Crowley, Louisiana.

Speaking of details, "Where's my suntan lotion?"

The parade is rolling. Finally, a pep talk to his cheering section that will ride on the truck float ahead of him. There are few in-betweeners in this crowd. Many of the whites cheer loudly as the truck float approaches while the blacks boo. "This is the future," a young Dukester yells out to booing blacks.

About a block ahead, the Edwards van simply rolls as the candidate waves. No truck float. No song. No convertible. No one within six feet. No sticker detail. No warm-up man.

Warm-up man?

Ten feet ahead of the Dukemobile, a young man runs up to the crowd on the sidewalk and waves his hands and cheers. The people on the sidewalk get the idea and cheer back just as Duke passes and waves. The cheerleader skips the crowds of blacks, who don't need a boo leader to let Duke have it. He smiles and waves back.

*He's the work-ing man's best friend.*
*Oh how I want to be in that number*
*When David Duke comes marching in.*

The parade goes down and back up Parkerson. The barely visible Edwards gets a few waves and cheers. Duke gets a rabid reception, pro or con, nearly every step of the way. On the second pass around the square, the prisoners in the second-floor jail jeer and wave their hands through the wooden slats at Duke. Everybody in Crowley is getting a piece of this one.

Within minutes of the parade's end, Edwards is on his way out of town. Climbing out of the Thunderbird, Duke, still pumped, shakes hands with the gang on the truck float. "Now I just want to ask you one more favor. I'm heading to Tiger Stadium. We're gonna work the crowd before the LSU game. Will you follow me there?"

In a small dining room at Baton Rouge General Hospital, 15 members of the Baton Rouge Ministerial Alliance struggle with a moral and political dilemma. The group of preachers, priests and rabbis plan to issue a statement to be read from pulpits this weekend that would urge churchgoers to vote against David Duke. But they don't want to mention Edwin Edwards. They feel they can stretch their moral authority only so far.

This is one for situational ethics. Pastors are rightly squeamish about defining ethical choices in politics. Can you denounce the greater of evils without promoting the lesser? Is bigotry worse than corruption? Does equality among the flock mean we all must be fleeced together? Again? Does what preachers say even matter? David Duke has been denounced by the President and the archbishop and it's only seemed to make him stronger. Would a pastoral endorsement of Edwin Edwards help Duke even more?

What does the Bible say? Before the meeting begins, Methodist minister Jeff Daye seeks clues in Jeremiah to the sinking feeling he has that nothing the group does now matters. "Nebuchadnezzar is at the door," reads Daye of the fall of Jerusalem to the evil Persian king. "God sent Nebuchadnezzar to chasten you and get you back to your senses." Daye fears that we in Louisiana, like the people of Jerusalem in 597 B.C., are so steeped in corrupt politics and bad living that "you have forgotten how to blush."

If David Duke is at the door, concludes Daye, "We have to prepare to live in exile. We have to redefine what it means to be children of God. We've been smug. Now we must learn 'how to pray in a strange land.' "

# 18. New Edwin

**M**orning *Advocate* editorial writer John LaPlante closes his notebook as the Edwards victory party swirls around him in the ballroom of the Monteleone.

"Beer, LaPlante?"

"Nah, I've gotta go back and write the Edwards endorsement."

"Already?"

"I don't think we're gonna wait around on this one."

The *Morning Advocate* has been nearly as constant and implacable an Edwards critic as the *Picayune* or the *Shreveport Times,* but, like the other papers' editorial boards, it knows there simply is no choice. So let's get it over with. Within days, all of Roemer's daily-newspaper endorsements transferred to Edwards. Republican leader Dave Treen, who considered running himself to stop Edwards, endorses the man who retired him from politics. Chambers of commerce and business groups fall into place too. Public figures and institutions, who had devoted the last decade to standing against everything Edwin Edwards stood for, now line up shoulder to shoulder for him. At this point, silence in the face of David Duke is taken as complicity, a cover for his growing hidden vote coming out of hiding.

Ten days after the primary, the two biggest voices have not been heard. No one doubts that the *Picayune*, disagreeable as it will find the task, will come out for Edwards. And surely Buddy Roemer will too. Won't they?

Edwards displays public indifference. In his suite at the Monteleone, he says his own polling shows that the endorsement by Dave Treen, as the state's most respected Republican, is more important than Roemer's. As for the *Picayune*, there was the earlier brave talk in the heady closing days of the primary of telling the paper to keep its endorsement and stay out of the race, but the politician in him prevails. By Halloween, with the Duke surge into the middle class showing no signs of ebbing, no word has come from Edwards' two old foes.

While Edwards waits, he seems to be taking to his odd new role as the good-government, establishment candidate. Without warning any aides, he arrives at a press conference and announces that he will reappoint his oldest enemy, Bill Lynch, to the post of state inspector general. "He didn't say a word about that this morning when I picked him up," says a shocked Andrew Martin. Probably because Edwards did not want to hear their wailings and the screams from his most loyal backers. They would come soon enough. "He doesn't have to take the calls," complains Martin. "I've been taking them all day. Our people are hot." Of course they are. Bill Lynch is more than an enemy—he tops the list.

During his former reporting career at the *Picayune*, Lynch was the first in the press to begin investigating Edwards, and did not let up for 15 years. In return, Edwards never missed an occasion to revile Lynch. Once at a Gridiron Show, Edwards in his rebuttal tossed out the customary insults to reporters in the cast, but spent more time personally attacking Lynch, who was sitting in the audience. After Governor Roemer hired him as the ethics watchdog, Lynch's official investigations created uproars at several state universities and drew fire from Edwards, who called them witchhunts and promised, once back in power, to not just fire

Lynch but to abolish the office. Now, to tap Lynch as his first appointee shocks Edwards' old supporters and angers many. Edwards could not choose a more dramatic way of debuting the New Edwin. Lynch, the honoree, was not on hand for the announcement. "He's still going over the papers of my last administration to try to find something before January 13 (inauguration day)," Edwards says. "He won't."

The job is unnecessary and Lynch is wholly unqualified to fill it, jabs Edwards, who really knows how to motivate his employees. But he knows he has a long way to go to allay Roemer voters' fears, which are considerable. But when he does, he tells reporters, "then I'll be the next reform governor who is not reelected."

New Edwin sweeps the business circuit. At the Baton Rouge City Club, he works the room while brother Marion follows him, collecting checks. This group formed a big part of Roemer's financial base. They were used to Buddy's difficult ways, but few can forgive him for blowing their best shot this century at reform. They may not trust Edwards, but they at least admire the personal touches Buddy ignored. Former state Senator Tommy Hudson guides Edwards to one young attorney whose mother has just died. Edwards offers his condolences and says some nice things about the man's family. When Edwards moves on, the lawyer makes a point: "Buddy Roemer would never do that."

Besides the New Edwin, the candidate is trying out some new attack lines tonight, courtesy of Roemer's unused research on Duke. "Whether you like affirmative action or not, the state can ill afford to lose $350 million in federal highway funds" if the state adopts Duke's plan to ban minority contract set-asides. "When I was 16, a federal affirmative action program brought electricity to my home in rural Louisiana. It was called the Rural Electrification Administration." Duke wants drug testing for welfare recipients. Edwards calculates that would cost $59 million to save $3 million in payments. Food stamps? That comes from federal funds on which local grocers make money.

On the subject of making money off government programs, Edwards promises that some old friends "who took advantage of my trust" will not be able to enrich themselves in his fourth administration. It will be his signature slogan of forgiveness and redemption: "I may not be as good a friend as I was, but I'll be a better governor than I've ever been."

Finally, Edwards flatters the crowd by asking that they urge their employees to vote for him, knowing full well that the last people employees heed on politics are their employers.

But it isn't votes he came looking for. When they depart, Marion estimates the take at $250,000, which is probably wildly inflated. Yet even a third of that, which is likely, would make it one hell of a cocktail hour.

On to the environmentalists. David Duke touts himself as a world ecologist while Edwards was best known for standing up for Rollins and Marine Shale. But this crowd gathered at the Baton Rouge Sheraton operates in a broader, moral environment. Mike Milkey of the Coastal Coalition introduces Edwards as "the only candidate with the ability to meet the problem" of the state's slow erosion into the sea. Edwards promises this crowd he will not cut back on the funding levels and authority for the Department of Environmental Quality, which grew up under Roemer. About the time he says, "My environmental record is not all that bad," the hotel fire alarm goes off. A politically weary environmentalist looks up, "I didn't know they installed lie detectors."


The voters' unhappiness and frustration with the choice left them fuels Duke's maverick assault against the established political disorder.

From a barstool at DiGiulio's, Tom Baxter of the *Atlanta Journal-Constitution* sees something bigger than Duke, past or present: "David Duke is a small man riding a very large animal." From his state representative race only three years ago until now,

Duke has held on as the beast picked up speed. Where will it stop? Who can stop it?

Ten days after the primary, the *Times-Picayune* finally weighs in. Figuring it will take more than one editorial to explain why it is backing Edwin Edwards, the New Orleans daily kicks off a week-long front-page series of editorials, called "The Decision of Our Lives," expressing its cautious reservations about Edwards and its outright contempt for Duke. This goes on for five days — endorsement by breech birth. On the news side, the *Picayune* embarks on a crusade to throw everything it has at Duke, including the Roemer research it requests from Raymond Strother.

On the day of Halloween, Buddy Roemer calls a press conference in order to make his final political statement that anyone will pay much attention to. "I have sat at my desk and cried at the anger, and shock and shame" because of the choice facing him and his supporters. But what's a guy to do? "I cannot, will not, must not vote for David Duke. It would be suicide for Louisiana. And since my choices are only two, Edwards gets my vote. He does not get my endorsement." For the next 1,500 words, he slams Duke as he never did in the campaign, defends his own record, worries about Edwards and comes down to this: "Duke has no chance to help our state. Edwards has one chance. I pray to God that he takes it."

Edwin Edwards sneers at the television set in the Monteleone suite. "Talk about damning with faint praise," he says. This is not the first time he has heard Roemer's speech. "I'll tell you what happened." After he called Roemer on the day after the election, says Edwards, "He called me back to set a meeting. He said he was still talking to people about what to do. Which is silly because he knew there was nothing else he could do. We set a meeting. He calls back. He's not finished talking to people. Okay. Fine. Finally, I go to meet with him. He has a legal pad of notes." Edwards waves his arms: "He's going through all these machinations and details, like he's writing the fucking U.N. charter. He says he's not ready. I say, 'Okay, that's fine, do what you want to do.'

"Then he calls me at night and says, 'Let me read this to you.' I say, 'Buddy, I don't give a shit.' He says, 'No, I want to get it right.' So he reads the whole fucking thing. And then he says he may want to change a few phrases. Fine, I say, whatever you want. Then he calls back the *next* morning and wants to read over more changes." Edwards is incredulous. "I've got phones in my ear, people all over are talking to me and he's going on and on and on. He should know that no one's going to pay any attention to what he says except he's going to vote for Edwin Edwards but he's not endorsing him. That's all. Man!" Edwards shakes his head as he looks out over the rooftops of the French Quarter on this brilliant fall afternoon. He did find one bright spot in the governor's speech. "At least he didn't put the children first."

George Ackal Jr., last seen standing onstage next to David Duke and accepting his endorsement in his unsuccessful state Senate race, now stands in front of the TV monitors in the Edwards suite, sifting through the effluvium of the news. Ackal never stopped helping Edwards, even while he was going to Duke rallies. Edwards knew about it and approved. After all, he wanted to help Duke as much as he could. In the primary. Now Ackal is working full-time on Edwards fundraising. In a day or two, he will go to Los Angeles to represent the boss at a little fundraiser Steven Stills and Dan Aykroyd are throwing. "Can you believe?" he says, watching a CNN report. "There are parents taking the kids trick or treating wearing little Klan outfits. Are people sick or what?"

Edwards touches bases around the state, but he is concentrating where the votes are and where the fear of Duke is greatest. A reception/rally sponsored by the New Orleans Young Businessmen's Association attracts over 500 well-dressed business and professional men and women, many of whom never thought they would vote for Edwin Edwards, much less be working for him. Some have organized themselves into phone banks in the large downtown law offices. Bob d'Hemecourt marvels at the crowd nibbling on the fruit and cheese at the Hilton. "This is Halloween night. People here have kids."

Edwin Edwards is relishing the return of his prodigal supporters, regardless of the reason. Onstage, he is revisiting the theme of tolerance. "When he's through with the minorities and Jews, who's next? Irish and the Italians. What about disabled people? People who can't see or hear or get out of a wheelchair?"

He sounds like Earl Long vilifying the budget-cutters for being against "the spastics." Anyone who can remember the tired, bitter harangues from the summer see a renewed candidate now. "Look at him. He's having a ball," nudges d'Hemecourt. "The B-12 shot is kicking in."

"Someone is saying because you can't produce you should be shunted aside and not cared for," preaches Edwin the Tolerant. "We're a better people than that." The last time Edwards could share that pronoun with a group of yuppies, the term had not yet been coined.

Edwin is loving this more than the crowd, which is more pumped to beat Duke than to restore the reign of the Sun King. Many of these are people who have voted for Edwin Edwards two or three times in the last 20 years, especially in the early years when they saw Edwards as the social liberal with oil revenues to pay for his populism and for his friends. When his oil and their luck ran out in the '80s, they turned hard on him. After the trials, after the depression, after the Revolution, they saw Edwards as lower than a crook, as old news. Now they are giving him money, applauding him, working for him. Some even want to believe him, but most don't care.

"What choice do I have?" The young attorney at the rally has done more than vote against Edwards in the past. She once testified against him. Kathryn Lichtenberg, a former employee of Hospital Services Development Corporation, testified for the prosecution that co-defendant Jim Wylie had told her "the gravy train will really come in when Edwards is back in office." From her 1985 testimony, you would think there is no one she regarded as lower than Edwin Edwards. Apparently there is.

Edwards brims with confidence, but many in the audience are very nervous. They have seen the consensus candidate of the decent, progressive New Orleans Uptown community get trashed before in the rural parishes. It's a different world out there and a young female journalist is getting that inkling. "I'm hearing people I *know* saying Duke will win."


Who hasn't endorsed Edwin Edwards so far? Today is the turn of the state's student government associations. No, answers Tracy White of LSU, there was no vote by student bodies but there was "the consensus of student leaders who are concerned about the future of higher education." Edwards looks on approvingly: "That was pretty good. You ought to run for governor."

The students laugh. Edwards enjoys the light moment with the leaders of tomorrow before disappearing down the hallway of the Baton Rouge headquarters. In the back of the conference room, Sam Jones is not smiling. The Franklin mayor came by to endorse Edwards today too, throwing the full moral weight of his .76 percent showing behind the Democrat. But not with great confidence. "I told him, 'You're not going to like what I have to say,' when I met him this morning. He told me, 'I have to listen to you. You've been right all along.' "

He hopes he's wrong. "All I'm hearing is Duke," Jones says later over pasta at Maggio's. "I told him that all these endorsements are not helping and they could be hurting. The message people are getting from these endorsements is business as usual and these people don't want anything the hell to do with business as usual."

So what should Edwards do?

"I advised him to show himself as caring and compassionate, and concerned about people. I told him, 'You've got to prove to people that you understand suffering, that you've been there too.' "

Did he listen?

"I don't think so."

The student of history doesn't like the pattern of this election. "All revolutions start in the countryside and spread to the cities." Roemer may have started the revolution, says Jones, but then, "All revolutions eat their children. Duke took Roemer's revolution to the next level and devoured him. He gutted Roemer and took his issues."

And Edwin has Roemer's endorsements. "You remember what Edwin said about waiting by the river long enough to see your enemy's dead body float past? Edwin's problem is he's hitching a ride on Buddy's corpse."

He pulls out a large binder, the full report from the McKeon poll that first charted Duke's hidden vote. "I tried to show this to Edwin, but he wasn't interested," says Jones, adjusting his napkin tucked in at the neck as he flips through the cross-tabs. He finds the Duke-Edwards matchup poll from last August. It shows Edwards winning 42-30 percent while 28 percent are won't say/undecided. Only a third of whites in the poll say they would vote for Edwards against Duke. Duke also polled over 40 percent of people who make more than $40,000 a year. "That's where the hidden vote hid out in the primary," concludes Jones. Nothing Edwards has said or done in the runoff addresses what people are mad about. "People have lost faith in institutions and they've lost money in S&Ls. Electronic preachers are on trial. Their confidence is not broken, it's in intensive care. Anything could break it."

What Duke says works for him because people see it. "They see people buying hamburger with food stamps while they're buying

Hamburger Helper." Calling welfare a federal problem instead of a state one doesn't matter to voters who are trying to get someone's attention, says Jones. And Duke knows there is not much he can do about the problems: "The worst thing that would happen to him would be to be elected."

The Duke campaign has unveiled a new t-shirt — a heroic David Duke in front of an American flag — and it is selling fast before the big Monroe rally. The police have shut the front doors of Brown Auditorium on the Northeast Louisiana University campus, leaving about 400 true believers and the curious to wait and shiver in the cold night air.

About 1,000 people are jammed into the small auditorium. Two young Roemer voters — one a college student, the other a salesman — lean against the wall on the side aisle. "I came to listen," says the salesman, wearing an Alabama t-shirt, his alma mater. "I could vote for Duke. I mean, considering the alternative."

Monroe is the white-hot center of Duke support. Duke carried the city despite its 40 percent minority population. Duke cut a wide swath through North Louisiana, stopped only by Edwards in the black parishes in the Delta and around Shreveport.

Suddenly, David Duke emerges from backstage, followed by an army of two dozen cameramen, photographers, reporters, supporters and two state policemen, who jostle to stay ever at Duke's side. The crowd is on its feet: "Duke, Duke, Duke."

Tonight's rally will begin with a slide show prepared by local supporters. The lights go down. The music of Randy Newman's "Louisiana" comes up. Forest scenes. Cotton fields. Sunrise over Lake D'Arbonne. NLU Stadium. A green meadow. A green meadow with a Duke sign in it. The crowd roars.

*Loo-wee-ziana, Loo-wee-ziana*

Now we see David Duke's smiling face. The crowd cheers loudly with each Duke appearance on the screen. There will be many. Here's David Duke with arms around his children. David Duke at a country fair. David Duke signing autographs. Cheer. David Duke aiming a shotgun. Very big cheer. David Duke kneeling in prayer. A cheer for that too.

*They're tryin' to wash us away,*
*They're tryin' to wash us away.*

The montage runs about 10 minutes too long, enough for the crowd to hear "Everything I Do" and "Wind Beneath My Wings" to accompany repeats of the slides. Duke views with great interest. This has potential. Fortunately, it also has an ending. This crowd is ready for the real thing.

As Duke starts to speak, a young woman stands and shouts, "We love you, David."

Duke blinks. "I love you too." She squeals and sits down.

He runs through the usual litany of ills facing the Gret Stet, with "women on welfare having more illegitimate children" eliciting the loudest response. That's followed by his new platform plank, to prohibit welfare recipients from buying lottery tickets.

He draws a bead on Edwards' establishment support, holding up the endorsement from the *Baton Rouge Morning Advocate*. "The *Advocate* said they don't like the things Edwards has done, but we need to elect him because he gets things done. Great. Edwards believes in government of, by and for the special interests."

Duke, who has swallowed Roemer's Revolution, now is chewing on Edwards' populism. "People have been waiting so long for someone to stand up. The media and the liberal opposition say America doesn't like what's going on here." ("Bullll-shit," yells someone from the back.) "The people of America love what's going on here. Louisiana has been at the bottom of the heap for so long. It's about time we are in first place in waking up this country."

As the crowd roars again, some of the shivering fans locked outside begin beating on the metal doors near the stage. They hear the screaming and they want to come in.

Duke is pacing the stage now. With each pivot and turn, troopers Beau Torres and Brad Stewart keep in step, following him around the stage. With each applause line, folks stand, yell, stomp their feet, stand on chairs and in general carry on like this is a rock concert.

"I don't think you came to hear me speak. You came to celebrate."

"We love you, David."

With the polls going his way, the money coming in and this crowd going crazy, David Duke is at the peak of his political experience.

Just as he is getting into the story of the 94-year-old woman beaten to death in her living room on the Fourth of July, there are angry rumblings in the rear of the hall. Four people in a back row are holding up red "No Dukes" signs. The people around them are booing. Now those in the front rows see the signs and they are standing and booing and chanting "Duke." A woman screams, "You better get out of here."

The four dissenters, two men and two women in their 30s, sit placidly through the insults and curses hurling at them. Duke needs to reclaim his supporters' attention. "Now, now," he extends his arm while clutching the microphone. "That's okay. I admire their courage." The crowd mutters and stirs between Duke and the silent protest. "There was a time that people like us were small and they were many. Now we are many and they are few." That gets the crowd yelling the right way again. The new majority. "Duke, Duke, Duke."

Having incited the crowd into a frenzy, the speaker revels in tolerance: "When I'm governor, I will have an open door and I will even talk to them. . . . I don't hate them. I don't want you to hate them. If someone flips the bird at you" — he pauses and smiles — "blow them a kiss."

A new chant starts up, "Duke for President, Duke for President." The beating on the metal doors resumes from the outside.

Just when it's about time to start the collection, the sound system fails. Duke moves to the front of the stage and raises his volume. "A few times in my life I've had my mike cut off. It's not stopped me before and it won't now. We got a lot of problems with equipment tonight. I hope we won't with the voting machines. Now I have a few things to ask you to do for me."

A middle-aged woman from the side shouts, "You can have anything you want, babe."

"I want you to go home tonight and get out your phone book and call everyone." The oyster buckets are passing through the audience without the candidate's instructions on playing Doubloons for Dollars. His mike is back on, so he can say softly, "And one more thing. Before you go to sleep tonight, say a prayer for me and my family. . . ."

The candidate gives himself to his audience as he walks along the front of the stage, shaking the outstretched hands. A woman in her early 20s comes away holding her right hand: "I touched him!"

The camera-lit entourage in tow, Duke heads out the side door to talk to about 400 people waiting in the clear cold night air.

"You know why I'm for David Duke?" Carl Beatty sits on the edge of the stage as the crowd flows out. He is a farmer from Winnsboro. "My great-grandfather was a slavedriver. He was poor and it was the only job he could get. When the war started, he went to hide in the woods and he was found by the Union troops and he was starving."

Mr. Beatty's odd family history apparently is meant to establish his credentials on the minority question. "I have a hired man who is living in a housing project with a girlfriend and two children. She's pregnant again. They hide him when the welfare people come. I gave him $3 because he said he had to take his boy to the doctor. Then I saw him the same day, buying a six-pack. I'm just telling you what I see, you understand? My black friends need someone like David Duke. They're drowning."

David Duke, man of the people, forgiving of his enemies, the black people's great white hope. Reality in the heart of Duke country.


Bob d'Hemecourt opens each envelope, inspects each check and places it in a little pile.

"What are you looking for?"

"The zip code," answers d'Hemecourt, tearing open the next envelope. "As long as it has a complete address and a zip code for the campaign finance report, it goes there," he motions to the check pile. You figure if Carlos Marcello sent a $5,000 check, as long as it contained the magic five numbers, it would land there.

"What's the difference raising money this time and in 1971?"

D'Hemecourt looks over the littered glass-top table. "In 1971, this was all cash. Checks take up much less room."

George Fischer and George Ackal are working the phones. Fischer is pleased he is down to only a handful of tickets for the one big New Orleans fundraiser. Ackal is distressed, "Can you believe someone stole my Mont Blanc pen?"

Edwin Edwards has been running appointments through his bedroom all day. A couple of trial lawyers have just departed. A couple of insurance lobbyists wait on the couch.

Since Roemer's statement, Edwards continues to promise business, civic and environmental groups that he will maintain and enhance Buddy Roemer's reforms. He has had to stop trashing Roemer and has even choked out a word or two of praise for the late dragonslayer. D'Hemecourt feels sorry . . . for Edwards. "Edwin had to say things he thought he would never have to say. Everything he wanted to say about Roemer is still in the file cabinets."

A visitor asks for Edwards' prediction.

"It'll be 60-40," Edwards says matter-of-factly, ushering the insurance lobbyists in.

D'Hemecourt grimaces, "I wish he'd stop that."

Pete Babin is concerned with more than predictions. "Don't get too overconfident with all those endorsements and cut off your grass roots." The labor leader worries that the business endorsements are eating into the few blue-collar white votes that Edwards got in the primary.

Edwards already has got that message and has put the word out to cool the endorsements. According to his polling, the most important blessing came from Dave Treen, a straightforward endorsement. Roemer's and the *Picayune*'s were of some value. "The rest were forced on us, overkill," says d'Hemecourt. It's been so long since he's got one, though, Edwards is loath to hurt someone's feelings by discouraging any endorsement, especially the ones that come with checks.

In the face of Edwards' blithe confidence stands the large undecided bloc in the polls of former Roemer voters, still angry over the election, still unreconciled to Edwards. After his early fumbling start in the runoff, Edwards now seems to be warming up to the economic argument. So too are some business groups buying third-party commercials to warn of the hazards of Duke. The Louisiana Coalition runs a full-page ad of Duke before and after plastic surgery with the headline: SOME CHANGE IS ONLY SKIN DEEP. And now the *Picayune* is into the act, detailing the national associations that say they will cancel their planned New Orleans conventions if Duke is governor.

The economic argument will work best in New Orleans, which understands and depends on trade and tourism from the rest of the world. It falls off, though, the farther upstream you go into deepest, whitest Louisiana. Plantworkers along the river don't believe for a moment that the multinational corporations, who daily deal with the world's greatest despots, would abandon or curtail operations because of one more crazy governor. In North Louisiana parishes, the heart of Duke country, the non-agricultural economy can't get any worse — the prospect of hard times in New Orleans moistens few eyes.

There's another problem. Surrogates can warn of economic doom. Third-party commercials can hammer home Duke's Nazi connections. But it takes a candidate to face the enemy. So far, Edwin Edwards has not been the match of David Duke, whether before live audiences or cameras. Edwards, at his physical and political peak the week of the primary, has yet to get the measure of his strange young opponent. He's been so busy promoting his new mature, humble incarnation — with mixed results — that he's neglected what he does best in a campaign: make his opponent look worse. The state has seen enough governors fail for lack of personal power. That's what being governor is about. When is Edwin Edwards going to show he can take on David Duke?

Beth Courtney stands in the WLPB parking lot, tapping her foot. The director of Louisiana Public Broadcasting is surrounded by reporters and cameras, all waiting for David Duke to show up for his live statewide televised debate with Edwin Edwards. He has five minutes.

Campaign schedules are pretty crazy, but this is stretching it. "I wonder if he'll make it," says Courtney. Some around her wonder if he cares. Duke has grown more cavalier to the local media. Who needs them? He's in hot demand on national TV and radio. The adoring crowds at his own rallies grow larger and wilder with each event. So far, in two meetings, he's handled Edwards with ease. Why should he get worked up over one more debate with the old man?

The old man is there early for extra time in makeup. He is patiently waiting, on the set. Nearly everyone else is in the parking lot. A pair of headlights beams down the entrance road. "This must be him." Instantly the corner of the parking lot is illuminated by the camera lights flashing on. The white car wheels around the corner and slams to a halt. Duke and two bodyguards jump out and race for the entrance. The gaggle of reporters and lights run with him, nearly trampling some slow-moving print reporters at the door. We are 30 seconds to airtime.

Edwards gets in the opening salvo: "While my opponent is going around the country to advance his national agenda, my only interest is in being your governor." The born-again economic developer is name-dropping through the list of CEOs he has conversed with recently, from Exxon to Louisiana Land & Exploration to Freeport-McMoRan. "Things will settle down after November 16 and we can go on with what we're doing."

"You're right," adds Duke. "Business as usual, which is not good for business." The reputation of the governor is hardly relevant, he says. "Companies will come if there is no corruption and higher taxes." Duke repeats his claim that Edwards is selling positions.

"Name one," Edwards shoots back.

"Jim, get that list." Duke takes a news clip from McPherson's off-camera hand. It's a *Shreveport Times* story from 1983 about a contributor pushing for an appointment to the Mineral Board.

Edwards takes the clip and points out that he did not give him the board seat and returned the $20,000 contribution. "You see, that's about *not* selling positions."

To its credit, the panel does not ask the candidates sleep-inducing questions on their plans for education and the environment.

"Mr. Duke, can you tell us what jobs you have held."

Duke bristles. "I've been a small-businessman and I've worked hard. You suggest that if you're a small-businessman, you're not working. That insults small-businessmen. I sell mailing lists, I do computer consulting. I am the national president of a nonprofit organization, the NAAWP."

Edwin Edwards, a lawyer and a politician, cannot resist jumping in. "The truth is he's never had a job. He worked as a substitute interpreter in Laos and he was fired because he couldn't understand anyone." Duke doesn't even do a good job as a perennial candidate. "He ran eight times and he won one. That's no way to run a government if we win one out of eight."

It's Norman Robinson's turn. "Mr. Duke, I'm a concerned citizen and member of a minority," begins the news anchor from WWL. "I heard you say that Jews belong in the ashbin of history, that horses have made greater contributions to American history than have blacks. How can one govern with that evil, vile mentality? How can you convince me why I should entrust to you the lives of our children?"

Duke slips into Wronged Innocence mode: "Mr. Robinson, you're not being fair. I regret the things I've said. It's not the way I live today."

Robinson won't back off. "You've talked of political genocide. Are you willing to apologize to the people you've insulted?"

"Of course I apologize. I repudiate the Klan and the Nazis and anyone who discriminates. Mr. Robinson, you're not being fair."

"Mr. Duke, you're not being honest."

Experienced moderator Robert Collins has never had to rein in a reporter on one of these debates. As the bitter exchange escalates, says Collins later, "I could see my life flashing before my eyes."

With Duke off-balance, Edwards adds his own body blow. "I've heard that members of the Klan in Texas and Iowa are coming to town to help Duke in the election." He looks coldly at the camera. "If you come, I hope you behave yourselves. I've talked to the sheriffs and told them to be on the lookout. If any of them intimidate anyone or treat anyone harshly, they will be dealt with harshly."

Edwards has Duke unnerved. Before he can get on the offensive, it's Norman Robinson's turn again. He brings up Duke's failure to pay state income taxes for several years and the soft-porn sex manual Duke wrote, *Finderskeepers.* "Are these the actions of a man of public integrity?"

Duke is coming unglued. "I've only got one minute to respond. That is a cheap shot and I don't appreciate it," he complains to moderator Robert Collins, which only wastes a few more of his seconds. Hastily, he explains that his income at that time was far below the reporting threshold. And that he only wrote part of the book. "I stuck to exercise and diet. I wrote no pornography."

This little event, its time running short, is in bad need of some levity. Edwin Edwards is holding up a copy of the infamous map of America Resettled from the *NAAWP News*. "He has his plan to divide the country. Part of the plan is to send the Cajuns to Vermont. As a spokesman for the Cajuns, we aren't going to go. It's cold up there."

It's getting hotter down here. "I won the Cajun vote," snaps Duke in his best comeback, though it's not completely accurate. "I may not speak French, but I speak their language."

Since we're taking cheap shots, Duke gets at least one in. "After you mocked the crucifixion of Christ, I hope you get right with Christ."

Now Edwards bristles: "I never mocked the crucifixion," also only partly true. "I may lose this election because of your lies, but I will not lose my soul. I did say I had concerns (about Christ's death and resurrection), but I overcame that with faith." In 1984, in the midst of the firestorm over his statements expressing doubts about the very foundation of Christianity, Edwards was getting so worked over by the fundamentalists that he went onstage after the Alexandria Gridiron Show, ketchup smeared on his shirt front, lipstick on the palms of his hands, and stretched out his arms in a crucifixion tableau. That was funny. But the *Daily Town Talk* published the photo. That was not funny.

After Duke's limp closing, Edwards revs up his indignation: "While David Duke was burning crosses, I was building hospitals to heal. While he was wearing a Nazi uniform, I was in a National Guard uniform helping flood victims. While David Duke was selling Nazi hate literature, I was providing free textbooks. While

Duke was writing porn books, I was passing anti-pornography laws. After you've done community service for 20 years, come back and show how you've changed. Until then, don't let him divide us and make a mockery of us."

As the credits roll, Duke stands up, clearly disgusted. The media enter the studio and crowd around both candidates. Duke, of course, has the larger group, but Edwards doesn't seem to care. Tonight, he had Duke's number. It was not the same old Edwin. For the first time, he was focused on his enemy and, more important, he was funny. He succeeded in making Duke look foolish instead of ghoulish. Duke's boyish charm works for him when he is being attacked as a monster. But get people laughing at him, and he looks like a kid out of his league.

Tonight he was hit from both sides, from Edwards and the panel. With mixed results.

"I thought Norman Robinson just elected David Duke," says CNN's Charlie Zewe.

For months, Duke's opponents have criticized the press for helping establish Duke's credibility by accepting him as just another political candidate. Norman Robinson knows he stepped over the line of impartiality, but he's glad he did. "I'll not be on a panel and roll over like Larry King."

In the lobby, Beth Courtney is reading over a big stack of callers' comments: "Hope you fold," "Worst debate ever," "Poor choice of panelists," "Robinson is a racist."

The Edwards crowd takes up three tables at Ruth's Chris Steak House tonight. They are in a boisterous mood as they celebrate a turning point. The reporter notes, "You guys must be happy about the debate." The look on one supporter's face seems to say *What debate?*

"Naw," says the supporter. "Today we just raised the three millionth dollar. We've got our street money. It's in the bag."

For three weeks now, Jimmy Long has been sponsoring an open breakfast on Saturday mornings in the black section of Natchitoches. A six-term veteran of the House of Representatives and a cousin of Huey and Earl, Jimmy Long finds himself in the fight of his political life. Political currents he thought would never reach this rural North Louisiana parish have about capsized his career. The anti-incumbent vote, the Year of the Woman, Duke fever and hard-hitting direct mail have forced Long into a runoff with Police Juror Betty Hilton, an attractive widow, retired schoolteacher and thoroughly modern campaigner.

Hilton flat outworked Long in the primary, finding every door she could knock on in Natchitoches Parish. She found a few other things. "I saw a deer just standing on a front porch, plain as day." She found basic voter intolerance from one woman who sprayed her with Lysol. She also found enough discontent with politics in general — whether among blacks or Dukesters — to turn Long's six terms in the Legislature around on him. You can't be known as Mr. Education in this state — Long chairs the House Education Committee — for too many years without it coming back to haunt you.

In the runoff, Hilton has momentum and Long has a lot of work to do. The parish went to Duke and may go for him again in the runoff. Though Hilton in no way supports Duke, she shares many white voters with him and benefits from the same anti-incumbent mood. Long should get the black vote, but Long's alliance with Buddy Roemer and Hilton's aggressive campaigning enabled her to run well in black precincts.

That was the deepest cut of all: to take a big chunk of the black vote away from a Long. Worst of all, says Long, he was victimized by one of the oldest tricks in the hills. Someone, says Long, reproduced the sample ballot of the Natchitoches Voters League and substituted Betty Hilton's number next to Long's name and picture. Mr. Education was almost done in by his own constituents' illiteracy.

That won't happen again. To make sure, Jimmy Long, who owns the Dixie Dandy grocery store, is serving up breakfast and politics one week before the election. The battle lines in the runoff will be different. Only 60 percent of the black vote showed up for the primary. That will have to change. The election has polarized the state, but it has unified the black community. The governor's race touches every other contest, and Jimmy Long wants to make it clear that he alone is the politically safe choice.

That will take a little work. Ms. Hilton has done a good job of slamming her opponent in both communities. She complains that Jimmy Long "can walk a sewing thread from here to Alexandria," but she did uncover one Long misstep: in 1990, he voted for David Duke's anti–affirmative action bill. Explaining that curious vote in the black community will require more credibility than the Long name alone. For today's breakfast, Long has imported a ringer: state Representative Raymond Jetson of Baton Rouge, who is African-American, articulate, dynamic and a former standout lineman at Grambling.

Citizens filter in early on this cold Saturday morning to the Ben Johnson Auditorium, which is an old gym converted into a community center and named for the 86-year-old local black leader. Paying respects to Mr. Johnson, a local school principal warms up the crowd for the task next Saturday: "Please don't neglect to do your job just because you didn't get paid. Get up early, go through your neighborhood, tell your neighbors. The Lord blessed most of us who have an automobile, but some of your neighbors do not. We know we won't have a problem with the ballots this time."

"Oh yes," answers the audience.

"It's dishonorable to give someone a ballot with the wrong information on it."

Councilman John Winston makes the key linkage between the local and state races: "These are the most terrible times since I've been alive. Imagine having David Duke and Betty Hilton. Look at the returns in Provencal, Goldanna and East Natchitoches. Everywhere she did well, so did David Duke." The audience murmurs angrily.

The crowd is building and it is getting hungry, but they know the drill: no bacon and eggs until the speeches and prayers are done. The keynote speaker, Representative Jetson, has been making good money in this campaign advising white candidates how to get black votes. Today's trip, he says, "comes out of my own pocket" and out of loyalty to "a man who has been there over and over again for us." He says Long came to him for advice on that anti-affirmative action bill. Since the bill had been rendered toothless by committee amendments, it outlawed affirmative action in title only. In the heat of the Duke Senate campaign, with the bill on the floor, many rural white legislators felt pressured to vote for it. "But Jimmy was concerned about how blacks would react. I told him, 'Jimmy, the bill doesn't do anything. It doesn't matter.' So he voted for it. Then he came back to me and said the roof has fallen in, that the blacks are mad at him. Well, let me tell you something," Jetson leans his massive frame onto the rostrum. "When someone tells you your friends are not your friends, it's like me telling you your family is not your family."

"Amen."

"I don't know Ms. Hilton," continues Jetson. "She might be a fine lady. But the possibility that David Duke is your next governor is very real. In the last three weeks I have not seen a poll that gives Edwin Edwards a lead larger than the margin of error. You can change that. Any black person who does not vote next Saturday might as well vote for Duke. And if Duke is elected, God forbid, people like Jimmy Long will be more important than ever. Please send Jimmy back . . ."

So much for the politics. Jetson shifts into his sermon: "Do you realize what time it is? It is time to wake up. The dream has become a nightmare. We are all preoccupied with time; we have clocks everywhere. Some folks have clocks in their bathrooms. But do you really know what time it is? We live in a state where a man who was grand dragon of the Ku Klux Klan can say he made some mistakes and then be elected governor. Do you know what time it is?"

Onstage, the councilman winks at the preacher — the outside talent is pretty good.

Jetson is beyond politics now and into the real issues: "There are more black men 18 to 24 years old in prison than in college. There are more black women 18 to 24 years old on welfare than in college. Do we know what time it is? David Duke talks about the welfare issue because there really is a problem, but he has no solution.

"You can go out on the streets of Baton Rouge and see folks selling cocaine. You may not have it here . . ."

"Oh, yes we do."

"There was a time we got by without welfare, when we had neighbors who would help. Now, we don't know our neighbors and we are scared if we do. There was a time we had respect from children."

The audience laughs.

"Do you know what time it is? It is time we start addressing our problems."

The crowd has worked up a real appetite to vote now. The last word belongs to the elderly Ben Johnson, who clearly frames the challenge: "We've created a monster in this state. Duke is only one man. One man can't destroy us. But there are 44 percent other little Dukesters. David Duke talks about sterilization. I know he's not talking about sterilizing white folks. I know we have our problems, but we didn't create them ourselves. This monster must be stopped now, regardless of who wins. Bush knows that too. There's gonna be a national monster. And I'm concerned. I don't want to go through another bloodbath."

A distinct political alignment is taking place in this runoff in minority communities throughout the state. The lines were not clear in the primary, and, besides, in the governor's race, black folks voted all over the place. Now, from the top of the ballot on down, state to local, fair or not, black voters will be pairing every set of candidates with either Edwin Edwards or David Duke. Jimmy Long, a reform ally of Buddy Roemer, is hardly close to Edwards, but today he is close enough. The lines have been drawn around David Duke, and in Natchitoches, Betty Hilton finds herself on the wrong side.

# 19. Matters of Faith

John Breaux pointed to David Duke's face on the TV screen and said, "If you hit him right there, his whole face will fall apart." *Morning Advocate* correspondent Joan McKinney's account of the returns party in Washington reflects what interviewers have been trying to do throughout his public life: land that one punch that cracks Duke into pieces. Despite the barrage of shots taken over the years, Duke has maintained remarkable control of the image he wants to project: the man who has rechanneled his radical passions into the brave new conservative mainstream. The eventual sucker punch turned out to be a long left hook from Tim Russert of NBC News on *Meet the Press*, the Sunday before the election.

"Mr. Duke, can you name the top three manufacturing employers in Louisiana?"

Duke's face goes blank. "Um." Interminable seconds tick by. Finally: "We have a number of employers in our state. I couldn't give you the names right off."

"You're talking about economic development and you don't know?" presses Russert.

"I'm not sure . . ."

So we mark a little zero on that one. Next question: "In terms of economic development and the condition of your state, how many people in your state live below the poverty line?"

"A great percentage," answers Duke, struggling from the mat. "We have the highest per capita percentage in the country just about.... I don't carry around an almanac with me."

Aren't those the kind of things a governor should know? asks Russert.

"I think a governor should know how to make businesses work, and I think we do know—we all know we have a horrible poverty problem. That's not the issue." The issue, of course, is welfare, which he latches onto and talks about as long as he can.

Sitting next to him, Edwin Edwards looks like he's about to pop. He says later, "I wanted to raise my hand and say, 'Teacher, teacher, I know.'" He did. Asked after the debate, he responded: Avondale, General Motors and AT&T. Twenty-four percent of Louisianians live below the poverty line.

Russert wasn't through with Duke. Unlike the infotainment crowd, he spent the show peppering Duke with hard-line questions on his not-so-past anti-Semitic statements, his Nazi activities, his failure to file state income taxes and to pay property taxes.

Duke had fielded those questions before and responded with his usual disclaimers that those charges were in his past or taken out of context. But the manufacturing question (it had been sent by the LPB debate panel as one of its unused questions) stopped him cold. It made him appear to be lightweight and out of his league. With the Roemer voters, getting over the initial shock and the anger of the choices left them, Duke's flimsy showing struck a chord. They had seen what happens to governors who do not measure up to the power of the office.

Edwards had clearly bested Duke in the LPB debate and, despite his incredible claim that he was not a gambler, fared far better on *Meet the Press*, their first and only live national debate. In their earlier encounters Duke was able to make Edwards' past the issue, but now Duke, his past and lack of presence — his integrity — are in the spotlight. Edwards enjoys the enviable position of a side attraction. Instead of carrying the attack himself, Edwards has the press, the Dukewatchers and the business leadership acting as a kind of establishment goon squad to work over Duke constantly and mercilessly. The third-party anti-Duke multimedia offensive is slamming its prey with more commercials from new directions.

David Duke still occupies the countryside but his invasion of the middle class has stopped at the cities' gates. Many anti-Edwards Roemer voters who last week were saying they could vote for Duke are just keeping their mouths shut now. Edwin Edwards is personally offensive to many. He has burned them not once but twice. On their own they would never vote for him. But they are not on their own. The whole world is watching. Duke's image is firmly fixed among middle-class urban voters as both a lightweight and a pariah. It's taken some time but the economic argument is bearing down harder, and the pressure is not felt merely in the pocketbook. Most Louisianians outside of the tourism business do not seriously feel an anti-Duke backlash will diminish their livelihoods any more than will Edwin Edwards' predictably bad government. The stronger motivation for the Roemer voter is the fear of shame at electing a man the rest of the world has branded as morally repugnant. To the yuppie mind, the only thing more odious than bad government is bad taste.

As long as Roemer, then Edwards, were the issues, Duke's acceptance grew with voter discontent. Now the table is turned and tilted, and all the knives and forks are coming at him.


Sunday night Edwin Edwards sweeps into the big ballroom of the New Orleans Hilton for one of those good old-fashioned $1,000 fundraisers, well-catered and well-boozed, and filled with not only all the members of the extended Democratic tribe but also many of the business and social elite last seen lining up for pictures with

George Bush. It's been eight years since Edwards has been able to throw this kind of bash like in the old days, when the power train was whistling out of the station with the crush of passengers scrambling to get on board.

Edwards knows why they are here. He would have liked to have seen them in the primary, but that's just his pride. His politics couldn't be happier. He knows what he owes these people and they know the deal too. Maybe it wasn't Confucius, but some wise man said, "If you're with me in the primary, you get what you want. If you're with me in the runoff, you get good government." For Edwards, for once, the latter group is so much greater than the former that he may really have the freedom to be this New Edwin — within reason, of course.


Far from the twinkling cocktail hour, a few determined journalists navigate the back roads between Franklinton and Folsum in that isolated region of the Florida parishes that might as well be Mississippi. At the end of the dark, dusty road in the woods shine the light poles of the Yates Rodeo Arena, featuring David Duke Night.

"Whoa, hold up, get that car out of here." With long strides big John Yates moves in to round up the errant journalists.

"They said at the gate we could park here," says the female photographer.

"Don't you raise your voice to me. I own this place." Yates glowers with authority and resentment. The photographer shrugs. "We just parked where they told us to."

Yates eases up. "Well, all right. Look, I just got ticked off. It's you people in the press and what you're doing to David Duke. If you'd just give him a chance and write something fair about him. I know him. He's my buddy."

Properly stroked, Mr. Yates is just an old pussycat. He's taken a real liking, for instance, to the French news film crew, with its comely, dark-haired correspondent in fashionable ear muffs, and is squiring them about his spread. "I run about $50 million in livestock through here each year," he explains as he leads the Gallic press toward the horses.

There really will be a rodeo tonight, drawing a larger-than-usual crowd, observes one cowboy. "One girl I know rode her horse since 2 o'clock this afternoon to get here to see David Duke." The cars are still coming through the gates, where they pay $5 apiece for adults, and about 400 folks are filling up the bleachers. The rodeo was supposed to start 15 minutes ago, but the guest of honor has not yet arrived. The concession booth is keeping the hot chocolate and hot coffee pouring for the rodeo fans clustered in little groups behind the stands. Some are talking politics, the chief topic being the President's latest denunciation of Duke and his comment, dragged out of him by the press, that he would advise Louisianians to vote for Edwin Edwards.

"That Bush, he lost my vote. He didn't have to come out like that. He should have just kept his mouth shut."

"Yeah. I was crazy enough to vote him in, I'm crazy enough to vote him out."

"I voted for Duke," says a young fan. "Don't blame me."

"We mean for president."

"So do I," the young man stands his ground. "I voted for him for president in '88."

As for the governor's race, these guys see Duke taking the rodeo vote big but Edwards having the upper hand, overall. "You look at it," says one. "He's got the blacks, the people who're in jail or should be, the liberals and the gangsters. That's a pretty sizable vote."

David Duke is on the grounds. The fellows by the concession stand crane their necks to spot the candidate's car, surrounded by fans, TV cameras and a woman on horseback. It passes by and deposits Duke at a small building around the side of the stands that Yates uses for an office. The folks in the stands, having paid $5 apiece to shiver and wait for David Duke to start the show, will just have to wait a little longer. The candidate will have his picture taken by *Time* and will chat with the French news producer before emerging again for showtime.

Yates has prepared a special entrance. A mule-drawn covered wagon pulls around in position before the arena gates. Duke gingerly mounts and stands on the riding board next to the driver. His bodyguard, in order to ride along, holds on at the back of the wagon. The gates open, the driver snaps the reins and away we go. The reporters and cameramen run alongside the wagon like so many rodeo clowns while Duke holds his balance and waves to the cheering crowd. This may be the silliest moment of Campaign '91. No it isn't. Just when Duke begins speaking, one of the mules takes a huge dump. Guy Coates of the Associated Press marvels at the scene: "I wish I could put that in my lead."

Standing on the wagon, Duke is able right away to get this once-shivering crowd red hot, standing up and roaring. David Duke's message tonight is one of compassion for the underclass: "My gosh, just take a look. All the children that are born without loving fathers, born into a climate of drugs and poverty and crime, and the problems are growing. Ladies and gentlemen, I'm not against the poor people of this state. I want to help the poor people of this state, help them break the cycle of poverty they've been in for so long. But I tell you this, the people who really need the help are the people who have worked all of their lives, the elderly people who have worked and paid taxes." The rest of the social welfare system Governor Duke is going to clean up and fast, starting with the latest moral outrage that he's promoting as a major issue, that is, "these people cashing welfare checks and turning around and buying lottery tickets. I'm gonna change that." The crowd hoots and hollers through the rest of the monologue, until Duke lowers his voice for a sensitive moment. "Finally, ladies and gentlemen, there's one more thing I want to say to you. A lot has been said against me in the press, in the liberal media. Yes, I've done things in life I'd change. . . ."

"Don't apologize," a voice booms out from the stands.

"...But I've never been charged with any corruption in government, ladies and gentlemen. Ladies and gentlemen, all of us have been intolerant at some times in our lives . . ."

"Damn right!" hollers a young woman.

"...But with the power of Jesus Christ, we can all change and get better in our lives. But I want you to notice a double standard. The *Times-Picayune* has run 15 years of editorials against the corrupt policies of Edwin Edwards. But suddenly you don't hear any of that, do you? I'll give you an example. A lot has been said about statements I've made in the past, a lot of it taken out of context, changed around. The man I'm running against, when he was governor of Louisiana . . ."

"Okay, you've got him by the balls!"

"...He did an interview with the *Alexandria Daily Town Talk*" (it was the *Shreveport Journal*) "and the governor of our state was asked if he believed in the life, death and resurrection of our Lord Jesus Christ. And that man answered no."

"Boooooo."

"He told us the Bible was a lie. He may be right with Christ now. I don't mean to judge. As a Christian I give him the benefit of the doubt. But then he went onstage and put lipstick on the palm of his hands to signify he was crucified. He took ketchup and put it on his shirt and he mocked the crucifixion of Christ to howling laughter and derision before the Gridiron Club in Alexandria. Ladies and gentlemen, can you imagine for a moment what would be said in the press if I did something like that? And we've not heard one word from the liberal media about that. Why is there a double standard in the press?"

"They're scared!"

"It's not because of my past that they are attacking me, but it's because of the issues I'm talking about today in Louisiana that the liberal press can't stand. And with your help and God's help we're gonna turn Louisiana around and we're gonna send a message all around this country... ."

The mules maintain remarkable composure despite hundreds of rodeo fans screaming right at them. At the conclusion of Duke's remarks, they respond crisply on command, gallop in a wide turn around the arena and toward the gate, with the bodyguard clinging on the back and the press corps in hot pursuit. What a rush.

As the riders line up for the big show-opening Cowboy Roundup, David Duke, safe on the ground, signs Duke signs for admiring fans, mostly young women. At the edge of the crowd, a tow-headed, pudgy youth, all of ten years old, tells a friend, "My dad went to school with him."

"Oh, yeah?" says his friend.

"Yep, went to LSU with David Duke. My dad said he was the smartest guy there."


Marion Edwards can't resist getting in on this just a little. Now a corporate lobbyist, uninvolved in his brother's campaign, he answers the phone on the glass-top table because everyone else is busy on their lines. Marion is genetically incapable of putting someone on hold who wants to give money.

"Do you have a PAC?" he asks. "We're maxed out on PACs." (Roemer's rules put a $50,000 cap on total PAC contributions accepted.) This is not a problem.

"I want you to write the check to DemoPac. They are coordinating election day activities. You can make it out to them and send it to us here. And come down for the election, we're gonna have some fun. Thank you and good luck to Walgreen's."

From Main Street to the Strip: Bob d'Hemecourt is on the phone with a *Morning Advocate* reporter who is asking about a $5,000 check Edwards has received from the Nevada Hilton Corporation. D'Hemecourt remembers getting a Nevada Hilton check, sending it back and asking them to reissue from the New Orleans Hilton. That seems a rather brazen admission, but d'Hemecourt had no problem with it as long as all the zip codes were in order. The

*Morning Advocate,* already activating its casino sensors, runs a small item on the Nevada contribution. D'Hemecourt later asks Edwards if he wants to send the check back.

"Hell, no."

Money isn't all that's pouring in. There are so many requests for TV interviews, someone suggests: "We could sell interviews."

"You're about 20 years behind," pipes up old-timer George Fischer. Back then, even the candidate's wardrobe was a profit center. "What do you think happened to those ties he'd wear once and throw away?"

The press, of course, always was and forever will be a big pain in the ass. D'Hemecourt is chapped that Channel 4 pounced on Edwards for a live interview when he had just hurried up three flights of stairs (waiting for a Monteleone elevator was not an option) and caught him out of breath. "I only did it once before," steams d'Hemecourt, "but I was standing right there by the power switch on that camera and I was tempted to turn it off." Bobby will say things like that because he generally likes reporters.

"No, no, you just tell them they're doing a great job," cautions Fischer, who despises them all.

State Police Lieutenant Terry Shirley is worried about real threats. He has a picture to go out to other units of a gentleman who was arrested in 1984 lurking about the Edwards transition office with a .22 with a silencer and a list of political names. The security detail supervisor is worried about more than threats to Edwin: "I'm afraid of Duke. It could take out two troopers if someone goes for him." He's not alone. "The NOPD told us our job is easy. 'If there's trouble, you just have to close off the floor,' they said. 'If Duke wins, New Orleans will burn down.' "

The Baton Rouge Ministerial Alliance finally decides to urge their flocks to vote against David Duke without actually asking them to vote for Edwin Edwards. The neat bit of sophistry was only necessary because political elections are hardly ever mentioned in white churches, and endorsing Edwin Edwards was not seen as the right way to start. The point is made without really rubbing anyone's nose in it. Most of the ministers personally have little problem with supporting Edwin Edwards, for whom else do you send out against the Antichrist but the old devil himself ?

Duke's charge of Edwards' mocking Christ is hardly getting as much airplay as his own "ashbin of history" quote, in his own voice, in the Louisiana Coalition's radio and TV commercial. The television commercial actually ends with a shot of Hitler in military uniform giving the Nazi salute. The caption: VOTE FOR DUKE. CREATE A FUEHRER.

The stuff on Edwards' doubts about Christ's death and resurrection occurred eight years ago and he's done his public penance for it. As for the ill-advised photograph, Edwards turns the Good Book back on his attacker: "Duke is showing he doesn't know his Scripture. I had a mark on my chest. If he had read his Scripture, he would know that Jesus was not stabbed in the chest but in the side, fulfilling the biblical prophecy: 'Not a bone will be broken but He will be pierced in the side so the blood and water will flow.' "

Reporters wink at the response. No one bothers to ask just whom he was mocking with his stigmata tableau. No one really cares. By now, issues — if you can even call the religious issue that — count for little in this election. Anyone who hasn't firmly made up his or her mind at this point doesn't need issues to decide whom they fear more.

All this debate over Christ and the crucifixion in a political campaign may be more than Jimmy Swaggart can take shutting up. The evangelist breaks his silence in a taped broadcast, the final one before all Louisiana stations drop him. He promises, "We're coming back in His time, and it won't be long. He already told me that." Swaggart discloses details of his most recent conversation with the

Holy Ghost: "He said, 'You're quitting? Why are you quitting? You had a bad day.' The Holy Spirit can underestimate things at times, or understate them." We'll have to take his word for that. It is a shame, though, as *Picayune* columnist James Gill points out, that "God only talks to Jimmy after he gets in trouble."

Swaggart does not endorse in the governor's race. He did, however, before his TV image went dark, make one last plea for money: "I wouldn't ask this now, for me. How could I? How crass, how brassy would one be? But you see there are millions and millions fighting the same devil I'm fighting . . ."

Had Duke just said he gets his religion on the radio, had he just used Jimmy's description of churches ("They are as sepulchers — outside polished but inside full of dead men's bones"), he might have saved himself a lot of bad ink and loss of integrity in the runoff. Instead, Duke began to work his Christian faith into more and more comments in the governor's race, especially the runoff, after barely mentioning the subject in the Senate race. He claimed in the LPB debate that he went to the Evangelical Bible Church, which doesn't exist, and later said he meant to say he belonged to an evangelical Bible study group. He claimed the closest pastor in his life was Jim Rungsted, a Lutheran minister who has not pastored a church in 14 years but who gives Duke spiritual guidance while doubling as the campaign photographer and pilot.

In the last two weeks of the runoff, the *Times-Picayune* reveals in a front-page story that Duke earlier told a Monroe Christian station that he belonged to the Carrollton Avenue Church of Christ in New Orleans, though it turns out he was baptized there when he was 13 and has not been back in years. Duke even subjects himself to a panel of four evangelical ministers and a lay leader to determine his sincerity — three of the five came away unconvinced.

This leads to one more third-party anti-Duke commercial by conservative Christians that begins by quoting Matthew in the New

Testament: "Beware of false prophets who come to you in sheep's clothing but inwardly are ravenous wolves. . . . We can pray for David Duke, but we should not vote for him."

The Jesus card is not working as well as Duke needs to overcome the backlash from those who think he's a hypocrite. The final embarrassment comes when aide Bob Hawks, a former Tennessee legislator, quits the campaign in the last week and tells WDSU-TV that Duke's claim to be a devout Christian was "a hoax." Hawks tells a Memphis newspaper, "I would hear it in his words where he was stage center . . . but failed to hear it from his daily life." Hawks is no jewel himself. He has not held office in 18 years and was fired from a county job in 1980 for using inmate labor on his private property. He was not particularly liked among the longtime staffers at headquarters, though they distrusted all outsiders. Duke appears shocked when WDSU breaks the news to him about Hawks' defection and comments: "I don't know why he would say anything bad. . . . He doesn't know my heart." It can't be a happy place right now.

To know David Duke's heart is to know Livingston Parish. He's always been well received here, as a Klansman and as a candidate. This is his base, for votes, for money, for approval. As Edwin Edwards closes his campaign concentrating on the Roemer voters in the cities, Duke draws back deeper into his rural base. You don't get much deeper than the rustic old gym-auditorium on the Livingston Parish Fairgrounds, out where people call Denham Springs "the city."

Warming up the crowd are Kid Mixon and the Sonny Strickland Band, whose musical message for the evening is:

*What this world needs is a few more rednecks*
*People up front to take the lead*
*A little more peace and little more action*
*And a few more rednecks is what we need.*

In the audience is national columnist and commentator Robert Novak, who has prevailed upon Julia Reed to show him the Duke Phenomenon, though she's seen about all she can take. Novak just wants to blend in, but they do have cable TV in Livingston, and a steady stream of admirers ask him to autograph the backs of their Duke fans. "When they started cheering and holding up their fans," says Reed, "all I could see were these Robert Novak signatures waving all around me."

KSLA-TV reporter Rick Masters feels safer here, where he's not known, than at home. "I'm just glad to get out of Shreveport," says the Iowa native. "The station endorsed Edwards this week and so far I've had 10 death threats. The security guard has to walk me to my car at night."

One other person who looks out of place tonight is the blond-headed gentleman who is wearing a cleric's collar. It's Jim Rungsted, David Duke's pastor, pilot and photographer, here to offer witness to the candidate's Christianity. He tells the audience that his first assignment as a Lutheran minister was a small mission in a black neighborhood in downtown Selma, Alabama, in 1965. As he talks about getting to know and getting to believe in David Duke, one of these rednecks the world needs more of belts out, "I came to hear David Duke, not no reverend!" And so he will, after the prayer, during which one woman in the front row makes the sign of the cross while the lady behind her holds a hand aloft and silently moves her lips.

Campaign manager Howie Farrell bemoans the campaign of "economic blackmail" being waged by outsiders and the press. "They're saying if we don't succumb, they won't bring their businesses here. . . . "

"Boooooooo."

". . . Or they will take their conventions somewhere else."

"Go somewhere else!"

With the crowd warmed up, the main attraction hits the stage and right away begins working damage control: "Edwin Edwards will do anything in these final days. We've met with people who tell that Edwin Edwards was going to go out of state and bring in people to act like Klansmen and try to hurt our campaign. I've had people tell me Edwin Edwards was going to plant people in our organization. You can expect anything and everything from Edwin Edwards in the closing days."

"He's desperate!" someone yells.

"And he's got every endorsement known to man. I'm waiting for Mikhail Gorbachev to endorse him. After him, who's next? Maybe Magic Johnson."

No speech is complete now without the usual sop to Clarence Thomas and a jab at Ted Kennedy, which he flubs. "They have a sign at the Kennedy compound that says, 'Violators will be trespassed.' I mean . . ."

They know what he means. It's Us against Them, and inside the Free State of Livingston, it's not much of a contest.


Andrew Martin and Bob d'Hemecourt no longer cringe when Edwin Edwards blithely predicts a 60-40 blowout. Is that wise? asks the reporter. "It's not wise or unwise," Edwards shrugs. "I've seen three polls. It's what I think." The certainty of winning big is settling in up at the Monteleone. "We've got it won," says the candidate. "We just got to stay alive." Terry Shirley and Harry Lee are still working on that. Peering out over the rooftops of the French Quarter, the lawmen speculate on the weapon needed to hit Suite 1545 from the top of the Maison Blanche building.

The pollsters see the same numbers Edwards does. They just can't believe them. Twice burned on Duke, they appear to be overheating their thermal indexes to bring his hidden vote to the surface. Pollster Susan Howell's raw figures show Edwards with a 26-point lead, which can't be right. So she cooks the numbers a little longer. "We bent over backwards to find anyone who could be a Duke voter" and she comes out with a 55-45 projection for Edwards, and still hedges on that. Ed Renwick sees it a little closer at 54-46, while Mason-Dixon remains stubbornly short of a majority, 49-42 with 9 percent undecided. Market Research Institute shows the only runaway, 57-43.

"The only poll I'm listening to is Robert J. d'Hemecourt's," states Julia Reed, spreading roasted garlic cloves over French bread at Upperline Restaurant. The *Vogue* writer and Roberto Suro, *New York Times* correspondent, agree that Edwards and company have stirred a dark enough "gumbo of fear" to swamp Duke. "Edwin's got it in the bag," she says. She's just waiting on d'Hemecourt's prediction before she places her bets in New York. "No one up there believes me when I tell them Edwards will beat Duke bad."


"Come in here. Let me tell you something." Edwin Edwards pauses on his way into his suite's bedroom to stoop down, pick up a penny and put it in his pocket. "Someone has taped a carphone conversation with Duke talking about pulling $196,000 out of his campaign. NBC has it."

Edwards says the conversation was picked up by a Lafayette businessman on his scanner, and turned over to a lawyer who knows Edwards. Later that day, transcripts and tapes of the conversation are in circulation in newsrooms.

Duke made the call from his car phone to Jim McPherson and Howie Farrell at his Metairie headquarters just after he was confronted by a WDSU-TV reporter investigating a story that Duke was siphoning campaign money out of a paper corporation he controlled.

On the tape, the three talk about how Duke will respond if the issue is raised on his appearance the next day on *Good Morning, America*. The company, Stirling Publications, was set up by McPherson's law partner P. K. Wallace, who listed McPherson as the president, which is news to McPherson.

McPherson: "You see, I didn't know I was president until I was told that today."

Duke: "You didn't know that?"

McPherson: "I didn't know it until today."

Duke: "Man, I can't believe all this. I didn't know P.K. brought you into this. So you get blindsided in the media."

McPherson: "Well, that's all right. The important thing is (TV investigative reporter Richard) Angelico says, 'We have no problem if you (McPherson) made a reasonable fee. We're just trying to see if it's a conduit to Duke.' "

Duke would later amend his financial disclosure report to show that most of the money, $168,912, was paid to a St. Louis printing firm that had wanted to remain unmentioned. Duke, however, is also concerned about other payments to Mississippi state Senator-elect Mike Gunn, who helped to prepare the mailing piece. "They asked me about Gunn and his relationship to Stirling and I said I didn't know of a relationship, which was fair for me to say."

McPherson: "What if we just give them the checkbook?"

Duke: "Noooo. Then they'll investigate and we have to have that confidentiality. We can't expose them. We should talk to them in the morning. In the meantime, on *GMA*, if they ask, first I say I have no financial dealings with Stirling and never received one penny."

McPherson: "Yeah, say, 'The money goes through this company and they (McPherson and Wallace) provide service and they paid the bills.' And they charged $7,000."

Duke: "$7,000 apiece?"

McPherson: "Yes, $14,000 total."

Duke: "Man!"

These lawyers are expensive. Howie Farrell then gets on the phone to say the arrangement is no different than "Edwin Edwards doing business with an advertising firm owned by his daughter." Edwards did that in 1983, but not through a dummy corporation.

Farrell then reviews issues Duke needs to counterattack on — Edwards' links to Champion Insurance and its owners the Eichers, who are now in jail, and to Carlos Miro, of defunct Anglo-American Insurance, who is in Spain awaiting extradition. Farrell rolls through detailed allegations while Duke repeats the phrases, practicing turning them into sound bites.

"Here's another thing," says Farrell excitedly. "We've already leaked it to the news: Edwards was never in the Navy!"

"How do you know that?"

"We checked with the Navy. We have documentation. There was no Edwin Edwards in the Navy from 1943 to 1947."

Duke is highly skeptical. "He wasn't in the Reserves?"

"Nothing. But you don't have to worry about that. We've leaked that to the news. We've got people with relatives. They will handle it."

Nothing comes of Farrell's scoop. (Edwards served in the Navy 1945-46. His honorable discharge is on file in the Acadia Parish Clerk of Court's office.)

Duke is approaching overload on Howie's facts. He wants to savor tonight's rally. "We had three or four thousand people at Evangeline Downs. Very enthusiastic. It was great."

Farrell says, "My friend Frank Salter left a meeting in Lake Charles. He says you'll carry Calcasieu."

"Wow."

"Yeah, they say you're getting 80 percent of the Roemer vote."

"Wow," repeats Duke. "If we carry Calcasieu, we're gonna carry the whole damn state. Everything but Orleans and some river parishes."

"They say if Edwards doesn't get 75 percent of the vote in New Orleans, he can't win," adds Farrell.

"Oh, he'll get 75 percent of the New Orleans vote," says Duke. "He'll come out of there 70,000 votes ahead. Then we'll make it up in Jefferson with 25,000 to 30,000, then 10-15,000 in St. Tammany, 10-15,000 in St. Bernard and Plaquemines together, and about

5,000 in St. John. By the time we get out of New Orleans, we'll have a 10-15,000 deficit. Then we get into the Florida parishes, we'll kill Edwards there. Then we get to Houma and Thibodaux and we'll be gone."

The Edwards caravan moves out of the Monteleone and rolls through the streets of the French Quarter at dusk. What used to be Edwards and one driver making country festivals has turned into five autos with security and press and friends along for the ride. In the front seat, the frontrunner is working on revising history, lest anyone get the impression that Duke once had his number. He really didn't start courting the Roemer voters in earnest until two weeks ago. "I had to let people settle down and get over their astonishment and shock and hurt."

Even the first shaky debate performances were—would you believe?—intentional. "I deliberately fumbled around and didn't do as good as I could. I know that no one remembers anything except what happens in the last two weeks. I gave that guy a false sense of security and he fell for it hook, line and sinker, like a choupique."

He interprets. "A choupique, that's a fish only the poorest people eat. It's a scum-sucking parasite, sort of like a lawyer. The only way to eat it is with lots of onions, parsley and garlic. I ate my share."

Back to campaign history. "He took an asswhipping in the second debate. Then another asswhipping on *Meet the Press*. He hung out there two or three minutes, like an eternity. He couldn't name one major employer. He could have at least guessed Popeye's."

Duke has been almost too easy. They didn't even bother to chase down the rumor that Duke was once on welfare. "Now that's a ballbuster," says Edwards.

As the caravan crosses the Industrial Canal into St. Bernard Parish, Edwards returns a call on the car phone from Louisiana Republican National Committeewoman Ginny Martinez. "Thank you. I need your vote and your support." He hangs up. "You should write a thesis about why people vote for Edwards. This one wants to protect George Bush. She thinks Duke could make a difference in four states."

He checks back with Suite 1545, where all is quiet. "You and George can go eat. I'll tell the wives you were there to midnight making calls. I'll cover for you."

Suburban blue-collar St. Bernard Parish belongs to David Duke, who won over half the vote here in the primary and polled a whopping 71 percent in the Senate race. Tonight, Judge Leander Perez Boulevard is lined with rows of recently planted Duke signs.

"They're all illegal," says d'Hemecourt, punching in a call to his sign man. "We need a rake. We can get rid of all of them."

"No, no," waves Edwards, "don't bother."

"I can't stand that big bodyguard of Duke's," says Cecil Brown, who's no bigger than Edwards. "I want to whip his ass."

"You be careful," warns Edwards. "He's a big son of a bitch."

Talking into his portable phone, Lieutenant Shirley gets a report of 50 Duke supporters waiting at the corner by the Civic Center, where Edwards is headed.

"Do we have Mace?" Shirley asks into the phone.

"No, no, forget it," Edwards says, agitated. "We'll just get out and talk to them."

"Governor!"

"You're taking all the fun out of it."

"You're keeping it in, boss."

We pass more Duke signs. Cecil Brown can barely contain himself. "I really want to whip that bodyguard's ass."

"Hey, that's a tough mother," says Edwards. "That's what Duke told me."

"I don't care," growls Cecil. "I want to shove this telephone up his ass."

"Have you voted absentee?"

"Yes sir."

"Then you go right ahead."

The caravan makes a brief stop at Sammy Nunez's insurance agency office so Edwards can privately huddle with the Senate President and St. Bernard Sheriff Jack Stephens. Bodyguards, deputies and a few reporters wait outside in the chilly night air. Across the street, a teenage girls' marching team rehearses their routines. When Edwards reemerges, he goes over to greet the young ladies. As the candidate says a few friendly words, a four-year-old girl, the team mascot, looks up at him in wonderment. Edwards smiles at her. She asks, "Are you David Duke?"

Minutes later, Edwards waves to the Duke supporters, including one woman on horseback, as the caravan wheels into the Civic Center. The St. Bernard political establishment, led by Nunez and Stephens, welcomes Edwards before he goes into the big dance and political rally. Edwards congratulates the politicos on the turnout: "I understand you've allowed some black people into Chalmette tonight just for this."

Legendary bar owner Bud Rip, a former Republican legislator, says he's been with Edwards for three months. Though pictures of Reagan and other GOP luminaries line the interior of his place, a large Edwards sign hangs on the outside wall of Bud Rip's, which is in a black neighborhood of the Ninth Ward in New Orleans. He likes Edwin. Besides, he didn't have much choice. "If I had put a Duke sign up, theyda boint me down."

Before he heads into the dance, Edwards does a quick interview with CNN's Charles Zewe, who started out years ago covering Edwards in New Orleans.

"What about the Vote for the Crook signs?" the newsman asks.

"It hurts."

Zewe asks Edwards to clarify his *Meet the Press* statement that he is not a gambler.

"I ride horses 40 times more than I gamble, but I'm not a cowboy. I do gamble, but I'm not a gambler. I go to Las Vegas a few times a year and that's it. I don't bet on horses, I don't bet on football."

Well, not in the last month, perhaps.

"You're not the same," notes Zewe.

"This is a different campaign. This is my last shot, my last best chance, and I don't want to blow it."

Anyway, says Zewe, he hears that Duke has eclipsed Edwards as a womanizer.

"Duke is not a womanizer," says Edwards icily. "He's a little-girlizer."

Edwards addresses the crowd very briefly and turns the stage back to the band. The second-to-last night's campaigning is done.

An hour later, following a late-night supper at Brennan's with Ms. Candy Picou and four bodyguards and a financial report from Bob d'Hemecourt — $330,000 today, $340,000 yesterday — the candidate and his lady stroll hand in hand up Royal Street back to the hotel. Four years ago he was a political dead man. Even six months ago, he could barely get anyone to take his comeback seriously. Two weeks ago, the spotlight was shining dangerously on his own record, until it turned, just in time, to the integrity of David Duke and the consequences of his election. Tonight, walking the streets of the French Quarter, not only are victory and vindication within his grasp, but this city is too — and he has big plans for it. For now, though, if he has a problem, it's that he can't get down a bet.

# 20. Victory Laps

Gary Burke looks sort of embarrassed as he tries to console the black woman crying softly in the lobby of the Monteleone. D'Hemecourt sent him down from 1545 to intercept the Opelousas woman who has been stalking the Edwards campaign. Yesterday she hand-delivered a letter at the front desk. Entitled "REQUEST FOR REVENUE," her letter begins, "I was to do work, politicking, etc. for your opponent for $25,000 and up to $50,000." Despite the lure of big bucks, she knows that the godly thing would be to help Edwin Edwards. But so far, as she takes about two pages to explain, he has not responded to her offers of assistance. Now she needs his help: "I am homeless. There is a God. This is the one chance I have to make big money. I need to live and to do God's work. But again I trusted you."

Burke grins sheepishly as he tries to comfort or quiet the crying woman while curious conventioneers pass by them. She'll get about $200. There's plenty. Minutes earlier across the lobby, Edwards, on his way out, runs into Hippo Katz, on his way up. "More ammo," says Katz, handing Edwards a wad of checks.

A friend of Katz has brought along a camera to capture the moment. Edwards punches Katz at his side. "Suck it up, Hippo."

331

On the 15th floor, the end game is on automatic pilot. Bob has again collected all the room keys for the 15th floor. Harry Lee is sitting on the sofa eating Oreo cookies and reading *Spy Magazine*. Hotel workmen are bringing up a new commode for room 1544, the room across the hall which Edwards often uses for private conferences or the acceptance of money delivered in person. The commode may not be all that needs replacing, notes d'Hemecourt. "If someone throws one more envelope or suitcase on that bed, it's gonna collapse."

The absentee vote count is in: 77,559, a 50 percent increase over the primary. Since 83 percent of the absentee voters were white, this indicates a big jump in white turnout tomorrow, which is good news for David Duke.

Again, the black turnout remains a major question mark. They did not turn out against Duke in his last two elections, or even that well for Edwards on October 19. What will make a difference this time? Two things: the real possibility that David Duke could get elected this time, and about $2 million in street money.

The state Democratic Party's PAC has doubled the contributions it's received since the primary and has already cut the street money checks for drivers, canvassers, coordinators, printing, mailing lists and postage. All Democrats, especially statewide candidates, are receiving a big boost from this rare, coordinated and well-financed party effort. The state Republican Party, left with David Duke at the top of its ballot for the second straight year, practically abandoned its fundraising efforts in 1991.

After years of struggling to cope with the polarizing effect of the open primary and the resulting gains by Republicans, the Democratic Party has adjusted to their role as a super political action committee. That was only made possible by Edwin Edwards' dominating his rivals and emerging as the consensus Democrat in the primary, which enabled the party, with only one major candidate, to get behind Edwards early. The other enormous boost came from former Democrat Buddy Roemer, whose campaign finance reform capped direct contributions but allowed unlimited donations to noncandidate groups. It's a loophole big enough to drive a schoolbus through.

So on this Friday before the election money is flowing out to voter groups, not just in New Orleans, but in other cities and rural parishes that received no Edwards funds in the primary. Some newspaper columnists will question why black groups need to be paid in order to mobilize against their enemy David Duke. From the Democratic Party's point of view, the groups are working for all Democratic candidates, not just Edwin Edwards. From Edwards' point of view, the money is a reward as much for the October 19 primary as for runoff at hand. Blacks turned out fairly well for him in the primary when he needed them more and had far less street money to put out. With the money pouring in for the runoff, he could have dumped it all on TV (which is the blacks' view of how the white vote is bought), he could have socked more away for future political activity (he will have a cool million left over as it is), or he could have given something back to those who have been so good to him.

So the Edwards campaign has the money taken care of, as well as the voter groups and, for the most part, David Duke. This just leaves the press. Edwards has laid down an ironclad rule that he will not go live with any TV station until he goes downstairs to the ballroom to claim victory. But Leslie Hill of WDSU is at the door to ask for special consideration.

"She'll win," predicts d'Hemecourt, counting checks.

"What are you doing at 8 o'clock tomorrow night?" the reporter asks Edwards.

"I have a date. I'm not going on at 8. I'm going out to eat."

"Where?"

"Burger King."

Maybe a little later, she suggests, but before everyone else.

"We'll see," says Edwards.

D'Hemecourt nods in mid-count: "See?" This is why Edwards needs so many tough guys around him: he can't say no.

Late-breaking news: there's word of someone willing to bet Duke can get within five percentage points. "Call and see if you can get down a bet," Fischer urges. "To hell with all this other stuff."

Robert J. d'Hemecourt is ready with his election prediction, which he scribbles on a scrap of yellow notebook paper: EWE 1,165,000 DUKE 685,000. Julia Reed heads for the Walgreen's on the corner to buy a cheap calculator before she places her New York bets.


Bombshell alert. WWL Radio is about to go live to a David Duke press conference which promises to drop a "bombshell" on Edwin Edwards. Duke has followed Farrell's urging from the car-phone conversation to try to redirect public attention to the "real issues" of Edwards' alleged corruption. Instead of two recent issues — the Eichers of Champion Insurance or Carlos Miro of Anglo-American Insurance — Duke resurrects an old allegation by Edwards' late aide and accuser Clyde Vidrine that Edwards sold state positions in 1971. Why? Perhaps because the job-selling charge comes with video. At the hastily called news conference at Augie's Restaurant, Duke unveils his last TV commercial, which is mostly re-edited excerpts from a 1983 60 *Minutes* interview between Ed Bradley and Edwin Edwards. On the tape, when Bradley asks Edwards if he sold a Mineral Board seat to Jerome Glazer in 1971 for $75,000, Edwards says no. "It was $45,000. I think Clyde skimmed $30,000."

"Was it a sale or not?" asks Duke. "It seems to me he admitted it." Reporters look at each other wearily as they close their notebooks. Some bombshell. Duke has dredged up a 20-year-old allegation that was aired on national television eight years ago.

Edwards does not break a sweat in responding that it was not illegal in 1971 to take money in exchange for promising to consider someone for a job. In fact, it was a time-honored practice. CBS is quick to follow with a demand that Duke halt airing the commercial because it shows "out of sequence and out of context" excerpts from 60 *Minutes*.

"Out of context" — that's Duke's usual response to old quotes that surface from his past, including the current Louisiana Coalition commercial of Duke's collegial chat with Nazi crazy Ed Fields. If they can do it . . .

Leaving his press conference, AP reporter Guy Coates asks about his response to quoted remarks by Duke's old white supremacist pal Tom Metzger that Duke was "a terrible womanizer," used cocaine and once hired a prostitute. "That's totally untrue," Duke answers angrily. "Anybody will say anything at this point."

No kidding.

Duke's been saying today that Edwards admitted snorting cocaine in *The Last Hayride*. Edwards made a crack like that as a joke about the wild stories people tell about him. It was out of context and, hence, fair game.

The Japanese film crew prepares for its stand-up in front of David Duke's Cypress Street headquarters. Activity in the quiet Metairie neighborhood is normal for the day before a David Duke election. Volunteers come in and out as reporters mill about under the carport, waiting for Duke. Four sheriff's deputies' cars, lights flashing, screech to a halt, and officers race inside. Bomb threat. No one seems to pay much mind.

The sign on the wall inside reads: "David will beat Goliath." An out-of-town reporter, sitting patiently in the waiting room, overhears two staffers discussing turnout.

"They say it's gonna rain in North Louisiana."

"That's good," says another. "Niggers hate to vote in the rain."

They notice the reporter and giggle nervously. It's too late to matter.

A local writer stringing for an out-of-town paper is unimpressed with the *Picayune*'s all-out runoff offensive on Duke. "If Duke wins, (editor) Jim Amoss should go in the closet and find a clothes hanger and hang himself," he says. "They sat on the Duke stuff so long and came out with it so late, people don't believe it."

Some Duke workers are just as displeased with Mr. Amoss, but for other reasons. "What the *Picayune* has done is shameless," bristles Michelle Shauer on the *Picayune*'s daily shelling of Duke. The Roemer expatriate's night job is at a local hotel, so she should be especially ripe for the *Picayune*'s dire economic argument against Duke. But she doesn't buy it. "People are still calling for Mardi Gras and Jazzfest. It might hurt a little at first but not in the long run." One thing is certain: the election itself has been good for tourism. "We've got people extending their stay through the weekend just to see this election."

About the time the bomb squad departs, the Duke caravan slams to a halt. The candidate, surrounded by state troopers and bodyguards, rushes into headquarters while more reporters and photographers are left to mill about the carport.

Minutes later, Duke reemerges, ready to roll, but his driver has gone to gas up. In typical behavior, he paces around the carport and driveway, from the gaggle of newsmen to doting volunteers, back into the office and back out again. Photographers are tripping over themselves trying to follow Duke, but the long-haired shooter from *Black Star* has it figured out: "Duke is always moving, always pacing. I know if I just plant myself, he will come to me." The photographer compares the two campaigns' press relations: "The Edwards people are far more courteous than Duke's people, but you get far less access to Edwards." The Duke people, by comparison, are pretty surly, but it's not hard getting close to the guy. *Black Star* concludes, "It would be a lot harder to knock off Edwards."

The car's back. Duke slips into the front seat. Gotta run.


The sun sets on the race from Hell. The Edwards caravan glides through the streets of the Quarter toward its last swing around the city.

The candidate checks his entourage at the door of the Greater St. Stephen Baptist Church on South Liberty Street. "This is a tough neighborhood," says d'Hemecourt, looking over his shoulder. "We lose two or three voters a night over here."

Inside, Reverend Paul Morton is laying hands on a kneeling Edwin Edwards. It will make a fitting final front-page picture for the *Picayune* tomorrow morning—no candidate could ask for a better election day visual message: God and the *Times-Picayune* urge you to vote for Edwin Edwards.

Out on the sidewalk, the white street gang is smoking cigarettes while the last parishioners file in. "This looks terrible," says d'Hemecourt. "This is just the scene Edwin wanted to avoid." He lights another cigarette. A dark car rolls slowly down the street and stops in front of them. Out steps Republican City Councilwoman Peggy Wilson, a candidate for state insurance commissioner. She warily approaches the Edwards gang and greets d'Hemecourt with reserve.

"I'm sorry you backed the wrong candidate," says Wilson, who, before the massive DemoPac alliance coalesced, thought she had a shot at carrying her hometown.

"We thought we needed a change," says d'Hemecourt tersely.

At least there is one gentleman in this gang. Token Republican George Ackal oozes up to shake Peggy's hand. "Mrs. Wilson, I'm George Ackal Jr. and I voted for you."

The two exchange pleasantries, which makes d'Hemecourt want to puke. "Listen to this lying motherfucker," he groans, turning away. "I tell ya Edwin will get more votes in her home precinct than she will. You watch."


It's a ten-foot-high Marilyn Monroe holding an Edwards sign. Behind her, a huge, fearsome gorilla is doing the same thing. Led by the Landry High School Marching Band, Edwin Edwards waves from his mini-float rolling through Blaine Kern's float barn in Algiers. The fantastic icons of Carnivals past ring the huge barn, including giant busts of Harry Lee and Edwin Edwards, right over there in front of the Joker's. Edwards' final campaign appearance of 1991 — perhaps ever — appropriately, is a parade, albeit indoors. The last word belongs to Edwin Lombard, who offers the standard Democratic benediction: "Go vote early and often."

Across the river, Duke is outside the American Legion Hall in Metairie talking to the fans who were smart enough not to squeeze inside the hot, cramped hall. As Todd Gillman of the *Dallas Morning News* and Ron Brownstein of the *Los Angeles Times* watch and listen, a Dukester passes behind and says, loud enough, "Hymie liberal press." With Duke railing against the hatchet job on him in the press, his crowd starts the chant, "Boycott the *Picayune*."

Duke predicts an upset win tomorrow, in line with "the trend of Republican victories in Mississippi and Pennsylvania."

"The Democrats won in Pennsylvania," notes a female Tulane student, a liberal Democrat, out political joyriding on this spooky election eve. Things get a little blurred toward the end.

Now this is more like it. Bill Schultz counts 25 people standing in line at 8:30 a.m. outside of the garage voting booth on Mandolin Street in the Seventh Ward, among them Cybil Morial, the widow of New Orleans' first black mayor. Over 27 percent of the black middle-class precinct has voted. It's getting better. Generally, the poorer the neighborhood, the worse the turnout. Yet, 23 percent have voted by 9 a.m. at Guste High Rise, a housing project, compared to only 20 percent at Holy Name School in one of the wealthiest Uptown neighborhoods. A WYLD Radio van unloads voters at Crocker School in the predominantly black Twelfth Ward. The station is just one of several black-owned businesses joining the volunteer get-out-the-vote effort, including an airport transportation company that has shut down for the day and turned its vehicles and drivers over to the cause.

Schultz slows down to get a better look at a young black man who has fashioned two of the ubiquitous red-and-white STOP

DAVID DUKE signs into a sandwich board that he wears as he walks the streets. "Wear it all day, my brother," says Schultz, who rolls on. "I don't think we'd have to lift a finger and they would come," he says. But nothing like being sure. Cruising past the Fairgrounds, he whistles. "We're runnin' like Risen Star."

Morning skies in New Orleans are overcast, but no rain is expected. Meanwhile, Schultz hears on his car phone that it's raining in North Louisiana. This election is rewriting all the rules. "If it rains, it's better for us," reasons Schultz. "Our vote is coming out, no matter what" while the Roemer voters now leaning to Duke may well just stay home. In fact, says Schultz, getting pretty cocky, "I'd like to beat this guy in the rain and the sleet. That would show we're not bumpkins."

At nearly every stop, every turnout count, every report of extreme volunteer action, Schultz marvels, "I've never seen anything like this," or "Now I've seen it all." But now, hitting his brakes on St. Charles Avenue, he *has* seen it all. "Junior Leaguers putting up Edwards signs . . . on the corner of St. Charles and Jefferson . . . in violation of the law . . . in broad daylight. Unreal."

"David's got a wild burr up his ass that he wants a parade," says press secretary Glenn Montecino. So cue the parade. In the parking lot of the Clearview Shopping Center in Metairie, Duke climbs up on the back seat of a convertible with his daughters and signals for the last charge to begin. Edwin Edwards has an army of several thousand paid drivers out rounding up voters in every corner of the state. David Duke has a parade. It's not really a parade. No spectators line the six-lane road to watch him pass. It's more a horn-honking caravan of about 60 cars on Veterans Highway as Duke and daughters wave to startled motorists in the Saturday morning traffic. This is the end of a long road, and he's determined to spend these last hours with his public.

A man wearing an Edwards campaign t-shirt stands at the counter of the South Galvez office, demanding his work assignment. "You told me to come back."

"I don't know who told you to come back, but everyone's been hired from the ones who worked last time," says the volunteer coordinator firmly.

"But I worked last time," he insists.

But his name is not on the list. "We had our last meeting two nights ago," says the coordinator.

He tries staring her down, but she's not budging. Edwards' cash may be flowing on the streets of New Orleans, but it's no open-ended deal.

The headquarters operation is organized down to the colored pins on the map in the war room, signifying turnout and vote in the primary. Stockbroker Bruce Feingerts is on the phone checking for problems at precincts. "We have people with parole power standing by if any of our workers get arrested. But it's not likely this time."

It's not. From the Uptown mansions to the downtown projects, the city is galvanized to stop, no, stomp David Duke.


Reports are coming into Suite 1545 of massive turnout all over the state. The Duke boxes aren't doing shabbily either. One report has 55 people in line to vote at the St. Bernard Firehouse. And volunteer activity too: a cross has been burned in Coushatta in front of the house of black leader Johnny Cox. The afternoon counts are extraordinary. Blacks have broken their pattern by voting heavily in the morning. They are still voting heavily into the afternoon. At 4 p.m., the turnout at the Fisher Project in Algiers hits 76 percent, and it was only 43 percent in the primary.

"You still at 53, dummy?" Edwards asks a reporter who bet a cautious victory margin. Many candidates get in the way on election day, when there is nothing for them to do but vote. Edwards knows the drill. In midafternoon, he and d'Hemecourt slip out to go look at boats and propellers on the West Bank. Passing a polling place, he rolls down his window to take a sample ballot from a shocked Democratic worker. The legend spreads: *He's everywhere.*

"Gus, you haven't lost an ounce." The candidate greets friends who begin filling the small suite by 6:30 p.m. The old faces are reappearing in force tonight. Mijalis and Billy Broadhurst both show up early with their new, young wives. Edmund Reggie, longtime Edwards friend and future father-in-law to Ted Kennedy, breezes in ahead of Mike O'Keefe, the former president of the state Senate, who had to interrupt his political career for a brief stint at a federal prison. Bernie Cyrus is wearing EWE pins from all five gubernatorial races going back to 1971. Harry Lee eases in on the couch next to Dorothy Mae Taylor. It's a real family affair.

The room is filling much faster than time is passing. Lieutenant Terry Shirley's elaborate security system of color-coded stickers has broken down completely. People just say at the door, "Edwin told me to come up"—which he's been telling people for a year—and Shirley has no choice but to let them in.

Fortunately for the state police, it won't be a long night. At precisely 8 p.m., Bob Schieffer comes on with a "CBS News Special Report": "In Louisiana, Edwin Edwards has been elected governor over David Duke." The room rocks.

The more delicious moment comes with the reaction from David Duke at his victory party in Baton Rouge: "If they can't poll me accurately in polls, I don't see how they can poll me in exit polls." Howls and catcalls and a good bit of profanity ensue in 1545.

How does it feel? the governor-elect is asked.

"It looks like Duke's been double-crossed."

He wants to save his remarks for the crowd downstairs, though he does let Leslie Hill of WDSU have her short exclusive at 8:45. Then it's time to get ready to go downstairs. "First," says Edwards, "I have to say hello to my girlfriend" as he sits on Dorothy Mae

Taylor's lap. "She was the first person in Orleans to come out for me." We're talking 20 years ago. The circle, once more, is unbroken.

The exit polls are dead on. This is a rout. Edwards has reclaimed Bayou Country and Acadiana, sweeping every French parish. Duke hoped to hold Edwards' victory margin to 70,000 votes in New Orleans. It comes in at 150,000 — Edwards polls 87 percent of the votes in the city. Duke carries his St. Bernard stronghold by 3,800 votes but loses his home parish of Jefferson by 32,000. Edwards carries Baton Rouge 2-1 with a 50,000-vote margin. It goes on like that across the state, with Duke carrying only 18 parishes — none by more than 6,000 votes — to Edwards' 46.

The final returns:
Edwin Edwards — 1,057,031
David Duke — 671,009

Duke gained 180,000 votes from the primary (60,000 more than he received in the U.S. Senate race), while Edwards added 534,000. The turnout is 79.9 percent of registered voters, a hair off the state record. What may be a record, black turnout is slightly higher than white. Turnout is higher in South Louisiana than in the north, where many Roemer voters leaning to Duke just stay home. Duke wins 55 percent of the white vote, but exit polls show that Edwards beats Duke 3-1 among Roemer voters.

The final victory margin is 61-39 percent. Edwards was right all along with his 60-40 prediction. D'Hemecourt was close too: about 90,000 votes high on Edwards and only 14,000 off on Duke. Julia Reed cleans up in Gotham.

The election turns out to be a referendum on Duke instead of on Edwards, which is the only way the ex-governor could win. Edwards, a man as low as the people, recognized their modest expectations of him — that his next term would not be as bad as his last — and he was able to promise that much. The electorate seemed to believe that neither man's past was too far behind, but that the state could bear the reemergence of Edwards' more than it could Duke's.

Finally, downstairs, Edwards can afford to be gracious. "I said four years ago that God is not finished with Edwin Edwards," he tells the cheering, boozing hordes in the ballroom. "I promise not to let you down."

The party has spilled out onto Royal Street. And Edwards leads his party out there too. Victory is best savored in the streets. This ancient street has seen the great ones come, from Alejandro O'Reilly and Andy Jackson to Huey and Earl. But no great ones have come back like Edwin Edwards has tonight.

# 21. The Way They Were

I wish I liked politics more. I wish I looked at the procedure more. I wish I'd used more tact." That's as close to a confession as anyone could expect from Buddy Roemer. Not that he's exactly apologizing as he bids farewell to the press on the third day of the new year. "I stepped on a lot of toes, but there were a lot of toes hanging out there naked." At least he is not wallowing in denial. "I underestimated the Duke thing too long," he tells about 40 reporters and cameramen standing in a semicircle around him while he sits in a chair in the Mansion parlor. "Look, I would have run a different campaign had I felt he was anyone to take seriously. This guy has zero substance. Zero. What's the Elton John song? 'Less Than Zero'? But the people like that. I realized that too late. I give him that, he knew his politics. He had it over me."

Later, he would pinpoint the one thing Edwin Edwards had over David Duke: of all things, integrity. The man, who "for 20 years created a hunger for integrity," he says, "was saved in the end by having a man run against him who had less integrity. If Duke had integrity, he would have beaten Edwin Edwards. You can just write it down."

For all Roemer's shortcomings, integrity was the one thing he had over both candidates at the start of this campaign. But he allowed the reputation of not being able to work with others and of not delivering on his promises to be hung on him in the primary. Whether the charges were true or not mattered less than the fact that they went unanswered through the long, negative primary campaign against him. That precious, nonrenewable resource of personal integrity — can you do what you say you're going to do? — flowed out of Buddy Roemer from a thousand unsalved nicks and cuts, inflicted by his own hand and by others. And when it's gone, can you get it back? Or, as a reporter asks: "Will he run for office again?"

"Probably. I never had a plan for such things." For the next six months Roemer is headed back to the intellectual womb, Harvard, to teach a course and to take a few. In his ample spare time, he says, he will be doing some consulting at the White House. A few reporters exchange curious glances. "They'll take one day a week of my time. I'm not sure what they want me to do. They have a long list."

Roemer does not see David Duke as a real problem for George Bush. "How can people take him seriously?" he launches one last tirade. "People say his past is his past. His past is last Wednesday. Give me a break."


So little time, so much to do. Two days after the governor's race, David Duke informally announces at his Metairie office that he is running for President of the United States. It took people by surprise and it didn't. The start of the presidential campaign is news to Jim McPherson, as was his presidency of Stirling Publications. Only days before, in the final week of the gubernatorial race, Duke had told audiences at his rallies, "George Bush has nothing to worry about from David Duke." In a way, then, he was telling the truth.

Money is seen as the primary motivation by critics. Duke raised $2.5 million in the Senate race and another $2 million in the governor's race. The *Times-Picayune* already has published an estimate that Duke could raise $5 million to $10 million running for president, including federal matching funds. Campaign defector Bob Hawks, who dropped a few choice bombs on Duke in the final week of the race, tells *Reader's Digest* that while traveling to Baton Rouge with Duke in the heat of the governor's race, the candidate told him, "I'm gonna run for president next year." Hawks says he argued that Duke should wait until 1996, or at least until this governor's race was finished. But Duke dismissed his concerns. "I don't care whether I win or not," Hawks quotes Duke. "I'm not doing it to get elected. I'm doing it to get those funds out of Washington. Man, that'll be clear money."

So cynicism abounds, but the iron is hot, and so is Duke. The prospect of a true wild card candidacy from the Most Politically Incorrect Man in America draws a crush of reporters, spectators and protestors to his official announcement at the National Press Club in Washington. Duke unveils his new national agenda of opposition to free-trade pacts with Mexico and Canada and retaliation against Japanese trade barriers. "You no buy our rice," he quotes a Louisiana billboard, "we no buy your cars." He also calls for reducing foreign aid, the military budget and taxes and, the old standard, for ending affirmative action.

He leaves open the possibility that he will run as a third-party candidate in the November election. "I'm going to say to George Bush that whether I run third-party or not depends on what he does."

Along with the crush of reporters, James Stovall from the Louisiana Coalition Against Racism and Nazism is there, ready for a new campaign. He has company. Hecklers pepper Duke with barbs throughout his address and a New York rabbi breaks the security cordon to rush the podium with his sign DAVID DUKE NAZI OF THE 90s, which is the moment the TV networks capture.

Duke declares he will skip the New Hampshire primary in February but will run "in every primary campaign where I can get on the ballot in the next few weeks." Without realizing it, he has just offered his opponents a challenge they can rise to.

A few days before Christmas, Duke fidgets with items on his desk as he tries to get off the phone with a reporter. "Of course I regret those things I said in my youth, and I'm sure you've said some things you would take back . . ." Another interview awaits and Duke would sure like to get in a racquetball match with Jim McPherson before it's too late.

The wounds of the last two weeks of the campaign and the drubbing he took from Edwin Edwards are fading as a new campaign opens up to him.

How far can he go?

"I don't know," says Duke, "but my politics are coming in America. You can see that every day. In the Democratic debate Sunday, they mentioned my name four times. Four times! In a Democratic debate! The one great accomplishment I've had so far is I've caused a national debate on my issues. Whether I'm elected president or governor, and I think we'll be moving more toward that in the future."

But how does he go national so quickly?

"We're doing pretty well. We have so many people on mailing lists around the country, about 120,000 names and 50,000 or 60,000 contributors. Other candidates don't have nearly our grass-roots organization. I'm getting a lot more signatures in Massachusetts and Rhode Island. People are coming out of the woodwork to help."

And many more will come, he predicts. "This will be like the first race, the Senate race, when we drew those big crowds. This will be new to people. And the press will be huge. So if we go to like Birmingham we can fill up that civic auditorium. We can put 5,000-10,000 people in a meeting."

And pass the ol' oyster bucket. "We can pass the oyster bucket. We can take cash in a federal campaign. It's already started. In the last five weeks, we've got in about 50,000 letters. Many of them sent money, small amounts. Most said they want to help in some way. We have about $230,000 on hand. That's a pretty good start. When we do mailings, we should be able to raise $5 million by the end of the primary season. And that's all matched."

The Louisiana Coalition has announced that it will follow Duke into the presidential primaries, but that, he says, hardly bothers him. "It's gotten now to where the negatives create more positives for me. A lot of philosophy goes into that, the philosophical position that you become what you resist to. When you resist something strongly, you make it stronger. Beth Rickey and them have made me much stronger."

He can feel it changing, especially the more people meet him through the infotainment medium. "When they told the audience on *Donahue* before the show I'd be on they booed. I came on and it was like walking into a lion's den. By the end of that show, they were cheering for me. They were cheering for my cat." (He told the audience he had a tabby cat and loved her.) "By the end of it, these Jewish women in the front row—I talked to them during the breaks and they told me they were Jewish—were telling me they wanted me to meet their daughter."

As usual, Duke exaggerates. "At my press conference (in Washington), press from the whole country was there and there weren't two questions on my past. It was all issues. So we have definitely moved on. There's still going to be the spite from the Coalition and these other guys. They were there too. Stovall was there. But it didn't make any difference. I've moved beyond that. People are now talking about my issues."

So, for the first time, are his rivals, like Pat Buchanan.

"He's a good TV commentator and I agree with most of his positions, but I don't think he's the candidate. I think I have a lot more voter appeal. CNN did a Gallup poll and had me leading

Buchanan. That's one reason why he wants to have a debate with me."

A few weeks before, Duke told the National Press Club he would enter every Republican primary that allowed crossover voting, and some others, rattling off the 17 states, from New York to California, where he was sure to run. Since then, the realities of nationwide campaigning and the roadblocks many state Republican parties already were erecting have given him pause. Now he's rethinking plans.

"We've got to figure out our strategy in the next couple of days. We either concentrate on a lot of primaries or just run in four or five and drop out of the others. I have a chance to win a majority of delegates in some states. Texas is a perfect example. George Bush's home. I can clean up in Texas. Texas is proportional representation. Plus crossover voting. With a crossover state, I can beat George Bush."

The phone rings. "Hey, Erika. How're you doing?" He'll be going to see his teenage daughters in Florida over Christmas. "No, I might not drive straight through. I'm going by Sea World. I'm gonna see Shamu. . . . No, I don't think so." Erika wants to see Shamu too. "No, we can't. That's in opposite directions. . . . Yes, it is. Look, I'll call you later tonight."

Where were we? The Alamo. "We want to go into Super Tuesday on a positive note. We want to go into a state that has proportional representation for one thing. You don't have to run in every state to have a national candidacy. Georgia is before Super Tuesday, so is South Carolina. Those are states we have to look at."

Duke apparently has considered every option. "A lot of people say I should run as a Democrat." It's been suggested that could lure Jesse Jackson into the nomination race.

Duke smiles at the thought. "I wish I had talked to him. . . . We're talking about arranging a nationally televised debate with Jesse. We're talking to Jackson's people and we're talking to the networks because they would want to do it during ratings sweeps.

They'd be crazy if they didn't. They say it would be the biggest-rated TV program of the year. The possibilities are enormous."

The show, of course, will have to be worked around his planned trip to the Orient to get in those foreign policy credentials. "I've always been big in the Japanese press. Japanese officials said they would talk to me."

Duke's eyes are alight with the prospects. The candy store of celebrity lies before him. What to grab next?

"Every talk show in the country wants me. . . . I'll do my book too. It's autobiographical. That's what they want. I've got some people in New York trying to help me out. They say it will sell four million copies, easy. That's hard copies."

There will have to be sacrifices. "I had all these speaking engagements, $10,000 a throw, foreign engagements and tours, book offers, and you just can't do that and run in primaries at the same time. You've got to strike while the iron's hot." And the primaries are not just a warmup to run for Congress in Louisiana in the fall. "I'm ruling out a race for Congress. They're every two years anyway, so it's not like . . ."

The tabby cat hops on his desk and Duke shoos her off. Campaigning practically nonstop for nearly three years now has been a strain and a wild ride. For the past month he's been coasting on his peaking celebrity. On his recent skiing trip to Crested Butte, Colorado, "I couldn't even get to the slopes, I was out signing autographs. A few were negative, but much more were people saying, 'I'm 100 percent for you' and the rest were very polite and wanted autographs." Just the other night, he was walking through the French Quarter after an event, "People were screaming, 'Duke, Duke.' Girls were coming up screaming. Now I think it's stupid, but I never thought in my life I'd be in a position where I'd have girls coming up screaming. Not against you but for you. It's never been more than right now, after the governor's race."

Even positive celebrity status is not carefree. "Sometimes it feels very good, but it's so constant now that it's hard to deal with it. You can't hardly have a conversation, you can't hardly have a dinner, you can't hardly go anywhere without—sometimes we get to a theater and I'm signing autographs for 40-45 minutes. It feels good and it helps me deal with some of the negatives."

He will deal with it. David Duke is bigger than ever. From Louisiana's small stage he's vaulted into the national arena. A recent poll shows his name recognition is greater than that of any candidate for president except the incumbent. The White House girds for hurricane-force winds. The next few months for Duke can only bring in more money, more discussion of his issues, more acceptance for himself, greater distance from his past.

When it's all over, whether it's George Bush or a Democrat in the White House, Duke's goal is to be the established true conservative voice and a threat to be dealt with in every national election. Duke is focused. "All I can do this year is run for president. Then I'll just be the Jesse Jackson of the conservative cause for a while and we'll see what occurs."


This is not the happiest of Christmases at Jimmy Swaggart's little spread on Highland Road, which is up for sale to satisfy a $417,000 IRS lien for personal and ministry taxes. Swaggart's TV audience, once over 2.1 million homes, has shrunk to 143,000 households in the November sweeps. Nearly 300 workers have been laid off, shrinking the payroll to about 400 from its peak of 1,500. A professor at the Jimmy Swaggart Bible College says fewer than 250 students were expected back on campus, down from 1,450 in 1987. The ministry's radio station is carrying word of a big piano sale: six grand pianos, three baby grands and 16 uprights are offered, says band director Thomas Sloan: "They're a real good deal."


Instead of coming in the old way, through the side basement entrance, Governor-elect Edwards has the car pull up at the circular driveway. He enters the Mansion through the front doors. "Just for the feeling." And? "It feels good." Not much else is said as he surveys the entrance hall. The floor needs some work. The interior pillars have been painted a godawful kelly green. "Not my color," sniffs Edwards as he continues his inspection.

During the transition, the setup at LSU's Pleasant Hall was a far cry from the Monteleone. One day, Harry Lee actually was found *waiting* in the waiting room. Edwards had to ask Bob d'Hemecourt to come up to make sure his New Orleans business allies would not get shuffled and neglected in the New Order.

A week before the inauguration, the governor-elect has not formally announced all his top staff positions. Those closest to him today still wonder who will be there next week. Edwards' instructions to his entourage on his Mansion visit should give them a clue: "I want things back just the way they were."

That would mean the New Orleans boys would be on their way back to New Orleans. And 32-year-old Sid Moreland, not around much during the campaign while he studied law at Southern, would resume his old post as gatekeeper. Moreland had started as a driver eight years before, but, unlike some other aides and friends, had not used his closeness to Edwards for his personal agenda. "Stay low, stay long," says Moreland — it's his personal motto — as he starts early on his wakeup calls around Louisiana. "Gillis Long used to say that if you call someone early in the morning, they won't stay on the phone long because they have to go to the bathroom."

Just the way things were.

"Who will live here?" asks the slightly impertinent reporter at Edwards' first Mansion press conference.

"I will live in the Governor's Mansion," Edwards answers evenly. "My daughter Anna will live here and will gratuitously take over the stewardship of the Mansion and save the taxpayers $40,000 a year. No one else will live here."

The cocktail glasses tinkle at Ruth's Chris Steak House in Baton Rouge, the dining room of the Tribe. It's the night before the inauguration but it feels like Christmas Eve here. "Just the way things were" means a Baton Rouge judge would issue an injunction against enforcing the new lobbyist disclosure law before it took effect in the new year. It would mean Louisiana would continue being one of three states in the Union in which lobbyists do not disclose how much they spend entertaining legislators. And they spend a lot. Says a chemical company lobbyist over his filet, "I called the home office and told them the cheap dates are over." That's all right. Buddy Roemer is gone. It's okay to be a politician again.

Christmas in New Orleans serves as Advent to the Mardi Gras season, which begins with a succession of winter night parades leading up to the wild pageant and bacchanalia in February. New Orleans is ready to get the political year behind it and to get on with the historic celebration that brings blacks and whites together in the streets, costumed and besotted, equals in excess. This year there is all the more reason in that the whole city has united to turn back the race menace and economic threat posed by the Duke campaign. That's the way white folks look at it, anyway. Blacks in the city aren't so sure. In columns and letters in the *Times-Picayune*, blacks ponder the meaning of Duke's winning 55 percent of the white vote statewide. Sure, even a majority of whites in the city of New Orleans voted against Duke, but how much of that was in response to the gun at their head in the form of economic retribution and ostracism from the rest of the nation. Many blacks still feel troubled by the Duke phenomenon and the given explanations of white frustration and pent-up anger. Tell the people in the projects about frustration and anger.

Just as the city prepares to settle in for the party, City Councilwoman Dorothy Mae Taylor lobs a bomb at the way things were. She introduces an ordinance to deny parade permits to any Carnival krewe that discriminates on the basis of race, religion or sex. The city gasps. It doesn't take long for tempers on both sides to overheat. Taylor and her supporters say it is unconscionable for the rich and high-born to be able to parade their privilege on the city streets. The all-white krewes — the older the more secret — are outraged that their presentation of this massive street pageant, free to the people and vital to the tourist economy, would be threatened by insipid political correctness. Even the ancient black Krewe of Zulu, which admits whites, objects to being forced to admit women.

The issue is delayed for one year, but two of the oldest white krewes, Momus and Comus, call off their parades for 1992. Krewes holding the two big Shrove Tuesday parades, Zulu and Rex, announce they will roll, but traditionalists mourn the passing of something sacred and irreplaceable. What makes Mardi Gras and New Orleans truly different is an element of institutionalized social discrimination. This sort of thing would never happen in progressive Atlanta, which claimed the title Queen City of the South when it went northern after the war. Atlanta will have the Olympics but never Mardi Gras. Though the bottom lines don't match, old New Orleans would have their city no other way.

But it's not their city anymore. The white middle class, which held the balance, has long since fled for the suburbs, leaving the white upper class and a majority-black lower class behind. Still, New Orleans, having ducked the racial conflagration of the '60s, appeared able to maintain a separate peace with its traditions. The old families thought they would never see the day when the king and queen of Comus would not be welcomed on the streets. But then blacks never thought they would see an ex-Klan leader running for governor.

"This sort of feels like a high school reunion," says Glenn Montecino, David Duke's old press secretary, surveying the crowd at the Duke rally on the eve of Super Tuesday. Judging from attendance it wasn't a big school, or the graduates stayed away in droves. Duke rallies and the primary night victory party in the governor's race have packed rooms in the cavernous Pontchartrain Center. Tonight, less than 150 people, counting the media, turn out for what should have been the high point of Duke's race for the Republican presidential nomination.

It's been a rough three months for the man the whole world was watching at Christmas. Indeed, from Georgia to Massachusetts, they saw him coming and were waiting for him. The Japanese trip never came off. And, apparently, Jesse Jackson or the networks or both were not interested in the ratings bonanza a debate with David Duke would bring. There were no giant rallies in Birmingham or the Astrodome.

Instead, Duke's campaign has spent three months in Pat Buchanan's stormy shadow while flailing about in the paper traps state Republican parties set for him across the country. From the start, Duke faced GOP roadblocks getting onto ballots in prime states with crossover voting. He quickly found out that Republican parties in other states are not as toothless as the Louisiana group in controlling their own primaries. In some states where the party blocked him, like Massachusetts, he even failed at the alternative method of getting enough signatures on petitions. The weakness of his own organization and the old desire of Duke voters to remain in the closet showed when Howie Farrell mounted a petition drive there and received a lot of media attention but far less than the 2,500 signatures he needed. His only ally turned out to be one of his favorite whipping boys, the American Civil Liberties Union, which weighed in on Duke's behalf by threatening to sue the secretary of state to put the candidate's name on the ballot. He was not as fortunate in critical states like Florida and Georgia, where state laws allowed party officials to determine who could be on primary ballots. On the other hand, he was welcomed in some places he needed to avoid. For instance, on the day the Georgia Republicans denied him ballot access, South Carolina officials sent him information about their party primary. Was the hand of the White House moving behind the scenes? Georgia is a Super Tuesday state with crossover voting. South Carolina, voting three days before Super Tuesday, is a closed primary state, with one of the strongest Bush organizations in the country. Duke abandoned his fight in Georgia and signed up for the South Carolina primary. The paper trap.

Working around the petition obstacles was all the harder with no money. The well had gone dry. Duke claims the mailing house he used, bending to client pressure, delayed his big mailing for over a month, from which he never recovered. His past regular contributors from around the country either were tapped out, turned off or scared off when reporters began calling. The Louisiana News Bureau did a brisk business through the winter in photocopying and mailing out Duke's campaign finance report with all the names and addresses of his contributors nationwide. Newspapers in other states began doing stories profiling Duke's contributors in their areas. Talk about a severe chilling effect.

The real ice man, though, is Patrick J. Buchanan, the hard sound-biting conservative TV commentator with all of Duke's firepower and little of the baggage. Buchanan brings more national stature and issue relevance to the campaign. He can strike the base notes of human nature just as deftly as Duke without being accused of speaking in codes. The presence of Buchanan does not so much discredit Duke as it makes him irrelevant. Even a target. Buchanan can make a protest voter feel doubly good to vote against Bush *and* Duke. People can vote for Buchanan, even tell their neighbors and pollsters, without fear of ostracism.

The money and the crowds may be absent from this campaign, but Duke's enemies remain ever faithful. The Coalition's updated resource packets are in hot demand in newsrooms all over the country. "Presidential candidate and former Ku Klux Klan leader" is still a favored label in most news stories on him. The *Dallas Morning*

*News* quotes him saying that though not as intolerant as he once was, "Fundamentally, yes, I haven't changed." Another paper has fun with Duke's admission that he keeps his Klan robes stored in a closet at home — something to show the grandkids one day. Even the old props are acting up. James Meredith, from whom Duke has gained a lot of mileage, now offers to join Duke and run as his vice president. "The future of the black race, particularly the black male, is now absolutely tied to the David Duke phenomenon," says Meredith, who wants to tie into it too. The Duke campaign does its best not to comment.

Duke's decision to bypass New Hampshire and hunker down for Southern Super Tuesday backfires on him as it has on Southerners in the past. New Hampshire works for protest candidates the same as it does for frontrunners. Grabbing a third of the first-in-the-nation vote, Buchanan gets very hot very fast in the South.

Duke, meanwhile, gets a fever. In February, the *Times-Picayune* reports that Duke is hospitalized in Metairie with a bad case of the flu. An unidentified friend who took him to the hospital is quoted as saying, "He had a temperature of 104 degrees, was red as a beet in the face, was sweating, had chills and was a little bit delirious." Some friend.

His opening primary races, the ones he could enter, are disasters. Buchanan plows Duke under at less than 5 percent in the closed South Carolina primary on the Saturday before Super Tuesday.

Duke limps into Super Tuesday without any of the huge rallies he predicted for the South. His Super Tuesday closer in Kenner is especially pathetic. Babs Wilson is selling a few t-shirts. Howie Farrell looks lost: "It's tough when you don't have the money and can't get your campaign kickstarted." Donal Milton of Jena is ready to announce his own race for Congress while continuing to work hard for Duke in the piney woods. What about Buchanan? The John Birch leader snaps, "He worked for the very same people who ran the Trilateral Commission." It always helps to have someone who knows history.

Tonight's crowd is part old guard, part rank-and-file blue-collar loyalists, part freak show. A young man sports a diamond earring and a Rebel flag t-shirt with the inscription "It's a white thing. You wouldn't understand." He's standing next to the Elvis impersonator, who introduces himself as "Bobby Blaze from Oldies 106." He is quick to explain, "I don't vote. I'm an entertainer. I'd like to help him raise money."

He's a bit late. Someone other than David Duke has figured out a way to make money from his name. Longtime country music huckster Jay Chevalier is hawking a cassette of songs extolling Duke. Reporter Tyler Bridges wants to know how many he thinks he will sell.

"About 250,000," answers Chevalier.

"Oh, come on, how many?"

"I'm serious. Look, I sold 15 already tonight." And just wait, he says, until "I get them into truckstops. Last year I would have sold a million." And that's the point.

No Duke class reunion would be complete without Tyler Bridges, who has been tracking this campaign in remission around the South. After the three years the *Picayune* reporter has been dogging Duke and unearthing his past, Tyler was rewarded when he happened upon his very first Ku Klux Klan rally on the road to Anderson, South Carolina.

The faithful cheer and clap loudly when Duke enters the meeting room. This is bigger than most crowds he's been seeing this winter, and they are louder—but it's far off in size and intensity from those he drew in his state rep race when he started on this long, wild ride not 30 months before. The cheers subside. Instead of going to the mike, Duke circles the room and shakes a few hands. Just a few. Mostly, he's looking at the crowd and smiling before a handful of photographers and cameramen. He seems in no rush to get this over with.

During this interlude, the audience is being entertained by Duke's new musical accompanist, Traci Fruchtnicht, a strikingly attractive blonde, who sings — to recorded background music — "Sweet Love," then "Desperado," then, of course, the classic, "Wind Beneath My Wings."

"She's really good," notes the admiring Bobby Blaze.

As Traci finishes her last number, the stirring "Proud to Be an American," Duke takes back the mike. "She sounds good and she looks even better," he smarms as Traci blushes. "Ladies and gentlemen, let's give her a big hand."

The candidate bows his head as the Reverend Driscoll from Crescent City Baptist Church prays, "Bless David especially in this role of leadership you have called him to do."

Howie Farrell fills in the crowd on how well the message is doing with other messengers. "Duke came out for a flat tax. Now Jerry Brown has. George Bush stole his platform on welfare reform. So did Clinton." The crowd boos. "Pat Buchanan's message matches verbatim with David Duke's every single step." Sounds bleak, but actually, says Farrell, "I'm not worried. Because people want the real thing."

And for the last time they get him. You would think Duke would have a special valedictory for these troops who have followed him the whole way through. But it's just the warmed-over canned speech he's given several times in this building alone, spiced with a few sops to the trade issue — "No free trade before fair trade" — and immigration — "If we don't control our borders we will be invaded by a vast new army that is gathering there."

He ends by putting the best light on things. "We've done so much over the last two years. We've changed the whole scope of national politics. . . ."

There will be a few more primaries to campaign in after Super Tuesday, but Duke already is looking forward to the end, and a rest. "I don't think I'm going to run for a good while after this election," but he will be writing and lecturing about his cause. Perhaps that's what he should have been doing all along since November. Between hostile Republicans and his co-opted message, this presidential campaign has been a dud, and you have to wonder what damage it did to the marketability of David Duke — author, lecturer and infotainment celebrity.

But first there is an end game to play. "Tomorrow your vote will resonate across this country . . ."

Before the final passing of the oyster bucket, Duke calls Traci back up onstage. "You have to hear her sing 'Diamonds Are a Girl's Best Friend.' " She protests she doesn't have the music, but he insists. It's quite appropriate, actually. As the white buckets fan out through the small but giving crowd, Traci coos breathlessly, "A kiss on the hand may be quite continental . . ."

With Erika close at his side, Duke bids farewell to the faithful at the door. "You were great," he tells Traci. "I'll call you later." The crowd shuffles out. The cameras disappear. The press shows its limited interest in a single-digit candidate. The media wave has passed him by. Duke is reduced to talking to — *aaauugghh* — Tyler Bridges again. Duke keeps a cheerful face for the encounter while Erika, arms wrapped protectively around Daddy, glares malevolently at the young reporter. Bridges is doing his methodical excavation work as he asks Duke about a high school acquaintance of his Tyler has just interviewed.

The ever-hopeful Duke leads with his chin. "Yeah, we were friends. Did he tell you that?"

"No, he said he never much cared for you."

The Pontchartrain Center is almost empty. Tomorrow's vote will settle the nomination battles in both parties, but Duke's fate as a candidate has long been sealed. Louisiana, with a closed presidential preference primary, will give Duke his largest percentage in his campaign, a resonating nine percent.

# 22. Circus Maximus

Since the election, the governor publicly has soft-pedaled the casino measure and kept it under wraps for the first two-thirds of the spring legislative session. During the campaign, he had deflected specific casino questions by saying any such proposal would come from New Orleans Mayor Sidney Barthelemy's administration. His friends, however, were not so disengaged. Casino opponents howled, and most people smelled something familiar, when it was learned that Bob d'Hemecourt had been retained by Caesar's World and Billy Broadhurst by Hawaiian developer Chris Hemmeter, who, it was widely assumed, would form an alliance to hold the inside track on landing the license.

First Mardi Gras and now Little Las Vegas. More than ever, the right people in New Orleans are feeling the wrong people closing in on them. The *Times-Picayune*, having saved Louisiana from David Duke, now commits to killing the casino plan, with reporters Tyler Bridges and Peter Nicholas running daily bombing raids on the proposal once it surfaces in committee. They have a lot to work with. The bill gives the city of New Orleans no oversight on the casino and no direct share of revenues. The governor, meanwhile, would appoint the members of the casino corporation board and they would grant the 30-year exclusive license. Also, the state police will not be involved in any background checks on potential licensees or corporation officers — the board will police itself. *Picayune* columnist James Gill muses over the evolution of New Edwin: "He promised us Caesar's wife and he gave us Caesar's Palace." What's not so funny is the people of New Orleans feel a screw job coming. Incited by the *Picayune* and radio talk shows, they light up the switchboards at City Hall and the State Capitol in protest.

The reaction rattles Mayor Barthelemy, whom Edwards originally cast as the front man in this endeavor. Now the mayor is rolling and firing all over the deck, raising demands again that the city get a direct cut of the action and insisting that the administration first pass a constitutional limit of one casino in New Orleans, to save Canal Street from being overrun once the greed bug bites.

The governor's strategy, if there is any, appears to be unraveling when the showdown vote comes on the bill on a Thursday afternoon early in June. The opposition is ready to fire.

New Orleans representatives Mitch Landrieu, a liberal, and Garey Forster, a conservative, beg colleagues not to foist Edwards' scheme on unwilling Orleanians. "We would not do this to your cities," pleads Forster. Jim Donelon of Jefferson Parish asks rhetorically, "Why not let the people vote on this?" and then answers his own question: "Edwin Edwards has seen what crazy things happen when people vote — how do you think he got this job?" If the microphone would reach that far, he says, "I would get down on my knees and beg you: don't do this. Don't flush the Queen City of the South down the toilet because we don't think we can do better." Republican legislator Peppi Bruneau speculates on the patronage bonanza once this bill puts "the reins firmly in the hands of the ringmaster of Circus Maximus."

The governor's floorleader Bo Ackal is unable to keep his legendary temper in check. "They have the nerve to say, 'Don't do this to my city,' " he growls angrily. "They have done it to themselves."

Representative Sherman Copelin, the governor's choice as the new Speaker pro tem, is walking the aisles looking worried. Even the normally rock-solid votes of the Speaker-picked chairmen and vice chairmen are wavering. The governor isn't doing much better. His vaunted persuasive style isn't getting the same old respect from new legislators. Freshman legislator Melissa Flournoy breaks the code of silence to actually talk about her phone call from the governor. "You know the governor. He's so seductive," she tells the *Times-Picayune*. "It was kind of neat." Neat? The governor plays his casino hand and the representative from Shreveport acts like he's asked her to the prom? Neat? And she didn't even say yes.

Minutes before the big vote comes, Mayor Barthelemy angrily jumps ship and urges his three closest House allies to vote no. Copelin looks like he's been kicked. The rural legislators are getting colder and colder feet. Many have told the governor they would vote yes if their votes are needed, but they're not sure the administration will come close.

The most focused ten seconds in politics is the brief period the electronic voting machine is open for recording votes. Years of experience at close votes have taught legislators how to read a count in seconds. As Speaker John Alario instructs, "The clerk will open the machine," the giant electronic scoreboard behind the dais begins to light up green and red. Some wavering legislators are holding back their vote until they see which way the issue is going. Some opposing members are playing games with their lights. They hit the green light, which makes it appear to the waverers that their votes will not be needed and that they can vote no or not vote. Only Speaker Alario, with an electronic counter at his desk, can read the exact vote as it's cast. As he begins to say, "The clerk will close the machine," several green lights flash red. Alario double-takes. Later he will say his counter had hit 51 — very close on the first try for the 53 votes needed — but in an instant the switched votes knock the number down to 43 for and 52 against, with 10 not voting.

Casino opponents yelp as Garey Forster and Jim Donelon exchange high-fives. The administration has fallen embarrassingly short. Mitch Landrieu takes the mike to caution, "If you think the deals were hard before, just wait." But both sides know 10 votes is a lot to make up on an emotional issue, especially now with the mayor of New Orleans out in the open against the bill. It looks like Edwards bet high and busted. Had he trimmed back on some of his or the board of directors' control, as was expected he would do, he probably could have come close enough to hold the waverers and win. Surely the administration will come back, but some team members already are panicky. The bill's author, LaLa Lalonde, feels "rigor mortis is setting in" and John Alario admits he may be right. The sense around the House is that even with extra inducements and concessions the governor is going to have a very hard time getting this bill through. The Mansion is dark and silent.


The following Monday evening Garey Forster and conservative allies are in the House lobby celebrating yet another win over the hapless Edwards administration and his gang who can't count straight. Minutes earlier, organized labor has been turned back on its renewed quest, backed by Edwards, to gut the state's Right-to-Work law. It wasn't even close. The governor, who had advanced a very limited agenda, has yet to win a big one. And time is running out on this first session, which is his best hope for getting anything controversial done.

"Casino! Casino!" The word shoots through the foyer. Conservative legislators, like fighter pilots scrambling to an air raid alert, race back into the chamber just as LaLa Lalonde calls the question on an identical casino bill plucked from far down the calendar.

Debate is not necessary. Everyone knows what needs to be done. Some casino opponents finger their green buttons ready to switch back to red.

"The clerk will open the machine."

The big board lights up, with about a dozen legislators holding back their votes as they scan the lights for clues. There are more greens today, but it is very close. At least two casino opponents have punched their green buttons, but rest their fingers on the red one, waiting for John Alario to say:

"The clerk . . ."

Some legislators who haven't voted yet hit their red buttons. Representative Tim Stine could swear he had voted no from the start, but the light next to his name on the voting board is shining green. Stine punches the red button again, but nothing happens.

". . . will close the machine."

The Speaker, watching his instant counter, nods approvingly. "Fifty-three votes and the bill finally passes."

"Noo-o-o-o!" comes the roar from House members staring in shock and anger at the voting board, which has now gone dark. Clerk Butch Speer had closed the machine about five seconds earlier than usual, a virtual eternity in which lives would change and fortunes would be made. A huge uproar ensues as members stampede the front desk in protest, demanding to see the computer printout, which is not readily available. Some casino opponents, hoping to confuse their colleagues into briefly thinking their votes were not needed, ended up trapped with the green lights. Sherman Copelin clucks that those representatives "got caught with their hands in the cookie jar."

Edwin Edwards is sitting in his den-office at the Mansion listening to the commotion on the speaker there. Somehow he had gotten the mayor of New Orleans back on board, for Barthelemy, who still wanted the casino, had nowhere else to go. The committee chairmen and vice chairmen were rounded back into the fold. Now Alario just had to hold off the angry hordes on the House floor.

In the House, several attempts to reconsider the vote fail, which indicates more acquiescence if not support for the results. Many do not like the way it has passed, but they are not going to challenge the Speaker. The moral of the evening is: you don't play games with the man who runs the voting machine.

Some casino opponents listed as yes votes demand theirs be changed. That can only be done, according to House rules, if it does not change the final outcome of the vote. Once it is clear the majority will hold, legislators scramble for cover. Four nonvoting members agree to switch to yes in order that Stine and three others can be listed as voting no. Four other nonvoters change to no. The final printed tally sheet, with lines and arrows marking switched votes, "looked more like a play from Italian basketball," observes Gannett's John Hill. Lots of motion and confusion, going nowhere. The original 53-42 tally winds up at 53-50. Louisiana will have a casino.

The next day Edwards strolls into a press conference, the cat who swallowed New Orleans. "I knew we had 58 votes if we needed them," he begins, though "a number of legislators saw the validity of the bill, but they had a problem with a mother-in-law or a preacher or wife or someone else."

He brushes off several questions about the manner of the vote and acts offended at the suggestion that any deals were cut.

"Absolutely not," he protests. "No one can say I said anything was *quid pro quo*." He looks with mild contempt on *Picayune* reporter Peter Nicholas. "Poor Peter, he has been down there trying to find some legislators who said I did. It would be very important to him to find one. It would be as close to an orgasm as he has come. But, my man, you can't find that. I suggest you go on to a more productive cause."

He cites the folly of other critics. "I've told one of the opponents of the bill he will benefit more than anyone else. He owns four restaurants there," says Edwards of Ralph Brennan. "He may have to pay his dishwashers more, because the casino will cause those wages to go higher."

But today he can afford to be magnanimous with his critics because he is confident that time, like the voting machine, is on his side. "I would like to hear from them a few years from now. All of these misguided, well-intentioned souls will say, 'Man, if we had just listened to Edwards years ago we would be better off.' These are the people with their feet planted firmly in the eighteenth century, with their minds in the seventeenth century, with their bodies being propelled unwillingly into the twentieth."

"People in New Orleans say they've been cheated," a reporter prods.

"They are in the minority," Edwards bristles. "I am the governor. I received 87 percent of the vote in New Orleans, more than anyone in the past. No one has acknowledged that. No one knows the city of New Orleans as I do. I talk to the publishers of the newspapers, the news directors at the stations, the taxi cab drivers, the waiters and waitresses, the people in the streets and the people in the houses. No one knows the city of New Orleans like I do and the vast majority of people want this. The mayor wants it, the Council wants it, the Legislature wishes it to happen. It is unfair to suggest that all of us are involved in a giant conspiracy to damage the city. No one cares about the city more than I do."

If it isn't clear already, that's what this has been about. His insistence that New Orleans not even get a small slice of the casino pie is driven less by concern about opposition to the bill than by his own control. As passed, the new casino law would leave the casino corporation board, appointed by Edwards, to decide how much the city should be reimbursed yearly for the extra municipal services.

Though he will appoint them and set their salaries, Edwards insists the board members will be completely independent of him. As an example of the kind of "upstanding, pristine board" he will appoint, Edwards says he has asked Republican Party Chairman Billy Nungesser to be its first member. *Advocate* reporter Bill McMahon deadpans to a colleague: "I feel a lot better about this already."

Regardless of the board's real power, Edwards, in effect, will be a shadow mayor, the moving hand behind the newest economic force in town. Edwards has positioned himself as the economic liberator of the city's underclass, the font of thousands of low-skill, good-paying jobs. He could care less that the *Picayune* and the elite Boston Club and all the fine people locked up in their mansions — the ones who held their noses and voted for Edwards against Duke — still regard him as a lowlife trying to cheapen the unique character of their city. They may run Carnival, but they don't run the city anymore. Edwards has obtained a prize that has eluded Louisiana governors in the past. Huey Long tried to trample the city politically while it resisted him like an armed camp. John

McKeithen built the Superdome, but never felt fully appreciated there. Edwards, building on his base in the black community, was able to make the city come to him to save it from Duke. Now he has finished the deal. No other politician or business leader holds cards like his.

The Uptown elite can keep Momus and Comus to themselves. The king of the new carnival is Edwin Edwards.

"What brings you here?" asks the guy at the bar.

He does. The guy is David Duke. The bar is his, MacGillicuddy's, the new Irish bar in Metairie. "Well, it's more a restaurant than a bar," he says. And it really belongs to his old campaign manager Howie Farrell — "Howie's a professional Irishman" — and Duke has put in a little money and his name and some time as the guy at the bar.

On a tour of the place, Duke glides through the back room, greets a few diners and enters the kitchen. Now this should be interesting. Indeed. All the kitchen help is Asian.

The actual Celticity of the cuisine is confined to the names of the dishes on the menu, like the popular Belfast Burger. The drinks are more authentic, like the Half and Half he suggests, a dark, frothy combo of Guinness and Harp's, only $2. "The way I operate is I try to give people a good service for less money."

One happy diner agrees. Duke introduces Bill, who did his local printing, and Bill's wife. They are enjoying their steaks. "The price is right," says Bill.

"Bill tells great jokes," brags Duke. "You have a joke for us, Bill?"

"Sure," says Bill. "Do you know how the copper wire was invented?"

We give up.

"Two Jews trying to split a penny."

Duke grins and grimaces, "Well, you're not supposed to tell jokes like that."

There's Howie Farrell at the end of the bar, chatting with a young fellow wearing a muscle shirt. "David, he says you get him the flyers and he'll put them out."

"Great," says Duke. The place could use a bit more business for a Friday night. "We're doing okay and I haven't even sent out a mailing yet to my list."

MacGillicuddy's has benefited from some news stories about his new enterprise. Not everyone around him approved, such as Jim McPherson, who questioned if bar ownership fit the image Duke should project. Certainly some folks thought it was pretty funny, like his old tormentor Lance Hill, who calls the new establishment "the Klavern Tavern."

Let them laugh. Duke seems less bothered by jokes at his expense, especially when it's all that's keeping his name out there now. "Arsenio Hall does stuff on me all the time. I don't watch him, but people tell me about it. Whenever there's anything about the Klan, he hits me. And Jay Leno always has a joke on me. Did you see *Saturday Night Live* on election night? Oh, it was funny. Dana Carvey impersonated me. It wasn't a good impersonation, but he said some funny things, like 'Now is the time we need to bring people together and reunite them, like the Goebbels faction and the Goering faction.' It was pretty good."

If the laughter hasn't quite stopped, the whirlwind of 1991 has. The heady prospects, just after the election, of book deals, speaking engagements and Jesse Jackson debates evaporated along with his presidential campaign. He's written a chapter of his book, but apparently New York is not as hot for him now, for he is considering publishing it himself. Besides that, he says he is doing some computer consulting on mailing lists and "I'm working at getting involved with a telecommunications business, a long-distance company."

He's a family man again. Sixteen-year-old Erika comes up and hugs Daddy. Erika has moved back in with her father and will attend Crescent City Baptist High. "It's where she goes to school and it's where we go to church." Erika beams.

On the social front, Duke's latest female companion is a law student. "She's very smart," says her beau. "And she's Jewish." Duke smiles broadly at the shock effect. "Well, her father's Jewish. . . . Actually, she's adopted, so she's not . . ."

No, he doesn't miss campaigning. "What killed the presidential campaign was my mailing company got my mailing out a month and a half too late to help. They stiffed me. They got pressure from their Jewish customers." He has ruled out a congressional race in the fall, though he figures he could win in the new, whiter Fifth Congressional District in North Louisiana — "but then I'd have to move to Washington and there are other things I'd much rather do." As for state politics, he is appalled at the level of gambling being proposed, but he won't sign the recall petition being circulated against Edwin Edwards. "I won't sign the recall petition. And I don't think Edwin would sign it if I were governor. I guess I just believe too much in the democratic process." But he's not very hopeful about its future. "I won't rule out another political campaign. I think the country is in very bad shape and it's going to fall apart sooner or later. So we'll see."

A week later, he does get that mailing out. Not for the bar, but for himself. It's an appeal to his old contributors to give again "so I can keep up the fight for the conservative cause we share." He details the harassment he still endures, with continuing audits from the IRS, as well as state and parish government. Death threats to him and his daughters necessitate bodyguards, which are expensive. Though the cause he fights for is public, this gift would be private. "Since I am not a candidate for office, your contribution will not be reported and made public."

Then, just as Duke's enemies are charging that he's back on public welfare, he gets a job. The state manager for Physicians Mutual, a national insurance company, reveals that Duke has passed the state insurance exam and will become an agent for the company. Insurance industry sources estimate that Duke, with his personal following, mailing list and company affiliation, could net as much as $200,000 a year in income. Not bad for your first job. That is, until word of his new employment reaches the home office in Omaha, and the decision quickly is reversed.

Duke is bitter. "All this time these people are criticizing me for not having a job. When I get one, they want to run me out of it. I'm just trying to sell insurance." And he still will. "I'm going to be an independent agent and place insurance with different companies. This will work out better for me, but this is still pretty dirty."

Even out of public life, Duke's past sticks at his side. It's dawning on him what "Never forget" means.

It's a bad summer for old Louisiana politicians in federal court. Charlie Roemer and his son Danny, in a long-running investigation, are indicted on charges of defrauding a Leesville savings and loan on a $10 million development loan from 1985.

Marine Shale owner Jack Kent and two cousins both named Vince Sotile are indicted for trying to bribe U.S. District Judge with an offer of $2 million for favorable disposition of the federal charges against the waste recycler. The Sotiles plead guilty but Kent stands trial and is acquitted.

Edwin Edwards' longtime close friend and Ted Kennedy's new father-in-law, Edmund Reggie of Crowley, is convicted of misapplication of loan funds in a banking scandal that has been investigated for eight years.

In September, Buddy Roemer is sued in state court by a Hammond bank for a $71,000 note, part of which the ex-governor had used to pay for his son Chas' Harvard education.

Not to be outdone by David Duke, Jimmy Swaggart has a new mail appeal out, claiming that postal workers are opening envelopes addressed to him, stealing the cash and throwing away the checks. The Post Office responds that no stolen-mail complaints have been filed by Jimmy Swaggart Ministries.

The St. Amant High School Class of 1982 holds its 10-year reunion at the Governor's Mansion, hosted by classmate Candy Picou and her date, Governor Edwards.

Governor Edwin Edwards sits serenely in his den-office, gazing out over the Mansion's side lawn toward peaceful, polluted Capitol Lake, as he listens to the babble of the constitutional convention foundering a few blocks away.

When the photographer indicates he is ready for the cover shot, Edwards turns down the speaker volume and reflects on the campaign: "There have been three classic elections in Louisiana: Earl Long's in 1956, mine in 1983 and this one."

It did not always feel so classic. He at least admits there were times—dark days in the primary—when he felt he could not best Roemer in the final struggle. "That was hard, feeling here I am doing all this work and if things do not change, it will all be for naught." But those feelings passed.

"I know you don't believe it, but I would have beaten Roemer in the runoff. It would have been a different race, much closer, but I would have won."

That, indeed, was the classic showdown this state was waiting for, the chance to decide a mandate on where this state would go. But things don't work out so cleanly in politics, and certainly a runoff between two flawed and angry politicians, fighting over David Duke's alienated voters, would be anything but clean.

Under another governor, the personnel and priorities may differ, but the same giant problem that has broken the last three chief executives still exists: the inability to decide how to pay for even the people's lowered expectations. Compounding Edwards' situation is the reality that he, despite his landslide win, commands even less of a mandate than did Buddy Roemer four years before. He operates in the nearly untenable position of one of America's last liberal governors in one of its most virulently anti-tax states. In addition, he blew his New Edwin cover with the casino grab. So while the people and the politicians look to the powerful governor for answers, this one, this time, is not making the mistake of impaling himself on strong, decisive leadership. He seems to pursue a strategy favored by Chinese rulers in dangerous times: to relinquish authority so he may preserve power.

With a new budget storm bearing down on Louisiana (actually, it's just the same old one, never resolved) and with voter rage being restoked in the presidential contest, Edwards decides to cede the power to tax to the allegedly coequal legislative branch.

A few weeks earlier, he opened the constitutional convention (with legislators serving as delegates and Candy Picou sitting in a place of honor) with a hard-breaking curve: a call for all-out fiscal reform that sent tingles through the ranks of long-suffering good-government activists. A stunned Republican senator wondered if Edwards had joined their ranks. He was young. The *Picayune* and the *Advocate* found themselves praising the governor again. Can it be a Newer Edwin?

No. He knew, the delegates knew, even the people knew that the model good-government plan, with its "broadened" income and property taxes, was going nowhere.

After Hurricane Andrew passes, so has any legislative will for a long-term fiscal solution. The convention is stalled. Does the governor have a fall-back position? Actually, the governor has nothing more to say.

With the virtual collapse of the convention, the governor orders sweeping, painful, across-the-board cuts, which, because most spending is constitutionally mandated, falls most heavily on state colleges. Edwards knows higher education cuts are guaranteed to hit hardest on conservative, reform-minded legislators who opposed him most in the past. When they scream, he warns that worse reductions will come the following year, unless legislators can agree on how to raise taxes. He is giving them a free hand. With state finances approaching meltdown, with his own approval ratings below 50 percent, the governor acts with the quiet reserve of one who knows where this will end and is taking his time getting there.

One day, the state will learn how to live within its means, though it will lose a few sets of legislators doing so. Even in the tricky areas of ethics, education and economic development, odds are fairly good that the Bayou State will enter the twentieth century some time before it ends. But on its own terms.

Louisiana has played a risky game of revolution, resentment and anger, and what is it left with? With Edwin Edwards, with a casino, and with most of Roemer's reforms in jeopardy if not *in extremis*. As hard as the hardline reformers try to change it, Louisiana will never be like Iowa. If the Louisiana experience teaches anything, it's that its deeply formed, ancient character cannot be denied and purged, only experienced and exploited. It is destiny.

Which brings us back to the old business of Edwin Edwards. The man who said the best thing that could happen to him "would be to get elected and to die the next day" will have to settle for something else. He has been vindicated in the only way it counts for a politician. But can he be redeemed? Luckily for him, the people's expectations are not much higher than his approval ratings. The terms could be as modest as getting through four years unindicted, as reasonable as doing no harm, as challenging as leaving things better than how he found them. Perhaps it had to be this way. For if Edwin Edwards has a shot at redemption, there is hope for Louisiana.

And if there is hope for Louisiana . . .

There was time, after the Last Hayride crashed and burned, when it seemed that Louisiana politics would eventually sober up and begin to resemble that of the rest of the United States. But it's turning out to be the other way around.

In its off-center way, Louisiana's dangerous electoral politics of 1991 would foretell the nation's bizarre political year to follow. As more alienated voters respond to feelings and forces beyond the mainstreams of the political parties, there will be more, not fewer, races from Hell ahead. That large animal that thundered through Louisiana in 1990 and 1991 has galloped on. It has thrown several small riders since, and it's still out there, running loose.

**David Duke**

**Edwin Edwards**

**Buddy Roemer**

**October 19, 1991**
**Gubernatorial Primary**

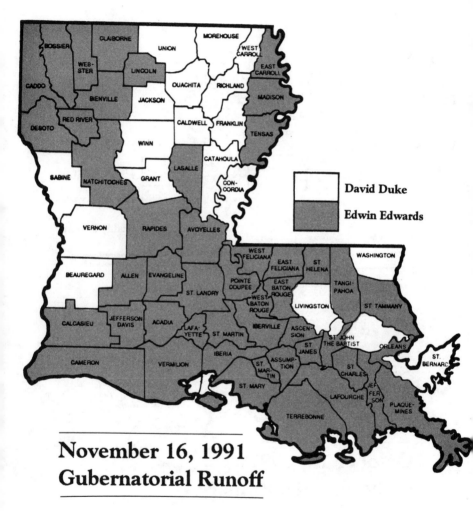

David Duke

Edwin Edwards

**November 16, 1991**
**Gubernatorial Runoff**

FOR DIRECT ORDERS OF

# CROSS to BEAR

and

## *THE LAST HAYRIDE*

Contact:

**DARK**HORSE **PRESS**

P.O. Box 6

Baton Rouge, Louisiana  70821

1-800-673-5577